Globalization and the Myths of Free Trade

T0320306

Globalization and the Myths of Free Trade critically examines the Washington Consensus, its history, theory, practice and its global outcomes. Two decades have passed since neoliberal globalization began to be implemented, and its highly uneven effects have given rise to a growing opposition. The present debate is not about the need to utilize international resources in the effort to enhance global development, but rather about the *manner* in which resources should be brought to bear on this project. Throughout the volume, contributors critically analyze whether free trade is the optimal path to development in the current global climate.

The book is organized in four parts, each dedicated to one of the four major issues that inform the debate. The first part focuses on the history and theory of the relationship between international trade and economic development. The second part is concerned with the linkages between globalization and economic development. It examines the actual experiences of various parts of the world in the neoliberal era, ranging from Asia and Latin America to Russia and Eastern Europe. The third part analyzes the effects of globalization on gender inequality and international poverty. And the final section looks at the impact of capital account liberalization, both on the developing world and on the developed countries themselves.

Anwar Shaikh is Professor of Economics at the Graduate Faculty of Political and Social Science of the New School University, USA.

Routledge Frontiers of Political Economy

Globalization and the Myths of Free Trade

History, theory, and empirical evidence

Edited by
Anwar Shaikh

Routledge
Taylor & Francis Group

LONDON AND NEW YORK

First published 2007
by Routledge
2 Park Square, Milton Park, Abingdon, Oxon OX14 4RN

Simultaneously published in the USA and Canada
by Routledge
711 Third Ave, New York, NY 10017

Routledge is an imprint of the Taylor & Francis Group, an informa business

First issued in paperback 2013

Typeset in Times by Keyword Group Ltd

British Library Cataloguing in Publication Data
A catalogue record for this book is available from the British Library

Library of Congress Cataloguing in Publication Data
A catalogue record for this book has been requested

ISBN13: 978-0-415-77047-7 (hbk)
ISBN13: 978-0-203-96638-9 (ebk)
ISBN13: 978-0-415-64804-2 (pbk)

Contents

Tables

Figures

Contributors

Ha-Joon Chang is Reader in the Political Economy of Development at University of Cambridge. His research interests include the role of the state in economic change; industrial policy, privatization, and regulation; theories of institutions and morality; the East Asian economies; globalization; economic development in historical perspective.

Andrew Glyn is University Lecturer in Economics at Corpus Christi College, Oxford University. His research interests are in postwar profitability, comparative development of advanced economies since Second World War, OECD unemployment and inequality, UK economic policy; UK coal industry and macroeconomic effects of environmental constraints.

Massoud Karshenas is Professor of Economics, School of Oriental and African Studies, University of London, and Professor of Development Economics, Institute of Social Studies, The Hague. His areas of interest are in oil economies, poverty and development, Middle Eastern economies and structural adjustment and labor markets.

Deepak Nayyar is Professor of Economics at Jawaharlal Nehru University, New Delhi and Chairman of the Board of Governors of the UNU World Institute for Development Economics Research, Helsinki. His research covers a wide range of subjects including trade policies, industrialization strategies, macroeconomic stabilization, structural adjustment, economic liberalization, trade theory, macro policies, international migration, the multilateral trading system, and economic development in India. Globalization and development is the area of focus in his present research.

Stephanie Seguino is Associate Professor and Chair, Department of Economics, University of Vermont. Her research explores the two-way relationship between income and well-being inequality and economic growth, and emphasizes the differential effects of gender, ethnicity, and class inequality on growth.

Anwar Shaikh is Professor of Economics at the Graduate Faculty of Political and Social Science of the New School for Social Research; and a Senior Scholar and member of the Macro Modeling Team at the Levy Economics Institute of

Bard College. His current research areas include globalization; exchange rates; US macroeconomic policy; finance theory; and sustainable development (in Ethiopia and Indonesia).

Ajit Singh is Professor of Economics at the University and Senior Fellow at Queens' College Cambridge. His research includes studies relating to the modern corporation, corporate organization, finance and governance and theories of the firm; "deindustrialization" in advanced economies; North–South competition and issues of employment and unemployment in the North and the South; industrialization and economic policy in emerging markets.

Lance Taylor is presently the Arnhold Professor of International Cooperation and Development at the Department of Economics, New School for Social Research, and the Director of Schwartz Center for Economic Policy and Analysis (SCEPA), New School. His current research includes macroeconomic stabilization and adjustment in developing and transition economies; reconstruction of macroeconomic theory.

John Weeks is Professor of Development Economics and Director of the Centre for Development Policy and Research at the School of Oriental and African Studies of the University of London. His main research interests are structural adjustment and stabilization programs; labor markets; effects of hyperinflation; classical theory of value and growth; his recent work has been on macroeconomic policies for poverty reduction in Moldova and Zambia.

Abbreviations

ACC	Advanced Capitalist Countries
CI	Crowding In
CMEA	Council for Mutual Economic Assistance
ECLAC	Economic Commission for Latin America and the Caribbean
EDB	European Development Bank
FAO	Food and Agricultural Organization
GATT	General Agreement on Trade and Tariffs
GDI	Gender Development Index
GDP	Gross Domestic Product
GEM	Gender Empowerment Measure
HDI	Human Development Indicator
HOS	Heckscher–Ohlin–Samuelson
ILO	The International Labor Organization
IMF	International Monetary Fund
ISI	Import Substituting Industrialization
LAC	Latin America and the Caribbean
LDCs	Least Developed Countries
LO	Landsorganisationen i Sverige
LSMS	Living Standard Measurement Surveys
MAI	Multilateral Agreement on Investment
NBFI	Non-Bank Financial Intermediary
NDCs	Now-Developed Countries
NICs	Newly Industrialized Countries
NGO	Non-Governmental Organization
NIFA	New International Financial Architecture
NIH	National Institutes of Health
OECD	Organization for Economic Cooperation and Development
OLS	Ordinary Least Squares
PMAI	Proposed new Multilateral Agreement on Investment
PPP	Purchasing Power Parity
RULC	Relative Unit Labor Costs
R&D	Research and Development
SOEs	State Owned Enterprises

TRIPs	Trade Related Intellectual Property Rights
UIP	Uncovered Interest Parity
UK	United Kingdom
UNCTAD	United Nations Council for Trade and Development
UNDP	United Nations Development Program
USA	United States of America
VERs	Voluntary Export Restraints
WTO	World Trade Organization
WWII	World War Two

Acknowledgments

The papers in the book were presented at the conference on "Globalization and the Myths of Free Trade" held in April 2003 at the New School for Social Research. I wish to thank Irene and Bernard Schwartz for their generosity in funding this conference as part of the Schwartz Center for Policy Analysis (SCEPA) Project on "Markets, Equality and Democracy". I am also grateful to my colleagues Lance Taylor and William Milberg for their support, and to Bhargavi Ramamurthy for her excellent assistance in editing the conference volume.

1 Introduction

Anwar Shaikh

1 Globalization and the effects of neoliberalism

The world has become a human laboratory for the momentous social experiment called neoliberalism. Its proclaimed purpose is to reduce global poverty. Its protocols are derived from the orthodox theory of competitive free markets. And its policies are enforced by the full weight of the rich countries and global institutions such as the World Trade Organization (WTO), the World Bank (WB), and the International Monetary Fund (IMF). This book is a critical examination of this ongoing enterprise, of its history, theory, practise and most of all, of its outcomes.

The annual Gross National Income per capita of the richest countries was about \$27,000 in 2001, whereas that of the poorest countries was about \$430 (World Bank 2003: 235, Table 1). But even the latter sum is misleading, because the distribution of income in poorer countries is appallingly skewed. Even according to World Bank estimates, some 1.2 billion people, one in every five people on Earth, are forced to live on less than \$370 per year, that is, on less than \$1 a day. Almost *half* the world's population lives on less than \$2 a day (World Bank 2001: 3).

Neoliberalism insists that unrestricted international trade and capital flows provide the best way to overcome such problems. It sees markets as self-regulating social structures that optimally serve all economic needs, efficiently utilize all economic resources, and automatically generate full employment for all persons who truly wish to work. Poverty, unemployment, and periodic economic crises in the world are thought to exist because markets have been constrained by labor unions, the state, and a host of social practices rooted in culture and history. Overcoming poverty therefore requires creating "market friendly" social structures in the poorer countries and strengthening existing ones in the richer countries. This involves curtailing union strength so that employers could hire and fire whom they choose, privatizing state enterprises so that their workers would fall under the purview of domestic capital, and opening up domestic markets to foreign capital and foreign goods (Friedman 2002, Stiglitz 2002). The job of international institutions is to oversee this task, for the good of the world, and particularly for the good of the poor. To quote Mike Moore, former Director General of the WTO, "the surest way to do more to help the [world's] poor is to continue to open markets" (cited in Agosin and Tussie 1993: 9).

Neoliberal globalization began to be implemented in the 1980s, and gathered great force in the 1990s. Yet in most countries, this latter period has been associated with increased poverty and hunger. Over this interval, more than 13 million children died from diarrhoeal disease. Even today, over half a million women die each year in pregnancy and childbirth, one for each minute of the day. More than 800 million suffer from malnutrition (UNDP 2003: 5–8, 40). Of the 50 countries with the lowest per capita GDP in 1990, 23 suffered declines, whereas the other 27 grew so modestly that it would take them almost 80 years just to achieve the level attained by Greece, which in 2002 was the poorest member of the EU (Friedman 2002: 1). In Latin America and the Caribbean, GDP per capita grew by a total of 75 percent in the two decades from 1960 to 1980, and only 7 percent in the subsequent two decades under neoliberalism. In Africa, the first period yielded a total growth of 34 percent, whereas in the second per capita GDP *fell* by 15 percent (Weisbrot 2002: 1). Only certain Asian countries escaped this pattern, and they did so by channeling the market mechanism rather than by following its dictates (see Chapter 2 of this book). Finally, international inequality also rose in the two decades of neoliberalism: in 1980, the richest countries had median incomes 77 times as great as the poorest but by 1999 this tremendous inequality had *increased* to 122:1 (Weller and Hersh 2002: 1).

The current debate is not about the need to utilize international resources in the effort to reduce global poverty. It is about the *manner* in which resources should be brought to bear. Neoliberalism provides one possible answer. Because it is also the dominant practise, the debate has focused on neoliberalism. Defenders of neoliberalism make a variety of points. They point to history, to the indisputable fact that the rich countries are market-based economies that developed in-and-through the world market (Norberg 2004: 1). They point to standard economic theory, to "the virtual unanimity among economists, whatever their ideological position on other issues, that international free trade is in the best interests of trading countries and of the world" (Friedman and Friedman 2004: 1; see also Bhagwati 2002: 3–4; Winters *et al.* 2004: 72, 78, 106). They point to empirical evidence indicating that global poverty has been reduced since the 1990s, and that trade liberalization reduces poverty by fostering growth (Winters *et al.* 2004: 106–7).[1] And they argue that if developing countries have not done as well as they should, it is because they have themselves failed to implement social and economic policies that are sufficiently market-friendly (Norberg 2004: 2).

Critics of neoliberalism dispute all of these points. They note that rich countries, from the old rich of the West to the new rich of Asia, relied heavily on trade protectionism and state intervention as they themselves developed, and that they continue to do so even now (Agosin and Tussie 1993: 25; Rodrik 2001: 11; Chang 2002; Stiglitz 2002). They claim that free trade theory is irrelevant because it is based on premises that do not hold even in the rich countries, let alone the poor ones. They argue that in the poor countries, trade liberalization has actually led to slower growth, greater inequality, a rise in global poverty, and recurrent financial and economic crises. And they fault the WTO, IMF, and World Bank for their cruel and inept actions in the face of such miseries (McCartney 2004; Friedman 2002: 3–4; Stiglitz 2002: 1; Weller and Hersh 2002; Weisbrot 2002).

2　Structure of this book

This book examines the preceding themes in greater detail. In addition to this introductory chapter, it is organized in four parts, each dedicated to one of the four major issues that cleave the debate.

- Part I: Globalization and free trade
- Part II: Globalization and economic development
- Part III: Globalization, gender, and inequality
- Part IV: Globalization, capital mobility and competition

2.1　Part I: Globalization and free trade

The first part of the book analyzes the theory and practice of free trade. *Ha-Joon Chang* (*Chapter 2*) examines the notion that the rich countries of the world climbed to the top of the economic ladder through neoliberal policies. This "official history of capitalism" maintains that it was eighteenth century Britain's adherence to free trade and market policies that enabled it to beat interventionist France, its main competitor. A new liberal world order followed, ushering in a period of unprecedented prosperity in the Western countries that lasted until the 1930s, when the Great Depression sparked a round of trade-destroying tariffs. From this point of view, the reign of free trade was not restored until the 1980s, when neoliberalism took the stage.

Chang shows that the real history is very different. He traces in some detail how Britain, the US, Germany, France, Sweden, the Netherlands, Switzerland, Japan, South Korea, and the most recent Asian Tigers used interventionist trade and industrial policies to promote and protect their own industries. He also shows how these very same countries took up the cudgel of free trade only after they were internationally competitive. For instance, Britain had high tariffs even two generations after the industrial revolution, and its repeal of the Corn Laws in 1846 came at a time when its manufacturers became confident that they would dominate world trade. The US, whom Bairoch has called "the mother country and bastion of modern protectionism" (Chang, Chapter 2 of this book, p. 23), openly rejected Britain's ideology of free trade as a threat to its own infant industries, and relied instead on high tariffs and extensive state intervention during its own process of industrialization. As in the case of Britain, the US substantially liberalized its international trade only after it had achieved industrial supremacy. Japan's entry onto the world stage follows a similar pattern of extensive state intervention, beginning with the Meiji Restoration of 1868. Its tariffs were low because punitive treaties prevented it from raising them. State-supported industrialization was therefore its main channel to success until these treaties ended in

1911, after which tariffs and quotas also became a part of its industrialization policy. This long period of steady development set the stage for its explosive growth after the Second World War. South Korea and the other successful East Asian countries (except for Hong Kong) followed this same path, relying heavily on interventionist trade and industrial policies.

For Chang, real history teaches us that successful development requires today's developing countries to fashion similar policies, possibly with even higher tariff barriers given that the playing field is vastly more unequal than it was in the past. The rules of the WTO should be rewritten to facilitate this, and international financial assistance should be redirected away from neoliberal policies toward real social and industrial development.

Some defenders of neoliberalism concede that the rich countries relied heavily on trade intervention and state supported industrialization. Nonetheless, they argue that economic *theory* proves that competitive international markets provide the best option for today's developing countries. They conclude that it is therefore essential to eliminate restrictions on markets, particularly in the developing world, so as to spread competition throughout the globe and allow free trade to work as promised (Bhagwati 2002: 9–12). But if the theory is itself wrong, such a prescription could be disastrous. So it becomes crucial to examine the theory of free trade itself. This is the task taken up by Shaikh and Nayyar in this book.

Anwar Shaikh (*Chapter 3*) focuses on the logic of free trade theory. He maintains that the basic theory is wrong even on its own grounds. It is not the *absence* of competition that produces underdevelopment alongside development but rather its *existence*. He argues that "real competition" between nations operates in much the same manner as competition within a nation: it favors the (competitively) strong over the weak. Thus, the collateral damage arising from globalization is exactly what one would expect to find. From this point of view, the rich countries were correct to recognize, when they were themselves on the way up, that unrestricted international competition was a threat to their own plans for development.

Shaikh argues that the fundamental error in the standard theory of free trade lies in its treatment of international competition. When economists discuss competition *within a nation*, they recognize that firms and regions with lower costs will tend to beat out those with higher costs. Thus, a region with low cost producers will be able to sell many of its products in the high cost region, without buying much from it. It will therefore enjoy a regional trade surplus, whereas the high cost region will suffer a regional trade deficit. Even when it comes to competition *between nations*, economists agree that when international trade is opened up a similar outcome obtains *at first*: The country with the initially lower costs of production will tend to enjoy a national trade surplus, and the other a trade deficit.

It is after this point that a critical divergence arises between standard trade theory and the theory of real competition. Standard trade theory says that in the country with an initial trade deficit, the terms of trade (the relative price of its exports to imports) will automatically fall. This would make its imports more expensive to domestic purchasers and its exports less expensive to foreign producers, so that if conditions (i.e. elasticities) are right, trade will automatically move toward balance. In this way, trade imbalances will be eliminated through automatic movements of a country's terms of trade. This is the essence of the *theory of comparative costs,* which is the foundation of standard trade theory. It is important to note, as David Ricardo did long ago, that such a movement implies a fundamental change in the determination of relative prices. Within a country, and even when trade first opens up between countries, relative prices are regulated by relative costs. But according to the theory of comparative costs, once trade has been established these same relative prices have to move away from their initial cost-determined values to new levels determined by the requirements of trade balance.

Shaikh argues that the theory of real competition comes to the very opposite conclusion. Competition forces prices, and hence terms of trade, to be regulated by relative real costs at all times. In a country that enjoys an initial trade surplus, the resulting inflow of funds would enhance the availability of credit, which would lower interest rates. Conversely, in the country with the initial trade deficit, the fund outflow would tighten the credit market, and raise interest rates. With interest rates lower in the surplus country and higher in the deficit country, profit-seeking capital would flow from the former to the latter. Thus the surplus country would become a net lender on the world market, and the deficit country a net borrower. Instead of eliminating the trade imbalances, free trade would cover them with capital flows. Trade imbalances would be *persistent*, and deficit countries in particular would be forced to run down their reserves and to depend on foreign borrowing (foreign capital inflows) to cover such deficits. In free trade, it is the profit-motive that regulates trade, and the (competitive) advantage goes to the *firms* with the real lowest costs. Nothing in this process ensures that the resulting outcomes will necessarily serve the needs of the developing world, however much it might serve those of the advanced firms of the rich countries.

Deepak Nayyar (Chapter 4) focuses on the history of the doctrine of free trade, with a particular focus on the interplay between economic theory and politics. He argues that Smith and Ricardo's emphasis on free trade was motivated by the desire to challenge mercantilist ideas. Mercantilism emphasized that trade should be managed to enhance national economic power. The classical economists countered with the claim that free trade would provide gains for all parties involved, and would enhance growth, employment, and incomes. This allowed them to associate free trade with a moral stance in favor of the general good and to cast the mercantilist doctrine as an outmoded fixation on domestic national power. The association between free trade and the general good has been a fixture ortho-dox theory of free trade ever since. As neoclassical economics emerged, it placed particular emphasis on the universal gains that free trade was said to provide. Inserted into the model of perfect competition, free trade also became optimal. And with the advent of the Heckscher–Ohlin model (which assumes away any technological differences among nations), it also led to the claim that wage rates and profit rates (factor prices) would be equalized across nations without any need for international movements of labor and capital. Hence the holy trinity of modern free trade theory: universal good through universal gains, efficiency through optimality, and equity through international factor price equalization.

Of course, the development of the doctrine of free trade was not without challenge. In the early nineteenth century, late industrializers such as the United States and Germany saw free trade theory as a thinly veiled expression of the self-interest of leading industrial producers such as England (see Chapter 2 of this book). Their opposition was manifested in a critique of the theory itself, with particular emphasis on the failure of market prices to incorporate all relevant social costs, and on the absence of perfect competition in the real world. Both market failure and imperfect competition have been standard elements of the critique of free trade theory ever since.

Nayyar points further that while economic theorizing abstracts from political power, the latter plays a decisive role in the real world. From this point of view, the flexible history of free trade policy signals that this doctrine is as much about the pursuit of political power as was the mercantilism it replaced. The classic case is Britain's varying stance on its textile trade: Britain protected its textile industry when it was inferior to the Indian one, then forcibly imposed "free" trade on India when British textiles became competitive. As Britain rose to industrial dominance, it sought to impose free trade on the rest of the world but the US was strong enough to resist. In the Great Depression all sides shelved free trade in the sake of national interest. And then in the postwar period, when the US was economically hegemonic, it revived the doctrine. Given this history, it is utterly predictable that the developed world and its international institutions would try to force free trade and its associated theoretical claims on the rest of the world. Nayyar argues that in this latest phase, globalization has disproportionately benefited advanced economies, large international firms, and individual asset-owners, profit-earners, rentiers, managers, and professionals. Yet even here, when globalization poses a hazard, these groups typically use their power to try to contain it. For instance, when industries in the rich countries face strong competition from abroad, the focus switches from "free trade" to "fair trade." This same struggle is played out in the "rules of the game" constructed by the WTO, which put almost complete freedom for capital mobility [side by side with] … draconian restrictions on labor mobility" (Nayyar, Chapter 4 of this book, p. 81). For real development to take place, such double standards and rigged rules must be set aside in favor of an ongoing process whose goal is not to level the playing field but rather the contest itself.

2.2 Part II: Globalization and economic development

Lance Taylor (*Chapter 5*) analyzes the experiences of 14 countries that have undertaken external (trade and capital flow) liberalization policies in the last quarter century. He classifies the countries into five groups:

- Steady growth countries: China, India, Singapore, and Vietnam
- Asian crisis countries: Indonesia, Korea, Malaysia, and Thailand

- Countries that experienced cyclical stagnation: Philippines, and Turkey
- Countries in which inflation stabilization was paramount: Brazil, and Russia
- Post-socialist transition countries: Hungary, and Poland

These countries have been implementing external liberalization policies since at least 1980, and even earlier in some cases. Taylor traces the economic effects of these policies, with a particular focus on productivity growth, effective demand, and employment. The first two have opposite effects on employment, because increased productivity growth by itself implies slower job growth whereas increased effective demand growth implies faster job growth.[2]

Trade liberalization typically removes any import quota and export subsidies, and replaces them with fairly low tariffs. Demand tends to shift toward imports because they are now cheaper, and because capital liberalization (see subsequent paragraph) has made credit more available. Fiscal policy becomes more restrictive, as required by the rules. Domestic firms in the traded goods sector tend to suffer declines in their profit margins, leading the survivors to raise productivity growth through workplace reorganization, downsizing, and foreign outsourcing. This tends to raise productivity growth in the traded goods sector but does not generally raise the rate of growth of this sector's effective demand. Thus, after trade liberalization employment growth in the traded goods sector is typically low or even negative. On the other hand, in the nontraded goods sector, productivity growth tends to be low or even negative, whereas employment growth depends on growth in the sector's effective demand. Unskilled workers tend to suffer relatively greater job displacement than do skilled workers, so inequality tends to rise.

Capital liberalization generally produces a surge of foreign capital inflows, with a corresponding rise in a country's foreign debt. Within a country, these capital flows add to the assets of a country's financial institutions, so that unless they are sterilized by the central bank, they tend to set off a domestic credit boom, including booms in housing and asset market. In some cases, this sets off a classic "mania-panic-crash," as in Latin America in the 1980s. Real exchange rates (nominal exchange rates relative to inflation) tend to rise. More than half the economies being considered suffered external crises. The typical (albeit not universal) scenario begins with high interest rates designed to attract foreign capital, followed by a surge in inflows, which causes the exchange rate to appreciate and domestic credit to boom. As the central banks attempt to offset the capital inflows by reducing the domestic money supply, interest rates rise even further. At some point the bubble bursts, short-term capital flees the country, and the real economy undergoes a severe contraction. By contrast, it is particularly interesting that three out of the four "steady growth" countries (China, India, and Vietnam) were relatively *dirigiste* in their policy stances: They retained strong control on capital movements, interventionist policies involving both industrial and export promotion, maintained consistent productivity growth in both traded and nontraded sectors, and managed to avoid the real exchange appreciation experienced by the others.

John Weeks (*Chapter 6*) examines the relation between external liberalization and economic growth in Latin America. It has become "an article of faith" that reorienting a country toward the world market will increase its growth rate. Because developing countries did indeed experience enhanced export growth and increased capital inflows in neoliberal era which began in the 1980s, the analytical question becomes: how do these enhanced external flows affect overall economic growth? More precisely, does export growth enhance or retard growth in other sectors, and does foreign investment enhance or retard domestic investment? In the latter regard, he reminds us that statistics on foreign direct investment (FDI) must be interpreted with care. Before the liberalization of capital markets in the 1980s, FDI was largely synonymous with fixed capital formation but after that a significant portion of FDI consists of portfolio investment. For instance, among the larger countries from 1985 to 1989, debt-equity swaps alone account for 46 percent of total FDI (Weeks, Chapter 6 of this book, Table 6.1).

Weeks develops an analytical framework to address these questions. He decomposes the overall growth rate of GDP into its export and nonexport components. He assumes that the growth rate of nonexports depends on the growth rate of domestic demand and, through a linkage parameter λ_1 ("the coefficient of export dynamism"), on export growth. As Weeks points out, the standard argument that export growth enhances overall economic growth requires a positive empirical value for λ_1. A similar argument is used to construct a test for the effect of FDI growth on overall economic growth, which results in a parameter ρ_1. The standard argument concerning a positive linkage between foreign investment and domestic investment then requires a positive empirical value for ρ_1.

Seventeen Latin American countries were studied over three intervals: the import-substitution era from 1960 to 1981, the debt-crisis era from 1981 to 1989, and the recovery era from 1990 to 1997. Weeks finds that the positive export linkages assumed by standard theory are not universal. Whereas nine countries generally exhibit positive linkages, another six do not. Of these six, three move from positive export linkages in the first period to lower positive ones in the second, and to negative or nonsignificant linkages in the third; and the other three exhibit neutral or negative linkages in both the second and third periods (Weeks, Chapter 6 of this book, Table 6.1).[3] In the case of foreign capital inflows, 52 countries are studied, beginning from 1970 for reasons of data availability. Thirty-four of these yield nonsignificant estimates of the FDI linkage parameter, ten yield negative parameter estimates (indicating that FDI crowds out domestic investment), and eight yield positive estimates (indicating that FDI stimulates domestic investment). Only the last set conforms to the standard assumption, which is once again shown to be a special case. In the end, the evidence is quite mixed. Neoliberal policies do lead to enhanced export growth and increased capital inflows but can also retard overall growth and displace domestic investment.

Massoud Karshenas (*Chapter 7*) examines the relationship between export performance and the flexibility of real exchange rates and real wages in developing countries. Standard trade theory claims that flexible real exchange rates and flexible real wages would jointly bring about full employment and balanced international trade. From this point of view, the persistence of unemployment and trade imbalances in developing countries must be due to "rigidities" in real exchange rates and wages (see Chapter 3).

Karshenas shows that this presumption is false. He studies 26 less developed economies in Asia, Latin America, Africa, and the Middle East during the 1970s and the 1980s. Over this interval, the Asian countries of Korea, Malaysia, Singapore, Hong Kong, and Thailand were the most successful, having achieved high growth rates and rising standards of living. Although wage shares were generally stable in these countries (Chapter 7, Figure 7.5), real wages were able to rise because productivity was growing (Chapter 7, Figure 7.6). But he finds that the success of these particular Asian economies cannot be attributed to greater flexibility in real exchange rates and real wages. On the contrary, he finds that both variables fluctuate substantially in most countries in the sample. Real exchange rate variations are not noticeably different between the successful countries and the others (Karshenas, Chapter 7 of this book, p. 146), although wage share fluctuations (often declines) are even greater in the other countries (Karshenas, Chapter 7 of this book, p. 164).

What *does* distinguish the successful economies from the others is their ability to achieve rapid export growth in manufactured goods (Karshenas, Chapter 7 of this book, p. 139). This leads Karshenas to examine the precise linkages between his two key variables and export growth. He begins by considering two different international relative prices; (1) the price of domestic manufactures relative to the price of international manufactures (RER), both expressed in U.S. dollars; and (2) the price of existing domestic exports relative to the price of the exports of competing countries (UVX), both in U.S. dollars. Because each domestic price can be expressed as the sum of its unit labor and material costs and its unit profit, the domestic unit labor cost (i.e. the wage rate over labor productivity) plays an important role in the determination of each price ratio (Karshenas, Chapter 7 of this book, pp. 140–142). Moreover, because all prices are expressed in U.S. dollars, the nominal exchange rate enters into each measure. Indeed, both indexes are types of real exchange rates, although Karshenas reserves the term for the former (RER).

A central finding is that real exchange rates (RER) exhibit strong comovement with corresponding real unit labor costs (Karshenas, Chapter 7 of this book, p. 146, and Figure 7.1). On the other hand, relative export prices are not responsive to variations in RER, except when the latter is associated with short or medium run changes in real wages (Karshenas, Chapter 7 of this book, pp. 156–157). There is an interesting connection between these findings and the argument advanced by Shaikh (Chapter 3 of this book). Shaikh argues that the theory of comparative costs, upon which the whole corpus of standard trade theory rests, is wrong because relative international prices *cannot* simply move around to bring about balanced trade. On the contrary, relative international prices are competitively determined in the same way as relative domestic prices: by relative real unit costs, of which real unit labor costs are a major component (Shaikh, Chapter 3 of this book, pp. 57–58). It follows Karshenas' RER, which are manufacturing relative prices expressed in a common currency, will exhibit strong comovements with manufacturing real unit labor costs. It also follows that devaluations will not permanently alter the terms of trade (relative export prices) except when they affect relative costs, particularly relative wage costs. This is what Karshenas finds, and it is directly contrary to the expectations of standard trade theory.

A second finding is that export growth is highly sensitive to changes in relative export prices (RERX). This holds across countries, and across time (Karshenas, Chapter 7 of this book, p. 156). On the other hand, export growth is not sensitive to changes in the RER, precisely because the latter does not significantly affect relative export prices except when it affects real wages. In other words, devaluations in the real exchange rate (declines in RER) "seem to be only effective in promoting exports to the extent that they lead to a [medium run] decline in the share of wages in output during the process of adjustment" (Karshenas, Chapter 7 of this book, p. 159). However, over the longer run there does not seem to be any statistically significant association between changes in wage shares and export performance. If we recall that the successful Asian countries had rapid export growth but stable wage shares, this latter result is not surprising. Finally, export growth also responds strongly to the growth of investment. Karshenas interprets this latter variable as an index of technological dynamism and production flexibility. But we could also read this in a more traditional manner, in which investment is viewed as a proxy for aggregate demand.

2.3   Part III: Globalization, gender and inequality

Stephanie Seguino (*Chapter 8*) analyzes the effects of 30 years of globalization on gender inequality in Latin America and the Caribbean. Supporters of globalization tend to believe that it will facilitate economic growth and spur employment. Because women get paid relatively lower wages, it is argued that they will benefit relatively more from a surge in employment in a competitive environment. Thus, globalization should reduce gender inequality. Women in the Latin American and Caribbean (LAC) region would be particularly advantaged, because they rank higher in health and education than women in most other regions of the developing world. Critics of globalization have different expectations. They argue that liberalized trade, investment, and financial flows can put women at a disadvantage. This is because unemployment often increases under such circumstances, and women are generally the first to suffer. Similarly, the social expenditures that can help offset negative effects such as these, as well as preexisting disadvantages, are often reduced under such policy regimes. Finally, job growth need not automatically favor industries with higher female employment. The LAC region provides a good ground for the testing of these competing hypotheses, because it has undergone economic liberalization for quite some time. The consequent shift in economic structure has tended to favor manufacturing industries and which tend to be female-intensive.

Seguino first develops a set of indicators that track the trends in relative female well-being in the LAC from 1970 to 2000. These are grouped along three dimensions: *capabilities* measured through education, health, and nutrition; *resource access,* measured through income and employment; and *empowerment,* measured through the degree of women's share of parliamentary seats and of professional, technical, and managerial employment. As she notes, there is likely to be feedback among these categories, with improvement in any one spilling over to the others. Most of the changes in these individual measures point to an improvement in women's well-being. Notable among these are a decline in the number of children borne (fertility), and increases in female–male school enrollment rates and female shares of labor force and total employment. On the other hand, women's access to work worsened, as reflected in a rise in their relative unemployment rates.

The next step is to develop an aggregate measure for each of the 21 countries in the sample. This is accomplished by assigning each country points for each indicator according to the country's ranking in that indicator (21 points for the highest rank and 1 point for the lowest), and then summing the points to obtain an aggregate country score (Borda Rule scoring). El Salvador then ranks the highest in terms of improvements in women's relative well-being, and Colombia the second. This is quite striking, because both countries have undergone long period of conflict. On the other hand, the countries with the highest per capita growth in the sample, Chile and the Dominican Republic, ranked among the lowest.

To assess the overall impact of growth on women's well-being, Seguino first regresses each country's aggregate index on growth in per capita income, to control the level of its initial per capita income. By contrast, the World Bank uses single indicators of well-being (e.g. educational gaps), and does not control for initial income. Seguino is thus able to distinguish between income level and growth effects on distribution, and finds that while the former had a positive impact on gains in women's well-being, the latter had a *negative* impact. She concludes that where there were aggregate gains in women's well-being, these were due to factors other than growth. To get a better sense of the factors involved, she proceeds to regress the individual well-being indicators against four main explanatory variables: economic growth, production structure (manufacturing value-added as a share of GDP), the growth rate of government spending, and women's share of the labor force. Of these, the latter three have generally positive effects on gender well-being measures. But economic growth, the primary variable in the proglobalization argument, has mixed results: it has no effect on gender gaps in education; it has a negative effect on female–male population ratios, a stock variable taken as an indicator of female health; but it has a positive effect on relative female–male mortality, which is a flow variable also indicative of relative female health. Once again, the standard neoliberal claims do not stand up to detailed scrutiny.

Massoud Karshenas (Chapter 9) returns with a *tour-de-force* on the measurement of poverty in the least developing countries. The depth of world poverty is appalling, and virtually every modern social agenda has made poverty reduction a central theme. Indeed, even neoliberalism proclaims that its very purpose is to reduce global poverty. Yet it has become increasing evident that official poverty measures, such as those from the World Bank, are unreliable and may even be seriously flawed (Reddy and Pogge 2005). Karshenas tackles the problem head-on, by constructing a new set of poverty estimates that are consistent with country national income accounts. He begins with the survey data from which the World Bank draws its own $1-a-day and $2-a-day estimates of poverty, and adjusts it to make it consistent with data from corresponding national income accounts. He shows that the resulting estimates exhibit powerful structural patterns, and this allows him to extend his estimates to low-income countries excluded from his initial sample. Thus *even* using the World Bank's own data set, and accepting its own (strongly criticized) poverty thresholds of $1-a-day and $2-a-day, he finds that the World Bank measures "systematically underestimate poverty in poorer countries and overestimate it for the richer ones" (Karshenas Chapter 9 of this book, p. 225).

Karshenas starts by noting that the kinds of survey-based measures of income and expenditure used by the World Bank are often highly inconsistent with national income account data for the same country. For instance, in Tanzania, Ethiopia, and Mali, survey-based measures of per capita consumption are two to three times *higher* than those derived from national income accounts. On the other hand, in countries such as Bangladesh, India, Indonesia, Pakistan, and Thailand, they are two to three times *lower*. Similar glaring inconsistencies appear in comparisons of trends. Karshenas argues that while survey measures reflect method-ologies and sample designs that vary across time and space, national accounts are built around a given set of methods and concepts. Thus for comparisons across countries and across time, the latter are more reliable. Of course, survey methods also produce information on the *distribution* of income and expenditures, which national accounts do not. Accordingly, he uses the latter to calibrate the scale of the former, by adjusting the average per capita income of survey-based measures of expenditures to match those of national accounts. Thus his country expenditure measures exhibit the same distributions as those of the World Bank, but their levels are consistent with country national accounts. With this, he is able to provide new measures of "headcount poverty," that is, of the numbers of people living below the $1-a-day and $2-a-day poverty thresholds. These new poverty estimates indicate that the World Bank estimates underestimate poverty in the poorer developing countries and overestimate it in the relatively richer ones.

A striking feature of Karshenas' new measures is that his measures of head-count poverty exhibit a strongly nonlinear (logistic) pattern in relation to per capita income. These patterns vary by region but appear stable across time. He performs a number of validation tests on the robustness of these patterns. For instance, he drops individual observations from the sample, fits the curve for the reduced sample, and compares the estimated poverty headcount with the actual one, and finds that the two are quite close. He also finds that his measures are highly correlated with measures of the undernourished population produced by the Food and Agriculture Organization of the United Nations (FAO), and with the Human Development Index provided by the United Nations Development Program

(UNDP). The World Bank poverty measures, on the other hand, are not. The robustness of his fitted curves then allows him to estimate headcount poverty in those developing countries that lack distribution data, by using national income account data on their per capita incomes in conjunction with appropriate regional curves.

In his concluding section, Karshenas considers the implications of his findings for the ongoing debate about the relation between economic growth and poverty reduction. A common perspective, issued from the World Bank, is that there is a stable relation between growth in per capita incomes and poverty reduction, the "growth elasticity of poverty reduction." He notes that most of these estimates are based on regressions of changes in poverty measures on changes in per capita consumption or GDP. The estimated elasticities vary greatly, but Karshenas is more concerned here with their meaning. He argues that in a rich country, economic growth is neither necessary nor sufficient for poverty reduction. It is not necessary because rich countries can afford to directly fund poverty alleviation programs. And it is not sufficient because without such programs, growth by itself will leave those it does not pick up in poverty, and usher some newly displaced into it. Rich countries therefore need the kinds of social programs characteristic of postwar European Welfare States. In poor countries the situation is different, because the resources for redistribution are more limited. This does not preclude redistribution (e.g. land reform) in poor countries. It only implies that growth must play a relatively greater role than in rich countries. But then, can we presume that there exist stable links between growth and poverty reduction? Karshenas shows that there is indeed a stable relation, for both the $1-a-day and $2-a-day poverty measures. But as shown earlier, because the relationship between per capita income and headcount poverty is highly nonlinear, the relationship between their respective growth rates is equally nonlinear: *the "elasticities" are not constant.* Moreover, they are critically dependent on the exact poverty threshold chosen. The fatal difficulty with the World Bank's "growth elasticity" approach is that it confuses the stability of the underlying relation with the constancy of the resulting elasticities.

2.4 *Part IV: Globalization, capital mobility, and competition*

Ajit Singh (Chapter 10) provides a detailed and searching analysis of the debate about capital account liberalization (free flows of portfolio and direct investment). His primary objective is to review the theoretical, historical, and empirical arguments on this issue. While these arguments are of interest as part of the greater debate on the neoliberal agenda, they also have important implications for current discussions on the creation of a New International Financial Architecture (NIFA), and on the post-Doha agenda in the WTO in relation to FDI flows. Singh is concerned with fostering economic development within the context of current and future global rules of the game. In particular, he seeks to identify the kinds of rules about capital flows that would best serve the interests of developing countries.

Singh examines two main topics: (1) capital liberalization in general and (2) the particular impact of FDI. In each case, he begins with the traditional theoretical arguments, proceeds to the counter-arguments, and then examines the empirical literature on the issue. His overall conclusion is that neither history nor econometric investigation supports the neoliberal claim that free trade and capital flows will automatically lead to economic development. The main message of this chapter is that one needs to fashion particular developmental paths that account for a country's history, resource endowments, and public and private capabilities. One-size-fits-all rules will not work.

The traditional case for capital account liberalization rests directly on the case for free trade. And this in turn derives from the claim that a perfectly competitive equilibrium is optimal. Free trade is then presented as the logical extension of this same argument to the sphere of international competition. Of course, many neoclassical economists recognize that this story is based on highly unrealistic assumptions. They concede that real markets are neither perfect nor efficient. Nonetheless, they generally maintain that free trade is still the best practical policy, on the "sadder but wiser" grounds that free trade is the best "rule of thumb in a world whose politics are as imperfect as its markets" (Krugman 1987 cited in Singh in Chapter 10 of this book, p. 262). Singh points out that this so-called practical approach cannot be grounded in the theory itself, because once the assumptions are contravened, there is no longer any universal rule of thumb. Instead the gains and losses from various market "imperfections" and "externalities" would have to be balanced against the gains and losses of government intervention, on a case-by-case basis (Singh in Chapter 10 of this book, p. 262). Moreover, the putative trade benefits identified by the standard model require that there be full employment in each trading country (see Shaikh, Chapter 3 of this book). In the real world, particularly in the developing world, even this condition would require state intervention. Thus, the central lesson is that trade openness is most beneficial when there is an appropriate set of policies to manage domestic production, foreign trade, and international access to knowledge and technology. He cites Japan and Korea as the modern instances of this path to economic development, although one could also cite every other developed country. In all such cases, exports were promoted and imports were generally controlled, all in the context of comprehensive policies designed to foster rapid technological and industrial development (see Chang, Chapter 2).

The standard case for free trade also leads directly to an argument in favor of free capital flows. Just as the former is said to optimally allocate commodities across nations, the latter is said to optimally allocate capital. Thus at a theoretical level, capital account liberalization should allocate world savings to those who could use them most productively, thereby enhancing global economic efficiency and social welfare. As in the case for free trade, the free capital argument requires many theoretical assumptions that differ markedly from real world conditions. Many neoclassical economists concede this. They even admit that capital liberalization contains special risks, such as the possibility of currency crises. Yet most orthodox economists continue to favor both free trade and free capital flows (Bhagwati being an important exception, because he does not favor the latter). As

Stanley Fischer, the former Deputy Managing Director of the IMF, puts it, "capital movements are mostly appropriate: currency crises do not blow up out of a clear blue sky, but rather start as rational reactions to policy mistakes or external shocks. The problem is that once started, they may sometimes go too far." (Fischer 1997: 4–5, cited by Singh in Chapter 10 of this book, p. 264). For Fischer, the solution lies in establishing economic policies and institutions, particularly financial institutions, which are well adapted to function in a world of free capital flows.

Many counter-arguments exist. The first two are already familiar from the discussion of free trade theory. Even within neoclassical theory, the consideration of real world characteristics, which appear to the theoreticians as "imperfections" and "externalities," tend to vitiate the case for unrestricted international capital flows. Moreover, full employment is a necessary condition for the standard argument on the benefits of free capital flows but is hard to find in the developing world. Third, even within the neoclassical tradition itself, economists such as Stiglitz (2000) argue that free capital flows are fundamentally different from free commodities, because capital flows are intrinsically characterized by asymmetric information, agency problems, adverse selection, and moral hazard. Various heterodox economists (e.g. Davidson 2001) advance even stronger criticism, arguing that financial speculation is inherently unstable because the future is fundamentally unknown. The standard emphasis on greater transparency and better information would not resolve this (Singh in Chapter 10 of this book, pp. 265–266).

In addition to these problems with the standard argument, there is the previously mentioned association between the liberalization of short-term (portfolio) capital flows and deep economic and financial crises in Asia, Latin America, and Russia in the 1990s (Singh in Chapter 10 of this book, pp. 259–260). Such crises have arisen even in the developed world, including the US, the UK, and various Scandinavian countries, but they have invariably been deeper and more destructive in the developing world. Many economists (e.g. Stiglitz 2000 cited by Singh in Chapter 10 of this book, p. 265) recognize that this record provides a serious reason for avoiding precipitous liberalization of short-capital flows, although the official position continues to portray these problems as being induced by "policy mistakes or external shocks" (see the previous quote by Fischer). At an econometric level, the results of studies of costs and benefits are decidedly mixed: some indicate that financial liberalization has a positive impact on domestic investment; others point to a close causal connection between financial liberalization and banking and currency crises in the developing world. Similarly, the econometric link between financial liberalization and growth is quite tenuous (Singh in Chapter 10 of this book, p. 000). On the other hand, studies indicate that the real economic costs of financial crises are substantial, ranging from an estimated 3.2 percent of GDP in the U.S. savings and loans crisis of 1984–91 to 55.3 percent of GDP in the banking crisis in Argentina from 1980 to 82 (Table 10.1). And of course the Asian economic crisis of the late 1990s had devastating effects on employment, poverty, and inequality. Singh attributes these crises to the characteristic instability of financial markets, not to some "inflexibility" of labor markets because real wages were typically quite flexible (see also Karshenas, Chapter 7, on this issue).

In the final section of this chapter, Singh analyzes the particular impact of FDI. He notes that FDI is generally viewed much more favorably than short-term capital flows, because it is supposedly less volatile and because it supposedly creates access to resources, technology, markets, and knowledge (Stiglitz 2000). It should be noted that *measured* FDI includes retained profits and financial flows associated with derivatives and hedge funds, and these elements can be quite volatile. Even leaving these aside, it is important to recognize that the positive net demand for domestic currency induced by current FDI has to balance against a negative net demand arising from associated future dividend and repatriated profit outflows, which could trigger a liquidity crisis in the future. Finally, the empirical evidence on the technology transfer and spill-over effects (on national productivity and investment) of FDI is quite mixed. The general finding is that technology transfer and productivity are best captured when FDI is integrated into a national plan for industrial development. As for the effect of FDI on domestic investment, it appears to have been strongly positive in Asia, negative in Latin America, and essentially neutral in Africa. This is contrary to standard expectations, because the positive effect appears in the *less* liberalized region (Asia), whereas the negative effect appears in the *more* liberalized one (Agosin and Mayer 2000: 27–8). Lastly, there appears to be no consistent empirical link between FDI and enhanced economic growth (Singh in Chapter 10 of this book, p. 275). Singh's overall conclusion is that, like short-term capital flows, FDI too should be regulated with an eye toward extracting maximum benefits for the country's development.

Andrew Glyn (*Chapter 11*) turns the discussion to the impact of globalization on the advanced world itself: on its internal profitability and on its internal politics. His focus is mainly on four advanced countries (USA, Japan, Germany, and the UK), with an excursion into the profitability patterns of selected developing countries. Glyn considers two main questions. First, has globalization led to a convergence in profitability among the advanced countries? And second, did the increased exchange rate volatility that accompanied globalization also show up in profitability?

Profitability is defined in two ways: as profit shares and as profit rates. Profit shares are in turn measured in two ways, conditioned by the availability of data. At a national level, in the first section of the paper, they are constructed as pretax net profits relative to net national product; and at the level of manufacturing industries, in the second section, they represent the ratio of gross (of depreciation) pretax profits to gross value added. Profit rates, on the other hand, are measured as pretax profits relative to the total capital stock, the latter being the sum of the net fixed capital stock and inventories. Since inventories decline from a range of 18% to 40% of fixed capital in the 1970s, to 12%–15% in the 1990s, their presence in the total capital stock affects both the level and trend of the profit rate. It should be added that because Glyn's data is not adjusted for cyclical fluctuations, the well-known cyclical variations of inventory-sales ratios undoubtedly increases the volatility of his profit rate measures.

Glyn finds that profit rates not only generally decline over the postwar period but also tend to converge. Moreover, the declines themselves are heavily concentrated in manufacturing, and over time this relatively more rapid fall in manufacturing profit rates eliminates the differential between them and profit rates in non-manufacturing. He interprets this as an effect of increased international competition in manufacturing that has been unleashed by globalization. Because the profit rates of nonmanufacturing sectors also fall, albeit at a slower rate, he notes that there must be other causes at work. Indeed, by considering the profit rate as the ratio of the profit share and the capital-output ratio, he shows that both components contribute to the overall decline in profit rates.

In his analysis of the variability of profitability, Glyn analyzes the gross profit share (profit relative to value added, both being gross of depreciation) in manufacturing across 16 OECD countries. Looking profit shares *within* countries, decade by decade, he finds that their volatility increases sharply from the 1960s to the 1970s, declines a bit in the 1980s, and then increases back to the previous level in the 1990s. *Across* countries, manufacturing profit shares are somewhat less dispersed in the 1980s than they are in the 1970s or the 1990s. Glyn ties both of these patterns to globalization, through the volatility in exchange rates induced by sharply increased capital flows. He connects exchange rates to profitability by means of an index of relative unit labor costs in manufacturing, because unit labor costs are important to profits, and because this index is dominated by movements in the nominal exchange rate. His regressions indicate that changes in relative unit labor costs have a major effect on gross profit shares, although the magnitude of this effect varies across countries. In a brief concluding section, he examines the evolution of profit shares for a small selection of developing countries which exhibit some suggestive patterns.

On the whole, Glyn discerns two phases to postwar globalization in the advanced capitalist countries. The first lasts until the 1970s, exhibiting increasing competition, particularly in manufacturing. Because workers are strong enough to maintain and enhance their positions in this era, profits end up been squeezed by the increased competition. But starting in the 1980s, capital mobility becomes more prominent, unemployment increases, and workers increasingly come under political attack. This erodes worker bargaining positions to such an extent that wage shares fall, and hence profit shares generally rise, despite increased international competition. In addition, increased capital flows make exchange rates very volatile, and this volatility is transmitted to profitability.

Notes

1 These authors of a recent major survey called "Trade Liberalization and Poverty: The Evidence So Far" also note that "there is ... a surprising number of gaps in our knowledge about trade liberalization and poverty" (Winters *et al.* 2004: 107).

2 Taylor uses the national income accounting identity $Y = C + I + G + \text{Exp} - \text{Imp} = C + S + T$, where the variables used represent GDP, investment, government spending, exports, imports, savings, and taxes, respectively. Following Godley (1999), he uses this to derive the aggregate sectoral balances identity $(I-S) + (G-T) + (\text{Exp}-\text{Imp}) = 0$, where

the terms in parentheses represent the private, government, and external balances, respectively.
3 Weeks (*op. cit.*) finds that Bolivia and Venezuela are anomalous. They both show negative linkages during the first period (1960–81), and either positive (Bolivia) or neutral (Venezuela) thereafter. But these are also the only two countries for which there is no consistent data for the 1960s.

References

Agosin, M. R. and Tussie, D. (1993) *Trade and Growth: New Dilemmas in Trade Policy*, London: Macmillan Press.

Agosin, M. R. and Mayer, R. (2000) 'Foreign Investment in Developing Countries: Does It Crowd In Domestic Investment?', United Nations Conference on Trade and Development, Discussion Paper No. 146, February 2000.

Bhagwati, J. (2002) *Free Trade Today*, Princeton, NJ: Princeton University Press.

Chang, H.-J. (2002) 'Kicking Away the Ladder', *Post-autistic Economics Review*, no. 15, September 4.

Davidson, P. (2001) 'If Markets are Efficient, Why Have There Been So Many International Financial Market Crises Since the 1970s?' in P. Arestis, M. Baddeley, and J. McCombie, (eds.) *What Global Economic Crisis?*, London: Palgrave.

Fischer, S. (1997) 'Capital Account Liberalisation and the Role of the IMF', Paper presented at the seminar Asia and the IMF, Hong Kong, China, September 19, 1997.

Friedman, B. M. (2002) 'Globalization: Stiglitz's Case', *The New York Review of Books*, August 15, 49(13).

Friedman, M. and Friedman, R. (2004) 'The Case for Free Trade', Globalization and World Capitalism: A Debate, *Cato Institute*, May 25. Online. Available HTTP: <http://www.cato.org/special/symposium/essays/norberg.html> (accessed September 20, 2004).

Godley, W. (1999) 'Seven Unsustainable Processes: Medium-Term Prospects and Policies for the US and the World', Annandale-on-Hudson, NY: Jerome Levy Economics Institute, Bard College.

Krugman, P. R. (1987) 'Is Free Trade Passé?', *Journal of Economics Perspectives,* 1(2): 131–43.

McCartney, M. (2004) 'Liberalisation and Social Structure: The Case of Labour Intensive Export Growth in South Asia', *Post-autistic Economics Review,* no. 23, January 5. Online. Available HTTP: <http://www.btinternet.com/~pae_news/review/ issue23.htm> (accessed September 20, 2004).

Norberg, J. (2004) 'How Globalization Conquers Poverty', Globalization and World Capitalism: A Debate, *Cato Institute*, May 25. Online. Available HTTP: <http://www.cato.org/special/symposium/essays/norberg.html> (accessed September 20, 2004).

Reddy, S. G. and Pogge, T. W. (2005), 'How *Not* to Count the Poor', Version 6.1, October 3. Online. Available HTTP: <www.socialanalysis.org> (accessed October 15, 2005).

Rodrik, D. (2001) 'The Global Governance of Trade: As if Trade Really Mattered', Background paper to the UNDP project on Trade and Sustainable Human Development, October, New York: United Nations Development Program (UNDP).

Stiglitz, J. (2000) 'Capital Market Liberalization, Economic Growth, and Instability', *World Development*, 28(6): 1075–86.

—— (2002) 'Globalism's Discontents', *The American Prospect*, January 1–14, 13(1): 16–21.

UNDP (United Nations Development Program) (2003) *Human Development Report*, New York: Oxford University Press.

Weisbrot, M. (2002) 'The Mirage of Progress', *The American Prospect*, January 1–14, 13 (1): 10–12.

Weller, C. E. and Hersh, A. (2002) 'Free Markets and Poverty', *The American Prospect*, January 1–14, 13(1): 13–15.

Winters, L. A., McCulloch, N., and McKay, A. (2004) 'Trade Liberalization and Poverty: The Evidence So Far', *Journal of Economic Literature*, 42(1): 72–115.

World Bank (2001) *World Development Report 2000/2001: Attacking Poverty*, New York: Oxford University Press.

—— (2003) World Development Report 2003: Sustainable Development in a Dynamic World, New York: Oxford University Press.

Part I
Globalization and free trade

2 Kicking away the ladder: the "real" history of free trade

Ha-Joon Chang[1]

1 Introduction

Central to the neoliberal discourse on globalization is the conviction that free trade, more than free movements of capital or labor, is the key to global prosperity. Even many of those who are not enthusiastic about all aspects of globalization – ranging from the free-trade economist Jagdish Bhagwati advocating capital control, to some NGOs accusing the developed countries for not opening up their agricultural markets – seem to agree that free trade is the most benign, or at least the least problematic, element in the progress of globalization.

Part of the conviction in free trade that the proponents of globalization possess comes from the belief that economic theory has irrefutably established the superiority of free trade – well, almost, as there are some formal models which show free trade may not be the best (although even the builders of such models as Paul Krugman will argue that free trade is still the best policy because interventionist trade policies are almost certain to be politically abused). However, even more powerful is their belief that history is on their side, so to speak. After all, the defenders of free trade ask, isn't free trade how all the world's developed countries have become rich? What are some developing countries thinking, they wonder, when they refuse to adopt such a tried and tested recipe for economic development?

A closer look at the history of capitalism, however, reveals a very different story (Chang 2002). As we shall establish in some detail in this chapter, when they were developing countries themselves, virtually all of today's developed countries did not practise free trade (and *laissez-faire* industrial policy as its domestic counterpart) but promoted their national industries through tariffs, subsidies, and other measures. Particularly notable is the fact that the gap between the "real" and the "imagined" histories of trade policy is the greatest in relation to Britain and the USA, which are conventionally believed to have reached the top of the world's economic hierarchy by adopting free trade when other countries were stuck with outdated mercantilist policies. As we shall show in some detail, these two countries were in fact often the pioneers and frequently the most ardent users of *interventionist* trade and industrial policy measures in their early stages of development.

By debunking the myth of free trade from the historical perspective, this paper shows that there is an urgent need for a thorough rethink on some key conventional wisdoms in the debate on trade policy, and more broadly on globalization.

2   The "official history of capitalism" and its limitations

The "official history of capitalism," which informs today's debate on trade policy, economic development, and globalization, goes like the following.

From the eighteenth century, Britain proved the superiority of free-market and free-trade policies by beating interventionist France, its main competitor at the time, and establishing itself as the supreme world economic power. Especially once it had abandoned its deplorable agricultural protection (the Corn Law) and other remnants of old mercantilist protectionist measures in 1846, it was able to play the role of the architect and hegemon of a new "Liberal" world economic order. This Liberal world order, perfected around 1870, was based on:

1   *laissez-faire* industrial policies at home;
2   low barriers to the international flows of goods, capital, and labor; and
3   macroeconomic stability, both nationally and internationally, guaranteed by the Gold Standard and the principle of balanced budgets.

A period of unprecedented prosperity followed.

Unfortunately, according to this story, things started to go wrong with the First World War. In response to the ensuing instability of the world economic and political system, countries started to erect trade barriers again. In 1930, the USA also abandoned free trade and raised tariffs with the infamous Smoot–Hawley Tariff, which the famous free-trade economist Jagdish Bhagwati called "the most visible and dramatic act of anti-trade folly" (Bhagwati 1985: 22 fn 10). The world free trade system finally ended in 1932, when Britain, hitherto the champion of free trade, succumbed to the temptation and re-introduced tariffs. The resulting contraction and instability in the world economy and then finally the Second World War destroyed the last remnants of the first Liberal world order.

After the Second World War, so the story goes, some significant progress was made in trade liberalization through the early GATT (General Agreement on Trade and Tariffs) talks. However, unfortunately, *dirigiste* approaches to economic management dominated the policy-making scene until the 1970s in the developed world, and until the early 1980s in the developing world (and the Communist world until its collapse in 1989).

Fortunately, it is said, interventionist policies have been largely abandoned across the world since the 1980s with the rise of neoliberalism, which emphasized the virtues of small government, *laissez-faire* policies, and international openness. Especially in the developing world, by the late 1970s economic growth had begun to falter in most countries outside East and Southeast Asia, which were already pursuing "good" policies (of free market and free trade). This growth failure, which often manifested itself in economic crises of the early 1980s, exposed the limitations of old-style interventionism and protectionism.

As a result, most developing countries have come to embrace "policy reform" in a neoliberal direction.

When combined with the establishment of new global governance institutions represented by the WTO, these policy changes at the national level have created a new global economic system, comparable in its (at least potential) prosperity only to the earlier "golden age" of Liberalism (1870–1914). Renato Ruggiero, the first Director General of the WTO, thus argues that, thanks to this new world order, we now have "the potential for eradicating global poverty in the early part of the next [21st] century – a utopian notion even a few decades ago, but a real possibility today" (1998: 131).

As we shall see later, this story paints a fundamentally misleading picture but no less a powerful one for it. And it should be accepted that there are some senses in which the late nineteenth century can indeed be described as an era of *laissez faire*.

To begin with, there was a period in the late nineteenth century, albeit a brief one, when liberal trade regimes prevailed in large parts of the world economy. Between 1860 and 1880, many European countries reduced tariff protection substantially (see Table 2.1). At the same time, most of the rest of the world were forced to practise free trade through colonialism and through unequal treaties in the cases of a few nominally "independent" countries (such as the Latin American countries, China, Thailand [then Siam], Iran [then Persia], and Turkey [then the Ottoman Empire], and even Japan until 1911). Of course, the obvious exception to this was the USA, which maintained very high tariff barriers even during this period (see Table 2.1). However, given that the USA was still a relatively small part of the world economy, it may not be totally unreasonable to say that this is as close to free trade as the world has ever got.

More importantly, the scope of state intervention before the First World War was quite limited by modern standards. States had limited budgetary policy capability because there was no income tax in most countries[2] and the balanced budget doctrine dominated. They also had limited monetary policy capability because many of them did not have a central bank,[3] and the Gold Standard restricted their policy freedom. They also had limited command over investment resources, as they owned or regulated few financial institutions and industrial enterprises. One somewhat paradoxical consequence of all these limitations was that tariff protection was far more important as a policy tool in the nineteenth century than it is in our time.

Despite these limitations, as we shall soon see, virtually all of today's developed countries – or now-developed countries (NDCs) – actively used interventionist trade and industrial policies aimed at promoting – not simply "protecting," it should be emphasized – infant industries during their catch-up periods.[4]

3   History of trade and industrial policies in today's developed countries

3.1 Britain

As the intellectual fountain of the modern *laissez-faire* doctrines and as the only country that can claim to have practised a total free trade at least at one point,

Table 2.1 Average tariff rates on manufactured products for selected developed countries in their early stages of development (weighted average, in percentages of value)[a]

	1820[b]	1875[b]	1913	1925	1931	1950
Austria[c]	R	15–20	18	16	24	18
Belgium[d]	6–8	9–10	9	15	14	11
Denmark	25–35	15–20	14	10	na	3
France	R	12–15	20	21	30	18
Germany[e]	8–12	4–6	13	20	21	26
Italy	na	8–10	18	22	46	25
Japan[f]	R	5	30	na	na	na
The Netherlands[d]	6–8	3–5	4	6	na	11
Russia	R	15–20	84	R	R	R
Spain	R	15–20	41	41	63	na
Sweden	R	3–5	20	16	21	9
Switzerland	8–12	4–6	9	14	19	na
UK	45–55	0	0	5	na	23
US	35–45	40–50	44	37	48	14

Source: Bairoch 1993: 40, Table 3.3.

Notes:

R, numerous and important restrictions on manufactured imports existed and therefore average tariff rates are not meaningful.

a   World Bank (1991: 97, Box Table 5.2) provides a similar table, partly drawing on Bairoch's own studies that form the basis of the above table. However, the World Bank figures, although in most cases very similar to Bairoch's figures, are *unweighted* averages, which are obviously less preferable to *weighted* average figures that Bairoch provides.

b   These are very approximate rates, and give range of average rates, not extremes.

c   Austria–Hungary before 1925.

d   In 1820, Belgium was united with the Netherlands.

e   The 1820 figure is for Prussia only.

f   Before 1911, Japan was obliged to keep low tariff rates (up to 5 percent) through a series of "unequal treaties" with the European countries and the USA. The World Bank table cited in note 1 above gives Japan's *unweighted* average tariff rate for *all goods* (and not just manufactured goods) for the years 1925, 1930, 1950 as 13 percent, 19 percent, 4 percent, respectively.

Britain is widely regarded as having developed without significant state intervention. However, this cannot be further from the truth.

Britain entered its postfeudal age (thirteenth to fourteenth centuries) as a relatively backward economy. It relied on exports of raw wool and, to a lesser extent, of low-value-added wool cloth to the then more advanced Low Countries (Ramsay 1982: 59; Davies 1999: 348). Edward III (1312–77) is believed to have been the first King who deliberately tried to develop local wool cloth manufacturing. He only wore English cloth to set an example,[5] brought in the Flemish weavers, centralized trade in raw wool, and banned the import of woolen cloth (Davies 1999: 349; Davis 1966: 281).

Further impetus came from the Tudor monarchs. The famous eighteenth century merchant, politician, and the author of the novel, *Robinson Crusoe*, Daniel Defoe, describes this policy in his now-almost-forgotten book, *A Plan of the English Commerce* (1728). In this book, he describes in some detail how the

Tudor monarchs, especially Henry VII (1485–1509), transformed England from a raw-wool exporter into the most formidable woolen-manufacturing nation in the world (pp. 81–101). According to Defoe, from 1489, Henry VII implemented schemes to promote woolen manufacturing, which included: sending royal missions to identify locations suited to wool manufacturing; poaching skilled workers from the Low Countries; increasing duties on the export of raw wool; and even temporarily banning the export of raw wool (Ramsay 1982 provides further details).

For obvious reasons, it is difficult to establish the exact importance of the afore-mentioned infant industry promotion policies. However, without them, it would have been very difficult for Britain to make this initial success in industrialization, without which its Industrial Revolution may have been next to impossible.

The most important event in Britain's industrial development, however, was the 1721 policy reform introduced by Robert Walpole, the first British Prime Minister, during the reign of George I (1660–1727). Before this, the British government's policies were in general aimed at capturing trade and generating government revenue. Even the promotion of woolen manufacturing was partly motivated by revenue considerations. In contrast, the policies introduced after 1721 were deliberately aimed at promoting manufacturing industries. Introducing the new law, Walpole stated, through the King's address to the Parliament: "it is evident that nothing so much contributes to promote the public well-being as the exportation of manufactured goods and the importation of foreign raw material" (as cited in List 1885: 40).

The 1721 legislation, and the supplementary policy changes subsequently made, included the following measures (for details, see Brisco 1907: 131–3, 148–55, 169–71; McCusker 1996: 358; Davis 1966: 313–14). First, import duties on raw materials used for manufactures were lowered, or even altogether dropped. Second, duty drawbacks on imported raw materials for exported manu-factures were increased. Third, export duties on most manufactures were abol-ished. Fourth, duties on imported foreign manufactured goods were raised. Fifth, export subsidies (then called "bounties") were extended to new export items such as silk products and gunpowder, whereas the existing export subsidies to sailcloth and refined sugar were increased. Sixth, regulation was introduced to control the quality of manufactured products, especially textile products, so that unscrupu-lous manufacturers would not damage the reputation of British products in for-eign markets. What is very interesting is that these policies, as well as the principles behind them, were uncannily similar to those used by countries like Japan, Korea, and Taiwan during the postwar period (see below).

Despite its widening of technological lead over other countries, Britain contin-ued its policies of industrial promotion until the mid-nineteenth century. As we can see from Table 2.1, Britain had very high tariffs on manufacturing products even as late as the 1820s, some two generations after the start of its Industrial Revolution.

By the end of the Napoleonic War in 1815, however, there were increasing pressures for free trade in Britain from the increasingly confident manufacturers. Although there was a round of tariff reduction in 1833, the big change came in

1846, when the Corn Law was repealed and tariffs on many manufacturing goods abolished (Bairoch 1993: 20–1).

The repeal of the Corn Law is these days commonly regarded as the ultimate victory of the Classical liberal economic doctrine over wrong-headed mercantilism. Although we should not underestimate the role of economic theory in this policy shift, it is probably better understood as an act of "free trade imperialism" (the term is due to Gallagher and Robinson 1953) intended to "halt the move to industrialization on the Continent by enlarging the market for agricultural produce and primary materials" (Kindleberger 1978: 196). Indeed, many leaders of the campaign to repeal the Corn Law, such as the politician Robert Cobden and John Bowring of the Board of Trade, saw their campaign precisely in such terms (Kindleberger 1975; Reinert 1998).[6] Cobden's view on this is clearly revealed in the following passage:

> The factory system would, in all probability, not have taken place in America and Germany. It most certainly could not have flourished, as it has done, both in these states, and in France, Belgium, and Switzerland, through the fostering bounties which the high-priced food of the British artisan has offered to the cheaper fed manufacturer of those countries.
>
> (*The Political Writings of Richard Cobden* 1868 William Ridgeway, London, vol. 1, p. 150, as cited in Reinert 1998: 292)

Symbolic the repeal of Corn Law may have been, it was only after 1860 that most tariffs were abolished. However, the era of free trade did not last long. It ended when Britain finally acknowledged that it has lost its manufacturing eminence and re-introduced tariffs on a large scale in 1932 (Bairoch 1993: 27–8).

Thus seen, contrary to the popular belief, Britain's technological lead that enabled this shift to a free trade regime had been achieved "behind high and long-lasting tariff barriers" (Bairoch 1993: 46). And it is for this reason that Friedrich List, the nineteenth-century German economist who is (mistakenly – see Section 3.2) known as the father of modern "infant industry" theory, wrote the following passages.

> It is a very common clever device that when anyone has attained the summit of greatness, he *kicks away the ladder* by which he has climbed up, in order to deprive others of the means of climbing up after him. In this lies the secret of the cosmopolitical doctrine of Adam Smith, and of the cosmopolitical tendencies of his great contemporary William Pitt, and of all his successors in the British Government administrations.
>
> Any nation which by means of protective duties and restrictions on navigation has raised her manufacturing power and her navigation to such a degree of development that no other nation can sustain free competition with her, can do nothing wiser than to *throw away these ladders* of her greatness, to preach to other nations the benefits of free trade, and to declare in penitent tones that she has hitherto wandered in the paths of error, and has now for the first time succeeded in discovering the truth [italics added].
>
> (List 1885: 295–6)

3.2 USA

As we have just seen, Britain was the first country to successfully use a large-scale infant industry promotion strategy. However, its most ardent user was probably the USA – the eminent economic historian Paul Bairoch once called it "the mother country and bastion of modern protectionism" (Bairoch 1993: 30). This fact is, interestingly, rarely acknowledged in the modern literature, especially coming out of the USA.[7] However, the importance of infant industry protection in US development cannot be overemphasized.

From the early days of colonization, industrial protection was a controversial policy issue in what later became the USA. To begin with, Britain did not want to industrialize the colonies and duly implemented policies to that effect (e.g. banning of high-value-added manufacturing activities). Around the time of the independence, the Southern agrarian interests opposed any protection, and the Northern manufacturing interests wanted it, represented by, among others, Alexander Hamilton, the first Secretary of the Treasury of the USA (1789–95).

In fact, it was Alexander Hamilton in his *Reports of the Secretary of the Treasury on the Subject of Manufactures* (1791) who first systematically set out the infant industry argument, and not the German economist Friedrich List as it is often thought (Corden 1974 chapter 8; Reinert 1996). Indeed, List started out as a free trade advocate and only converted to the infant industry argument following his exile in the US (1825–30) (Henderson 1983; Reinert 1998). Many US intellectuals and politicians during the country's catch-up period clearly understood that the free trade theory advocated by the British Classical Economists was unsuited to their country. Indeed, it was against the advice of great economists like Adam Smith and Jean Baptiste Say that the Americans were protecting their industries.[8]

In his *Reports*, Hamilton argued that the competition from abroad and the "forces of habit" would mean that new industries that could soon become internationally competitive ("infant industries")[9] would not be started in the USA, unless the initial losses were guaranteed by government aid (Dorfman and Tugwell 1960: 31–2; Conkin 1980: 176–7). According to him, this aid could take the form of import duties or, in rare cases, prohibition of imports (Dorfman and Tugwell 1960: 32). He also believed that duties on raw materials should be generally low (p. 32). We can see close resemblance between this view and the view espoused by Walpole (see Section 3.1 above) – a point that was not lost on the contemporary Americans, especially Hamilton's political opponents (Elkins and McKitrick 1993: 19).[10]

Initially, the US did not have a federal-level tariff system, but when the Congress acquired the power to tax, it passed a liberal tariff act (1789), imposing a 5 percent flat rate tariff on all imports, with some exceptions (Garraty and Carnes 2000: 139–40, 153; Bairoch 1993: 33). And despite Hamilton's *Reports*, between 1792 and the war with Britain in 1812, the average tariff level remained around 12.5 percent, although during the war all tariffs were doubled to meet the increased government expenses due to the war (Garraty and Carner 2000: 210).

A significant shift in policy occurred in 1816, when a new law was introduced to keep the tariff level close to the wartime level – especially protected were cotton, woolen, and iron goods (Garraty and Carnes 2000: 210; Cochran and Miller 1942: 15–6). Between 1816 and the end of the Second World War, the USA had one of the highest average tariff rates on manufacturing imports in the world (see Table 2.1). Given that the country enjoyed an exceptionally high degree of "natural" protection due to high transportation costs at least until the 1870s, we can say that the US industries were literally the most protected in the world until 1945.

Even the Smoot–Hawley Tariff of 1930, which Bhagwati in the aforementioned quote portrays as a radical departure from a historic free-trade stance, only marginally (if at all) increased the degree of protectionism in the US economy. As we can see from Table 2.1, the average tariff rate for manufactured goods that resulted from this bill was 48 percent, and it still falls within the range of the average rates that had prevailed in the USA since the Civil War, albeit in the upper region of this range. It is only in relation to the brief "liberal" interlude of 1913–29 that the 1930 tariff bill can be interpreted as increasing protectionism, although even then it was not by very much (from 37 percent in 1925 to 48 percent in 1931 – see Table 2.1).

In this context, it is also important to note that the American Civil War was fought on the issue of tariffs as much as, if not more than, on the issue of slavery. Of the two major issues that divided the North and the South, the South had actually more to fear on the tariff front than on the slavery front. Abraham Lincoln was a well-known protectionist who had cut his political teeth under the charismatic politician Henry Clay in the Whig Party, which advocated the "American System" based on infrastructural development and protectionism – thus named on recognition that free trade was in "British" interest (Luthin 1944: 610–1; Fraysse 1994: 99–100). Moreover, Lincoln thought the blacks were racially inferior and slave emancipation was an idealistic proposal with no prospect of immediate implementation (Garraty and Carnes 2000: 391–2; Foner 1998: 92) – he is said to have emancipated the slaves in 1862 as a strategic move to win the War rather than out of some moral conviction (Garraty and Carnes 2000: 405).[11]

It was only after the Second World War, with its industrial supremacy unchallenged, that the US liberalized its trade (although not as unequivocally as Britain did in the mid-nineteenth century) and started championing the cause of free trade – once again proving List right on his "ladder-kicking" metaphor.[12] The following quote from Ulysses Grant, the Civil War hero and the President of the USA during 1868–1876 clearly shows how the Americans had no illusions about ladder-kicking on the British side and their side.

> For centuries England has relied on protection, has carried it to extremes and has obtained satisfactory results from it. There is no doubt that it is to this system that it owes its present strength. After two centuries, England has found it convenient to adopt free trade because it thinks that protection can no longer offer it anything. Very well then, Gentlemen, my knowledge of our

country leads me to believe that within 200 years, when America has gotten out of protection all that it can offer, it too will adopt free trade.

(Ulysses S. Grant, the President of the USA,
1868–76, cited in Frank 1967: 164)[13]

Important as it may have been, tariff protection was not the only policy deployed by the U.S. government to promote the country's economic development during its catch-up phase. At least from the 1830s, it supported an extensive range of agricultural research through the granting of government land to agricultural colleges and the establishment of government research institutes (Kozul-Wright 1995: 100). In the second half of the nineteenth century, it expanded public educational investments – in 1840, less than half of the total investment in education was public, whereas by 1900 this figure had risen to almost 80 percent – and raised the literacy ratio to 94 percent by 1900 (p. 101, especially fn 37). It also promoted the development of transportation infrastructure, especially through the granting of land and subsidies to railway companies (pp. 101–2).

And it is important to recognize that the role of the U.S. federal government in industrial development has been substantial even in the postwar era, thanks to the large amount of defense-related procurements and R&D spending, which have had enormous spillover effects (Shapiro and Taylor 1990: 866; Owen 1966 chapter. 9, Mowery and Rosenberg 1993).[14] The share of the US federal government in total R&D spending, which was only 16 percent in 1930 (Owen 1966: 149–50), remained between one-half and two-thirds during the postwar years (Mowery and Rosenberg 1993, Table 2.3). The critical role of the US government's National Institutes of Health (NIH) in supporting R&D in pharmaceutical and biotechnology industries should also be mentioned. Even according to the US pharmaceutical industry association itself (see http://www.phrma.org/publications), only 43 percent of pharmaceutical R&D is funded by the industry itself, whereas 29 percent is funded by the NIH.

3.3   Germany

Germany is a country that is today commonly known as the home of infant industry protection, both intellectually and in terms of policies. However, historically speaking, tariff protection actually played a much *less* important role in the economic development of Germany than that of the UK or the USA.

The tariff protection for industry in Prussia before the 1834 German customs union under its leadership (*Zollverein*) and that subsequently accorded to German industry in general remained mild (Blackbourn 1997: 117). In 1879, the Chancellor of Germany, Otto von Bismarck introduced a great tariff increase to cement the political alliance between the *Junkers* (landlords) and the heavy industrialists – the so-called "marriage of iron and rye." However, even after this, substantial protection was accorded only to the key heavy industries, especially the iron & steel industry, and industrial protection remained low in general

(Blackbourn 1997: 320). As it can be seen from Table 2.1, the level of protection in German manufacturing was one of the *lowest* among comparable countries throughout the nineteenth century and the first half of the twentieth century.

The relatively low tariff protection does not, however, mean that the German state took a *laissez-faire* approach to economic development. Especially under Frederick William I (1713–40) and Frederick the Great (1740–86) in the eighteenth century, the Prussian state pursued a range of policies to promote new industries – especially textiles (linen above all), metals, armaments, porcelain, silk, and sugar refining – by providing monopoly rights, trade protection, export subsidies, capital investments, and skilled workers from abroad (Trebilcock 1981: 136–52).

From the early nineteenth century, the Prussian state also invested in infra-structure – the most famous example being the government financing of road building in the Ruhr (Milward and Saul 1979: 417). It also implemented educational reform, which not only involved building new schools and universities but also the reorientation of their teaching from theology to science and technology – this at a time when science and technology was not taught in Oxford or Cambridge (Kindleberger 1978: 191).[15]

There were some growth-retarding effects of Prussian government intervention, such as the opposition to the development of banking (Kindleberger 1978: 199–200). However, on the whole, we cannot but agree with the statement by Milward and Saul (1979) that

> [t]o successive industrializing countries the attitude taken by early nineteenth-century German governments seemed much more nearly in touch with economic realities than the rather idealized and frequently simplified model of what had happened in Britain or France which economists presented to them
>
> (p. 418).

After the 1840s, with the growth of the private sector, the involvement of the German state in industrial development became less pronounced (Trebilcock 1981: 77). However, this did not mean a withdrawal of the state rather a transition from a directive to a guiding role. During the Second Reich (1870–1914), there was a further erosion in state capacity and involvement in relation to industrial development, although it still played an important role through its tariff policy and cartel policy (Tilly 1996).

3.4   France

Similar to the case of Germany, there is an enduring myth about French economic policy. This is the view, propagated mainly by British Liberal opinion, that France has always been a state-led economy – some kind of an antithesis to *laissez-faire* Britain. This characterization may largely apply to the pre-Revolutionary period and to the post-Second World War period in the country's history, but not to the rest of it.

French economic policy in the pre-Revolutionary period – often known as *Colbertism*, named after Jean-Baptiste Colbert (1619–83), the famous finance minister under Louis XIV – was certainly highly interventionist. For example, in the early eighteenth century, the French state tried to recruit skilled workers from Britain on a large scale and encouraged industrial espionage.[16]

The Revolution, however, significantly upset this course. Milward and Saul (1979) argue that the Revolution brought about a marked shift in French government economic policy, because "the destruction of absolutism seemed connected in the minds of the revolutionaries with the introduction of a more *laissez-faire* system" (p. 284). Especially after the fall of Napoleon, the *laissez-faire* policy regime got firmly established and persisted until the Second World War.

For example, challenging the conventional wisdom that pitches free-trade Britain against protectionist France during the nineteenth century, Nye (1991) examines detailed empirical evidence and concludes that "France's trade regime was more liberal than that of Great Britain throughout most of the nineteenth century, even in the period from 1840 to 1860 [the alleged beginning of full-fledged free trade in Britain]" (p. 25). Table 2.2 shows that, when measured by net customs revenue as a percentage of net import values (which is a standard measure of protectionism, especially among the historians), France was always less protectionist than Britain between 1821 and 1875, and especially until the early 1860s.

What is interesting to note is that the partial exception to this century-and-half-long period of "liberalism" in France under Napoleon III (1848–70) was the only period of economic dynamism in France during this period (Trebilcock 1981: 184). Under Napoleon III, the French state actively encouraged infrastructural developments and established various institutions of research and teaching (Bury 1964, chapter 4). It also modernized the country's financial sector by granting limited liability to, investing in, and overseeing modern large-scale financial institutions (Cameron 1953).

On the trade policy front, Napoleon III signed the famous Anglo-French trade treaty (the Cobden–Chevalier treaty) of 1860, which heralded the period of trade liberalism on the Continent (1860–79) (see Kindleberger 1975 for further details). However, as we can see from Table 2.2, the degree of protectionism in France was already quite low on the eve of the treaty (it was actually *lower* than in Britain at the time), and therefore the resulting reduction in protectionism was relatively small.

The treaty was allowed to lapse in 1892 and many tariff rates, especially ones on manufacturing, were raised. However, this had little positive effects of the kind that we saw in the similar move in countries like Sweden at the time (see Section 3.5 below), because there was no coherent industrial upgrading strategy behind this tariff increase.[17] Especially during the Third Republic, the French government was almost as *laissez-faire* in its attitude toward economic matters as the then very *laissez-faire* British government (Kuisel 1981: 12–13).

It was only after the Second World War that the French elite got galvanized into reorganizing their state machinery to address the problem of the country's (relative)

Table 2.2 Protectionism in Britain and France, 1821–1913 (measured by net customs revenue as a percentage of net import values)

Years	Britain	France
1821–25	53.1	20.3
1826–30	47.2	22.6
1831–35	40.5	21.5
1836–40	30.9	18.0
1841–45	32.2	17.9
1846–50	25.3	17.2
1851–55	19.5	13.2
1856–60	15.0	10.0
1861–65	11.5	5.9
1866–70	8.9	3.8
1871–75	6.7	5.3
1876–80	6.1	6.6
1881–85	5.9	7.5
1886–90	6.1	8.3
1891–95	5.5	10.6
1896–1900	5.3	10.2
1901–05	7.0	8.8
1906–10	5.9	8.0
1911–13	5.4	8.8

Source: Nye (1991: 26 Table 1).

industrial backwardness. During this time, especially until the late 1960s, the French state used indicative planning, state-owned enterprises, and (what is these days somewhat misleadingly known as) "East-Asian-style" industrial policy to catch up with the more advanced countries. As a result, France witnessed a very successful structural transformation of its economy, and finally overtook Britain (see Shonfield 1965; Hall 1986).

3.5. Sweden

Sweden did not enter its modern age with a free trade regime. After the end of the Napoleonic wars, its government enacted a strongly protective tariff law (1816), and banned the imports and exports of some items (Gustavson 1986: 15). However, from about 1830 on, protection was progressively lowered (p. 65), and in 1857 a very low tariff regime was introduced (Bohlin 1999: 155; also see Table 2.1).

This free trade phase, however, was short-lived. Sweden started using tariffs as a means to protect the agricultural sector from American competition since around 1880. After 1892, it also provided tariff protection and subsidies to the industrial sector, especially the newly emerging engineering sector (Chang and Kozul-Wright 1994: 869, Bohlin 1999: 156). Despite (or rather because of) this switch to protectionism, the Swedish economy performed extremely well in the following decades. According to a calculation by Baumol *et al.* (1989), Sweden was, after Finland, the second fastest growing (in terms of GDP per work-hour) of the 16 major industrial economies between 1890 and 1900 and the fastest growing between 1900 and 1913 (p. 88, Table 5.1).[18]

Tariff protection and subsidies were not all that Sweden used in order to promote industrial development. More interestingly, during the late nineteenth century, Sweden developed a tradition of close public–private cooperation to the extent that was difficult to find parallel in other countries at the time, including Germany with its long tradition of public–private partnership. This first developed out of state involvement in the agricultural irrigation and drainage schemes (Samuelsson 1968: 71–6). This was then applied to the development of railways from the 1850s, telegraph and telephone in the 1880s, and hydroelectric energy in the 1890s (Chang and Kozul-Wright 1994: 869–70, Bohlin 1999: 153–5). Public–private collaboration also existed in certain key industries, such as the iron industry (Gustavson 1986: 71–2; Chang and Kozul-Wright 1994: 870). Interestingly, all these resemble the patterns of public-private collaboration for which the East Asian economies later became famous (Evans 1995 is a classic work on this issue).

The Swedish state made great efforts in facilitating the acquisition of advanced foreign technology, including through state-sponsored industrial espionage. However, more notable was its emphasis on the accumulation of what the modern literature calls "technological capabilities" (see Fransman and King 1984 and Lall 1992 for pioneering works on this issue). It provided stipends and travel grants for studies and research, invested in education, helped the establishment of technological research institutes, and provided direct research funding to industry (Chang and Kozul-Wright 1994: 870).

Swedish economic policy underwent a significant change since the electoral victory of the Socialist Party in 1932 (which has been out of the office for less than ten years since then) and the signing of the "historical pact" between the union and the employer's association in 1936 (the *Saltsjöbaden* agreement) (see Korpi 1983). The policy regime that emerged after the 1936 pact initially focused on the construction of a system where the employers will finance a generous welfare state and high investment in return for wage moderation from the union.

After the Second World War, the use was made of the regime's potential for promoting industrial upgrading. In the 1950s and the 1960s, the centralized trade union, LO (*Landsorganisationen i Sverige*) adopted the so-called Rehn–Meidner Plan (LO 1963 is the document that set out the strategy in detail). This introduced the so-called solidaristic wage policy, which explicitly aimed to equalize wage across industries for the same types of workers. It was expected that this would generate pressure on the capitalists in low-wage sectors to upgrade their capital stock or shed labor, while allowing the capitalists in the high-wage sector to retain extra profit and expand faster than it would otherwise have been possible. This was complemented by the so-called active labor market policy, which provided retraining and relocation supports to the workers displaced in this process of industrial upgrading. It is widely accepted that this strategy contributed to Sweden's successful industrial upgrading in the early postwar years (Edquist and Lundvall 1993: 274).

3.6   The Netherlands

The Netherlands was, as it is well known, the world's dominant naval and commercial power during the seventeenth century, its so-called "Golden Century", thanks to its aggressive "mercantilist" regulations on navigation, fishing, and international trade since the sixteenth century. However, it showed a marked decline in the eighteenth century, the so-called "Periwig Period" (*Pruikentijd*), with its defeat in the 1780 Fourth Anglo-Dutch War marking the symbolic end to its international supremacy (Boxer 1965, Chapter 10).

A policy paralysis seems to have gripped the Netherlands between the late seventeenth century and the early twentieth century. The only exception to this was the effort by King William I (1815–40), who established many agencies providing subsidized industrial financing (Kossmann 1978: 136–8; van Zanden 1996: 84–5). He also strongly supported the development of modern cotton textile industry, especially in the Twente region (Henderson 1972: 198–200).

However, from the late 1840s, the country reverted to a *laissez-faire* regime, which lasted until the Second World War. As we can see in Table 2.1, except for Britain in the late nineteenth century and Japan before the restoration of tariff autonomy, the Netherlands remained the least protected economy among the NDCs. Also, the country abolished the patent law (which was first introduced in 1817) in 1869, inspired by the antipatent movement that swept Europe at the time, which condemned patent as just another form of monopoly (Schiff 1971; Machlup and Penrose 1950). Despite international pressures, the country refused to re-introduce the patent law until 1912.

On the whole, during this extreme *laissez-faire* period, the Dutch economy remained rather sluggish, and its industrialization remained relatively shallow. According to the authoritative estimate by Maddison (1995), measured in 1990 dollars, it was the second richest country in the world even after the UK in 1820, after a century of relative decline ($1,756 vs. $1,561). However, a century later (1913), it was overtaken by no less than six countries – Australia, New Zealand, USA, Canada, Switzerland, and Belgium – and almost nearly by Germany.

It was largely for this reason that the end of the Second World War saw the introduction of more interventionist policies (van Zanden 1999: 182–4). Especially up to 1963, rather active trade and industrial policies were practiced. These included: financial supports for two large firms (one in steel, the other in soda); subsidies to industrialize backward areas; encouragement of technical education; encouraging the development of the aluminum industry through subsidized gas; and the development of key infrastructures.

3.7   Switzerland

Switzerland was one of the earliest industrializers of Europe – starting its Industrial Revolution barely 20 years later than Britain (Biucchi 1973: 628). It was a world technological leader in a number of important industries (Milward and Saul 1979: 454–55), especially in the cotton textile industry, where it was deemed technologically more advanced in many areas than Britain (Biucchi 1973: 629).

Given this very small technological gap with the leader country (if at all), infant industry protection was not very necessary for Switzerland. Also, given its small size, protection would have been more costly for the country than what it would been the case for bigger countries. Moreover, given its highly decentralized political structure and very small size, there was little room for centralized infant industry protection (Biucchi 1973: 455).

However, Switzerland's *laissez-faire* trade policy did not necessarily mean that its government had no sense of strategy in its policymaking. Its refusal to introduce a patent law until 1907, despite strong international pressure, is such an example. This antipatent policy is argued to have contributed to the country's development, especially by allowing the "theft" of German ideas in the chemical and pharmaceutical industries and by encouraging foreign direct investments in the food industry (see Schiff 1971; Chang 2001a).

3.8 Japan and the East Asian NICs

Soon after it was forced open by the Americans in 1853, Japan's feudal political order collapsed and a modernizing regime was established after the so-called Meiji Restoration of 1868. The role of its state since then has been crucial in the country's development.

Until 1911, Japan was *not* able to use tariff protection, due to the "unequal treaties" that barred it from having tariff rates over 5 percent. Therefore, the Japanese state had to use other means to encourage industrialization. So, to start with, it established state-owned "model factories" (or "pilot plants") in a number of industries – notably in shipbuilding, mining, textile, and military industries (Smith 1955; Allen 1981). Although most of these were privatized by the 1870s, it continued to subsidize the privatized firms, notably in shipbuilding (McPherson 1987: 31, 34–5). Subsequently, it established the first modern steel mill, and developed railways and telegraph (McPherson 1987: 31; Smith 1955: 44–5).

Following the ending of the unequal treaties in 1911, the Japanese state started introducing a range of tariff reforms intended to protect infant industries, make imported raw materials more affordable, and control the imports of luxury consumption goods (McPherson 1987: 32). During the 1920s, under strong German influence (Johnson 1982: 105–6), it started encouraging "rationalization" of key industries by sanctioning cartel arrangements and encouraging mergers, which were aimed at restraining "wasteful competition," achieving scale economies, standardization, and the introduction of scientific management (McPherson 1987: 32–3). These efforts were intensified in the 1930s (Johnson 1982: 105–15).

Despite all these developmental efforts, during the first half of the twentieth century, Japan was on the whole *not* the economic super-star that it became after the Second World War. According to Maddison (1989), between 1900 and 1950, Japan's per capita income growth rate was only 1 percent per annum. This was somewhat below the average for the 16 largest NDCs that he studied, which was 1.3 percent per annum[19] – although it must be noted that part of this rather poor performance was due to the dramatic collapse in output following the defeat in the Second World War.[20]

Between the end of the Second World War and the early 1970s, Japan's growth record was unrivalled. According to the data from Maddison (1989: 35, Table 3.2), between 1950 and 1973, per capita GDP in Japan grew at a staggering 8 percent, more than double the 3.8 percent average achieved by the 16 NDCs mentioned above (the average includes Japan). The next best performers among the NDCs were Germany, Austria (both at 4.9 percent) and Italy (4.8 percent), while even the East Asian "miracle" developing countries like Taiwan (6.2 percent) or Korea (5.2 percent) came nowhere near Japan, despite the bigger "convergence" effect that they could expect given their greater backwardness.

In the economic successes of Japan and other East Asian countries (except Hong Kong), interventionist trade and industrial policies played a crucial role.[21] What is notable is the similarities between their policies with those used by other NDCs before them, including, above all, eighteenth-century Britain and nineteenth-century USA. However, it is also important to note that the policies used by the East Asian countries (and indeed those used by some other NDCs like France) during the postwar period were a lot more sophisticated and fine-tuned than their historical equivalents.

They used more substantial and better-designed export subsidies (both direct and indirect) and much less (actually very little) export taxes than in the earlier experiences (Luedde-Neurath 1986; Amsden 1989). Tariff rebates for imported raw materials and machinery for export industries were much more systematically used than in, for example, eighteenth-century Britain (Luedde-Neurath 1986).

Coordination of complementary investments, which had been previously done, if ever, in a rather haphazard way, was systematized through indicative planning and government investment programs (Chang 1993, 1994). Regulations of firm entry, exit, investments, and pricing intended to "manage competition" were a lot more aware of the dangers of monopolistic abuses and more sensitive to their impact on export market performance, when compared to their historical counterparts, namely, the late-nineteenth and early-twentieth century cartel policies (Amsden and Singh 1994; Chang 2001b).

The East Asian states also integrated human-capital- and learning-related policies into their industrial policy framework a lot more tightly than their predecessors had done, through "manpower planning" (You and Chang 1993). Regulations on technology licensing and foreign direct investments were much more sophisticated and comprehensive than in the earlier experiences (Chang 1998). Subsidies to (and public provision of) education, training, and R&D were also much more systematic and extensive than their historical counterparts (Lall and Teubal 1998).[22]

3.9 Summary

The following picture emerges from our examination of the history of today's developed countries.

First, almost all NDCs used some form of infant industry promotion strategy when they were in catching-up positions. Interestingly it was the UK and the

USA – the supposed homes of free trade policy – and not countries like Germany or Japan – countries which are usually associated with state activism – that used tariff protection most aggressively.

Of course, tariff figures do not give a full picture of industrial promotion efforts. During the late nineteenth and the early twentieth century, while maintaining a relatively low *average* tariff rate, Germany accorded strong tariff protection to strategic industries like iron and steel. Similarly, Sweden provided targeted protection for the steel and the engineering industries, while maintaining generally low tariffs. Germany, Sweden, and Japan actively used nontariff measures to promote their industries, such as establishment of state-owned "model factories," state financing of risky ventures, support for R&D, and the development of institutions that promote public-private cooperation.

The exceptions to this historical pattern are Switzerland and the Netherlands. However, these were countries that were already on the frontier of technological development by the eighteenth century and therefore did not need much protection. Also, it should be noted that the Netherlands had deployed an impressive range of interventionist measures up till the seventeeth century in order to build up its maritime and commercial supremacy. Moreover, Switzerland did not have a patent law until 1907, flying directly against the emphasis that today's orthodoxy puts on the protection of intellectual property rights. More interestingly, the Netherlands abolished its 1817 patent law in 1869 on the ground that patents were politically created monopolies inconsistent with its free-market principles – a position that seems to elude most of today's free-market economists – and did not introduce a patent law again until 1912.

It must be pointed out that tariff protection was in many countries a key component of this strategy, but was by no means the only, and not necessarily the most important, component in the strategy. There were many other tools, such as export subsidies, tariff rebates on inputs used for exports, conferring of monopoly rights, cartel arrangements, directed credits, investment planning, manpower planning, R&D supports, and the promotion of institutions that allow public–private cooperation. These policies are thought to have been invented by Japan and other East Asian countries after the Second World War or at least by Germany in the late nineteenth century, but many of them have a long pedigree.

Finally, despite sharing the same underlying principle, there was a considerable degree of diversity among the NDCs in terms of their policy mix, suggesting that there is no "one-size-fits-all" *model* for industrial development.

4 Comparison with today's developing countries

Those few neoliberal economists who are aware of the records of protectionism in the NDCs try to avoid the obvious conclusion – namely, it can be very useful for economic development – by arguing that, although some (minimal) tariff protection may be necessary, most developing countries have tariffs rates that are much higher than what most NDCs used in the past.

For example, Little *et al.* (1970) argue that

[a]part from Russia, the United States, Spain, and Portugal, it does not appear that tariff levels in the first quarter of the twentieth century, when they were certainly higher for most countries than in the nineteenth century, usually afforded degrees of protection that were much higher than the sort of degrees of promotion for industry which we have seen, in the previous chapter, to be possibly justifiable for developing countries today [which they argue to be at most 20 percent even for the poorest countries and virtually zero for the more advanced developing countries]

(pp. 163–4).

Similarly, World Bank (1991) argues that

[a]lthough industrial countries did benefit from higher natural protection before transport costs declined, the average tariff for twelve industrial countries[23] ranged from 11 to 32 percent from 1820 to 1980 ... In contrast, the average tariff on manufactures in developing countries is 34 percent

(p. 97 Box 5.2).

This argument sounds reasonable enough, but is actually highly misleading in one important sense. The problem with it is that the productivity gap between today's developed countries and the developing countries is much greater than what existed between the more developed NDCs and the less developed NDCs in earlier times.

Throughout the nineteenth century, the ratio of per capita income in PPP terms between the poorest NDCs (say, Japan and Finland) and the richest NDCs (say, the Netherlands and the UK) was about 2 or 4 to 1. Today, the gap in per capita income in PPP terms between the most developed countries (e.g. Switzerland, Japan, and the USA) and the least developed ones (e.g. Ethiopia, Malawi, and Tanzania) is typically in the region of 50 or 60 to 1. Middle-level developing countries like Nicaragua ($2,060), India ($2,230), and Zimbabwe ($2,690) have to contend with productivity gaps in the region of 10 or 15 to 1. Even for quite advanced developing countries like Brazil ($6,840) or Columbia ($5,580), the productivity gap with the top industrial countries is about 5 to 1.

This means that today's developing countries need to impose much higher rates of tariff than those used by the NDCs in earlier times, if they are to provide the same degree of actual protection to their industries as the ones accorded to the NDC industries in the past.

For example, when the USA accorded over 40 percent average tariff protection to its industries in the late nineteenth century, its per capita income in PPP terms was already about 3/4 that of Britain. And this was when the "natural protection" accorded by distance, which was especially important for the USA, was considerably higher than today. Compared to this, the 71 percent trade-weighted average tariff rate that India used to have just before the WTO agreement, despite the fact that its per capita income in PPP terms is only about 1/15 that of the US, makes the country look like a champion of free trade. Following the WTO agreement, India cut its trade-weighted average tariff to 32 percent, bringing it down to the level below which the US average tariff rate never sank between the end of the Civil War and the Second World War.

To take a less extreme example, in 1875, Denmark had an average tariff rate around 15–20 percent, when its income was slightly less than 60 percent that of Britain. Following the WTO agreement, Brazil cut its trade-weighted average tariff from 41 percent to 27 percent, a level that is not far above the Danish level, but its income in PPP terms is barely 20 percent that of the USA.

Thus seen, *given the productivity gap*, even the relatively high levels of protection that had prevailed in the developing countries until the 1980s do not seem excessive by historical standards of the NDCs. When it comes to the substantially lower levels that have come to prevail after two decades of extensive trade liberalization in these countries, it may even be argued that today's developing countries are actually even less protectionist than the NDCs in earlier times.

5   Lessons for the present

The historical picture is clear. When they were trying to catch-up with the frontier economies, the NDCs used interventionist trade and industrial policies to promote their infant industries. The forms of these policies and the emphases among them may have been different across countries, but there is no denying that they actively used such policies. And, in relative terms (that is, taking into account the productivity gap with the more advanced countries), many of them actually protected their industries a lot more heavily than what the currently developing countries have done.

If this is the case, the current orthodoxy advocating free trade and *laissez-faire* industrial policies seems at odds with historical experience, and the developed countries that propagate such view seem to be indeed "kicking away the ladder" that they used to climb up where they are.

The only possible way for the developed countries to counter this accusation of "ladder-kicking" will be to argue that the activist trade and industrial policies that they had pursued used to be beneficial for economic development but are not so any more, because "times have changed." Apart from the paucity of convincing reasons why this may be the case, the poor growth records of the developing countries over the last two decades makes this line of defense simply untenable. It depends on the data we use, but roughly speaking, per capita income in developing countries grew at 3 percent per year between 1960 and 1980, but has grown only at about 1.5 percent between 1980 and 2000. And even this 1.5 percent will be significantly reduced, if we take out India and China, which have *not* pursued liberal trade and industrial policies recommended by the developed countries.

So if you are a neoliberal economist, you are faced with a "paradox" here. The developing countries grew much faster when they used "bad" trade and industrial policies during 1960–80 than when they used "good" (at least "better") policies during the following two decades. The obvious solution to this "paradox" is to accept that the supposedly "good" policies are actually *not* good for the developing countries but that the "bad" policies are actually good for them. This gets further confirmation from the fact that these "bad" policies are also the ones that the NDCs had pursued when they were developing countries themselves.

Given these arguments, we can only conclude that, in recommending the allegedly "good" policies, the NDCs are in effect "kicking away the ladder" by which they have climbed to the top beyond the reach of the developing countries. I do accept that this "ladder-kicking" may be done genuinely out of (misinformed) goodwill. Some of those NDC policy makers and scholars who make the recommendations may sincerely believe that their own countries had developed through free trade and other *laissez-faire* policies and want the developing countries benefit from the same policies. However, this makes it no less harmful for the developing countries. Indeed, it may be even more dangerous than "ladder-kicking" based on naked national interests, as self-righteousness can be even more stubborn than self-interest.

Whatever the intention is behind the "ladder-kicking", the fact remains that these allegedly "good" policies have not been able to generate the promised growth dynamism in the developing countries during the last two decades or. Indeed, in many developing countries growth has simply collapsed.

So what is to be done? While spelling out a detailed agenda for action is beyond the scope of this article, the following points may be made.

To begin with, the historical facts about the developmental experiences of the developed countries should be more widely publicized. This is not just a matter of "getting history right," but also of allowing the developing countries to make informed choices. I do not wish to give the impression that every developing country should adopt an active infant industry promotion strategy like the eighteenth-century Britain, nineteenth-century USA, or twentieth-century Korea. Some of them may indeed benefit from following the Swiss or Hong Kong models. However, this strategic choice should be made in the full knowledge that historically the vast majority of the successful countries used the opposite strategy to become rich.

In addition, the policy-related conditionalities attached to financial assistance from the IMF and the World Bank or from the donor governments should be radically changed. These conditionalities should be based on the recognition that many of the policies that are considered "bad" are in fact not, and that there can be no "best practice" policy that everyone should use. Second, the WTO rules and other multilateral trade agreements should be re-written in such a way that a more active use of infant industry promotion tools (e.g. tariffs, subsidies) is allowed.

Allowing the developing countries to adopt the policies (and institutions) that are more suitable to their stages of development and to other conditions they face will enable them to grow faster, as indeed it did during the 1960s and the 1970s. This will benefit not only the developing countries but also the developed countries in the long run, as it will increase the trade and investment opportunities available to the developed countries in the developing countries. That the developed countries are not able to see this is the tragedy of our time.

Notes

1 This chapter draws heavily on my recent book, *Kicking Away the Ladder –
   Development Strategy in Historical Perspective* (2002 Anthem Press). I thank the
   research support from the Korea Research Foundation through its BK21 program at
   the Department of Economics, Korea University, where I was a visiting research professor when the first draft was written.
2 Britain was the first country to introduce a permanent income tax, which happened in
   1842. Denmark introduced income tax in 1903. In the US, the income tax law of 1894
   was overturned as "unconstitutional" by the Supreme Court. The Sixteenth Amendment allowing federal income tax was adopted only in 1913. In Belgium, income tax
   was introduced only in 1919. In Portugal, income tax was first introduced in 1922, but
   was abolished in 1928, and re-instated only in 1933. In Sweden, despite its later fame
   for the willingness to impose high rates of income tax, income tax was first introduced
   only in 1932. See Chang (2002: 101) for further details.
3 The Swedish Riksbank was nominally the first official central bank in the world
   (established in 1688), but until the mid-nineteenth century, it could not function as a
   proper central bank because it did not have monopoly over note issue, which it
   acquired only in 1904. The first "real" central bank was the Bank of England, which
   was established in 1694 but became a full central bank in 1844. By the end of the nineteenth century, the central banks of France (1848), Belgium (1851), Spain (1874), and
   Portugal (1891) gained note issue monopoly, but it was only in the twentieth century
   that the central banks of Germany (1905), Switzerland (1907), and Italy (1926) gained
   it. The Swiss National Bank was formed only in 1907 by merging the four note-issue
   banks. The US Federal Reserve System came into being only in 1913. Until 1915,
   however, only 30 percent of the banks (with 50 percent of all banking assets) were in
   the system, and even as late as 1929, 65 percent of the banks were still outside the system, although by this time they accounted for only 20 percent of total banking assets.
   See Chang (2002: 94–7) for further details.
4 Moreover, when they reached the frontier, the NDCs used a range of policies to help
   themselves "pull away" from their existing and potential competitors. They used measures to control transfer of technology to its potential competitors (e.g. controls on
   skilled worker migration or machinery export) and made the less developed countries
   to open up their markets by unequal treaties and colonization. However, the catch-up
   economies that were not (formal or informal) colonies did not simply sit down and
   accept these restrictive measures. They mobilized all kinds of different "legal" and
   "illegal" means to overcome the obstacles created by these restrictions, such as industrial espionage, "illegal" poaching of workers, and smuggling of contraband machinery. See Chang (2002: 51–9) for further details.
5 It is also said that George Washington insisted on wearing the then lower-quality
   American clothes rather than the then superior British one at his inauguration cere-
   mony. Both episodes are reminiscent of the policies used by Japan and Korea during
   the postwar period to control "luxury consumption," especially concerning imported
   luxury goods. On this, see Chang (1997).
6 In 1840, Bowring advised the member states of German *Zollverein* that they should
   grow wheat and sell it to buy British manufactures (Landes 1998: 521).
7 Even when the existence of high tariff is acknowledged, its importance is severely
   downplayed. For example, in what used to be the standard overview piece on U.S. economic history until recently, North (1965) mentions tariffs only once, only to dismiss
   it as an insignificant factor in explaining the US industrial development. He argues,
   without bothering to establish the case and by citing only one highly biased secondary
   source (the classic study by Taussig 1892), "while tariffs became increasingly protective in the years after the Civil War, it is doubtful if they were very influential in affecting seriously the spread of manufacturing" (p. 694).

8 In his *Wealth of Nations*, Adam Smith wrote:

> Were the Americans, either by combination or by any other sort of violence, to stop the importation of European manufactures, and, by thus giving a monopoly to such of their own countrymen as could manufacture the like goods, divert any considerable part of their capital into this employment, they would retard instead of accelerating the further increase in the value of their annual produce, and would obstruct instead of promoting the progress of their country towards real wealth and greatness
>
> (Smith 1937 [1776]: 347–8).

9 Bairoch (1993: 17) credits Hamilton for inventing the term, "infant industry."

10 According to Elkins and McKitrick (1993),

> "[a]s the Hamiltonian progress revealed itself ... – a sizeable funded debt, a powerful national bank, excises, nationally subsidised manufactures, and eventually even a standing army – the Walpolean parallel at every point was too obvious to miss. It was in resistance to this, and everything it seemed to imply that the 'Jeffersonian persuasion' was erected"
>
> (p. 19).

11 In response to a newspaper editorial urging immediate slave emancipation, Lincoln wrote:

> If I could save the Union without freeing any slave, I would do it; and if I could save it by freeing all the slaves, I would do it; and if I could do it by freeing some and leaving others alone, I would also do that
>
> (Garraty and Carnes 2000: 405).

12 However, it should be noted that USA never practised free trade to the same degree as what Britain did in its free trade period (1860 – 1932). It never had a zero-tariff regime like the UK and it was much more aggressively in using "hidden" protectionist measures. These included: VERs (voluntary export restraints); quotas on textile and clothing (through the Multi-Fibre Agreement); protection and subsidies for agriculture (cf. the repeal of the Corn Law in Britain); and unilateral trade sanctions (especially through the use of anti-dumping duties).

13 I am grateful to Duncan Green for drawing my attention to this quote.

14 Shapiro and Taylor (1990) sum this up nicely: "Boeing would not be Boeing, nor would IBM be IBM, in either military or commercial endeavours without Pentagon contracts and civilian research support" (p. 866).

15 Interestingly, the reorientation of teaching is similar to what happened in Korea during the 1960s. See You and Chang (1993) for further details.

16 However, this attempt backfired and propelled the British to introduce a ban on the emigration of skilled workers, and especially on the attempt to recruit such workers for jobs abroad ("suborning") in 1719 (see Chang 2001a for further details).

17 If anything, the new tariff regime was actually *against* such thing – the author of this tariff regime, the politician Jules Méline, was explicitly against large-scale industrialization, in the belief that France should remain a country of independent farmers and small workshops (Kuisel 1981: 18).

18 The 16 countries are, in alphabetical order, Australia, Austria, Belgium, Canada, Denmark, Finland, France, Germany, Italy, Japan, the Netherlands, Norway, Sweden, Switzerland, the UK, and the USA.

19 See footnote 18.

20 Japanese GDP (not per capita) in 1945 is estimated to have fallen to 48 percent of the peak reached in 1943. This was, however, less dramatic than what Germany experienced,

where 1946 GDP was only 40 percent of the peak reached in 1944 or Austria, where the 1945 GDP was only 41 percent of the peaks reached in 1941 and 1944. See Maddison (1989: 120–1, Table B-2).

21 There is an extensive literature on this now. See Johnson (1984) and Chang (1993) for the earlier phase of the debate. See Akyuz *et al.* (1998) and Chang (2001b) for the more recent phase.

22 With the recent crisis in Korea and the prolonged recession in Japan, it has become popular to argue that activist trade and industrial policies have been proved mistaken. While this is not a place to go into this debate, a few points may be made (for a criticism of this view, see Chang 2000). First, whether or not we think the recent troubles in Japan and Korea are due to activist ITT (industrial, trade and technology) policies, we cannot deny that these policies were behind their "miracle." Second, Taiwan, despite having used activist ITT policies, did not experience any financial or macroeconomic crisis. Third, all informed observers of Japan, regardless of their views, agree that the country's current recession cannot be attributed to government industrial policy – it has more to do with factors like structural savings surplus, ill-timed financial liberalization (that led to the bubble economy), and macroeconomic mismanagement. Fourth, in the case of Korea, industrial policy was largely dismantled by the mid-1990s, when the debt build-up that led to the recent crisis started, so it cannot be blamed for the crisis. Indeed, it may be argued that, if anything, the demise of industrial policy contributed to the making of the crisis by making "duplicative investments" easier (see Chang *et al.* 1998).

23 They are Austria, Belgium, Denmark, France, Germany, Italy, the Netherlands, Spain, Sweden, Switzerland, the UK, and the USA.

References

Akyuz, Y., Chang, H.-J., and Kozul-Wright, R. (1998) 'New Perspectives on East Asian Development', *Journal of Development Studies*, 34(6).

Allen, G. C. (1981; 4th ed.) *A Short Economics History of Modern Japan*, London and Basingstoke: Macmillan.

Amsden, A. (1989) *Asia's Next Giant*, New York: Oxford University Press.

Amsden, A. and Singh, A. (1994) 'The Optimal Degree of Competition and Dynamic Efficiency in Japan and Korea', *European Economic Review*, 38(3/4).

Bairoch, P. (1993) *Economics and World History – Myths and Paradoxes*, Brighton: Wheastheaf.

Baumol, W., Wolff, E., and Blackman, S. (1989) *Productivity and American Leadership*, Cambridge, MA: The MIT Press.

Bhagwati, J. (1985) *Protectionism*, Cambridge, MA: The MIT Press.

Biucchi, B. (1973) 'The Industrial Revolution in Switzerland', in C. Cipolla, (ed.), *The Fontana Economic History of Europe, Vol. 4: The Emergence of Industrial Societies-Part Two*, Glasgow: Collins.

Blackbourn, D. (1997) *The Fontana History of Germany, 1780–1918*, London: Fontana Press.

Bohlin, J. (1999) 'Sweden: The Rise and Fall of the Swedish Model', in J. Foreman-Peck, and G. Federico (eds.), *European Industrial Policy – The Twentieth-Century Experience*, Oxford: Oxford University Press.

Boxer, C. (1965) *The Dutch Seaborne Empire, 1600–1800*, London: Hutchinson.

Brisco, N. (1907) *The Economic Policy of Robert Walpole*, New York: The Columbia University Press.

Bury, J. (1964) *Napoleon III and the Second Empire*, London: The English University Presses Ltd.

Cameron, R. (1953) 'The Crédit Mobilier and the Economic Development of Europe', *Journal of Political Economy*, 61(6).

Chang, H.-J. (1993) 'The Political Economy of Industrial Policy in Korea', *Cambridge Journal of Economics*, 17(2).

—— (1994) *The Political Economy of Industrial Policy*, London: Macmillan Press.

—— (1997) 'Luxury Consumption and Economic Development', A report prepared for UNCTAD, Trade and Development Report, Geneva: UNCTAD.

—— (1998) ''Globalization, Transnational Corporations, and Economic Development', in D. Baker, G. Epstein, and R. Pollin (eds.), *Globalization and Progressive Economic Policy*, Cambridge: Cambridge University Press.

—— (2000) 'The Hazard of Moral Hazard – Untangling the Asian Crisis', *World Development*, 28(4).

—— (2001a) 'Intellectual Property Rights and Economic Development – Historical Lessons and Emerging Issues', *Journal of Human Development*, 2(2).

—— (2001b) 'Rethinking East Asian Industrial Policy – Past Records and Future Prospects' in P.-K. Wong and C.-Y. Ng (eds.), *Industrial Policy, Innovation and Economic Growth: The Experience of Japan and the Asian NIEs*, Singapore: Singapore University Press.

—— (2002) *Kicking Away the Ladder – Development Strategy in Historical Perspective*, London: Anthem Press.

Chang, H.-J. and Kozul-Wright, R. (1994) 'Organising Development: Comparing the National Systems of Entrepreneurship in Sweden and South Korea', *Journal of Development Studies*, 30(4).

Cochran, T. and Miller, W. (1942) *The Age of Enterprise: A Social History of Industrial America*, New York: The Macmillan Company.

Conkin, P. (1980) *Prophets of Prosperity: America's First Political Economists*, Bloomington: Indiana University Press.

Corden, M. (1974) *Trade Policy and Economic Welfare*, Oxford: Oxford University Press.

Davies, N. (1999) *The Isles – A History*, London and Basingstoke: Macmillan.

Davis, R. (1966) 'The Rise of Protection in England, 1689–1786', *Economic History Review*, 19(2).

Defoe, D. (1728; reprinted 1928) *A Plan of the English Commerce*, published by C. Rivington, Oxford: Basil Blackwell.

Dorfman, J. and Tugwell, R. (1960) *Early American Policy – Six Columbia Contributors*, New York: Columbia University Press.

Edquist, C. and Lundvall, B.-Å. (1993) 'Comparing the Danish and Swedish Systems of Innovation' in R. Nelson (ed.), *National Innovation Systems*, New York: Oxford University Press.

Elkins, S. and McKitrick, E. (1993) *The Age of Federalism*, New York and Oxford: Oxford University Press.

Evans, P. (1995) *Embedded Autonomy – States & Industrial Transformation*, Princeton: Princeton University Press.

Foner, E. (1998) *The Story of American Freedom*, New York: W. W. Norton & Company.

Frank, A. G. (1967) *Capitalism and Underdevelopment in Latin America*, New York: Monthly Review Press.

Fransman, M. and King, K. (eds.) (1984) *Technological Capability in the Third World*, London and Basingstoke: Macmillan.

Frayssé, O. (1994) *Lincoln, Land, and Labor*, trans. S. Neely, from the original French edition published in 1988 by Paris: Publications de la Sorbonne, Urbana and Chicago: University of Illinois Press.

Gallagher, J. and Robinson, R. (1953) 'The Imperialism of Free Trade', *Economic History Review*, 6(1).

Garraty, J. and Carnes, M. (2000; 10th edn.) *The American Nation – A History of the United States*, New York: Addison Wesley Longman.

Gustavson, C. (1986) *The Small Giant: Sweden Enters the Industrial Era*, Athens, OH: Ohio State University Press.

Hall, P. (1986) *Governing the Economy – The Politics of State Intervention in Britain and France*, Cambridge: Polity Press.

Henderson, W. (1972; 3rd ed.) *Britain and Industrial Europe, 1750–1870*, Leicester: Leicester University Press.

Henderson, W. (1983) *Friedrich List – Economist and Visionary, 1789–1846*, London: Frank Cass.

Johnson, C. (1982) *The MITI and the Japanese Miracle*, Stanford: Stanford University Press.

Johnson, C. (1984) 'Introduction', in C. Johnson (ed.), *The Industrial Policy Debate*, San Francisco: Institute for Contemporary Studies.

Kindleberger, C. (1975) 'The Rise of Free Trade in Western Europe, 1820–1875', *Journal of Economic History*, 35(1).

Kindleberger, C. (1978) 'Germany's Overtaking of England, 1806 to 1914', in *Economic Response: Comparative Studies in Trade, Finance, and Growth*, Cambridge, MA: Harvard University Press.

Korpi, W. (1983) *The Democratic Class Struggle*, London: Routledge and Kegan Paul.

Kossmann, E. (1978) *The Low Countries, 1780–1940*, Oxford: Clarendon Press.

Kozul-Wright, R. (1995) 'The Myth of Anglo-Saxon Capitalism: Reconstructing the History of the American State', in H.-J. Chang and R. Rowthorn (eds.), *Role of the State in Economic Change*, Oxford: Oxford University Press.

Kuisel, R. (1981) *Capitalism and the State in Modern France*, Cambridge: Cambridge University Press.

Lall, S. (1992) 'Technological Capabilities and Industrialization', *World Development*, 20(2).

Lall, S. and Teubal, M. (1998) 'Market Stimulating Technology Policies in Developing Countries: A Framework with Examples from East Asia', *World Development*, 26(8).

Landes, D. (1998) *The Wealth and Poverty of Nations*, New York: W. W. Norton & Company.

List, F. (1885). *The National System of Political Economy*, trans. L. Sampson, from original German edition published in 1841 by London: Sampson Lloyd, London: Longmans, Green, & Company.

Little, I., Scitovsky, T., and Scott, M. (1970) *Industry in Trade in Some Developing Countries – A Comparative Study*, London: Oxford University Press.

LO (Landsorganisationen i Sverige) (1963) *Economic Expansion and Structural Change*, T. Johnston (ed. and trans.) London: George Allen & Unwin.

Luedde-Neurath, R. (1986) *Import Controls and Export-Oriented Development: A Reassessment of the South Korean Case*, Boulder and London: Westview Press.

Luthin, R. (1944) 'Abraham Lincoln and the Tariff', *The American Historical Review*, 49(4).

Machlup, F. and Penrose, E. (1950) 'The Patent Controversy in the Nineteenth Century', *Journal of Economic History*, 10(1).

Maddison, A. (1989) *The World Economy in the 20th Century*, Paris: OECD.

Maddison, A. (1995) *Monitoring the World Economy*, Paris: OECD.

McCusker, J. (1996) 'British Mercantilist Policies and the American Colonies', in S. Engerman and R. Gallman (eds.), *The Cambridge Economic History of the United States, Vol. 1: The Colonial Era*, Cambridge: Cambridge University Press.

McPherson, W. J. (1987) *The Economic Development of Japan, 1868–1941*, London and Basingstoke: Macmillan Press.

Milward, A. and Saul, S. (1979; 2nd ed.) *The Economic Development of Continental Europe, 1780–1870*, London: George Allen & Unwin.

Mowery, D. and Rosenberg, N. (1993) 'The U.S. National Innovation System', in R. Nelson (ed.), *National Innovation Systems – A Comparative Analysis*, Oxford: Oxford University Press.

North, D. (1965) 'Industrialization in the United States', in H. Habakkuk and M. Postan (eds.), *The Cambridge Economic History of Europe, vol. VI. The Industrial Revolutions and After: Incomes, Population and Technological Change (II)*, Cambridge: Cambridge University Press.

Nye, J. (1991) 'The Myth of Free-Trade Britain and Fortress France: Tariffs and Trade in the Nineteenth Century', *Journal of Economic History*, 51(1).

Owen, G. (1966) *Industry in the U.S.A.*, London: Penguin Books.

Ramsay, G. D. (1982) *The English Woolen Industry, 1500–1750*, London and Basingstoke: Macmillan.

Reinert, E. (1996) 'Diminishing Returns and Economic Sustainability: The Dilemma of Resource-based Economies under a Free Trade Regime', in H. Stein *et al.* (eds.), *International Trade Regulation, National Development Strategies and the Environment – Towards Sustainable Development?*, Oslo: Center for Development and the Environment, University of Oslo.

—— (1998) 'Raw Materials in the History of Economic Policy – Or why List (the protectionist) and Cobden (the free trader) both agreed on free trade in corn', in G. Cook (ed.), *The Economics and Politics of International Trade – Freedom and Trade, vol. 2*, London: Routledge.

Ruggiero, R. (1998) 'Whither the Trade System Next?', in J. Bhagwati and M. Hirsch (eds.), *The Uruguay Round and Beyond – Essays in Honour of Arthur Dunkel*, Ann Arbor: The University of Michigan Press.

Samuelsson, K. (1968) *From Great Power to Welfare State*, London: Allen & Unwin.

Schiff, E. (1971) *Industrialisation Without National Patents – the Netherlands, 1869–1912 and Switzerland, 1850–1907*, Princeton: Princeton University Press.

Shapiro, H. and Taylor, L. (1990) 'The State and Industrial Strategy', *World Development*, 18(6).

Shonfield, A. (1965) *Modern Capitalism*, Oxford: Oxford University Press.

Smith, A. (1937, 1st edn 1776). *An Inquiry into the Nature and Causes of the Wealth of Nations*, edited, with an introduction, notes, marginal summary and an enlarged index by Edwin Cannan, with an introduction by Max Lerner, New York: Random House.

Smith, T. (1955) *Political Change and Industrial Development in Japan: Government Enterprise 1868–1880*, Stanford: Stanford University Press.

Taussig, F. (1892) *The Tariff History of the United States*, New York: G. Putnam.

Tilly, R. (1996) 'German Industrialisation', in M. Teich and R. Porter (eds.), *The Industrial Revolution in National Context – Europe and the USA*, Cambridge: Cambridge University Press.

Trebilcock, C. (1981) *The Industrialisation of the Continental Powers, 1780–1914*, London and New York: Longman.

van Zanden, J. (1996) 'Industrialisation in the Netherlands', in M. Teich and R. Porter (eds.), *The Industrial Revolution in National Context – Europe and the USA*, Cambridge: Cambridge University Press.

van Zanden, J. (1999) 'The Netherlands: The History of an Empty Box', in J. Foreman-Peck and G. Federico (eds.), *European Industrial Policy: The Twentieth Century Experience*, Oxford: Oxford University Press.

World Bank (1991) *World Development Report, 1991 – The Development Challenge*, New York: Oxford University Press.

You, J. and Chang, H.-J. (1993) 'The Myth of Free Labor Market in Korea', *Contributions to Political Economy*, vol. 12.

3 Globalization and the myth of free trade

Anwar Shaikh

1 Introduction

The world today is beset by widespread poverty and persistent inequality. Some developing countries have managed to advance in the face of these obstacles, but many others have not, and still others have slipped back (UNDP 2002, Chapter 1). How should we proceed in the face of all of these problems? What role should international trade play in all of this? It is obvious that access to international resources can greatly benefit economic development. But it is equally obvious that some forms of access can cause much "collateral damage." How then should a nation proceed to take advantage of the potential benefits while avoiding potential pitfalls?

The answer which currently dominates both theory and policy is that given by Mike Moore, the former Director General of the World Trade Organization (WTO): "the surest way to do more to help the poor is to continue to open markets" (Agosin and Tussie 1993: 9). Thus, the powerful countries are pressing the developing world to adopt wholesale trade liberalization, on the grounds that the best way to raise global living standards is to maximize trade (Rodrik 2001: 5, 10).

But there has been a growing reaction to this agenda. From those outside the so-called Washington Consensus and its variants has come a mounting attack on its various theoretical and empirical claims. It has been argued that the empirical evidence does not support the claim that trade liberalization leads to faster growth. Rather, it is concluded that almost all of successful export-oriented growth has come with selective trade and industrialization policies. So much so that there "are no examples of countries that have achieved strong growth rates of output and exports following wholesale liberalization policies" (Agosin and Tussie 1993: 26; Rodrik 2001: 7). This holds not only in recent times but even in the distant past when the currently rich countries were themselves climbing the ladder of success. For they themselves relied heavily on trade protection and subsidies, ignored patent laws and intellectual property rights, and generally championed free trade only when it was to their economic advantage. Indeed, the rich countries do not follow many of these policies even today (Agosin and Tussie 1993: 25; Rodrik 2001: 11).

Such sentiments have begun to show up even in the principal agencies pushing for dominant agenda. Joseph Stiglitz's stinging critique of WTO and IMF policies continues to reverberate throughout the world (Stiglitz 2002). And most recently, even the IMF itself has grudgingly conceded that, contrary to the rosy predictions of its theoretical models, a systematic examination of the empirical evidence leads to the "sobering" conclusion that "there is no proof in the data that financial globalization has benefited growth" in developing countries (Prasad *et al.* 2003: 5–6).

So if global trade liberalization has not lived up to its theoretical claims, where does the basic problem lie? In this paper I will argue that the deficiency lies within the theory of free trade itself, in the very principle of comparative costs upon which it is founded. From this point of view, it is not the real world that is "imperfect" because it fails to live up to the theory but rather the theory that is inadequate to the world it purports to explain. Indeed, I will argue that globalization has been working out as would be expected from the point of view of what I will call the classical theory of "competitive advantage." That is to say, it generally favors the developed over the developing, and the rich over the poor.

Section 2.1 of this paper will trace out the fundamental role played by the theory of comparative costs in current policies of trade liberalization, and will discuss the many empirical problems this theory encounters. Section 2.2 will examine the two main branches that have developed from standard trade theory in reaction to its empirical weaknesses. And Section 2.3 will outline the classical theory of *competitive* advantage as a third alternative, and develop some of its principal implications.

Section 3 of the paper then addresses the relation between trade liberalization and the historical record. Section 3.1 will show that the developing countries themselves did not follow the very policies they now espouse, and in many cases do not follow them even today. Section 3.2 will argue that even in the modern era there is no convincing link between trade liberalization and economic development. Section 4 will then summarize the preceding historical and empirical evidence, and relate it to the classical theory of competitive advantage.

2 The theoretical foundations of trade policy

2.1 *The theory underlying the policy of trade liberalization*

Conventional economic theory concludes that trade and financial liberalization will lead to increased trade, accelerated economic growth, more rapid technological change, and a vastly improved allocation of national resources away from inefficient import-substitutes toward more efficient exportable goods. It admits that such processes might initially give rise to negative effects such as increased unemployment in particular sectors. But any such negative consequences are viewed as strictly temporary; to be addressed by appropriate social policies until the benefits of free trade begin to take hold. From a policy point of view, this means that the best path to economic development involves opening up the country to the world market: the elimination of trade protection, the opening up of financial markets, and the privatization of state enterprises.

It is quite striking to note that this powerful panoply of claims is actually based on two crucial premises: (1) the premise that free trade is regulated by the principle of comparative costs; and (2) the premise that free competition leads to full employment in every nation.

The principle of comparative costs is so familiar that it has come to be seen as a truism. It is most often presented in the form of the proposition that a "nation" would always stand to gain from trade if it were to export some portion of the goods it could produce comparatively more cheaply at home, in exchange for those it could get comparatively more cheaply abroad. It is the *comparative* costs of production which are said to be relevant here, not the absolute costs, so that a nation is enjoined to focus on producing and exporting goods that are comparatively cheaper at home. Implicit in this presentation is the claim that the market will then ensure that exports will be exchanged for an *equivalent* amount of imports, *so that trade will be balanced* (Dernburg 1989: 3).

But a normative proposition such as this has little value unless it can be shown that free trade among market economies actually operated this way. After all, in the world market it is not "nations" which barter some goods for others,[1] but rather myriad firms in different countries who buy and sell goods for money, all with the aim of earning profits on the export and import of a ever shifting variety of commodities. Therefore when (if) conventional trade theory seeks to appear more realistic, it moves to a second stage in the argument in which a quite different positive claim is substituted for the previous normative one. And here, it is argued that in free trade the terms of trade of a nation *will* always move in such a way as to eventually equate the values of exports and imports. Thus even when multitudes of profit-seeking firms are the actual agents of international trade, the end result is said to be the same as if each nation directly barters a particular quantity of exports for an equivalent value of imports (Dornbusch 1988: 3). Because this applies equally to advanced and developing economies, no nation need fear trade due to some perceived lack of international competitiveness. In the end, free trade will make each nation equally competitive in the world market (Arndt and Richardson 1987: 12). Note that for this positive proposition to hold, it is necessary to claim that the terms of trade fall whenever a country runs a trade deficit and *also* that the trade deficit will diminish when terms of trade fall. Obviously, the opposite movements must occur in the case of a balance of trade surplus.

Finally, to complete the standard argument on the benefits of free trade, it is also necessary to assume that full employment is the norm in countries with competitive markets. Without this additional assumption, even automatically self-balancing trade would not necessarily lead to gains from trade for the nation as a whole. After all, who is to say that balanced trade constitutes a "gain" from trade if that outcome is achieved at the expense of sustained job losses?

The theory of theory of comparative *advantage* lies downstream of the theory of comparative *costs*. Because these two are frequently confused, it is worth dwelling on their difference. We have noted that the principle of comparative costs claims that the terms of trade of every nation will automatically adjust so as to balance international trade. In such a process, each nation will find that its cheapest goods, the ones in which it is presumed to specialize, are those in which it has the lowest relative (i.e. comparative) costs. For example, if trade were opened between nations with equal wages but great disparities in technology, comparative cost theory would say that even if one nation was absolutely more efficient in producing all goods, it would nonetheless end up with lower international costs only in those goods in which it was relatively (comparatively) most advanced. Conversely, the absolutely less efficient nation would nonetheless end up with lower costs in those goods in which it was comparatively least backward. Hence it is comparative efficiency, not absolute, which would ultimately rule free trade in this case. The Hecksher–Ohlin–Samuelson (HOS) model of comparative *advantage* takes this principle of comparative *costs* for granted, as it does the notion that full employment obtains in both nations. It then seeks to locate differences in national comparative costs in differences in national factor endowments, on the usual assumption of "perfect competition, international identity of production functions and factors, nonreversibility of factor intensities, international similarity of preferences, [and] the constant returns-to-scale" (Johnson 1970: 10–11). Two well-known conclusions emerge. First, that within a system of free trade, nations with capital-intensive factor endowments will have lower comparative costs in capital-intensive goods. Hence they will have a "comparative advantage" in the production of such goods, and will tend to specialize in them. And second, that international trade by itself, without any need for direct flows of labor and capital, will tend to equalize real wages and profit rates across countries (the factor price equalization theorem).

To summarize, three propositions are essential to the whole corpus of standard trade theory: the terms of trade fall when a nation runs a trade deficit; the trade balance improves when the terms of trade fall; and there is no overall job loss generated by any of these adjustments. All of these mechanisms are assumed to operate over some period short enough to be socially relevant.

The trouble is that each of these three foundational claims of standard trade theory has been widely criticized for its theoretical and empirical deficiencies. We will consider each proposition in turn, in reverse order, because this is the order in which they are best known.

Let us begin with the claim that full employment is a natural consequence of competitive markets. The International Labor Organization (ILO) reports that as much as one-third of the world's workforce of three billion people are unemployed or underemployed (ILO 2001: 1). Even in the *developed* world, the unemployment rate has ranged from 3 percent to 25 percent across countries in the last decade. Matters are much worse, of course, in the *developing* world, where there are 1.3 billion unemployed or underemployed people at the current time (ILO 2001), many of whom with no prospects of reasonable employment in their lifetime. It does not take much reflection to recognize the linkages between persistent unemployment and intractable poverty. Given such patterns, it is hardly surprising that there remain a significant body of analysts who argue that there is no automatic tendency for full employment even in the advanced world. Indeed, this has long been the foundation of Keynesian and Kaleckian thinking.

Consider next the claim that a fall in the terms of trade will improve the balance of trade, at least after some initial negative effect, the so-called J-curve (Isard 1995: 95). This proposition that the balance of trade will ultimately improve lies at the root of the famous "elasticities problem" which has long been the subject of great controversy[2] (Isard 1995: 90–6).

We come finally to the most important claim of all, namely that the terms of trade automatically move to eliminate trade imbalances. As noted earlier, this hypothesis requires that terms of trade continue to fall in the face of a trade deficit, and continue to rise in the face of a trade surplus, until "trade will be balanced so that the value of exports equals the value of imports" (Dernburg 1989: 3). To put it another way, it says that this particular real exchange rate will adjust to make all freely trading nations *equally competitive, regardless of the differences in their levels of development or of technology.* At an empirical level, this leads to the expectation that "on average, over a decade or so, ebbs and flows of competitive 'advantage' would appear random over time and across economies" (Arndt and Richardson 1987: 12).

The trouble is that this proposition has never been empirically true: not in the developing world, not in the developed world, not under fixed exchange rates, not under flexible exchange rates. On the contrary, persistent imbalances are the *sine qua non* of international trade. This will come as no surprise to those familiar with the history of developing countries. *But it is equally true in the developed world.* For instance, over most of the postwar period the United States has run a trade deficit, and Japan has enjoyed a trade surplus (Arndt and Richardson 1987: 12). Similar patterns hold for most other OECD countries.

Because the HOS theory rests on the assumption of comparative costs, it is not surprising that it too has had grave difficulties at an empirical level (Johnson 1970: 13–18). In addition to the empirical difficulties it inherits from the theory of comparative costs, it has further problems that it fails to correctly predict trade patterns about half of the time, that technologies differ markedly across countries, and that real wages remain persistently unequal even across developed countries. As Magee (1980: xiv) puts it, the "history of postwar international trade theory has been one of attempting to patch up either the Ricardo [comparative costs] or Hecksher-Ohlin model to fit the facts as we know them." It is acknowledged among experts that this persistent failure of the most fundamental propositions of standard trade theory has undermined confidence in its whole structure (Arndt and Richardson 1987: 12).

2.2   *Reactions to the problems of standard trade theory*

In the light of the many deficiencies of the standard theory, the question arises as to where the theory goes wrong, and how should we correct for that. Two general approaches are widespread, and we address them here. In Section 2.3 we will take up a third, alternative approach, which I will call the classical theory of "competitive advantage."

Of the two types of reactions to the problems of standard theory, the first one focuses on the fact that the basic predictions of the theory of comparative costs and/or Purchasing Power Parity (PPP) are supposed to hold over the long run. Therefore one tack has been to redefine this "long run" to be on the order of *75 years or longer* (Rogoff 1996: 647; Froot and Rogoff 1995: 1657, 1662). Keynes' pithy phrase about the long run comes quickly to mind in this regard. But in any case, that still leaves us with the problem of explaining what happens before then. And here the tendency has been to switch the focus to a host of short run (e.g. portfolio balance) models (Harvey 1996; Stein 1995; Isard 1995). But even so, the "evaluation of ... [these] contemporary models ... shows why economists have been so disappointed in their ability to explain the determination of exchange rates and capital flows" (Stein 1995: 182). The problems of the standard theory have become so acute that

> neoclassical economists have expressed increasing frustration over their failure to explain exchange rate movements ... Despite the fact that this is one of the most well-researched fields in the discipline, not a single model or theory has tested well. The results have been so dismal that mainstream economists readily admit their failure.
>
> (Harvey 1996: 567)

Nonetheless, "the notion of comparative advantage continues to dominate thinking among economists" (Milberg 1994: 224). Worse still, these very same failed models "continue to be offered as the dominant explanation of ... exchange rate determination [even though] most scholars are aware of the deficiencies of these models" (Stein *op. cit.* p. 185). And worst of all, these same models continue to have a major influence on economic policy, for they provide the underpinning for the current policies of the IMF and the World Bank (Frenkel and Khan 1993).

The other major reaction to the empirical troubles of standard theory has been to modify one or more of its assumptions concerning perfect competition, factor mobility, and returns to scale. This New Trade Theory approach assumes that the crucial weakness of standard theory lies in the fact that actual competition, indeed the actual world itself, is "imperfect." It therefore situates itself within the problematic of "imperfect competition," and seeks to fill the gap between theory and the empirical evidence by incorporating oligopoly, increasing returns to scale, and various strategic factors into the standard analysis (Milberg 1993: 1). New Trade Theory shares the standard view that trade openness is generally good, but admits that it is not always so. Therefore, the focus shifts to identifying particular conditions under which trade can produce real gains and act as an engine of growth. The task is to explain why, in contradistinction to standard theory, the bulk of international trade was between countries with similar levels of development, was intraindustry and mostly in intermediate rather than final goods, was under apparently oligopolistic conditions, and took place without any appreciable resource reallocation or income distribution effects (Krugman 1981, 1983). To explain these phenomena, increasing returns to scale and imperfect competition are introduced into the traditional HOS framework.[3] This allows the principal of comparative advantage to be consistent with specialization in goods within an industry rather than specialization in whole industries. Thus, countries might end up exporting a particular type of automobile while importing another type of automobile, so that its international trade would be intraindustry. Similarly, economies of scale in the face of larger market could potentially overturn the HOS prediction that free trade would serve to equalize international factor prices (real wages and profit rates). In addition, the composition of trade, as opposed to its mere volume, becomes important because it may lead to significant effects such as differential elasticities of demand (the Prebisch–Singer thesis),[4] or differential transfers of technology. Finally, differences in knowledge (which includes technology) also modify the standard results. Once the notion of "factor endowment" is expanded to include accumulated and/or institutionalized human knowledge, then this changes the predicted patterns of comparative advantage, benefits of trade, and international rates of growth (Romer 1986; Lucas 1993). All of these give rise to a set of possible exceptions to the standard results, which in turn provide some (limited) room for state intervention in certain strategic sectors and certain strategic activities such as R&D. But "the models involved in the new trade theory, even with a few factors, are extremely complicated in terms of their outcomes – potentially generating multiple equilibria and complex patterns of adjustment to or around them" (Deraniyagala and Fine 2000: 11) and in the end the theory provides "few unambiguous conclusions" (ibid. p. 4).

2.3   The classical theory of "competitive advantage"

We have seen that the problems of standard trade theory have led to two basic types of reactions. The first of these is to argue that standard long run propositions such as balanced trade and/or PPP only hold over periods of 75 years or more. The focus then shifts to "short run" models, of which there is a considerable variety. The second reaction, on the other hand, argues that the real world fails to live up to the standard model. This in turn leads to focus on introducing various real world "imperfections" into the standard theory.

One purpose of this paper is to argue that the fundamental problem of standard theory is that it is wrong on its own terms. That is to say, it is flawed at its very root, in the analysis of competitive free trade between nations: the very principle of comparative costs is wrong even under competitive conditions.[5] The alternative argument, which I will call the classical theory of "competitive advantage",[6] rejects the standard theory altogether. In brief, the argument here is that relative prices of international goods, and hence a nation's terms of trade, are regulated in the same way as relative national prices. In both cases, high cost producers lose out to low cost ones, and high cost regions (nations) tend to suffer trade deficits which will tend to be covered by corresponding capital inflows (subsidies and borrowing). Unlike in the theory of comparative costs, there are no magic mechanisms that will automatically make all regions (nations) automatically equal. Indeed, persistent trade imbalances covered by foreign capital flows are the "normal" complement of international trade between unequally competitive trade partners. Thus, free trade does not make all nations equally competitive, as is argued within standard trade theory. Rather, it exposes the weak to the competition of the strong. And as in most such cases, the latter devour the former (Shaikh 1996, 1980; Milberg 1993, 1994).

The starting point of the classical competitive advantage approach lies in the classical theory of competition, which is very different from the conventional theory of "perfect" competition. In the classical tradition, competition means *real* competition, in the sense of business competition. Firms utilize strategy and tactics to gain and hold market share, and price-cutting and cost reductions are major feature in this constant struggle (Shaikh 1980).

Second, the Classical approach argues that this real competition regulates trade *between* nations operates in much the same manner as it regulates trade *within* a nation. In regard to the latter, it was a central theme of classical theory that competition within a country is driven by the law of *absolute costs*, that is to say, firms with higher unit costs of production enjoy suffer an absolute competitive disadvantage. From this point of view, firms within high-cost regions of any one country, if exposed to competition, would tend to suffer declining shares in the national market. Their higher costs would make it difficult for them to sell outside the region ("exports") and would leave their markets vulnerable to products originating in lower-cost regions ("imports"). In other words, in domestic free exchange, regions with higher costs would tend to have "balance of trade" deficits. Such deficits would of course have to be financed, either by running down some monetary stocks or by attracting other funds to cover its net import needs. This in turn implies that if such regions entered into trade with other more competitive ones within the same country, they would tend to suffer job loss and real wage declines – at least until they caught up or their labor migrated elsewhere.

The last step in the Classical approach is to extend these results of real competition to the case of free trade between nations. Because a nation's international terms of trade are merely international common-currency relative prices, they will be regulated in the same manner as any relative price: by relative real costs. However, the terms of trade will then not be free to automatically adjust to eliminate trade imbalances unless real costs themselves did so. The latter depends on real wages and productivity, and while international trade affects these, they also have many other social and historical determinants.[7] It follows that under unregulated trade, countries at a competitive disadvantage in the world market would tend to suffer trade deficits.[8] These in turn would have to be covered by foreign debt or subsidies. It is easy from within this framework to explain the familiar cycle of persistent trade deficits, periodic and ineffective exchange rate devaluations, and eventual debt crises (Shaikh 1999, 1996).[9]

Three crucial corollaries follow. First, trade liberalization will principally benefit the firms of the developed countries of the world, because they are the most technologically advanced. Without adequate time to prepare for this challenge, the developing world will largely fall back on to providing foreign access to cheap labor and cheap natural resources. Nothing in such a process promises that development, or poverty reduction, will automatically follow. On the contrary, cheap imports and capital-intensive foreign direct investment are likely to displace more jobs than they create, thereby intensifying poverty. Second, it is now easy to make sense of the industrial strategy followed by the *Western countries themselves*, as well as that subsequently followed by Japan, South Korea, and the Asian Tigers, as they moved up the ladder. We shall see that in both sets of cases, trade protection and state support to industry played a central role – the very roles that are forbidden under current WTO, IMF, and World Bank rules. It should be noted that the Classical approach provides much more room for government regulation of trade and industrial policy than does New Trade Theory, because it is no longer just a question of handling particular instances in which free trade fails to perform as it should. On the contrary, within the Classical approach what-you-see is what-you-get: free trade does what it is supposed to do, namely reward the strong. Conversely, if development is really the objective, then trade is merely one of many means to this end, not the end in itself.

To summarize, there are three basic types of responses to the failures of standard theory. The traditional approach, which remains within the standard framework, retains its faith in the virtues of free trade, but concedes that it might take 75 years or more to work. The imperfections approach, which argues that free trade does not always work as it "should" because of the effects of imperfect competition, economies of scale, and an uneven distribution of skills, knowledge, and institutions across countries. And the classical competitive advantage approach, which argues that free trade does indeed work as it should – which is to benefit advanced firms and advanced countries. All three approaches imply some room for government intervention, from a little for the first, so somewhat more for the second, and to possibly a great deal for the third (as in the historical rise of today's wealthy countries).

In what follows, we will turn to the actual practises in international trade. Section 3 focuses on the role of (the absence of) free trade in the historical rise of the Western countries themselves, and to the later rise of Japan, South Korea, and the Asian Tigers. In the subsequent section we will then turn to the more recent history of the effects of trade liberalization of developing countries. It will be argued in both cases that the actual outcomes in both cases are perfectly consistent with the classical theory of competitive advantage. This will shed a different light on the actual policies followed by powerful countries in any given epoch.

3   Trade liberalization and the historical record

3.1   *The role of managed trade in the rise of the advanced world*

The rich countries of the world are pushing developing countries to adopt policies of liberalized trade, foreign investment, and strong laws on intellectual property and patents. It is useful to note, then, that they themselves assiduously *avoided* such policies when they were climbing the ladder of success (Chang 2002).

For instance, Britain and the USA relied heavily on trade protection and subsidies in their own process of development. Even as early as the fourteenth and fifteenth centuries, Britain promoted its leading industry, which was the manufacture of woolen goods, by taxing the exports of raw wool to its competitors, and by trying to attract away their workers. In the heyday of its development from the early 1700s to the mid-1800s, it used trade and industrial policies similar to those subsequently used by Japan in late nineteenth and twenteeth centuries, and by Korea in the post-Second World War period. It was only when Britain was already the leader of the developed world that it began to champion free trade. This point was not lost on its rivals, such as Germany and the United States (Chang 2002: 1). Prominent thinkers in these countries argued instead for protection of newly rising industries. Indeed, even as Britain was preaching free trade after 1860, the United States "was literally the most heavily protected economy in the world," and remained that way until the end of the Second World War. In doing so.

> the Americans knew exactly what the game was. They knew that Britain reached the top through protection and subsidies and therefore that they needed to do the same if they were going to get anywhere ... Criticizing the British preaching of free trade to his country, Ulysses Grant, the Civil War hero and the US President between 1868–1876, retorted that "within 200 years, when America has gotten out of protection all that it can offer, it too will adopt free trade".
>
> (Chang 2002: 1)

And this, indeed, is exactly what happened.

Similar stories of protectionism and state intervention can be told for most of the rest of the developed world, including Germany, Sweden, Japan, and South Korea. Even countries like the Netherlands and Switzerland that adopted free trade in the late eighteenth century did so because they were already leading competitors in the world market and therefore could afford to do so. But even here.

> the Netherlands deployed an impressive range of interventionist measures up till the seventeenth century in order to build up its maritime and commercial supremacy ... and Switzerland and the Netherlands refused to introduce a patent law despite international pressure until 1907 and 1912 respectively, [so that they were free to appropriate] technologies from abroad.
>
> (Chang 2002: 2).

Table 3.1 The rising gap between rich and poor countries

Year	Ratio of rich-to-poor country GDP per capita
1820	3 to 1
1913	11 to 1
1950	35 to 1
1973	44 to 1
1992	72 to 1

Source: UNDP (1999: 38).

Table 3.2 Level of industrialization (manufacturing output per capita) 1800–1913 (UK 1900 = 100)

	1800	*1830*	*1860*	*1880*	*1900*	*1913*
Total developed countries	8	11	16	24	35	55
Total Third World	6	6	4	3	2	2
Memo						
UK	16	25	64	87	100	115
US	9	14	21	38	69	126

Source: Bairoch (1997: 404), vol. 1, as reproduced in Milanovic (2002: 12).

But this prior history of globalization is not just a matter of protectionism and state support as a means toward development in the West. There are also the small matters of colonization, force, pillage, slavery, mass slaughter of native peoples, and the deliberate destruction of the livelihoods of potential competitors (East India Company). "Globalization was brought to many at the "point of a gun" and many were 'globalized' literally kicking and screaming" (Milanovic 2002: 5–6). Gunboat diplomacy of the West was central in its treatment of Japan, Tunisia, Egypt and Zanzibar, and China, among others. Millions suffered in slavery and near slavery on plantations all across the world. According to recent conservative estimates, from 1865 to 1930 the "Dutch East Indies Company … pillaged … between 7.4 and 10.3 percent of Indonesia's national income per year" (ibid. p. 6).

Many other examples of such events can be adduced. What is striking is the cumulative impact led not only to widening inequality among nations (Table 3.1) but also to the early *deindustrialization* of the Third World in the face of the industrialization of the First World (Table 3.2).

We are therefore left with three central conclusions. First, that during their own process of development the rich countries relied heavily on trade protection and subsidies, that they did not generally abide by patent laws or so-called intellectual property rights, and that they generally championed free trade only when it was to their economic advantage. From this point of view, these countries are currently pushing the developing world to adopt the very policies that they themselves avoided. Second, that the policies of the rich countries included not only protectionism and state intervention but also colonization, pillage, slavery, and the deliberate deindustrialization of the Third World. And third, that the historic globalization of capitalism was attended by secularly rising international inequality.

How is one to interpret this history? It is clear that even as academic economic theory was trumpeting the universal benefits of free trade, advanced countries were not following its prescriptions. Should we say that policy makers lacked the confidence to wait three-quarters of a century or more for the theory to work itself out? Or should we say that the world was always beset with imperfections that negated the standard propositions, at least in practice? I would argue that neither of these readings is adequate nor even necessary. On the contrary, if free trade benefits the strong, then it is perfectly understandable that it would be championed in theory by the strong and resisted in practice by the up-and-coming.

But perhaps this is all in the past. Might we argue that the more recent history of trade liberalization in developing countries tells a different story?

3.2   Trade liberalization in recent times

The drive for wholesale trade liberalization rests on the assertion that the best way to raise global living standards is to maximize free trade (Rodrik 2001: 5, 10): "no protection is the best protection and that all economic decisions are best left to the market" (Agosin and Tussie 1993: 25). This means lowering of tariff and nontariff barriers and reduction or elimination of subsidies; adherence to WTO rules on intellectual property rights, customs procedures, sanitary standards, treatment of foreign investors; and various tax reforms, labor market reforms, and policy reforms designed to provide social support for displaced workers and technological support for displaced businesses (Rodrik 2001: 24).

All of this is grounded in two sets of claims. First, that the goal of the WTO is to increase consumer welfare through the expansion of trade. And second, that the expansion of trade will reduce poverty and raise general living standards in the developing countries.

On the WTO, it is important to recognize that in reality it "is an institution that enables countries to bargain about market access," not about poverty reduction. Indeed, its actual agenda was

> shaped in response to a tug-of-war between exporters and multinational corporations in the advanced industrial countries (which have had the upper hand), on the one hand, and import-competing interests (typically, but not solely labor) on the other. The WTO can best be understood in this context, as the product of intense lobbying by specific exporter groups in the United States or Europe or of specific compromises between such groups and other domestic groups.
>
> (Rodrik 2001: 34)

As for trade liberalization as the route to increased wealth, we have already seen that this prescription was not followed by the rich countries themselves in their own processes of development, and is not followed by them in many respects even today (Agosin and Tussie 1993: 25; Rodrik 2001: 11).

From this perspective, it should come as no surprise that even in recent times, the empirical evidence does not support the claim that trade liberalization or incentive neutrality leads to faster growth. It is true that higher manufacturing growth rates have been typically associated with higher export growth rates (mostly in countries where export *and* import shares to GDP grew), but there is no statistical relation between either of these growth rates or degree of trade restrictions. Rather, almost all of successful export-oriented growth has come with selective trade and industrialization policies. In this regard, stable exchange rates and national price levels seem to be considerably more important than import policy in producing successful export-oriented growth (Agosin and Tussie 1993: 26, 30, 31). Conversely, there "are no examples of countries that have achieved strong growth rates of output and exports following whole-sale liberalization policies" (Agosin and Tussie 1993: 26; Rodrik 2001: 7). Indeed, financial liberalization "leaves the real exchange rate at the mercy of fickle short-term capital movements" so that "even small changes in the direction of trade and capital flows can produce large swings in the real exchange rates." It also ties the domestic interest rate to that in international capital markets, which makes it difficult to have a lower rate for selective industrial development policies (*op. cit.* p. 23).

Japan, South Korea, and Taiwan are the classic cases of successful development through the application of "highly selective trade policies." On the other hand, Chile (1974–79), Mexico (1985–88), and Argentina (1991) did follow wholesale liberalization, which wiped out not only weak sectors but also potentially strong ones, often at great social cost over a long period of time. Chile's economy grew at less than 1 percent per capita from 1973 to 1989. Mexico suffered similar setbacks and slowdowns. And Argentina, which was lauded as being a good "globalizer" as recently as 2002 (World Bank 2002: 35, cited in Milanovic 2002: 30, footnote 29), is now of course mired in deep crisis (Agosin and Tussie 1993: 26–7).

What *is* true is that economic growth is correlated with reductions in poverty. In countries where the distribution of income is stable, growth benefits the poor. But because the income distribution does not generally stay stable in the developing world, growth does not necessarily produce poverty reduction. And at the other end, poverty reduction is generally good for growth. Thus, the high correlation between growth and poverty reduction does not tell us the causation, and certainly does not guarantee that the former will produce the latter (Rodrik 2001: 12).

4   History and policy from the perspective of competitive advantage theory

How then do we interpret the empirical evidence that trade liberalization does not automatically produce growth, and that growth does not automatically reduce poverty?

Well, the latest official response of the rich countries has been to say that the problem lies not in the basic theory, but in the lack of adequate institutions in the developing world (Rodrik 2001: 5, 9, 10). From the point of view of this "augmented" Washington Consensus view, successful integration into the world market requires the developing world to undertake further reforms that "include financial regulation and prudential supervision, governance and anti-corruption, legal and administrative reform, labor-market 'flexibility' and social safety nets." In return, the developed world is supposed to provide greater access to its own markets. As always, these reforms are driven by the aim of strengthening the integration of the developing countries into the world economy, on the premise that free trade will take care of the rest (*op. cit.* pp. 14–15).

It is a good thing that the Washington Consensus has begun to recognize the importance of institutions. Institutions clearly matter. The question is, are *these* the institutions and policies that matter? It is really true that they will somehow make free trade succeed where it has failed so far?

One way to address that question is to look back on the history of the developed world itself. We have already remarked that this is a history of protectionism and state intervention, not one of free trade and laissez faire. But it is also worth noting that the very institutions now being pushed on the developing world did not exist in the rich countries during their own rise. For example, in 1820, when the UK was more developed than India today

> it did not even have many of the most "basic" institutions that India has today. It did not have universal suffrage (it did not even have universal male suffrage), a central bank, income tax, generalised limited liability, a generalised bankruptcy law, a professional bureaucracy, meaningful securities regulations, and even minimal labour regulations (except for a couple of minimal and hardly-enforced regulations on child labour).
>
> (Chang 2002: 3)

The first real central bank, which was the Bank of England, came into being in 1844, well after England was an economic power. The United States only followed suit in 1913. And as for patent laws, "Switzerland and the Netherlands refused to introduce a patent law despite international pressure until 1907 and 1912 respectively, thus freely 'stole technologies from abroad" (*op. cit.* p. 3). And so we see once again the rich countries are pushing an agenda which they did not themselves follow: by and large, neither the trade liberalization policies nor its associated institutional extensions were central to their own development.

But the matter takes on a different cast when one interprets it in the light of the classical theory of competitive advantage. Institutions are important, but even more important is advanced technology and large-scale finance. And here, it is the developed countries of the time that possess the greatest advantage. Simply opening up the markets of a developing country exposes its businesses to powerful international competition, whether or not they are internationally competitive. And if they are not, they will lose out on a large scale. This can be offset to some extent by foreign investment attracted by natural resources and/or low wages. But even here, the unemployment created by the displaced domestic industries need not be absorbed by any new production by foreign firms, for the latter will generally be far less labor-intensive. Some countries, such as some oil producers, may be fortunate enough to have an export revenue large enough to offset these effects. But there is nothing in the market mechanism *per se* that guarantees this, and it is more likely that free trade and unfettered capital flows will leave developing nations in deficit, debt, unemployment, and underdevelopment. Without the intervention of appropriate institutions that *counter* these tendencies of free trade, the problems will tend to be chronic. From this point of view, the historical avoidance of free trade by the rich countries when they themselves were developing, as well as their current insistence on it now that they have climbed the ladder, make perfect sense.

Conversely, if trade liberalization is not a panacea, how should the developing countries try to proceed? If the goal is to reduce poverty and raise the general standard of living in the developing world, then *that* should be the direct focus of economic strategy capabilities (Rodrik 2001: 13). But as far as trade policy is concerned, both the history and competitive advantage theory suggest that the most appropriate procedure would be to consider trade liberalization in a selective manner, as individual industries become sufficiently competitive in the world market. To accomplish this would require a great social push, along with clear standards and deadlines on meeting the standards of the world market (Agosin and Tussie 1993: 25, 28). Of course, none of this would be possible without major change in current WTO rules and international conditions attached to financial assistance. Development must be brought back to the center of the picture, and a whole range of institutions and practises considered as alternatives (Rodrik 2001). In the final analysis, "[t]rade is a means to an end, not an end in itself" (Rodrik 2001: 29).

This has long been the focus of the opposition to the Washington Consensus, and it is precisely the right track. But, in my opinion, it needs to be freed from its residual dependence on the standard theory of trade and all of its trappings.

Notes

1 It is astonishing how easily even otherwise skeptical writers slide from a consideration of how trade actually operates to one of trade should operate. A standard example of this tendency is Magee's (1980, Chapter. 2) presentation of a Ricardian example of initial absolute advantage, in which each country produces two commodities but one country (the US) can produce both more cheaply than the other (Canada). Ricardo himself notes that in this case the more efficient country would enjoy an initial balance of trade surplus and the less efficient one a balance of trade deficit. This is because Canadian *consumers* will gain by buying the cheaper US products, and US *firms* will gain by exporting them. Ricardo then claims that the trade imbalances will change the real exchange rate in such a way as to raise the foreign prices of US goods and lower the foreign prices of Canadian goods, until at some point the two nations each have a cost advantage in one good. The motivations of consumers and firms remain the same throughout, but the US absolute cost advantage and the corresponding Canadian

absolute cost disadvantage are transformed into comparative cost advantages for both, in such a way as to eventually balance their trade. Magee jumps all of this, and simply asserts that "one of Ricardo's important contributions was to debunk the myth of absolute advantage; that is, the notion that the United States would *should* produce both products *and not engage in international trade*" because "it" can get both products more cheaply at home. From there he moves quickly to the claim that US consumers *should* engage in international trade, which he now presents as a form of barter run based on comparative costs (Magee 1980: 19, emphasis added). All of this from an author who says early on that he views the theory of comparative costs as "overrated" (Magee 1980: xiv).

2 The "elasticities problem" arises from the fact that a fall in the terms of trade, which implies a cheapening of exports relative to imports, has two contradictory effects. A lower relative export price implies that each unit of exports earns less for the country. Because the exports are thereby cheaper to foreigners, the quantity of exports should rise. This means that the *value* of exports could fall, stay the same, or rise, depending on the relative strengths of two effects. The obverse would apply to imports. Thus the overall response of the trade balance of trade to a fall in the terms of trade would depend on the combination of the two sets of responses, that is on the respective price elasticities of exports and imports.

3 For instance, money wages may be sticky, and even if they do adjust partially downward in the face of a trade deficit, this will worsen income inequality, may lead to social turmoil, and will worsen any problems of excess capacity (Milberg 2002: 242).

4 The Prebisch-Singer thesis posits three things. First, that free trade leads developing countries to specialize in primary goods and developed countries to specialize in manufactured goods. Second, that primary goods have low elasticity of demand, and manufactured goods have high elasticities of demand. Third, product and labor markets are imperfectly competitive in the center, but highly competitive in the periphery. Thus producers in the center are able to maintain high prices and workers are able to reap the benefits of technological change through rising wages; while in the periphery firms face declining prices in the face of competition from other primary producers and workers face stagnant or declining wages in the face of large pools of unemployed labor. Therefore the terms of trade of the developing countries deteriorate over the long run, which undermines their development process (Singer 1950; Prebisch 1959).

5 The Classical theory of competition encompasses both Smith and Ricardo. But whereas the former extends this theory to the case of international trade, the latter substitutes a different principle altogether when it comes to trade between nations – the principle of comparative costs. The logic of the two arguments, including their respective treatments of the exchange rate, the balance of trade, and the balance of payments, is developed in detail in Shaikh 1999, 1998, 1996, 1980).

6 Within the classical theory of "competitive advantage," just as real wages and production coefficients regulate relative prices within a nation, so too do they regulate international relative prices and hence international terms of trade. Hence it is the *differentials* in real wages and technologies across nations that determine their international competitiveness (Shaikh 1980; Cagatay 1993; Milberg 1993; 2002).

7 From the classical competitive advantage point of view, technological differences among nations play a central role. This provides an alternate theoretical foundation for the neo-Schumpeterian emphasis on technological differences between countries. Such models fall within the imperfect competition tradition, and focus on conditions in which absolute (competitive) advantages *dominate* over comparative advantages as determinants of trade flows, depending on the specific interactions between international differences in technology, wage rates, and market structures such as average firm size, concentration ratios, and the role of international oligopolies (Dosi *et al.* 1990; Milberg 1993; Milberg and Houston 2002).

8 For instance, a country with relatively higher real costs will suffer in international competition. Insofar as this leads to a fall in real wages (possibly abetted by state policies), this may temporarily improve the trade balance – at the expense of workers' standards of living. But this is at best a temporary solution, for if a nation's productivity growth rate is lower than that of its competitors, it will find its *relative* real unit labor costs rising once again after the wage adjustment is completed (Shaikh 1996).

9 At an empirical level, the Classical approach also allows us to explain the actual movements of real exchange rates. This also permits us to explain why Purchasing Power Parity theory does not work at an empirical level between countries with low or moderate inflation, and yet does appear to work in high inflation cases. And finally, it allows us to derive an empirically robust *policy rule* to judge the sustainability of a particular level of the exchange rate (Shaikh 1998).

References

Agosin, M. R. and Tussie, D. (1993) 'Trade and Growth: New Dilemmas in Trade Policy – An Overview', chapter 1 in Trade and Growth: New Dilemmas in Trade Policy, New York: St Martin's Press.

Arndt, S. W. and Richardson J. D. (eds.) (1987) *Real-Financial Linkages Among Open Economies*, Cambridge, MA: The MIT Press.

Bairoch, P. (1997) *Victoires and Deboires*, Paris: Gallimard (three volumes).

Cagatay, N. (1993) 'Themes in Marxian and Post-Keynesian Theories of International Trade: A Consideration with Respect to New Trade Theory', Essay 12 in M. Glick (ed.) *Competition, Technology and Money: Classical and Post-Keynesian Perspectives*, New Directions in Modern Economics Series, Aldershot, UK: Edward Elgar.

Chang, H.-J. (2002) 'Kicking Away the Ladder', *Post-autistic Economics Review*, no. 15, September 4, 2002, article 3. Online. Available HTTP: <http://www.btinternet.com/~pae_news/review/issue15.htm> (accessed September 20, 2004).

Deraniyagala, S. and Fine, B. (2000) 'New Trade Theory Versus Old Trade Policy: A Continuing Enigma', Working Paper Series No. 102, School of Oriental and African Studies (SOAS), London: University of London.

Dernburg, T. F. (1989) *Global Macroeconomics*, New York: Harper & Row.

Dornbusch, R. (1988) 'Real Exchange Rates and Macroeconomics: A Selective Survey', NBER Working Paper No. 2775, Cambridge, MA: NBER.

Dosi, G., Pavitt K., and Soete, L. (1990) *The Economics of Technical Change and International Trade*, New York: NYU Press.

Frenkel, J. A. and Khan, M. S. (1993) 'The International Monetary Fund's Adjustment Policies and Economic Development' in D. K. Das (ed.) *International Finance: Contemporary Issues*, London: Routledge.

Froot, K. A. and Rogoff, K. (1995) 'Perspectives on PPP and Long Run Real Exchange Rates', in G. M. Grossman and K. Rogoff (eds.) *Handbook of International Economics,* vol. III: 1647–88, Amsterdam: Elsevier.

Harvey, J. T. (1996) 'Orthodox Approaches to Exchange Rate Determination: A Survey', *Journal of Post-Keynesian Economics,* 18(4): 567–83.

ILO (2001) *World Employment Report 2001: Life at Work in the Information Economy*, Geneva: International Labour Organization.

Isard, P. (1995) *Exchange Rate Economics*, Cambridge, England: Cambridge University Press.

Johnson, H. G. (1970) 'The State of Theory in Relation to the Empirical Analysis', in R. Vernon (ed.) *The Technology Factor in International Trade*, New York: National Bureau of Economic Research, distributed by New York and London: Columbia University Press, pp. 9–21.

Krugman, P. (1981) 'Intraindustry Specialization and the Gains from Trade', *The Journal of Political Economy*, 89(5): 959–73.

Krugman, P. (1983) 'New Theories of Trade Among Industrial Countries', *The American Economic Review*, 73(2): 343–7.

Lucas, R. E. (1993) 'Making a Miracle', *Econometrica*, 61(2): 251–72.

Magee, S. P. (1980) *International Trade*, Reading, MA: Addison-Wesley.

Milanovic, B. (2002) 'The Two Faces of Globalization: Against Globalization As We Know It'. Online. Available HTTP: <http:/www.networkideas.org> (accessed March 23, 2004).

Milberg, W. (1993) 'The Rejection of Comparative Advantage in Keynes and Marx' *mimeo*, New York: Department of Economics, New School for Social Research.

—— (1994) 'Is Absolute Advantage *Passe?* Towards a Keynesian/Marxian Theory of International Trade', in M. Glick (ed.) *Competition, Technology and Money, Classical and Post-Keynesian Perspectives*, Aldershot, UK: Edward Elgar.

—— (2002) 'Say's Law in the Open Economy: Keynes's Rejection of the Theory of Comparative Advantage', Essay 14 in S. Don and J. Hillard (eds.) *Keynes, Uncertainty and the Global Economy*, Aldershot, UK: Edward Elgar.

Milberg, W. and Houston, E. (2002) 'The High Road and the Low Road to International Competitiveness,' in L. Taylor (ed.) *Globalization and Social Policy*, New York: The Free Press.

Prasad, E., Rogoff, K., Wei, S.-J., and Kose, M. A. (2003) 'IMF Effects of Financial Globalization on Developing Countries: Some Empirical Evidence', International Monetary Fund Occasional Paper 220, Washington, DC: International Monetary Fund.

Prebisch, R. (1959) 'Commercial Policy in Underdeveloped Countries', *American Economic Review*, 49 (May Supplement): 251–73.

Rodrik, D. (2001) 'The Global Governance of Trade: As if Trade Really Mattered', Background paper to the UNDP Project on Trade and Sustainable Human Development, October, New York: United Nations Development Programme (UNDP).

Rogoff, K. (1996) 'The Purchasing Power Parity Puzzle', *Journal of Economic Literature*, 34: 647–68.

Romer, P. (1986) 'Increasing Returns and Long run Growth', *The Journal of Political Economy*, 95(5): 1002–37.

Shaikh, A. (1980) 'The Law of International Exchange', in E. Nell (ed.) *Growth, Profits and Property*, Cambridge, UK: Cambridge University Press.

—— (1996) 'Free Trade, Unemployment and Economic Policy', in J. Eatwell (ed.) *Global Unemployment: Loss of Jobs in the 90's*, Armonk, New York: M. E. Sharpe.

—— (1998) 'Explaining Long Term Exchange Rate Behavior in the United States and Japan', Working Paper No. 250, New York: The Jerome Levy Economics Institute of Bard College.

—— (1999) 'Real Exchange Rates and The International Mobility of Capital', Working Paper No. 265, New York: The Jerome Levy Economics Institute of Bard College.

Singer, H. W. (1950) 'The Distribution of Gains Between Investing and Borrowing Countries', *American Economic Review*, 40: 473–85.

Stein, J. L. (1995) 'The Natrex Model, Appendix: International Finance Theory and Empirical Reality', in *Fundamental Determinants of Exchange Rates*, Oxford: J. L. Stein & Associates, Clarendon Press.

Stiglitz, J. E. (2002) *Globalization and its Discontents*, New York: W. W. Norton & Company.

UNDP (United Nations Development Program) (1999) *Human Development Report,* New York: Oxford University Press.

—— (2002) *Human Development Report*, New York: Oxford University Press.

World Bank (2002) *Globalization, Growth and Poverty: Building an Inclusive World Economy*, Policy Research Report (December), Washington, DC: World Bank.

4 Globalization and free trade: theory, history, and reality

Deepak Nayyar

1 Introduction

International trade is an integral part, if not the cutting edge, of globalization. In a positive sense, this is widely recognized. But international trade, which can be transacted under a wide range of institutional arrangements, is not the same as unrestricted ("free") trade. For all the theorizing, the rationale for international trade was always prescriptive. Recent years have witnessed the formulation of an intellectual rationale for globalization that has transformed globalization, together with free trade, into a "virtual ideology" of our times, so much so that both are perceived as a means of ensuring not only efficiency and equity but also growth and development in the world economy. This belief, I shall argue, is not validated by either theory or history let alone by reality.

The structure of the paper is as follows. First, it traces the origins of the free trade doctrine in classical political economy, so as to set out the fundamental propositions of orthodox trade theory, which provide the basis for the prescription that free trade would lead to both efficiency and equity. Second, it outlines the reasons for departures from free trade that seem to have been explored in economic theory but, despite history, set aside as exceptions that prove the rule. Third, it relates the economic theorizing to the political realities which have shaped the sequence of developments in the international trading system, since the early nineteenth century, to illustrate the flexibility of the free trade doctrine over time. Fourth, it situates free trade in the wider context of globalization, with an analysis of experience during the late nineteenth and the late twentieth centuries to show how uneven development has always excluded countries and people from development and prosperity. Fifth, it concludes that, despite the rhetoric, the invocation of the free trade doctrine is uneven in space and asymmetrical across sectors. This is because the multilateral system embodied in the WTO is characterized by double standards and rigged rules both of which need to be corrected.

2 Free trade doctrine

The analytical foundations of the orthodox theory of international trade, as it now exists, were laid in the era of classical political economy by Adam Smith, David

Ricardo, and John Stuart Mill. Smith (1776) enunciated the principle of absolute advantage to demonstrate that there were gains from trade, by extending his concept of the division of labor between men to a division of labor between countries. Ricardo (1817) formulated the theory of comparative advantage to develop an explicit argument against protection and an implicit argument for free trade. The concerns of Smith and Ricardo did not lie in abstract economic principles. Their economics was rooted in politics. Indeed, their intellectual pursuits were motivated by a strong desire to challenge the political dominance of mercantilist ideology. The doctrine of mercantilism was subjected to scathing criticism, which bordered on ridicule, for its pursuit of national economic power, at the cost of general economic welfare, to the neglect of plenty.[1] In doing so, the advocates of free trade adopted a moral stance claiming that their concern was the welfare of human beings and not of nation states.

At the same time, the economic thinking of Smith and Ricardo endeavored to provide a rationale, and also to analyze the conditions, for a transition from the prevalent feudalism to a prospective capitalism. Thus, for Adam Smith, free trade was simply one dimension of the case for *laissez faire* which confirmed his belief in the magic of the invisible hand. Similarly, for David Ricardo, the formulation of comparative advantage was not simply about the pattern of trade or the gains from trade, as contemporary textbooks would have us believe. It was as much, if not more, about the impact of international trade on income distribution, capital accumulation, and economic growth. The repeal of the Corn Laws and the adoption of free trade was advocated by Ricardo in the belief that it would redistribute incomes away from the reactionary landed gentry, who would at worst not save and at best invest in agriculture which promised diminishing returns, in favor of a progressive industrial capitalist class, who would earn more profits (given a lower corn wage) through cheap imports of wheat, and invest in manufacturing which promised increasing returns. The moral of the story was that, consequent on the removal of restrictions on trade, an increase in profits would lead to an increase in the rate of accumulation, which in turn would lead to a growth in employment, income, and wealth. Economics and politics were closely interwoven in this world, for the redistribution of incomes from rents to profits was bound to be associated with a redistribution of political power from landlords to capitalists.

Subsequent economic theorizing about international trade began to separate the economics from the politics. This process started with Alfred Marshall and Francis Edgeworth in the late nineteenth century. It was taken to its logical conclusion by Eli Heckscher, Bertil Ohlin, and Paul Samuelson during the first half of the twentieth century.[2] In retrospect, it would seem that economics, so divorced from politics, slowly but surely acquired a life of its own. The selectivity in the choice of problems and the abstraction in the choice of assumptions made this difficult task much simpler. These choices shaped a corpus of thought where elegant models based on restrictive assumptions reached strong conclusions. Orthodox trade theory, which began life in this mode, soon came to don the mantle of mainstream economics. In this milieu, seeking a different set of answers, let alone asking a different set of questions, was perceived as unorthodox. The intersection of economics and politics in the sphere of trade was of course set aside, as a model-fetishism captured the imagination.

The neoclassical paradigm, as it emerged, emphasized the gains from trade. The economic logic underlying the proposition was indeed simple. In the most elementary sense, there are gains to be derived from trade if it is cheaper for an economy to import a good than to produce it at home, in terms of domestic resources used, and pay for it by exporting another. The gains are attributable in part to international exchange when costs or prices differ among countries before trade is introduced, and in part to international specialization in production after trade commences. In a world where countries enter into international trade on a voluntary basis, each partner must derive some benefit to be in the game. The very existence of trade, then, becomes proof of its mutual benefit, irrespective of how the gains from trade are distributed between countries. It is clear, however, that the formal exposition of the gains from trade proposition was no more than an analytical contribution to economic theory. Its message was already widely accepted, as the mercantilist view about asymmetry in the gains from trade – exports were beneficial but imports were not – had been discredited much earlier in the mid-nineteenth century.

There were two other propositions which emerged from the theory of international trade in this phase and provided the basis for persuasive policy prescription: the free trade argument and the factor-price equalization theorem.

In terms of the orthodoxy, the economic logic of the proposition that there are always gains from trade combined with the assumption of perfect competition, establishes that free trade would be optimal. The reasoning is straightforward in a two-commodity model. Perfect competition ensures an equalization of the domestic price ratio with the marginal rate of substitution in domestic production. Free trade ensures an equalization of the domestic price ratio and the international price ratio. Thus, it is argued that free trade will enable the economy to operate with technical efficiency in production in terms of resource allocation. Given well-behaved utility functions, free trade, which equalizes domestic and international prices, would also enable the economy to optimize consumption through trade, by equalizing the marginal rate of substitution in consumption and the international price ratio, in terms of utility maximization. The neat conclusion derived from such theorizing was that free trade ensures efficiency.

The factor-price equalization theorem emerged as a corollary of the Heckscher–Ohlin formulation of comparative advantage. Samuelson (1948) set up a model in which there are two countries (America and Europe), two commodities (food and cloth) and two factors (land and labor). It is assumed that there is free trade in goods and that there is no factor mobility between the countries. The factor endowments are such that America has a higher ratio of land to labor than Europe and the production conditions are such that food requires a higher ratio of land to labor than cloth. Production functions, which differ between commodities, are identical across countries, and are characterized by constant returns and diminishing marginal productivity. There is perfect competition in both commodity markets and factor markets. These assumptions about production conditions ensure a unique relationship between the factor-price ratio and the commodity-price ratio. Because free trade equalizes commodity prices, as long as both countries continue to produce both commodities, the marginal productivities of the factors must be the same in both. Thus, if complete specialization is ruled out, commodity-price equalization necessarily leads to factor-price equalization. The abstraction in the assumptions of the model represents substantive departures from reality but yields a powerful conclusion to suggest that, even in a world where international factor movements are not possible, free trade would ensure equity through an equalization of factor prices across countries.

The free trade argument, formalized in the normative dimension of orthodox theory, served an explicit prescriptive purpose in stating that free trade is efficient. The factor-price equalization theorem, set out in the positive dimension of orthodox theory, carried an implicit prescriptive purpose suggesting that free trade is also equitable. It is clear that the free trade argument and the factor-price equalization theorem were not simply about abstract principles. Their prescriptive significance, whether explicit or implicit, is obvious.

3   Exceptions and the rule

The belief in free trade is almost a sacred tenet in the world of orthodox economics. Yet, from time to time, the economics profession has recognized that there are reasons which may justify departures from free trade.[3] Economic theory has analyzed these exceptions to the rule, mostly in response to developments in the real world that have challenged or questioned the free trade doctrine.

The earliest challenge to free trade came during the early nineteenth century, the era of classical political economy, even before the doctrine gained widespread acceptance. This thinking was prompted largely by the concerns of late industrializers, such as the United States and Germany who wished to follow in the footsteps of England and France,[4] and partly by the pursuit of economic interests rather than economic efficiency. It was recognized that there were two critical assumptions underlying the strong prescription of free trade: first, that market prices reflected social costs and, second, that a country's trade in a good was not large enough to influence world prices. If these assumptions did not hold, free trade could not ensure an efficient outcome. Market failure provided the basis of the infant industry argument, recognizing that free trade may prevent an economy from realizing its comparative advantage in manufacturing activities. Monopoly power provided the basis of the optimum tariff argument, recognizing that restricting the volume of trade may enable an economy to increase its real income at the expense of the rest of the world. These arguments were accepted as valid exceptions to the rule by Mill (1848), thus providing the intellectual foundation for legitimate departures from free trade.

A later, though similar, challenge to free trade emerged during the 1950s at the beginning of the postcolonial era. This was shaped by the aspirations of underdeveloped countries that were latecomers to industrialization and wanted to accelerate the catching-up process. In the realm of politics, of course, the strong sentiment against free trade stemmed from the perceived association between openness and underdevelopment during the colonial era. In the sphere of economics, however, the argument against free trade was based on market failure. It had two dimensions. First, it was argued that there were significant positive externalities in any process of industrialization which were difficult to identify, let alone capture. Second, it was argued that imperfections in factor markets, both labor and capital, would preempt the realization of potential comparative advantage in manufacturing. The infant industry argument was, thus, generalized into the infant manufacturing sector argument.[5] The industrial sector was protected from foreign competition. And the pursuit of industrialization in most developing countries was based on the strategy of import substitution.

The response of modern neoclassical economics was twofold. At one level, it accepted the infant industry argument, or the optimum tariff argument, as the basis of justifiable departures from free trade but reduced the validity of such arguments to a very demanding set of conditions.[6] At another level, it argued that if market prices did not measure social costs, whether on account of a divergence arising out of market failure or on account of a distortion arising out of government intervention, the optimum policy intervention is one which is applied at the point at which the divergence or the distortion arises; the simple solution which followed from this complex discussion was that, as a rule, intervention in the form of trade policies would be suboptimal.[7] In sum, such theoretical analysis sought to strengthen the case for free trade by accepting that there is market failure but arguing that protection is not the best corrective.

4   Flexible belief system

Economic theory is to political reality what the ivory tower is to the real world. The experience of the past two centuries provides ample confirmation. Economic ideas about free trade have not shaped political reality but political compulsions have shaped the contours of economic theory. However, economic interests, whether perceived or real, have exercised an important influence on the political objectives of nation states in the world economy. In this pursuit of national economic interests, the use of the free trade doctrine, with its emphasis on efficiency and equity, has been flexible over time and across space.

Economic theorizing about trade has always considered a world in which countries at similar levels of development are equal partners, thus ruling out the use of political power to foster economic interests. This abstraction simply does not conform to reality. It never did, as Joan Robinson (1974) wrote, even in Ricardo's world. In the now famous example, Portugal was to gain as much from exporting wine as England from exporting cloth. This was not quite true even in terms of economics. Once we introduce capital accumulation into the picture, it is clear that free trade promised growth for England and stagnation for Portugal, for investment in cloth would be associated with increasing returns whereas investment in wine would be associated with diminishing returns. But that is not all. In the realm of politics, as Joan Robinson puts it:

Portugal was dependent on British naval support, and it was for this reason that she was obliged to accept conditions of trade which wiped out her production of textiles and inhibited industrial development, so as to make her more dependent than ever.

Robinson (1974: 1)

It is patently clear that, despite the abuse of mercantilism, free trade was also about the pursuit of national economic power. Indeed, the moral stance adopted by the advocates of free trade was false insofar as the desire for affluence or plenty was motivated by a quest for economic power no less than by a concern for human welfare.

The consequences of imperialism in trade are brought home by another historical example which also illustrates the flexibility in the use of the free trade doctrine over time. To begin with, the British cotton textile industry in Lancashire grew up under protection from superior Indian imports. When it became competitive, free trade was imposed on India. A century later, Indian textiles were once more able to undersell Lancashire. In response, the British turned to protection again, this time through an international agreement to regulate trade in textiles. This multifiber agreement has been with us for more than five decades.

It is clear why free trade was in the interest of countries which were the pioneers in industrialization.[8] Their economic strength was perhaps a source of their political, even military, power which enabled them to impose free trade on the rest of the world. For this reason, the ideology of free trade went well with British imperialist expansion until the early twentieth century and with American political hegemony thereafter. The imposition of free trade on the underdeveloped world was simple enough because much of Asia, Africa, and Latin America were colonized either *de jure* or *de facto*. It was, however, difficult to impose on countries at similar levels of development, such as Germany and Japan, which were latecomers not only to industrialization but also to colonial empires. The exclusion of such rivals from sources of raw materials and from promising markets contributed to the tensions that led to the two world wars.[9]

The 1930s witnessed a different form of economic conflict between the advanced capitalist nations, attributable to similar reasons, as countries resorted to import controls, tariff wars, competitive devaluations and so on, to protect their own levels of income and employment at the expense of the outside world. The ideology of free trade ran into acute difficulties during the period from the Great Depression to the Second World War. So much so that the retreat from free trade was almost complete, even on the part of countries which were, until then, its most ardent advocates. The reason was simple enough. National economic interests were at stake. And the free trade doctrine was readily shelved for a while.

The lessons that emerged from this experience of economic chaos and political conflict were not lost on the architects of the international trading system that was created, with the General Agreement on Tariffs and Trade (GATT) as its centerpiece, in the late 1940s. Its basic foundation was the principle of nondiscrimination embodied in the most-favored-nation clause. The virtues of unilateral free trade were recognized in theory but not accepted in practise. It was agreed that trade barriers would be made transparent by a conversion into tariffs which, in turn, would be progressively reduced through negotiations. Thus, universal free trade was perceived as the ultimate objective, but the conceived transition path was characterized by an implicit reciprocity principle that was almost mercantilist. The contractual framework of the GATT meant that countries would negotiate market access and tariff reductions on a reciprocal basis, through bargaining among major trading partners, and this was to be multilateralized through the GATT system. Clearly, the countries of Western Europe seeking to reconstruct after the war, and conscious of American dominance, were not willing to accept trade at that juncture.

The acceptance came soon. The next 25 years witnessed trade liberalization among the major industrialized countries at a rapid pace. The *modus operandi* was successive rounds of multilateral trade negotiations, under the GATT umbrella, which brought tariffs in the industrialized countries to levels that were almost negligible. This process was facilitated in politics by American hegemony and in economics by rapid growth associated with full employment. The influence of these factors began to wane in the early 1970s, and there was a turn of the tide as the industrialized world resorted to increasing protectionism over the two decades that followed. Large segments of world trade such as agriculture and textiles were excluded from GATT discipline. Nontariff barriers proliferated and multiplied: some misused GATT rules (antidumping or countervailing duties), others circumvented GATT rules (gray-area measures like voluntary-export-restraints and orderly-marketing-arrangements), whereas a few were not even in the realm of trade (laws about standards or health regulations). The outcome was a steady erosion in the principle of nondiscrimination. The flexibility of the free trade doctrine, obviously, continued.

The surge of trade liberalization and the rise of protectionism in the second half of the twentieth century were both attributable to the pursuit of national economic interests by countries which had the requisite political power. In the first phase, the industrialized world led by the United States wanted free trade and had the political hegemony to achieve it. During this period, from the late 1940s to the early 1970s, the industrialized countries progressively dismantled barriers to trade among themselves. This was carried out, through negotiations, at a pace that was mutually acceptable. In the second phase, as growth slowed down, recession persisted and unemployment mounted in the industrialized economies, the United States and the European Community both turned to protectionism as a means of preserving their economic interests. The East Asian countries, led by Japan, wanted free trade but did not have the political strength to impose it on others. During this period, from the early 1970s until now, the industrialized countries essentially erected barriers to trade to restrain exports from the developing countries. This was done in a unilateral manner, which did not conform to the rules of the game. It is striking that the principle of free trade was preserved for trade within the industrialized world but diluted for trade between the industrialized countries and the developing world.

5   Globalization and free trade: winners and losers

The ideologues believe that globalization led to rapid industrialization and economic convergence in the world economy during the late nineteenth century. In their view, the promise of the emerging global capitalist system was wasted for more than half a century, to begin with by three decades of conflict and autarchy that followed the First World War and subsequently, for another three decades, by the socialist path and a statist world view. The return of globalization in the late twentieth century is thus seen as the road to salvation. The conclusion drawn is that globalization now, as much as then, promises economic prosperity for countries that join the system and economic deprivation for countries that do not.[10] For those who recall development experience in the late nineteenth century, it should be obvious that the process of globalization will not reproduce or replicate the United States everywhere just as it did not reproduce Britain everywhere a century earlier. It was associated with an uneven development then. It is bound to produce uneven development now, not only between countries but also within countries.

This is a lesson that emerges from history. The economic consequences of globalization in the late nineteenth century were, to say the least, asymmetrical. Most of the gains from international economic integration of this era accrued to the imperial countries which exported capital and imported commodities. There were a few countries like the United States and Canada – new lands with temperate climates and white settlers – which also derived some benefits. In these countries, the preconditions for industrialization were already being created and international economic integration strengthened this process. Direct foreign investment in manufacturing activities stimulated by rising tariff barriers combined with technological and managerial flows reinforced the process. The outcome was industrialization and development. But this did not happen everywhere. Development was uneven in the industrial world. Much of southern and eastern Europe lagged behind. This meant divergence rather than convergence in terms of industrialization and growth.[11] There was, in fact, an increase in economic inequalities between countries and within countries. The income gap between the richest and the poorest countries, for instance, which was just 3:1 in 1820, more than doubled to 7:1 in 1870, and increased further to 11:1 in 1913.[12] Countries in Asia, Africa, and Latin America, particularly the colonized, which were also a part of this process of globalization, were even less fortunate. Indeed, during the same period of rapid international economic integration, some of the most open economies in this phase of globalization – India, China, and Indonesia – experienced deindustrialization and underdevelopment. We need to remind ourselves that, in the period from 1870 to 1914, these three countries practised free trade as much as the United Kingdom and the Netherlands, where average tariff levels were close to negligible (3–5 percent); in contrast, tariff levels in Germany, Japan, and France were significantly higher (12–14 percent); whereas tariff levels in the United States were very much higher (33 percent).[13] What is more, these three countries were also among the largest recipients of foreign investment.[14] But their globalization did not lead to development. The outcome was similar elsewhere: in Asia, Africa, and Latin America. So much so, between 1860 and 1913, the share of developing countries in world manufacturing output declined from over one-third to under one-tenth.[15] Export-oriented production in mines, plantations, and cash-crop agriculture created enclaves in these economies, which were integrated with the world economy in a vertical division of labor. But there were almost no backward linkages. Productivity levels outside the export enclaves stagnated at low levels. They simply created dualistic economic structures where the benefits of globalization accrued mostly to the outside world and in small part to the local elites.

The growing inequalities between and within countries, particularly in the industrial world, were perhaps a significant factor underlying the retreat from globalization after 1914. John Maynard Keynes highlighted the benefits of globalization for some people and some countries, those included, but also recognized how economic and political conflicts associated with the process stopped what had seemed irreversible at the time:

> The projects and politics of militarism and imperialism, of racial and cultural rivalries, of monopolies, restrictions and exclusions, which were to play the serpent to this paradise, were little more than amusement of the daily newspaper, and appeared to exercise almost no influence at all on the ordinary course of social and economic life, the internationalization of which was nearly complete in practice.
>
> Keynes (1919)

The process of globalization has led to uneven development, now as much as then. The reality that has unfolded so far clearly belies the expectations of the ideologues. The development experience of the world economy from the early 1970s to the late 1990s, which could be termed the *age of globalization*, provides cause for concern, particularly when it is compared with the period from the late 1940s to the early 1970s, which has been described as the *golden age of capitalism*.

Available evidence suggests that the past 25 years have witnessed a divergence, rather than convergence, in levels of income between countries and between people. Economic inequalities have increased during the last quarter of a century as the income gap between rich and poor countries, between rich and poor people within countries, as also between the rich and the poor in the world's population, has widened.[16] And income distribution has worsened.[17] The incidence of poverty increased in most countries of Latin America and sub-Saharan Africa during the 1980s and in much of Eastern Europe during the 1990s. In the developing countries, employment creation in the organized sector continues to lag behind the growth in the labor force, so that an increasing proportion of workers are dependent on low productivity and casual employment in the informal sector. Unemployment in the industrialized countries has increased substantially since the early 1970s and remained at high levels since then, except in the United States, while there has been almost no increase in the real wages of a significant proportion of the workforce in many industrialized countries. Inequality in terms of wages and incomes has registered an increase almost everywhere in the world. Over the same period, the rate of growth in the world economy has also registered a discernible slowdown. And the slower growth has been combined with greater instability. It would seem that, in some important respects, the world economy fared better in the *golden age* than it has in the *age of globalization.*

It is obviously not possible to attribute cause-and-effect simply to the coincidence in time. But it is possible to think of mechanisms through which globalization may have accentuated inequalities. Trade liberalization has led to a growing wage inequality between skilled and unskilled workers not only in industrialized countries but also in developing countries.[18] As a consequence of privatization and deregulation, capital has gained at the expense of labor, almost everywhere, for profit shares have risen while wage shares have fallen.[19] Structural reforms, which have cut tax rates and brought flexibility to labor markets, have reinforced this trend. The mobility of capital combined with the immobility of labor has changed the nature of the employment relationship and has reduced the bargaining power of trade unions. The object of managing inflation has been transformed into a near-obsession by the sensitivity of international financial markets, so that governments have been forced to adopt deflationary macroeconomic policies, which have squeezed both growth and employment. The excess supply of labor has repressed real wages. Financial liberalization, which has meant a rapid expansion of public as well as private debt, has been associated with the emergence of a new rentier class. And the inevitable concentration in the ownership of financial assets has probably contributed to a worsening of income distribution.[20] Global competition has driven large international firms to consolidate market power through mergers and acquisitions which has made market structures more oligopolistic than competitive. The competition for export markets and foreign investment, between countries, has intensified, in what is termed "a race to the bottom," leading to an unequal distribution of gains from trade and investment.

Globalization has, indeed, created opportunities for some people and some countries that were not even dreamed of three decades ago. But it has also introduced new risks, if not threats, for many others. It has been associated with a deepening of poverty and an accentuation of inequalities. The distribution of benefits and costs is unequal. There are some winners – more in the industrialized world than in the developing world. There are many losers – numerous both in the industrialized world and in the developing world. It is, perhaps, necessary to identify, in broad categories, the winners and the losers.[21]

If we think of people, asset-owners, profit-earners, rentiers, the educated, the mobile, and those with professional, managerial or technical skills are the winners, whereas asset-less, wage-earners, debtors, the uneducated, the immobile, and the semiskilled or the unskilled are the losers. If we think of firms, large, international, global, risk-takers, and technology-leaders are the winners; whereas small, domestic, local, risk-averse, and technology-followers are the losers. If we think of economies, capital-exporters, technology-exporters, net lenders, those with a strong physical and human infrastructure, and those endowed with structural flexibilities are the winners; whereas capital-importers, technology-importers, net borrowers, those with a weak physical and human infrastructure, and those characterized by structural rigidities are the losers. It needs to be said that this classification is suggestive rather than definitive, for it paints a broad-brush picture of a more nuanced situation. But it does convey the simultaneous, yet asymmetrical, inclusion and exclusion that characterizes the process of globalization. It is not surprising, then, that the spread of globalization is uneven and limited both among people and across countries.[22]

6   Rules of the game

It should be recognized that the Uruguay Round agreement represents a return of free trade more in rhetoric than in reality. The axiom of unilateral free trade has obviously not been accepted, for the reciprocity principle remains overwhelmingly important. The object of universal free trade is no more than a fond hope on a distant horizon. But that is not all. The invocation of, and the adherence to, the free trade doctrine is uneven across space and asymmetrical across sectors.

In spite of the professed belief in the free trade doctrine, the industrialized world is reluctant to accept free trade with the developing world. This reluctance stems from concerns about real wages and employment levels at home. The economic foundation of such views is weak but the political appeal is strong.

First, there is a fear that free trade with developing countries would have an adverse impact on real wages of unskilled or semiskilled workers in the industrialized economies, which would not rise and may even fall as a consequence. In politics, the stagnation or decline in real wages in the industrialized world, particularly the United States, combined with the steady increase in real wages in some parts of the developing world, particularly East Asia, is cited as supporting evidence. In economics, the factor-price equalization theorem is invoked as a supportive argument. Orthodox economics, seeking to rehabilitate the free trade doctrine, is beginning to question the Samuelson result that it acclaimed not so long ago. Jagdish Bhagwati, for example, now says:

> It is time to remind ourselves that the original view of the factor-price equalization theorem was correct. Its assumptions are indeed extraordinarily demanding. It is not therefore a compelling, or adequate, guide to real world phenomena.
>
> Bhagwati (1994: 242)

Indeed, he goes further to cite scale economies, diversification, and competition as reasons why real wages in the North and the South will not converge as a result of free trade. It is ironical that the same factor-price equalization theorem, which was placed on a pedestal because it implied that free trade is equitable, is now pulled down to demonstrate that free trade cannot do anything as wicked as equalize wages across countries. What is more, this economic theorizing has not led to political persuasion.

Second, there is a concern that free trade with developing countries would mean unfair competition because environmental regulations are sparse and labor standards are poor. The demand, then, is for a level playing field. This, in turn, means that domestic economic policies on environment and labor must be harmonized across countries. In its political dimension, the argument is that developing countries have an unfair advantage in competition and that there must be fair trade before there can be free trade. In its economic dimension, the argument is that the high levels of unemployment in industrialized countries are attributable to imports of manufactured goods from developing countries. Such arguments are obviously exaggerated, if not false, and have been treated with some skepticism by most economists. For one, differences between economies, particularly in wages, are a source of gains from trade. For another, imports from developing countries constitute a miniscule fraction of consumption or income in the industrialized countries. Yet political considerations overrule economic reasons. The appeal extends beyond conservative politics because environment and labor are both good liberal causes. In fact, the "social clause" is already on the agenda for the world trading system. It is only a matter of time before an "environment clause" arrives on the scene.

In refuting such arguments, it is important to stress that the stagnation in real wages and the high level of unemployment in the industrialized countries are attributable to the nature of technical progress, which is replacing several unskilled workers with a few skilled workers, and the impact of macroeconomic policies, which have sought to maintain price stability at the expense of full employment. The source of these problems lies within the industrialized countries and not in their trade with developing countries. The red herring cannot be revealed by trade theoretic analysis.

In a world of unequal partners, it is not surprising that the rules of the game are asymmetrical in terms of construct and inequitable in terms of outcome. The strong have the power to make the rules and the authority to implement the rules. In contrast, the weak can neither set nor invoke the rules. The problem, however, takes different forms.

First, there are different rules in different spheres. The rules of the game for the international trading system, being progressively set in the WTO, provide the most obvious example. There are striking asymmetries.[23] National boundaries should not matter for trade flows and capital flows but should be clearly demarcated for technology flows and labor flows. It follows that developing countries would provide access to their markets without a corresponding access to technology and would accept capital mobility without a corresponding provision for labor mobility. This implies more openness in some spheres but less openness in other spheres. The contrast between the free movement of capital and the unfree movement of labor across national boundaries, lies at the heart of the inequality in the rules of the game.

Second, there are rules for some but not for others. In the WTO, for instance, major trading countries resort to a unilateral exercise of power, ignoring the rules, because small countries do not have the economic strength even if they have the legal right to retaliate. There is no enforcement mechanism, yet, that can be imposed on the powerful players who circumvent the rules. And the hegemonic powers, often, simply ignore the rules.

Third, the agenda for new rules is partisan but the unsaid is just as important as the said. The attempt to create a multilateral agreement on investment in the WTO, which seeks free access and national treatment for foreign investors with provisions to enforce commitments and obligations to foreign investors, provides the most obvious example. Surely, a discipline on restrictive business practices of transnational corporations, the importance of conformity with antitrust laws in home countries, or a level playing field for domestic firms in host countries, should also be in the picture.

The process of globalization, combined with these asymmetrical rules, is bound to significantly reduce the autonomy of developing countries in the formulation of economic policies in their pursuit of development.

The existing (and prospective) rules of the WTO regime allow few exceptions and provide little flexibility to countries that are latecomers to industrialization. In comparison, there was more room for maneuver in the erstwhile GATT, *inter alia*, because of special and differential treatment for developing countries. The new regime is much stricter in terms of the law and the implementation. The rules on trade in the new regime will make the selective protection or strategic promotion of domestic firms *vis-à-vis* foreign competition much more difficult. The tight system for the protection of intellectual property rights might preempt or stifle the development of domestic technological capabilities. The possible multilateral agreement on investment, when it materializes, will almost certainly reduce the possibilities of strategic bargaining with transnational firms. Taken together, such rules are bound to curb the use of industrial policy, technology policy, and trade policy as strategic forms of intervention to foster industrialization. It must be recognized that such state intervention was crucial for development in the success stories among late industrializers during the second half of the twentieth century.[24]

It need hardly be said that the nature of the solution depends on the nature of the problem. Where there are different rules in different spheres, it is necessary to make the rules symmetrical across spheres. Where there are rules for some but not for others, it is necessary to ensure that the rules are uniformly applicable to all. Where the agenda for new rules is partisan, it is imperative to redress the balance in the agenda.

There is a clear need for greater symmetry in the rules of multilateral trading system embodied in the WTO. If developing countries provide access to their markets, it should be matched with some corresponding access to technology. If there is almost complete freedom for capital mobility, the draconian restrictions on labor mobility should at least be reduced. The enforcement of rules should extend beyond the poor and the weak to the rich and the powerful. In addition, the agenda for the new rules needs careful scrutiny for it is shaped by the interests of industrialized countries while the needs of development are largely neglected. For instance, if the proposed multilateral agreement on investment is so concerned about the rights of transnational corporations, some attention should also be paid to their possible obligations. In any case, such an agreement should not be lodged in the WTO. The issue of labor standards, of course, is simply not in the domain of the WTO. And it is essential to reconsider the existing provisions of the unequal agreement on TRIPs, which was signed at a time when most governments and most people did not understand its economic implications. Such a reconsideration should endeavor to strike a balance between the interests of technology-leaders and technology-exporters in the industrialized world, which are the focus of attention, and the interests of technology-followers and technology-importers in the developing world, which are the object of neglect.

But that is not all.[25] Rules that are fair are necessary but not sufficient. For a game is not simply about rules. It is also about players. And, if one of the teams or one of the players does not have adequate training and preparation it would simply be crushed by the other. In other words, the rules must be such that newcomers or latecomers to the game, say, the developing countries, are provided with the time and the space to learn so that they are competitive players rather than pushover opponents.

Notes

1   See for example, Smith (1776) Book IV, Chapters I to VIII. This critique of mercantilism was developed further, in a longer term historical perspective, by Heckscher (1935).

2   The important contributions were Heckscher (1919), Ohlin (1933), and Samuelson (1939, 1948, 1962).

3   The challenges to free trade are discussed, at some length, by Irwin (1991) and Bhagwati (1994).

4   The origin of the infant industry argument is associated with Alexander Hamilton whose *Report on Manufactures* was published in the United States in 1791 and Friedrich List whose *Das Nationale System der Politischen Okonomie* was published in Germany in 1841.

5   This generalization is attributable, among others, to Myrdal (1956). It was also in keeping with List's conception of an infant economy argument.

6   See, for example, Corden (1974) who provides a meticulous analysis of the conditions under which the infant industry argument and the optimum tariff argument constitute valid arguments for protection.

7   Cf. Bhagwati and Ramaswami (1963) and Corden (1974). In this context, there are two points which are worth noting. First, appropriately chosen trade policy intervention, even if it is second-best or third-best, may result in a level of welfare higher than would be attainable under free trade. Second, the tax-cum-subsidy alternative may not be first-best if the taxes levied involve large collection costs or impose sizeable distortions elsewhere and if the disbursement costs of subsidies are significant.

8   For an interesting analysis of the interplay between ideology, interests, and institutions in the context of the political debate about free trade, both in Britain and in the United States, see Bhagwati (1988).

9   For a lucid discussion on economic conflicts during this period, see Diaz-Alejandro and Helleiner (1982).

10   The best example is Sachs and Warner (1995).

11   See Bairoch and Kozul-Wright (1996).

12   See Maddison (1995).

13   See Maddison (1989) and Bairoch (1982).

14   Cf. Maddison (1989).

15   Cf. Bairoch (1982).

16 For evidence, see UNCTAD (1997), UNDP (1999), and IMF (1997).
17 The ratio of the average GNP per capita of the richest quintile of the world's population to that of the poorest quintile rose from 31:1 in 1965 to 60:1 in 1990 (UNCTAD 1997: 81) and 74:1 in 1997 (UNDP 1999: 3). The ratio of per capita income in the richest country to that in the poorest rose from 35:1 in 1950 to 44:1 in 1973 and 72:1 in 1992 (Maddison 1995, UNDP 1999).
18 See UNCTAD (1997), Wood (1994, 1997), and Stewart (2000).
19 Some evidence is reported in UNCTAD (1997). Also see Stewart (2000).
20 This argument is developed in UNCTAD (1997).
21 Cf. Streeten (1996), who draws up a balance sheet of globalization.
22 For a discussion, and evidence, on this issue, see Nayyar (2000).
23 The asymmetry in the rules of the game for the international trading system, emphasized here, is examined in Nayyar (2002).
24 For a convincing exposition of this view, see Amsden (1989), Wade (1991), and Chang (1996).
25 For a more detailed analysis of the role of the state in a world of globalization, see Nayyar (2002).

References

Amsden, A. (1989) *Asia's Next Giant: South Korea and Late Industrialization*, New York: Oxford University Press.

Bairoch, P. (1982) 'International Industrialization Levels from 1750 to 1980', *Journal of European Economic History*, 11: 269–310.

Bairoch, P. and Kozul-Wright, R. (1996) 'Globalization Myths: Some Historical Reflections on Integration, Industrialization and Growth in the World Economy', Discussion Paper No. 13, Geneva: UNCTAD.

Bhagwati, J. (1988) *Protectionism*, Cambridge, MA: The MIT Press.

—— (1994) 'Free Trade: Old and New Challenges', *Economic Journal*, 104(423): 231–245.

Bhagwati, J. and Ramaswami, V. K. (1963) 'Domestic Distortions, Tariffs and the Theory of Optimum Subsidy', *Journal of Political Economy*, 71: 44–50.

Chang, H. J. (1996) *The Political Economy of Industrial Policy*, London: Macmillan.

Corden, W. M. (1974) *Trade Policy and Economic Welfare*, Oxford: Clarendon Press.

Diaz-Alejandro, C. F. and Helleiner, G. K. (1982) *Handmaiden in Distress: World Trade in the 1980s*, Ottawa: North-South Institute.

Heckscher, E. F. (1919) 'The Effect of Foreign Trade on the Distribution of Income', *Economisk Tidskrift*, 21: 497–512.

—— (1935) *Mercantilism*, London: Allen & Unwin.

IMF (1997) 'Globalization: Opportunities and Challenges', *World Economic Outlook*, Washington, DC: IMF.

Irwin, D. (1991) 'Challenges to Free Trade', *Journal of Economic Perspectives*, 5(2): 201–8.

Keynes, J. M. (1919) *The Economic Consequences of Peace*, London: Macmilan.

Maddison, A. (1989) *The World Economy in the Twentieth Century*, Paris: OECD.

—— (1995) *Monitoring the World Economy: 1820–1992*, Paris: OECD.

Mill, J. S. (1848) *Principles of Political Economy*, with an introduction by W. J. Ashley, London: Longmans.

Myrdal, G. (1956) *An International Economy: Problems and Prospects*, London: Routledge & Kegan Paul.

Nayyar, D. (2000) 'Globalization and Development Strategies', High-level Roundtable on Trade and Development, *UNCTAD X,* TD(X)/RT.1/4, New York and Geneva: United Nations.

Nayyar, D. (ed.) (2002) *Governing Globalization: Issues and Institutions.* Oxford: Oxford University Press.

Ohlin, B. (1933) *Interregional and International Trade*, Cambridge, MA:Harvard University Press.

Ricardo, D. (1817; 1973 edn.) *On the Principles of Political Economy and Taxation,* with an introduction by D. Winch, London: Dent.

Robinson, J. (1974) *Reflections on the Theory of International Trade*, Manchester: The University Press.

Sachs, J. and Warner, A. (1995) 'Economic Reform and the Process of Global Integration', *Brookings Papers on Economic Activity*, 1: 1–118, Washington, DC: The Brookings Institution.

Samuelson, P. A. (1939) 'The Gains from International Trade', *Canadian Journal of Economics and Political Science*, 5: 195–205.

—— (1948) 'International Trade and the Equilibrium of Factor Prices', *Economic Journal*, 58: 163–84.

—— (1962) 'The Gains from International Trade Once Again', *Economic Journal*, 72: 820–9.

Smith, A. (1776; 1970 edn.) *The Wealth of Nations*, with an introduction by A. Skinner, Harmondsworth: Pelican Books.

Stewart, F. (2000) 'Income Distribution and Development, High-Level Roundtable on Trade', *UNCTAD X,* TD(X)/RT.1/3, New York and Geneva: United Nations.

Streeten, P. P. (1996) 'Governance of the Global Economy', Paper presented to a Conference on Globalization and Citizenship, 9–11 December, Geneva: UNRISD.

UNCTAD (1997) *Trade and Development Report 1997*, Geneva: United Nations.

UNDP (1999) *Human Development Report 1999*, New York: Oxford University Press.

Wade, R. (1991) *Governing the Market: Economic Theory and the Role of the Government in East Asian Industrialization*, Princeton, NJ: Princeton University Press.

Wood, A. (1994) *North-South Trade, Employment and Inequality*, Oxford: Clarendon Press.

—— (1997) 'Openness and Wage Inequality in Developing Countries: The Latin American Challenge to East Asian Conventional Wisdom', *The World Bank Economic Review* 11(1): 33–57.

Part II

Globalization and economic development

5 External liberalization in Asia, postsocialist Europe and Brazil

Lance Taylor

This paper reviews the experiences of 14 countries with external liberalization and related policies, based on papers written by national authors following a common methodology. The focus is on transition and Asian economies, with Brazil as an illuminating comparator. The authors provide "thick descriptions" à la Geertz's (1973) famous Balinese cockfight about how diverse economies responded to rather similar "reform" packages and offer lessons about ongoing institutional change. They also suggest policy shifts that may help make economic performance better in the future than it has been in the past.

Somewhat arbitrarily, the countries can be classified into five groups:

- *Steady growth economies:* China, India, Singapore, and Vietnam
- *Asian crisis economies*: Indonesia, Korea, Malaysia, and Thailand
- *Cyclical stagnation economies*: Philippines and Turkey
- *Inflation stabilization economies*: Brazil and Russia
- *Post-socialist transition economies*: Hungary and Poland

Liberalization of trade and external capital flows in developing and post-socialist countries has been in full swing at least since the late 1980s and in some cases long before. Some of the Asian economies just listed were "early reformers." Before the 1997–98 crisis, growth and distribution in most of them appeared to be outstanding (the Philippines and Turkey being notable exceptions). However, the steadily growing Asian economies also performed well and were scarcely paragons of reform. They also managed to avoid the crisis, in part because they had *not* fully liberalized their capital and trade accounts.

From vastly different initial conditions, formerly socialist economies also opened dramatically in the 1990s. Their histories make interesting contrasts to those of the Asians, as also does Brazil's – a case of a "late reformer" with a substantial industrial base. Another dimension to the story is provided by the fact that Brazil, Turkey, and Russia engaged in drastic "exchange rate-based" attempts to stabilize high inflations with open capital markets. Their subsequent financial crises in many ways resemble the ones a few years earlier in East Asia.

Crises aside, the liberalization packages also had important implications for the generation of effective demand within economies, their patterns of productivity and employment growth (or in some cases, the lack of the same), and income distribution. The country case studies shed light on these questions as well.

1   Methodology

The studies are all "before and after" in the sense that they attempt to trace through the effects of liberalization over time in a specific national context. Depending on data availability, the authors carried out decompositions of shifts in effective demand and movements across sectors and time in labor productivity growth and employment. The algebraic details appear in Appendix I, but in brief the methodology of the decompositions goes as follows.

1.1   Effective demand

In any national economy, the level of activity is determined by effective demand. It is the outcome of the balance between demand "injections" – private investment in fixed capital and inventories, public spending, and exports – and "leakages" – private saving, taxes, and imports. In terms of the standard national income and product accounts (the NIPA system), the supply of goods and services that results is equal to the total value of goods and services produced (the gross domestic product or GDP) plus imports.

Following Godley (1999), one can ask hypothetically "what would have been" the level of supply had it been determined exclusively by an injection and leakage from just one of the three main sectors – private, government, and the rest of the world. For example, the government's injection of government spending is G and the corresponding leakage into taxation is tx, where t is the tax rate and X the total value of supply. If injections and leakages came only from the public sector, then because total injections must equal total leakages, we would have $G=tX$, or $X = G/t$. Similar calculations may be made for the private and foreign sectors. For the private sector alone, investment would have to equal savings, $I_p = s_p X$ or $X = I_p/S_p$, where S_p is the savings rate. For the foreign sector alone, exports (E) would have to equal imports, $E = mX$ or $X = E/m$, where m is the propensity to import.

In practise, X will be a weighted average of these terms, with the weights depending on the leakage rates s, t, and m. Because a financial deficit in one sector has to be balanced by a surplus elsewhere, macro financial balances have to satisfy the identity

$$(I-sX) + (G-tX) + (E-mX) = 0$$

1.2   Sectoral productivity growth

A fairly consistent pattern across countries has been an acceleration of productivity growth in traded goods following liberalization, with low or negative employment growth in the sector which can be traced to real appreciation and a shift in demand toward nontraded goods. Employment in nontraded goods went up or down according to the relative strengths of higher demand and (typically) slow or negative productivity growth.

To see the details, we can begin with a productivity decomposition. Suppose that one has data on employment and output for several sectors over time. Let $\theta_i = X_i/X$ be the share of sector i in real output, with $\sum X_i = X$. Similarly for employment: $\lambda_i = L_i/L$ with $\sum L_i = L$. The level of labor productivity in sector i is X_i/L_i, a with a growth rate $\varepsilon_i = \hat{X}_i - \hat{L}_i$ (with a "hat" over a variable signifying its growth rate).

After a bit of manipulation (see Appendix I), an expression for the growth rate ε_L of economy-wide labor productivity emerges as

$$\varepsilon_L = \sum_i [\theta_i \varepsilon_i + (\theta_i - \lambda_i)\hat{L}_i]$$

Overall productivity growth decomposes into two parts. One is a weighted average $\sum \theta_i \varepsilon_i$ of sectoral rates of productivity growth. The weights are the output shares θ_i. The other term, $\sum (\theta_i - \lambda_i)\hat{L}_i$, captures "reallocation effects" (Syrquin 1986). A sector with relatively high labor productivity will have a higher share of output than of the labor force, $\theta_i - \lambda_i$ so that if its employment growth is positive, $\hat{L}_i > 0$, reallocation of labor toward the sector generates a positive contribution to productivity growth economy-wide.

Two generalizations emerge when the productivity decomposition is applied to liberalizing economies:

If one disaggregates into traded and nontraded goods the productivity growth rate in the former is higher, and (as noted above) it tended to speed up after many countries liberalized. Insofar as nontraded sectors acted as labor sinks, their productivity growth rates declined.

With some exceptions, reallocation effects on productivity tended to be small, upsetting at least some traditional development economics dogmas.

Given these findings on productivity, it is tempting to look at growth rates of employment, which after all are driven by changes in productivity and demand. Very broadly following Pasinetti (1981), one can put together a two-step employment decomposition over time in terms of these forces.

Let P stand for the population, E the economically active population, L the total of people employed, and U the total unemployed or $U = E - L$. The participation rate is $\eta = E/P$ and the unemployment rate is $\upsilon = U/E$. The overall employment rate is $L/E = 1 - \upsilon = \phi/\eta$ with $\phi = L/P$ as the employed share of the population. Evidently, we have $E = L + U$. Dividing by P lets this expression be rewritten as $\eta = \phi + \eta\upsilon$. Taking growth rates and a bit of algebra show that

$$0 = (1 - \upsilon)(\hat{\phi} - \hat{\eta}) + \upsilon\hat{\upsilon} = -(1 - \upsilon)\hat{\eta} + \upsilon\hat{\upsilon} + (1 - \upsilon)\hat{\phi}$$

The terms after the first equals sign state that changes in the rates of employment and unemployment must sum to zero. The formula furthest to the right decomposes this condition in terms of the participation rate η, the unemployment rate υ, and the employed share of the population ϕ.

In a second step, ϕ provides a useful tool to analyze job growth across sectors. Along with the ratios defined above, let $x_i = X_i/P$ or sectoral output per capita. The labor or output ratio in sector i can be written as $b_i = L_i/X_i$, and let $\phi_i = L_i/P$. Then we have:

$$\phi = \Sigma(L_i/X_i)(X_i/P) = \Sigma b_i x_i$$

Transforming to growth rates gives

$$\hat{\phi} = \Sigma \phi_i (\hat{x}_i + \hat{b}_i) = \Sigma \phi_i (\hat{x}_i - \varepsilon_i)$$

so that the growth rate of the overall employment ratio is determined as a weighted sum across sectors of differences between growth rates of output levels per capita and labor productivity (the weights ϕ_i don't add up to one because they are ratios of each sector's employment to total population).

The last equation provides a framework in which sources of job creation can usefully be explored. In expanding sectors (relative to population growth), productivity increases do not necessarily translate into reduced employment; in slow-growing or shrinking sectors, higher productivity means that employment declines. Under liberalization, the interaction of nontraded and traded sectors can be traced in this fashion, along with the behavior of sectors acting as "sources" or "sinks" for labor (agriculture has played both roles recently, in different countries). The most common outcome is that productivity growth has exceeded output growth in traded goods sectors, to the detriment of creation of high-end jobs.

2　Stylized scenarios

Based on experiences of the preceding decade, generalizations about the effects of external liberalization began to appear around the year 2000.[1] The main points go as follows:

2.1　Capital account liberalization

With regard to the capital account of the balance of payments, countries liberalized for several reasons – to accommodate to external political pressures (Korea and other Asians), to find sources of finance for growing fiscal deficits (Turkey, Russia), or to bring in foreign exchange to finance the imports needed to hold down prices of traded goods in exchange rate-based inflation stabilization programs (Brazil and other countries in Latin America).

When they removed restrictions on capital movements, most countries received a surge of inflows from abroad. They came in subject to the accounting restriction that an economy's *net* foreign asset position (total holdings of external assets minus total external liabilities) can only change gradually over time through a deficit or surplus on the current account. Hence, when external liabilities increased as foreigners acquired securities issued by national governments or firms, external assets had to jump up as well. The new assets typically showed up on the balance sheets of financial institutions, including larger international reserves of the central bank. Unless the bank made a concerted effort to "sterilize" the inflows (selling government bonds from its portfolio to "mop up liquidity," for example), they set off a domestic credit boom. In poorly regulated financial systems, there was a high risk of a classic mania-panic-crash sequence along Kindleberger (2000) lines – the famous crises in Latin America's Southern Cone around 1980 were only the first of many such disasters.

When the credit expansion was allowed to work itself through, interest rates could be low. At times, however, other factors entered to push both levels of and the spread between borrowing and lending rates upward. One source of widening spreads is related to asset price booms in housing and stock markets, which forced rates to rise on interest-bearing securities such as government debt. Another source playing a role at times originated from central banks trying to sterilize capital inflows, and so pushing up rates as well. Finally, in noncompetitive financial markets, local institutions often found it easy to raise spreads. High local returns pulled more capital inflows, worsening the overall disequilibrium.

Unsurprisingly, exchange rate movements complicated the story. In countries with high inflation, the exchange rate was used as a "nominal anchor" in anti-inflation programs. Its nominal level was devalued at a rate less than the rate of inflation, leading to real appreciation. In several cases, the effect was rapid, with traded goods variable costs in dollar terms jumping upward immediately after the rate was frozen.

The same outcome also showed up via another channel. As countries removed capital controls and adopted "floating" rates, they lost a degree of freedom in policy formulation because now domestic interest rates and exchange rates are linked. Thus if the interest rate tended to rise, then the currency would appreciate. Or, the other way round, if the exchange rate strengthened over time, then interest rates would be pushed upward. This tendency would be amplified if real appreciation stimulated aggregate demand in the short run – the other side of the coin of the well-known possibility that devaluation can be contractionary in developing economies (Krugman and Taylor 1978). Abandoning capital controls made the exchange rate or interest rate trade-off far more difficult to manage. Some countries – notably in Asia – did succeed in keeping their exchange rates stable and relatively weak, though as discussed below that benefit ultimately fed into external crisis.

2.2 Current account liberalization

Current account deregulation basically took the form of transformation of import quota restrictions (where they were important) to tariffs, and then consolidation of tariff rates into a fairly narrow band, e.g. between 0 percent and 20 percent. With a few exceptions, export subsidies were also removed. There were visible effects on the level and composition of effective demand, and on patterns of employment and labor productivity.

Demand composition typically shifted in the direction of imports, especially when there was real exchange appreciation. In many cases, national savings rates also declined. This shift can partly be attributed to an increased supply of imports at low prices (increasing household spending, aided by credit expansion following financial liberalization), and partly to a profit squeeze (falling retained earnings) in industries producing traded goods. The fall in private savings sometimes was partially offset by rising government savings where fiscal policy became more restrictive. Many countries showed "stop-go" cycles in government tax and spending behavior.

Especially when it went together with real appreciation, current account liberalization pushed traded goods producers toward workplace reorganization (including greater reliance on foreign outsourcing) and downsizing. If, as assumed above, unskilled labor is an important component of variable cost, then such workers would bear the brunt of such adjustments via job losses. In other words, enterprises producing traded goods that stayed in operation had to cut costs by generating labor productivity growth. As discussed above, unless demand for traded goods grew rapidly, higher productivity growth meant that their total employment levels could easily fall.

The upshot of these effects often took the form of increased inequality between groups of workers, in particular between the skilled and unskilled.[2] With liberalization stimulating productivity increases leading to a reduction of labor demand from modern, traded-goods production, primary income differentials widened between workers in such sectors and those employed in nontraded, informal activities (e.g. informal services) and the unemployed.

2.3   *Crises*

More than half the economies considered herein went through external crisis. The basic pattern is familiar. A high internal return on financial assets is needed to bring capital from abroad. But then inflows surge and debt-financed public (Turkey, Russia) or private (Mexico pre-1994, the Asian economies pre-1997) spending follows in turn. The exchange rate appreciates. The central bank builds up reserves and attempts to sterilize them by cutting back on the domestic component of the money supply, with further upward pressure on interest rates. Eventually the bubble bursts, hot money flees the country, and onerous macro adjustment follows. The usual ingredients are very high real interest rates, big devaluations, and severe retrenchment of aggregate demand.

Although "basic," this scenario is a theme subject to notable national variations. Some countries did not have significant real appreciation before their crises; others kept interest rates under control. A relatively stable nominal exchange rate did appear to be a common element, as did mismatches in domestic financial institutions' balance sheets – especially between relatively short-term liabilities denominated in foreign currencies and long-term assets in national money. When, as was often the case, the short-term liabilities exceeded the central bank's foreign reserves, the situation was ripe for capital withdrawals and massive devaluation.

3 Country experiences

3.1 *Steady growth economies*

China, India, Singapore, and Vietnam maintained steady, moderate to high growth rates through the 1990s, in sharp contrast to most of the rest of the nonindustrialized world. These economies are all relatively *dirigiste* in their style of national management. In their own ways, all regulate international capital flows. On the whole they avoided the real exchange rate appreciation observed elsewhere and maintained productivity growth in both traded and nontraded sectors.

3.1.1 *China*

China, in fact, reports economy-wide productivity growth of more than 10 percent per year in the mid-1990s (with 15 percent in industry). Insofar as they are credible, such numbers can be attributed to several factors acting upon a large and diverse economy with a total GDP of around $1.1 trillion at current exchange rates and a population of 1.3 billion.

One was opening to international trade, with import and export shares of GDP rising from around 5 percent to more than 20 percent between 1978 and 2000 (average tariffs fell from around 40 percent to 15 percent during the 1990s).[3]

There was also a controlled liberalization of capital inflows. During the period 1985–2000, foreign debt increased almost nine-fold, from $16 billion to $146 billion; by 2000 total accumulated FDI of $346 billion was 32 percent of GDP (with perhaps a quarter of the total representing "round-tripping" of funds by mainland enterprises, another large portion coming from Hong Kong, Macao, and Taiwan, and the balance "from abroad"). Combined with selective capital controls, China was insulated from the 1997 financial crisis of East Asia.

Unsurprisingly, massive capital inflows and a current account surplus fed into both reserve accumulation (despite attempts at sterilization) and capital flight. Growth in the money supply correlated with a jump in the inflation rate to 24 percent in 1994 and 17 percent in 1995. To curtail monetary expansion, the central bank raised interest rates and reduced loans to domestic financial institutions which in turn slashed credits to state-owned enterprises (or SOEs). In a context of massive industrial restructuring, the results included lay-offs of 8 percent of the SOE labor force, a source of substantial political unrest.

Shifts in demand composition were directly related to liberalization. Before the drive to open the economy, the government was the major saver and investor, mandating the investment programs of the SOEs. After opening, resources were redistributed toward the private sector. Government revenue fell from over 30 percent of GDP around 1980 to 11 percent in 1996 and 15 percent in 2000. The personal income share rose from 50.5 percent in 1978 to 80.9 percent in 1997. Personal real income has grown in the 7–8 percent annual range, with consumption increasing at about 6 percent.

High household savings rates reflect the slower growth of consumption than income, in the presence of SOE lay-offs and absence of adequate pension and insurance schemes. Low private investments also contributed to a large private financial surplus which financed the current account surplus and the government deficit throughout the 1990s.

Employment shares have been reduced in agriculture (from 70 percent to 50 percent of the labor force between 1980 and 2000) and in urban SOEs. Overall employment growth was around 1 percent per year in the 1990s, with job destruction in traded sectors and job creation in nontradeds. There is still positive employment growth in the low productivity agricultural sector, so it contributes a negative "reallocation" effect to productivity growth economy-wide. The main engine for productivity increases has been the industrial sector (reported growth on the order of 15 percent during the 1990s), contributing to the labor shedding in traded goods just mentioned. The other sectors had positive productivity growth rates as well.

Rising income inequality accompanied liberalization. Nonwage income accounts for 55 percent of the total in urban areas, largely flowing toward high-income households (though there are also small transfer flows to former SOE workers). The urban Gini coefficient as estimated by the World Bank rose from 0.23 in 1990 to 0.30 in1999; the rural values were 0.30 and 0.34, respectively. The ratio of urban to rural household incomes declined from 2.57 in 1978 to 1.82 in 1983 (as the initial phases of deregulation favored agriculture) but then rose again to 2.79 in 2000. Income differentials across provinces also widened.

These changes were caused by several factors: an increasing share of nonwage incomes (as already noted), widening wage differentials by skill groups, lay-offs in traditional industries and SOEs, differential effects of liberalization across regions, a shift in the terms-of-trade against grain-producing agriculture, relatively slow urbanization, and a likely increase in illegally obtained income flows.

3.1.2   India

India is comparable to China in terms of population (a bit more than a billion people) but its GDP of about $500 billion is considerably less. The average GDP growth rate was around 6 percent in the 1980s and 1990s, tailing off toward the end.

Sporadic steps toward reducing state control and raising external openness date to the late 1970s, but much more decisive action came after a balance of payments crisis in mid-1991 (in part in response to pressure from the international financial institutions). There was an immediate effort at stabilization, followed by implementation of a package of "reforms."

Devaluation weakened the real exchange rate by about 10 percent after the crisis, with modest real appreciation subsequently. Most nontariff restrictions on capital and intermediate goods imports were removed. Import duties as a share of imports fell from 45 percent to 25 percent by the end of the decade, and export incentives were broadened and simplified. "Negative lists" of restricted imports (including defense- and health care-related imports, and some consumer and capital goods) were drawn up and subsequently shortened. The byzantine industrial "license raj" was dismantled and the financial sector deregulated. Portfolio and FDI flows were liberalized, though until 2001–02 strong controls remained in place on commercial borrowing and capital outflows. As in China, exchange controls helped insulate India from the Asian crises.

Using 1991 as the reference year, before-and-after comparisons suggest that the effects of the reforms have been decidedly mixed. The economy did open to foreign trade, with export and import shares rising several points to about 11 percent and 14 percent of GDP, respectively (numbers broadly comparable to China's if its re-export trade and overall trade surplus are not taken into account). The compositions of the import and export baskets have not changed, and the trade deficit rose in the 1990s.

Cumulated FDI in the 1990s was $15 billion, a pittance compared to China's inflows. At the end of the decade about 40 percent of FDI took the form of mergers and acquisitions of existing firms, without apparent technological spillovers.

In 1990–91, the combined central and state government budget deficit was over 11 percent of GDP. As a consequence of the stabilization program, this number fell to 7.5 percent in 1996–97, but then grew again to over 10 percent at the end of the decade. Contributing factors were interest payments on government debt (up from 3.8 percent to 4.7 percent of GDP) and a fall in indirect tax revenues of about 1.6 percent of GDP. Lower tariffs were a major factor behind this loss, which was partly offset by an increase of 0.7 percent in the GDP share of direct taxes.

Effective demand, unsurprisingly, was led by government spending, with $G > tX$ since the 1980s. The private demand contribution has closely tracked output, and foreign transactions have been contractionary. There was positive labor productivity growth 1993–2000 in all one-digit sectors, with job losses in the primary sectors of agriculture and mining, utilities, and social services.

Specific problem areas include agriculture and employment. Despite an unusual run of favorable monsoons, the trend growth rate of the index of agricultural production fell from 3.4 percent in the 1980s to 2.2 percent in the 1990s. Part of the problem can be traced to the shortfall of public infrastructure investment. Also, no attempt has been made to modify the institutions that generate landlessness and poverty in the countryside, where labor force participation rates have declined.

Elsewhere, there has been increasing informalization of labor markets and expansion of low wage female employment. Potentially tradable sectors such as parts of agriculture and manufacturing have not generated significant employment growth; rather, nontradables have seen the biggest employment and output gains.

Inequality has risen in both the personal and functional distributions of urban and rural incomes. Because of changes in methodology in the National Sample Surveys, there has been substantial debate about whether the incidence of poverty was affected by the reforms. The poor in India are concentrated among the rural landless, scheduled castes and tribes, and households in which all members are illiterate. Poverty tends to be reduced by labor-intensive nonagricultural output and employment growth in rural areas; all the poor are hit by higher food prices. They benefit from public food distribution and employment generation schemes, but spending on such programs as a share of GDP did not increase in the 1990s.

3.1.3   Singapore

Singapore, in one sense, is a successful long-term capital liberalization experiment, relying on FDI to deliver real resources and technological upgrading. On the other hand, its success has little to do with *laissez-faire*. The government has intervened continually in the foreign investment process, providing incentives and infrastructure for foreign firms and aggressively pursuing export promotion. The outcome has been annual GDP growth in the 7–9 percent range beginning in 1960 and continuing until 2000 (growth slowed thereafter), supported by a social contract under which the government devotes great effort to stimulating production while providing a package of social services to keep the labor force in line.

Singapore became a sovereign state in 1965 (seceding from the Malaysian federation), accompanied by substantial social unrest. Import substitution was practised under an Economic Development Board (EDB) that had been set up in 1961. With independence, the EDB's emphasis switched to export-led industrialization spearheaded by foreign investment attracted by an absence of restrictions on ownership or borrowing, enforced labor discipline, and public participation in setting up operations. Between 1961 and 1978, GDP increased by more than four times.

Leaving out re-export and entrepot activity, there was a consistent trade deficit until 1985, with the government and private sector alternating in providing stimulus to demand (the private sector's excess of investment over saving was especially important in the 1970s). The configuration switched markedly thereafter, with a trade surplus rising to nearly 20 percent of GDP. The balancing "twin surplus" within the system was the private sector's excess of saving over investment. Capital inflows continued, and some were transformed into Singapore's own foreign holdings abroad.

Historically, manufacturing has been the major source of productivity growth economy-wide, with financial services becoming important in the 1980s and 1990s.

The Gini coefficient as estimated on the basis of labor force surveys fell from 0.48 to 0.44 between 1973 and 1982, but since then has trended upward to 0.5. One cause is an increase in wage differentials for skilled workers. The estimates do not take into account housing subsidies and wealth distribution schemes for citizens that the government has put into place.

3.1.4   Vietnam

Vietnam went through a prolonged economic crisis in the 1980s, which catalyzed a 1989 *doi moi* package of external and domestic reforms. They placed the economy on the road to a market system, albeit subject to strong state control.

External liberalization covered the current but not the capital account, saving the country from the volatility that swamped its neighbors. Even current account liberalization was incomplete, for example in 2001 the IMF ranked Vietnam at 9 on a scale of 10 for trade restrictiveness. FDI was encouraged by Singapore-style legislation, and cumulated to $32 billion between 1988 and 1999 (GDP in 2001 was at about the same level). Despite its export dynamism, however, the "FDI sector" in 1998 still had a $685 million trade deficit (the deficit was $2.14 billion overall).

In comparison to postsocialist Eastern Europe and the former USSR, Vietnam went through a rapid transformation to steady growth at 7 percent per year in the 1990s, expansion of the external sector, and improvements in living conditions for many people. Total trade (including re-export) rose from 25 percent of GDP in 1988 to 111 percent in 2000. From 1993 to 1998, the proportion of people living below the poverty line fell from 58 percent to 37 percent.

"Externalization" intertwined with greater market orientation deserves partial but not full credit for Vietnam's strong macroeconomic performance during the *doi moi* years. The development of offshore oil resources, and favorable shifts in the geopolitical environment including domestic institutional changes in East Asian economies also played critical roles. Existing resource underutilization and misallocation were so great that the reforms produced substantial increases in output without requiring much by way of additional inputs. In the 1980s, output growth was constrained by a scarcity of imported inputs due to the international economic boycott ("before"), while the *doi moi* era was marked by changes in the post-Cold War international balance of power and Vietnam's more conciliatory foreign policy stance ("after"). The decision by non-CMEA countries to end the trade embargo probably contributed as much to the rapid expansion of exports and imports as Vietnam's actual lowering of trade barriers.

Aggregate demand was led by the private sector, especially before 1990 when estimated private saving was negative. By 2000, saving and tax leakage parameters were around 0.2 each, and the import coefficient was 0.6.

As in other countries that liberalized trade and shut down state enterprises, not many jobs were created in the higher value-added sectors of the economy because output growth could not compensate for the productivity increases that Vietnamese firms needed to survive the more competitive environment of the 1990s. The low productivity primary sector accounted for 60–80 percent of Vietnam's employment growth, with significant contribution from the services sector during the 1992–97 period.

At the same time, a geopolitical sea change and significant resource underemployment help to explain why the $ value of Vietnam's exports grew at an annual average rate of over 26 percent from 1989 to 2000, even though after the initial devaluation through 1995 there was a trend rise in the relative price of nontraded to traded goods. There was enough slack, despite widely reported shortages of skilled labor, to accommodate both greater export demand and greater growth of the nontraded goods and services sectors.

Overall income inequality increased marginally, with the Gini coefficient rising from 0.33 in 1992–93 to 0.35 in 1997–98. Theil T decompositions suggest that inequality rose in urban areas and fell in rural. Simulations with computable general equilibrium models suggest that upper income urban households have reaped a major share of the gains generated from sustained economic growth.

3.2   Asian crisis economies

The economies that fell into crisis shared common features – notably liberalized capital markets – but their histories are by no means uniform with regard to exchange rate movements, demand and productivity growth patterns, and other factors. The contrasts are as interesting as the similarities.

3.2.1   Korea

Korea, of course, was a superstar performer among developing economies in the second half of last century. It also followed the conventional wisdom that the sequence of liberalization should go from trade to domestic finance to the capital account. Korea's experience shows, however, that following the "correct" sequence by no means guarantees success.

Trade liberalization was implemented gradually since the 1980s, along with strategic protection of selected industries such as agriculture and automobiles and a gradual opening of the financial market to new commercial banks and nonbank financial intermediaries (NBFIs). Meaningful opening up to capital flows did not occur until the 1990s.

Nonetheless, the financial liberalization of the 1980s produced an important change in the financial structure – explosive growth of NBFIs such as securities, insurance, and investment trust companies and a fundamental change in the Korean model of development. Checks on *chaebol* (conglomerates that owned the NBFIs which could offer higher interest rates and attract deposits away from the banks) management by creditors and institutional investors were lacking, and the previously widespread government regulation regime was retreating. With the pace of liberalization gathering speed in the 1990s, the problem worsened.

The overriding policy theme for the 1990s was "responding to globalization." In practise, that meant accelerating liberalization and deregulation. By mid 1990s, industrial policy was wound down and controls on capital inflows were greatly weakened.

These measures proved disastrous. Liberalization policies in the end led to a rapid build-up of bad assets in the financial system and foreign debt that culminated in the exchange crisis of 1997.

In effect, the crisis was caused by an international bank run, triggered by a perception of bankruptcy risks of the major Korean banks. There was a steep increase in external debt in the mid-1990s. At the end of 1996, gross external liabilities were $164 billion, up two-and-a-half times from the end of 1993 and five times from the end of 1990. But the real source of vulnerability was that too large a proportion of the external debt was short term, amounting at the end of 1996 to 2.8 times foreign exchange reserves, leaving the financial system highly vulnerable to a run.

The rise in foreign debt was closely tied to capital account liberalization and the ensuing rise in capital inflows. From the end of 1992 to the end of 1996 foreign exchange liabilities of the commercial banks rose from about $62 billion to $140 billion, and those of the merchant banks from less than five to about $19 billion. A large part of the short-term capital inflow was used to finance long-term projects and risky investment abroad. Outflow of portfolio investment was also dramatic, as the financial institutions expanded their business in international finance including the extremely risky derivatives and junk bond markets. Foreign portfolio assets rose from only $0.5 billion in 1993 to almost $6 billion in 1996.

Corporate profitability had exhibited a declining trend in Korea since the early seventies, driven mostly by a decline in the output-capital ratio that was particularly pronounced in two periods of high capital formation: 1976–80 (related to the Heavy and Chemical Industrialization drive) and 1988–96 (associated with the mismanaged liberalization).

Despite falling profitability, firms continued to invest heavily. As a consequence, corporate indebtedness rose. The ratio of the corporate debt to GDP continuously increased from 1.09 in 1988 to 1.63 in 1996. The debt-equity ratio of the Korean companies rose from around 2.5 in 1989, to above 3.0 in the first half of the 1990s, to over 4.0 in 1997. Given their falling profitability and deteriorating balance sheets, the downturn in the economy since 1996 caused serious financial troubles for many firms. According to some estimates, the ratio of nonperforming loans to total loans increased from around 15 percent during 1988–90 to 26 percent in 1997. At the end of 1996, the ratio of nonperforming loans to capital for the merchant banks was as high as 31.9 percent while the ratio was 12.2 percent in the commercial banking sector.

The crisis hit Korea in November 1997, causing a V-shaped recession and recovery. The growth rate was −6.7 percent in 1998 (worsened by contractionary interest rate hikes and fiscal austerity imposed even more mindlessly than usual by the IMF). It rebounded to 10.7 percent in 1999 but then slowed thereafter. Meanwhile, labor productivity growth continued at about a 4 percent annual rate while real wage growth stagnated, shifting the functional income distribution against labor. On the other hand, spending on the social safety net was increased dramatically, from 5.1 percent of GDP in 1997 to 7.5 percent in 1999. It is noteworthy that this shift in social policy took place as Korea was being forcefully integrated into the world economy.

Leading into the crisis, the private sector's contribution to demand consistently exceeded total supply, accompanied by an external deficit and a neutral contribution by government. After the crisis, demand was supported by both government and an external surplus, with the private sector I_p/s_p falling sharply in 1997 and gradually recovering thereafter. Investment hovered around 27–28 percent during 1999–2001, or 10 percentage points below its level earlier in the 1990s.

The unemployment rate jumped from 2.6 percent in 1997 to 6.8 percent in 1998 and 6.3 percent in 1999. With the participation rate falling by 1.3 percent in 1998 and 1.5 percent in 1999, the economy moved sharply away from its earlier "full employment" (2–3 percent unemployment rate) situation.

Given these shifts in the wage structure, the shift in the functional income distribution mentioned above, and the spike in interest rates in 1997, it is not surprising that overall income inequality went up. Average monthly income in the bottom decile (of all persons receiving some labor income) fell by 6 percent 1997–2000 whereas that of the top decile rose by 19 percent. The lower five deciles all lost income whereas the upper five gained. Various studies show that the share of households in poverty roughly doubled.

Postcrisis policy reforms included attempts to enhance transparency and accountability in corporate management, increased financial regulation, a move toward corporatism via a tripartite labor or employer or government commission, and expansion of the social security programs. It remains to be seen how successful these changes will be in reining in the *chaebol,* establishing an effective state regulatory apparatus, reinvigorating economic growth, and reconstructing a social consensus on the distribution of income and power.

3.2.2   Indonesia

Indonesia had largely decontrolled its capital account as early as 1970. Other liberalizing moves – devaluations in the 30 percent range, trade and investment liberalization, tariff reductions, and removal of foreign investment restrictions – came in the 1980s in response to the oil price reduction in 1983. Bank deregulation came in 1988, though a few large banks linked to industrial groups continued to dominate the sector.

GDP growth at an average rate of 8 percent per year between 1987 and 1996 followed the policy changes. Capital inflows were a major driving factor, combined with a relaxed monetary policy at the end of the 1980s. Using a variety of tools, the central bank attempted to sterilize the inflows and restrict credit expansion in the first part of the 1990s. It basically failed, because off-budget borrowing by the government was monetized, and emission of export credits in foreign currency fed into growth of the money supply.

While all this was happening, there was slow depreciation of the real exchange rate, measured in terms of the differential between domestic and foreign inflation rates and the nominal depreciation rate. Domestic interest rates were driven along Uncovered Interest Parity (UIP) lines by foreign rates and the Indonesian risk premium.

From the early 1980s until 1994, effective demand was led by foreign and government deficits (with the latter partly financed by foreign borrowing). The private sector provided net lending to the others. This situation reversed dramatically during 1994–97, with the private sector pumping demand into the system. The private sector's saving rate fell from around 16 percent in 1996 to 9 percent in 1999, as its debt level soared. After the crisis in 1998–99, plummeting demand was supported by the external and private sectors in the face of strong fiscal contraction.

The employment share of tradables declined from the late 1980s through 1997, when the trend reversed. The employment share of agriculture was still 55 percent in 1985 but had dropped to 44 percent in 1995. As a consequence, services were the main sources of employment growth during the postliberalization boom.

The overall income distribution was fairly stable during the liberalization boom, although the data under-represent the high-income population, suppress regional differentials, and ignore cleavages between small business owners and conglomerates and the ethnic Chinese minority.

Before the crisis the poverty headcount ratio fell from 22 percent in 1984 to 11 percent in 1996, with roughly equal reductions in both urban and rural areas. Directed government policies (pricing policy for basic consumption goods, education, health, infrastructure investment) helped support these trends.

For Indonesia, the major cause of the 1997 crisis was financial, especially the mismatch between short-term foreign debt and the availability of international reserves. Despite apparently solid "fundamentals" (rapid growth, low fiscal deficit, slow inflation, real devaluation) leading into the crisis, its effects were devastating. GDP growth was −14 percent in 1998, and the exchange rate collapsed in the face of very high interest rates. Inflation surged by almost 80 points.

The poverty headcount ratio nearly doubled in 1998, offsetting the gains of a decade. Real wages fell sharply, but employment stayed stable (largely supported by job creation via reverse migration back to agriculture). Real consumption levels declined across the income distribution, with the biggest real reduction of 24 percent suffered by the top income quintile. In other words, the urban middle class was especially hard hit by the crisis.

3.2.3 Malaysia

Malaysia has run an open economy since colonial times, a policy stance that continued after the peninsula became independent in 1957; an expanded federation was formed in 1963, and Singapore seceded in 1965. Selective tariff protection was utilized for two rounds of import-substituting industrialization (or ISI) – for consumer goods in the 1960s and for heavier industries such as automotive in the 1980s. The capital account has also been relatively open, although the regulatory authorities did not allow easy access by nationals to foreign bank borrowing. In the crisis period, short-term loans were less of the problem in Malaysia than in Indonesia, Korea, and Thailand. The authorities also resorted to capital controls in two periods – to regulate destabilizing inflows in 1994 and outflows in 1998.

There has been a long-standing policy to attract FDI in manufacturing, with 84.5 percent of exports coming from that sector in 1999. As usual, there are questions as to how much value-added is generated by manufactured exports, owing to their high import content, but no recent empirical investigations seem to be available.

The propensity to import has risen steadily since the 1970s while tax revenues were less than 10 percent of total supply and the ratio tended to drift downward. Private saving fluctuates in the 20 + percent range. The government deficit, largely financed by domestic borrowing, has stimulated demand since the 1970s.

Before 1997, there tended to be a private sector surplus and an external deficit. Postcrisis, private and external stances changed signs, and after a brief period of fiscal contraction the government became a bigger net borrower.

Since the mid-1980s, manufacturing and services have generated employment growth with agriculture as the major supplier. Productivity growth has been balanced across traded and nontraded sectors.

Overall inequality declined in the 1980s and rose in the 1990s, with the Gini coefficient fluctuating between 0.45 and 0.5. With sustained growth, poverty incidence fell from 40 percent in 1976 to 6.8 percent in 1997, and then rose a point or two thereafter. Social policy has traditionally been biased in favor of the predominantly Muslim Malay Bumiputera – or indigenous – community, but liberalization has diluted its force. Agricultural support programs continue to exist.

As noted above, Malaysia's 1997 crisis was softened by preexisting restrictions on foreign borrowing (external liabilities did not exceed available reserves, as in other countries) as well as mechanisms for prudential regulation put into place after a banking collapse in the late 1980s. On the other hand, high levels of portfolio investment going into the crisis forced the Kuala Lumpur stock exchange to plummet when it started to flee. In effect, Malaysia was less beholden to its banking system than were its neighbors, and the system was in less trouble anyway. Recovery was not as spectacular or sustained as Korea's but was stronger than in Thailand and Indonesia.

3.2.4   Thailand

Thailand switched its development strategy from ISI in the 1960s to export promotion through subsidies and investment strategy thereafter. Imports were liberalized, with the ratio of tariff revenues to total imports falling from 18 percent in 1970 to less than 4 percent in 2000. The ratio of total trade to GDP rose from 27 percent in 1970 to 120 percent in 2000. FDI was encouraged, with an annual inflow of $2 billion in 1990 rising to $7 billion in 1998 (around 7 percent of GDP) when foreign investors acquired ailing Thai banks at fire sale prices. A great deal of FDI was directed toward assembly operations without high skill content.

Capital controls were relaxed in 1991 when Thailand accepted IMF Article VIII. In 1993, financial institutions were permitted to offer offshore banking facilities to domestic borrowers, in an attempt to establish Bangkok as a regional financial center. The ratio of capital inflows to GDP was 2 percent in 1970, 10 percent in 1990, and peaked at 12 percent in 1995, before collapsing at −13 percent in 1998. Maturity and currency mismatches in borrowing were severe by the mid-1990s.

Before the crisis, both private sector and government contributions to effective demand were slightly above the level of total supply; the external sector ran a deficit. These sectoral roles switched after the crisis, with the external sector propping up demand and the private sector strongly reducing it.

There was a substantial reduction in overall inequality between 1988 and 1998, with the Gini coefficient dropping from 0.48 to 0.41. The poverty headcount ratio was 32.6 percent in 1988, 11.4 percent in 1996, and then 15.9 percent in 1999. Poverty alleviation was aided by a steady increase in the agricultural terms of trade in the 1990s and modest extension of social service programs.

3.3   Cyclical stagnation economies

In different ways, the Philippines and Turkey have stagnated as a consequence of repeated business cycles tied to external liberalization. The malaise has affected the Philippines for decades and Turkey since the late 1980s.

3.3.1   Philippines

Philippines, among the populous Southeast Asian economies, is the one that has hewed most faithfully to traditional, conservative economic policy as advocated by the Bretton Woods institutions. It also has by far the worst record for economic growth. In 1960, Philippine per capita GDP was almost twice as high as Korea's and Thailand's. On the basis of its growth spurt in the 1950s and 1960s, Korea overtook the Philippines in the mid-1970s. Thailand pulled ahead in the late 1980s, and widened the gap with rapid growth prior to the Asian crisis while the Philippines went through a series of bust-recovery cycles.

The story of the 1950s was a prosperous decade based on ISI following a balance of payments crisis in 1949, but various rigidities of the regime and circumstances led to a crisis in 1960. Trade and liberalization policy got underway in 1962, with IMF assistance strengthened by the Washington-friendly Marcos regime that ascended to power in 1965.

Nevertheless, crisis-recovery cycles continued to recur, becoming steadily more frequent and with weaker recoveries. The economy deteriorated in the late 1970s and early 1980s due to corrupt, inefficient allocation of public investment financed by foreign debt, the second oil price shock, and the Volcker interest rate shock. GDP growth was negative in the mid-1980s (−7.6 percent growth in 1984 and 1985), 1991–93, and 1997 with the Asian crisis. The 1984–85 collapse led to intensified trade and capital market liberalization, which evidently did not succeed in boosting growth.

The Philippine 1997 crisis scenario followed the general pattern of countries in the region, in somewhat subdued fashion. The capital market was fully liberalized by 1993, and a familiar pattern of capital inflows associated with exchange appreciation and booming asset prices followed in train. GDP growth in the mid-1990s was in the 5 percent annual range; after the crisis, output contraction was less than in the other countries.

Throughout the 1980–2000 period, effective demand was led by the government and (especially in the 1990s) the private sector. There was a consistent external deficit, aggravated by a steady upward trend in the import coefficient that accelerated in the 1990s. The saving rate trended downward during the same period.

In the 1990s the service sector absorbed more labor than manufacturing, the latter having had to boost productivity because of its increasing exposure to competition brought about by real appreciation and external liberalization. Agriculture continues to decline in output and employment terms because of an absence of genuine agrarian reform and a neglect of infrastructure and investment in rural areas. Increasing output and employment shares of services, relatively constant shares of industry and manufacturing (since the late 1980s), and falling shares of agriculture can be explained by labor productivity and employment movements during the recession-recovery cycles of the economy. Because of the rising importance of services, low productivity growth in that sector increasingly drags down the growth rate overall.

In terms of distribution, an increasing share of income goes to the corporate sector after every bust-recovery transition. The informal household sector's operating surplus has fallen with external liberalization and as labor has moved out of agriculture. Government income inevitably improves during the growth periods and as a result of painful tax reforms. However during bad times of recessions and sharp currency devaluation, the contraction in imports and incomes reduces significantly tax revenues and results in the deterioration of the fiscal position. The general trend of tariff reductions aggravates this problem.

There is evidence of moderate but discernable shifts in labor employment from low-skilled workers to middle-level as well as managerial and professional workers. Together with the fall in real wages in the 1990s, this points to some deterioration in the income distribution within the household and labor sectors.

3.3.2   Turkey

Turkey witnessed severe fluctuations in its aggregate macroeconomic performance over the 1990s. In per capita terms its GDP had been left almost stagnant at its 1990 level by the end of the decade. Persistent disequilibria and ongoing price inflation for more than two decades finally led to the initiation of a comprehensive disinflation program in 2000, aimed at restructuring the domestic economy to fit the needs of external finance capital.

That effort took the form of an exchange rate-based anti-inflation package like those applied in Brazil and Russia, in this case designed, engineered, and monitored by the IMF. Unlike Brazil's Real plan and others around the world in 1990s, it dramatically failed in the short run. The causes lay with a financial cycle driven via a liberalized capital account – Turkey went through four such oscillations in the 1990s. The basic pattern resembles the one sketched above, featuring real appreciation and high domestic interest rates leading into the bust.

The unsuccessful stabilization package followed this pattern. With inflation running between 60 percent and 70 percent in 1999 (with growth in the wholesale price index rate below that of the consumer price index), the program targeted inflation rates in the 20–25 percent range at the end of 2000. Various restrictions on central bank activities effectively forced it to act as a mild currency board. A nominal devaluation rate of 20 percent was pre-announced as in the infamous Argentine *tablita* of the late 1970s.

Nonresident capital inflows totaled $15.5 billion in the first 10 months (in a $150 billion economy). Risk premia narrowed and internal interest rates fell. The current account deficit was $9.5 billion at year end, driven by deterioration in the trade balance. The bigger deficit was associated with real appreciation because prices rose between 30 percent and 40 percent over the year (in contrast to the pre-announced 20 percent nominal devaluation). The ratio of short-term debt to central bank reserves rose from 101 percent at the beginning of the year to 152 percent in December.

The IMF began to worry aloud about the macro situation in November, and nonresident investors responded by withdrawing assets rapidly. The central bank's reserves fell by $7 billion in two mid-November weeks. The bank broke its agreement to act as a currency board and provided Turkish lira liquidity to the banks. Emergency IMF funds were mobilized but failed to stabilize the economy. A political skirmish between the president and prime minister led to another attack on the lira in February 2001. In the final analysis, there was a capital flow reversal of almost $28 billion between the first 10 months of 2000 and the eight months that followed – almost 20 percent of GDP!

Turkey got into its present situation after widely trumpeted initial success as an "early reformer," with a liberalization push coming on the heels of an external crisis in the late 1970s. Developments in the 1980s and 1990s make an interesting contrast, as initial current account and labor market deregulation set up a jerky transition toward liberalized external and internal capital markets. The early 1980s witnessed a major export push, facilitated by rapid demand growth in Turkey's major trading partners and pushed on the domestic front by devaluation, aggressive export subsidies, and policies aimed at cutting real wages and the agricultural terms of trade (in contrast to India, higher agricultural prices appear to benefit – not harm – low-income peasant proprietors in the countryside). Despite rapid export growth, investment in traded goods sectors did not increase, so that capacity limits helped choke off the boom later in the decade. Moreover, higher exports were matched by imports so that demand was not externally led.

More fundamentally, the model broke down as repression of wages and the terms of trade could no longer be sustained – there was a wage explosion in 1988 accompanied be a marked political shift toward "populism" à la Turk. However, the government was unwilling or unable to raise taxes to fund its higher expenditures. Liberalizing the capital account was the expedient adopted to permit higher public borrowing. The pattern was for the banking system to borrow in external markets, and then relend the money to the government with a handsome interest rate spread. Along the lines discussed above, the rapid financial boom-bust cycles of the 1990s took over.

Throughout the 1990s, effective demand was led by the government, with private and external contractionary effects alternating in importance in tune with the cycle. Productivity growth has been slow, and fairly evenly balanced between traded and nontraded goods. Labor force participation has risen, accompanied by informalization and widening of wage spreads between skilled and unskilled labor. Although data are scarce, it is likely that poverty has increased. Shifts toward and away from populism on the political front were dramatic and the sequence of deregulation efforts was nonstandard, but otherwise Turkey exemplified the most familiar adverse effects of external liberalization.

3.4   Inflation stabilization economies

Reducing "high" inflation (annual rates in the two to four digit range) under a liberalized capital account was a principal goal in the 1990s in many countries. Besides Turkey, the ones considered here are Brazil and Russia – each a large economy with a significant industrial base. Both succeeded in reducing high inflations but then fell into financial crisis.

3.4.1   Brazil

Brazil enjoyed GDP growth of about 7.5 percent per year for more than three decades before the international debt crisis triggered by the Mexican default in 1982. In the 1980s – a "lost decade" – growth averaged 3.3 percent with an annual inflation rate (GDP deflator) of about 340 percent. Growth was 0.8 percent during 1990–94 and inflation reached 1,645 percent. The successful *Real* Plan stabilization in 1994 drastically cut inflation to 9 percent for the rest of the decade, with growth at 2.6 percent. However, the Real also ushered in an international financial crisis in 1999, from which the economy is still recovering.

The success of the anti-inflation package was directly tied to capital market liberalization. It shared many elements with half-a-dozen "heterodox" programs that had been attempted beginning in 1986. De-indexation was achieved by introducing a new nominal noninflationary unit of account tied to three price indexes; the unit was ultimately transformed into the *Real* which was pegged to the dollar. Residual inflation persisted so there was some real appreciation, but the major impetus for spiraling prices had been removed. The operation worked precisely because there was no pressure on the balance of payments. Capital inflows turned positive in 1990, and by 1995 they had reached a level of $30 billion per year (in a $500 billion economy).

The *Real* exercise had been preceded by several years of relatively tight fiscal policy, with primary surpluses of around 2–3 percent of GDP and operational surpluses (including interest payments) of −1 or −2 percent. But anti-inflationary success was not accompanied by concurrent fiscal austerity. Primary surpluses were near zero in 1995–97 and rose to about 3 percent in 1999–2000. Operational surpluses, however, were consistently negative as public debt rose from $30 billion in 1995 to $50 billion in 2000 (and much higher thereafter). High internal interest rates, largely driven by external rates and risk premia along UIP lines, were the principal cause of the fiscal deterioration. The liberalized capital market that was essential for inflation stabilization carried its own seeds of fiscal destruction.

During the 1980s demand was strongly export led, with E/m running three times as large as X. This situation rapidly reversed as imports grew at 14 percent per year in the 1990s while exports grew at 6 percent. It is difficult to separate public and private saving and investment accounts in Brazil, but after 1994 demand was clearly domestically led, probably with private investment and government consumption as the main contributing factors.

Brazilian proponents of liberalization argued that FDI and importation of "modern" (that is, foreign-made) intermediate and capital goods would lead to a jump in productivity, leading to export expansion. As already noted, the export surge did not happen. The productivity growth rate did rise from 1 percent before the Real plan to 2.6 percent in the second half of the 1990s. Both developments are consistent with real appreciation under a liberalized trade regime. FDI increased to about $5 billion per year by the end of the decade, but econometric tests suggest that it had negligible effects on productivity growth and domestic capital formation.

The 1999 crisis was followed by real depreciation and (still) higher interest rates, in the usual fashion. The output contraction was less sharp than in East Asia and Russia, and prior bank restructuring kept financial disruption to a minimum. However, the recovery that began in 2000 remains weak.

In six major metropolitan regions, total unemployment ("open" and "hidden") went from 10.3 percent in 1990 to 17.7 percent in 2000. As in other countries, demand growth was insufficient to offset faster productivity growth so there was negative net job creation. Informality in the labor market also increased.

3.4.2 Russia

The Russian transition doubtless has more acts to play, perhaps as dramatic as the ones that have already been staged. The opening featured orthodox liberalization shock therapy in 1992. The outcomes were a huge drop in output, rapid inflation as a vehicle for limiting demand by slashing real incomes, chaos in the public finances, distortion of the financial system, and an explosion of enterprise arrears. There were massive and often corrupt redistributions of property rights, resources, and political commitments.

The second act was "depressive stabilization." The inflation rate declined from almost 1000 percent in 1993 to 10 percent in 1997 in response to a tightly maintained exchange rate corridor and negative or zero growth. As in Turkey, the fiscal deficit was not monetized but rather financed by short-term bonds, with a large proportion sold abroad. The exchange rate became overvalued and there was capital flight on the order of $25–30 billion per year (larger than the trade surplus and almost 10 percent of Russia's $300 billion GDP). In the mid–1990s came a series of internal financial bubbles and Ponzi games.

External financial crisis hit in August 1998, as foreign funds that had been invested in government bonds and the stock market abruptly departed. GDP fell by 4.6 percent that year and the nominal exchange rate went from 5.96 rubles per dollar at the end of 1997 to 20.65 at the end of 1998.

Act Four was less unpleasant. Devaluation helped slow and possibly reversed deindustrialization, and higher world energy prices boosted the current account surplus from \$2–3 billion to around \$20 billion. Due in part to tighter enforcement, capital flight fell to the \$5 billion range. GDP growth rose to 5.4 percent in 1999, 9 percent in 2000, and 5.1 percent in 2001. Demand was led by foreign transactions as the government swung toward fiscal balance. Russia's high saving rate (about 30 percent of GDP) and lagging investment demand meant that the private sector was the economy's net lender.

Real wage and pensions payments suffered through the first three phases of liberalization described above. By 1997 they had fallen to one-half their levels in 1991, and by 1999 to one-third. Slow recovery began in 2000, but its prospects obviously depend on future growth of GDP. The overall Gini coefficient is near 0.4, and in 1998 over 40 percent of the population had incomes below the official poverty line.

More fundamentally, before its demise, the Soviet system had two main proto-classes, the *nomenklatura* in charge of the party or state governing apparatus and the rest of the population. The (former) *nomenklatura* were the clear gainers from liberalization, as in connection with the criminal "mafia" they seized control of the major productive assets in a blatantly rigged privatization process, and engaged in massive capital flight. The only Russians (the so-called "new Russians") whose real earnings rose were people in upper income strata who benefited from forced saving and the rapid, corrupt privatization. The production structure shows sharp duality between activities that may survive under the new economic regime and those that will not, and while Soviet-style industrial organization has been obliterated, a truly market-based system has not emerged in its place. At best, it will be many years before globalization and liberalization in Russia produce happy results for the population at large.

3.5   Postsocialist transition economies

In their own historical contexts, Hungary and Poland shared much of Russia's fate of the 1990s. But the phasing and repercussions of shock therapy were milder, following non-Soviet paths.

3.5.1   Poland

Poland in the 1980s had already taken steps toward a market system, with a multifaceted pricing system based on diverse values and/or rationing for the "same" commodity in different markets. This crutch was reinforced by the fact that agriculture had never been collectivized, leaving a farmer population with a significant social role.

The economy was pulled out of the initial contractionary effects of shock therapy in 1991 by fiscal stimulus, devaluation, and a strong export response. Moreover, "liberalization" during 1992–95 was incomplete. Imports were controlled through tariffs and other means; exports were (clandestinely and selectively) promoted by subsidies. In contrast to Russia, investment went up, pulling the economy out of its initial postshock recession. Higher economic activity meant that public sector deficits could decline without reductions in spending.

After 1995, the story was different. Policy shifted toward steady liberalization of imports along with strongly reduced levels of support for exports. Less controlled capital inflows failed to bring down domestic interest rates. The still shallow foreign exchange (forex) market was given a bigger role in setting the exchange rate. Unsurprisingly there has been strong real appreciation, growth slowed, and recently may have crossed the threshold of contraction. Unemployment has risen, foreign debt has accumulated. A "supply-side" fiscal policy misfired, resulting in big public deficits. Financial crisis may lurk in the wings.

The effective demand configuration also reversed around the transition year 1995. The government's demand contribution G/t has consistently exceeded the supply level X, falling until 1996 and increasing thereafter. The financial counterpart shifted from monetization to borrowing from the private sector, with the interest burden now running at 3 percent of GDP. In the latter part of the 1990s the trade surplus evaporated due to rising imports, and the private sector became a net debtor to the rest of the world and lender to the government. Post-1995, GDP growth slowed by a percent point on average.

Overall income inequality did not increase in the pre-1995 "illiberal" period, and rose significantly thereafter. Farmers' incomes rose before 1995, but confronted with import competition from Western Europe, they became the main losers thereafter in both relative and absolute terms. Retirees and the unemployed also suffered. Generally, the overall position of wage-earners improved but wage inequality increased strongly in the post-1995 "liberal" period. Employers and self-employed fared well in both periods but certainly better under liberalization. In the late 1990s there has been a visible increase in poverty, largely due to rising unemployment.

There has been positive productivity growth, the consequence of high capital formation in previous years and the overall evolution of ownership structure, management practises, etc. So falling employment (and strongly rising unemployment) in recent years reflects an overall slowdown in effective demand. While it is difficult to single out any clear productivity leader, in both periods agriculture was certainly the lagging sector. The foreign-owned sector – which has exhibited impressive rates of growth of output and employment – appears to have been a productivity laggard. Reallocation of labor from the domestic to foreign-owned corporations has reduced the overall productivity gain.

3.5.2 Hungary

Hungary's liberalization during the 1990s concentrated on the current account. Adverse impacts of large capital inflows were mitigated by sterilization and partial, gradual deregulation of the capital account. The country escaped the kind of "big bang" experienced by Poland and Russia. The mode of external liberalization, as well as the implementation of institutional changes in Hungary in the early years of the transition, may best be characterized as "shock therapy in slow motion," followed by true shock therapy in a stabilization package in 1995. As elsewhere, the outcomes of liberalization were deeply intertwined with both the accompanying economic policies and exogenous shocks at the time.

Hungary opened up its formerly strictly controlled trade system in 1989 without any temporary protection whatsoever, and combined the liberalization of imports with significant real appreciation. Abrupt changes in the institutional and legal framework included the introduction of strict legislation on bankruptcy procedures, driving potentially viable companies out of business. In practise, liberalization turned out to be an economic time bomb, which exploded in 1993. Its adverse effects on the trade balance were concealed because the Hungarian economy suffered a deep ("transformational") recession between 1990 and 1992. In 1993, as the recession began to subside, the trade balance and the current account deteriorated very sharply.

Demand decomposition exercises reveal that the fall in output had a close relationship with the fall in exports due to the collapse of trade with East-European partners, with whom Hungary had a special trading framework. The jump in the external deficit in 1993–1994 had to do with deterioration of the fiscal position and an increase in private investment.

By 1994, the deterioration of the current account reached such proportions that a correction became inevitable. However, the direct importance of the stabilization package of 1995 involving trade, exchange rate, and fiscal policy measures was negligible compared to a ten-point jump in the inflation rate, with a corresponding drop in real wages and social transfers.

In the partly deregulated capital account, FDI increased (with gross flows possibly amounting to 7–8 percent of a $50 billion GDP in the late 1990s) and apparently fed into higher gross domestic capital formation. While there were benefits from FDI-inflows – growth in investments, exports and GDP – disturbing inequalities and strains also emerged within Hungary. The emergence of excessive regional and sectoral disparities has been closely related to the presence (extent) of foreign capital. While the central and western part of Hungary which received large FDI-inflows has been prospering since 1996, counties in the northeast – only recently penetrated by FDI – have been characterized by high unemployment, slow growth, or recession. By 1999–2000, however, the sharp divergence in regional performances had started to subside.

Also by 1999, real GDP had returned to its level of the late 1980s, with consumption a bit over 60 percent of GDP (unchanged from its earlier share), investment at 26 percent (up from 16 percent) and government spending at 14 percent (down from 18 percent). The economy is quite open, with import and export GDP shares in 2000 of 65.6 percent and 61.6 percent, respectively.

Between 1992 and 2000, traded goods output grew by 5.3 percent per year, and nontraded by 2.2 percent. During the same period, employment in traded goods fell at a 3.3 percent rate, and grew at 0.8 percent in nontradeds. Labor productivity nearly doubled in traded goods over the period, but increased by only 12 percent in nontradeds. The traded goods employment or population ratio fell by 25 percent in 1992–95, and then gradually rose by about 5 percent (in part due to a population decrease of 2 percent, 1992–98). In nontraded goods, the ratio grew by 35 percent over 1992–98. This increase made up for about one-third of the employment loss in the traded goods sector.

On a final note, macro policy in 2001 switched toward reducing a 10 percent annual inflation rate using the currently popular set of tools – exchange rate appreciation and fully opening the capital account. The liberalization measures are in line with recommendations or requirements made by the EU (as well international financial institutions), and, in the optimistic case, they may contribute to the convergence of Hungary's inflation to that of the euro-region. However, it is by no means clear whether it will also support the country's real convergence – maintaining its relatively high growth rate – as well. As noted repeatedly above, exchange rate-based stabilizations carry their own perils.

4 Conclusions

The liberalization packages we have discussed, all represent attempts at integration of diverse developing and transition economies into the evolving world capitalist system. Under the aegis of the vintage-1980s Washington Consensus and later reformulations, all nations not members of the "old" OECD (as it stood before the entry of Mexico, Poland, South Korea, Turkey, etc.) faced great and increasing pressure to adopt a set of "good policies" together with "good institutions." As we have seen, good policies included a conservative macroeconomic stance, liberalization of the international trade and capital flows, privatization, and deregulation. Good institutions meant "sound" banking and financial policies with prudential regulation, protection of property rights, market-oriented governance, and transparent accountability of government bodies.

Outcomes were decidedly mixed. Of the 14 countries discussed herein, only four managed steady growth of a period of a decade or more and (attempts at prudential financial regulation notwithstanding) nine went through financial crises. In general, growth and productivity, performances were sub-par by historical standards.

With regard to employment and distribution, the record was also mixed. In at least seven country cases, output per capita in the traded goods sector grew less rapidly than labor productivity, forcing the overall employment structure to shift toward less attractive jobs in the nontraded sector (consistent with a broad tendency toward real appreciation). The shift went the other direction in four countries which had successful export performances.

Similarly, liberalization tends to shift the employment structure toward more highly skilled workers, an outcome observed in seven countries. Where data were available, there was just one exception.

Four countries reported increased "informality" of employment. Skilled or unskilled, urban or rural, and formal or informal pay differentials tended to rise, with increases in some or all such measures in eight countries.

Consistent with worldwide trends toward growing income inequality, increases in the Gini coefficient and/or shifts against labor in the functional income distribution showed up in eight cases, with one exception.

Contrary to all these findings, orthodox neoclassical theory asserts that increased integration of world commodity and capital markets is conducive to growth and is expected to be welfare-improving. On the side of trade, standard comparative advantage arguments are interpreted to mean that liberalization will raise economic efficiency and thereby growth. But mainstream commentators rarely acknowledge that the assumptions underlying standard trade theory – in particular Say's Law and a predetermined trade balance – are not satisfied in practise (Ocampo and Taylor 1998). In their absence, liberalization is likely to mean demand slumps and job losses in traded good sectors, perhaps exacerbated by productivity gains on the part of previously protected firms that manage to survive lost protection. As has been emphasized, these adverse effects are often worsened by real exchange rate appreciation, a possibility not contemplated in standard models which presume all goods are traded.

Capital flows are supposed to expand investors' possibilities for portfolio diversification, while simultaneously enabling households to smooth their consumption-saving decisions over their life cycle. Historical experience suggests otherwise. The recent crisis episodes across Latin America and Asia demonstrate the dangers of deregulation which in practise subjects weak indigenous financial systems to short-term foreign capital which is excessively liquid, excessively volatile, and always subject to herd psychology.

Besides liberalization aimed at raising developing and transition economies' integration with global commodity and capital markets, they are also asked to adopt or maintain contractionary monetary and fiscal policies. The goal is to secure investor confidence and international creditworthiness (Grabel 1996). Central banks are supposed to be "autonomous" and concentrate all their efforts on "inflation targeting." Fiscal policies are to be directly focused on the objective of "budget with a primary surplus." As Rodrik (2001) argues, this policy mix signifies reduced political autonomy in the developing world in exchange for market access to the industrialized North, and is itself a bad bargain as far as development is concerned. Robust growth is not likely to emerge in an economy perpetually subject to contractionary policy and in which the government is forced to eschew any attempt at creating a developmentalist state.

Alternative institutions such as developmentalism and policies such as intelligent capital controls, directed protection coupled with industrial policy, maintenance of sensible levels of macro prices (real interest rate, real wage, real exchange rate), and judiciously expansionary macro policy are of course possible – at least in principle. Whether principle can become practise in the coming years will depend on many factors. The two most important are greater possibilities for autonomous action on the part of governments in nonwealthy countries, and the ability of national economic policy makers to respond to the challenges that great autonomy would present. The constellation of forces will not be completely under the control of "emerging" nation states, but they certainly can play some role in influencing its shape.

Appendix I: Productivity and demand decompositions

Because macro data are available for discrete periods of time (typically years), the analysis is set up with variables for period beginning at time t indicated by a subscript. For simplicity equations are stated with t taking only the values 0 and 1 corresponding to the beginning and end of a period, respectively.

To begin with a productivity decomposition, suppose that one has data on employment and output for several sectors over time. Let $\theta_0^i\, X_0^i/X_0$ be the share of sector i in real output in period zero, with $\sum_i X_0^i = X_0$. Similarly for employment: $\lambda_0^i = L_0^i/L_0$ with $\sum_i L_0^i = L_0$. The level of labor productivity in sector i is X_0^i/L_0^i with a growth rate of

$$\varepsilon_L^i = (1 + \hat{L}^i)^{-1} (\hat{X}^i - \hat{L}^i) \approx \hat{X}^i - \hat{L}^i,$$

in which $\hat{X}^i = (X_1^i - X_0^i)/X_0^i$ and similarly for other variables with "hats." The term $(1 + \hat{L}^i)^{-1}$ captures "interaction" effects on growth rates arising from their calculation in discrete time.

After a bit of manipulation, an exact expression for the rate of growth of economy-wide labor productivity emerges as

$$\varepsilon_L = (1 + \hat{L})^{-1} \sum_i [\theta_0^i (\hat{X}^i - \hat{L}^i) + (\theta_0^i - \lambda_0^i) \hat{L}^i]. \tag{1}$$

Another expression for productivity growth comes out after some manipulation of (1),

$$\varepsilon_L = (1 + \hat{L})^{-1} \sum_i [\lambda_0^i (\hat{X}^i - \hat{L}^i) + (\theta_0^i - \lambda_0^i) \hat{X}^i]. \tag{2}$$

In (2), sectoral productivity growth rates are weighted by employment shares, and the reallocation effect is stated in terms of output growth rates. The message is basically the same as in (1).

Growth rates of employment are driven by changes in productivity and demand. The relevant decomposition (expressed in terms of continuous time for simplicity) appears in the text.

The decomposition procedure for effective demand draws on Godley (1999). At the one-sector level (ignoring intermediate outputs and sales along with the distinction between wage and profit income flows), the aggregate supply of goods and services available for domestic use (X) can be defined as the sum of total private income (Y_p), net taxes (T), and "imports" or (for present purposes) all outgoing payments on current account (M):

$$X = Y_p + T + M \tag{3}$$

In NIPA categories, we have GDP $= Y_p + T = X - M$ so the accounting in (3) is nonstandard insofar as X exceeds GDP. The aggregate supply and demand balance can be written as:

$$X = C_p + I_p + G + E \tag{4}$$

that is, the sum of private consumption, private investment, government spending (on both current and capital account) and "exports" or incoming foreign payments on current account. It is convenient to define leakage parameters relative to aggregate supply, yielding the private savings rate as $S_p = (Y_p - C_p)/X$, the import propensity as $m = M / X$, and the tax rate as $t = T / X$.

From all this one gets a typical Keynesian income multiplier function

$$X = (I_p + G + E)/(S_p + t + m) \tag{5}$$

which can also be written as

$$X = (S_p / \lambda)(I_p / S_p) + (t / \lambda)(G / t) + (m / \lambda)(E / m) \tag{6}$$

in which $\lambda = S_p + t + m$ is the sum of the leakage parameters, and I_p / S_p, G / t, and E/m can be interpreted as the direct "own" multiplier effects on output of private investment, government spending, and export injections with their overall impact scaled by the corresponding leakage rates (respectively, savings, tax, and import propensities). That is, aggregate supply is equal to a weighted average of contributions to demand from the private sector, government, and the rest of the world. If two of these contributions were zero, then output would be equal to the third.

Another representation involves the levels of $I_p - S_p X$, $G - tX$, and $E - mX$ which from (6) must sum to zero. Moreover, the economy's real financial balance can be written as

$$\dot{D} + \dot{Z} + \dot{A} = (I_p - s_p X) + (G - tX) + (E - mX) = 0 \tag{7}$$

where $\dot{D}$ ($= dD/dt$), $\dot{Z}$, and $\dot{A}$ stand respectively for the net change per unit time in financial claims against the private sector, in government debt, and in foreign assets.

Equation (7) shows how claims against an institutional entity (the private sector, government, or rest of the world) must grow when its demand contribution to

X exceeds X itself. So when $E < mX$, net foreign assets of the home economy are declining, while $G > tX$ means that its government is running up debt. A contractionary demand contribution from the rest of the world requires some other sector to be increasing liabilities or lowering assets, for example the public sector when $G > tx$. Because from (7) it is true that $\dot{D} + \dot{Z} + \dot{A} = 0$, such offsetting effects are unavoidable.

Notes

1 See, for example, Taylor (2001) and Vos, et al. (2003).
2 As discussed endlessly in the literature, this outcome runs counter to predictions from the Stolper–Samuleson (1941) theorem. But since that theorem presupposes Say's Law and ignores the real exchange rate and the distinction between traded and nontraded goods, there is no reason to expect it to apply.
3 Roughly half of this foreign trade takes the form of "re-export" or export-oriented processing and assembly activities.

References

Geertz, C. (1973) *The Interpretation of Cultures*, New York: Basic Books.

Godley, W. (1999) *Seven Unsustainable Processes: Medium-Term Prospects and Policies for the US and the World*, Annandale-on-Hudson, NY: Jerome Levy Economics Institute, Bard College.

Grabel, I. (1996) 'Marketing the Third World: The Contradictions of Portfolio Investment in the Global Economy', *World Development*, 24(11): 1761–76.

Kindleberger, C. P. (2000; 4th edn.) *Manias, Panics, and Crashes: A History of Financial Crises*, New York: John Wiley & Sons.

Krugman, P. and Taylor, L. (1978) 'Contractionary Effects of Devaluation', *Journal of International Economics*, 8: 445–56.

Ocampo, J. A. and Taylor, L. (1998) 'Trade Liberalization in Developing Economies: Modest Benefits but Problems with Productivity Growth, Macro Prices, and Income Distribution', *Economic Journal*, 108: 1523–46.

Pasinetti, L. (1981) *Structural Change and Economic Growth*, Cambridge: Cambridge University Press.

Rodrik, D. (2001) 'The Global Governance of Trade As if Development Really Mattered', Paper presented at the UNDP Meetings New York, October 13–14, 2000.

Stolper, W. and Samuelson, P. A. (1941) 'Protection and Real Wages', *Review of Economic Studies*, 9: 58–73.

Syrquin, M. (1986) 'Productivity Growth and Factor Reallocation' in H. B. Chenery, S. Robinson, and M. Syrquin (eds.), *Industrialization and Growth*, New York: Oxford University Press.

Taylor, L. (ed.) (2001) *External Liberalization, Economic Performance, and Social Policy*, New York: Oxford University Press.

Vos, R., Taylor, L., and Paes de Barros, R. (2003) *Economic Liberalization and Income Distribution: The Case of Latin America*, Northampton, MA: Edward Elgar.

6 Exports, foreign investment and growth in Latin America: skepticism by way of simulation

John Weeks

1 Introduction

The prevailing development strategy places emphasis on the 'outward orientation' of countries, with particular emphasis on export growth and attracting direct foreign investment. If 'outward-oriented economies really do grow faster' (Dollar 1992), one would expect this to be transmitted through exports imparting a dynamism to the economy as a whole, and by direct foreign investment stimulating increased total investment in an economy or, at least, not reducing it. This paper investigates the role of exports and foreign investment in the economic growth of the Latin American countries over the last four decades. The procedure is to evaluate the extent to which export growth, on the one hand, and direct foreign investment, on the other, have contributed to overall economic growth. Once this evaluation is made, the purpose is to demonstrate that the liberalization policies in Latin America in the 1980s resulted in a significant and substantial decline in the contribution of exports and FDI to the region's economic growth.

All decisions involving the allocation of resources have an opportunity cost, and this applies as much to export growth and foreign investment as to other economic variables. Rational policy involves maximization of both subject to relevant constraints. To foster export growth unconstrained by any objective function is mercantilism, discredited by Adam Smith over two centuries ago. Similarly, a policy regime that seeks to maximize foreign direct investment flows as if these were costless is non-rational. The basic strategy issue is what policy framework is likely to maximize the benefits of each.

2 Policy considerations

Recent literature on growth of developing countries has stressed the importance of exports and foreign direct investment for stimulating growth. For developing countries both exports and foreign investment grew faster in the 1980s and 1990s than previously (on FDI see Brewer and Young 1995; Greene and Villanueva 1991; Mallampally and Sauvant 1999), but it does not necessarily follow that the faster growth of these countries implies faster GDP growth. Whether faster economic growth results depend on a number of factors, the two most important of which are: (1) whether, on the one hand, export growth substitutes for or enhances non-export growth, and, on the other, whether foreign investment crowds-out or crowds-in domestic investors; and (2) if either relationship is negative, whether the growth-inducing effect of exports (foreign investments) is greater than for the non-exports (domestic investments) they replace.

The two questions are closely related, and much of the discussion of these issues has focused on the role of foreign investment, both in its investment-enhancing role and its function as a vehicle for export growth. Professional opinion shifted on this issue in the 1990s. For example, the 1992 *World Investment Report* of UNCTAD expressed some skepticism. After pointing out that FDI as a share of domestic investment in development countries was typically low, below five percent, it went on to observe:

> ... [T]here may be circumstances in which transnational corporation activities may not contribute to sustained long-term growth ... For example, transfer pricing may reduce the potential for growth through trade. Similarly, abuse of market power by transnational corporations can stifle the growth of local entrepreneurs.

> (UNCTAD 1992: 14)

In the abstract, a government can either pursue a neutral policy toward foreign direct investment and international trade or an interventionist one. In practise, all governments intervene to some degree. With regard to FDI, the dichotomy between policy neutrality and intervention became an anachronism in the 1990s. Before the debt crisis of the 1980s, most Latin American countries had varying degrees of capital controls, restrictions on external participation in domestic asset and bond markets (which were relatively underdeveloped), and regulations on foreign corporations acquiring domestic firms. In this context, direct foreign investment tended to result in the creation of new assets; indeed, a major motivation for the package of regulations was to ensure this. As a result, until 1980, the balance of payments entry 'foreign direct investment' could, for practical purposes, be interpreted as resulting in subsequent capital formation.

With the liberalization of capital accounts and privatization associated with the so-called Washington Consensus, the nature of FDI underwent substantial change. To varying degrees in all countries privatization took the form of debt-equity 'swaps', in which public assets were sold to foreign firms. This is demonstrated in Table 6.1 for the first, second, third, and sixth largest economies in the region in 1990. For the four countries together, well over 40 percent of foreign direct investment involved acquisition of domestic assets through privatization. Acquisition by international corporations of domestic private sector firms represented a second major change in the form of FDI in Latin America after 1980, though its extent was more difficult to quantify.[2]

Table 6.1 Debt-equity swaps in four Latin American countries, 1985–89 (millions of current U.S. dollars)

Country	Total FDI	FDI by debt-equity	DE/FDI (%)
Brazil	7,687	4,529	59
Mexico	10,098	3,052	30
Argentina	3,464	731	20
Chile	3,947	3,160	80
Totals	25,196	11,472	46

Source: UNCTC (1991).

These changes in mode of entry of FDI had important consequences. With regard to statistics, after 1980 FDI balance of payments flows must be read differently than before: it was no longer valid to infer that the FDI balance of payments entry in a given year would result in capital formation in a subsequent year. Specifically, it could no longer be assumed that all or even most FDI resulted in net creation of assets (see Brazil in Table 6.1). It follows that the interpretation of Figure 6.1 is not straightforward. The chart shows a dramatic increase in the share of FDI in regional GDP from the end of the 1980s (also showing the percentages excluding Brazil and excluding Brazil, Mexico and Venezuela). There are at least two reasons that the raw percentages overstate the growth of FDI. First, after 1980 the meaning of the percentage is different, due to asset acquisitions. Second, GDP grew slower in the 1990s than in the 1970s, while the growth rate of FDI was much the same.[3]

From the perspective of neoclassical theory, to find that FDI was not net asset creating would not be interpreted as a problem requiring action. If an economy is in full employment general equilibrium, the typical starting point of neoclassical 'stories', then an ex-post inflow of capital to construct physical capital would necessarily reduce some form of expenditure by an equal amount. If government expenditure and exports were constant in real terms, the capital inflow would result in 100 percent 'crowding out' of domestic private investment or domestic consumption. If the capital inflow prompted a rise in the real interest rate, the crowding out could be greater than 100 percent (total investment could fall).

This analysis is not consistent with the empirical evidence, which indicates that for most countries and decades the relationship between FDI and domestic investment was non-significant, and significantly positive almost as frequently as it was negative. In practise the empirical evidence supports the primary motivation of Latin American governments for their FDI policies during 1960–80: to ensure that foreign investment would bring a net addition to domestic investment, either by entering into sectors domestic capital was incapable of efficiently developing, or by creating complementary linkages to domestic capital.

With capital account deregulation and its associated domestic asset acquisition by international firms, the emphasis on the advantages of FDI shifted from the

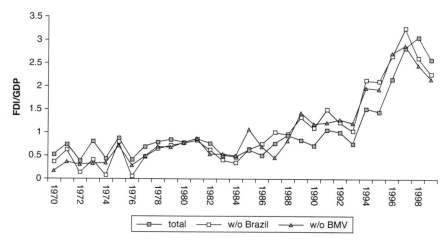

Figure 6.1 Foreign Direct Investment in 18 Latin American countries, percentage of GDP, 1970–99.

straightforward contribution to capital accumulation to more speculative outcomes. These include the possibility that FDI: (1) might provide technologies and skills not otherwise available; (2) access to new export markets; and (3) generate spread affects within an industry that raises the managerial or technical efficiency of domestic firms (UNCTAD 1999: 34–5). Empirical evidence suggests that no general conclusion could be drawn about these outcomes, which seemed to depend on the specifics of each country.[4] An argument sometimes encountered is that the inflow of FDI resulting from deregulation of capital flows can substitute for policy interventions to generate more competition in domestic markets. This is an empirical assertion about which no general conclusion can be drawn, and expert opinion is mixed.[5]

One can conclude that the most general argument in favor of FDI, both analytically and empirically, is that it fosters economic growth in as far as it increases total investment, and, slightly weaker, that its total effect is more likely to be positive if it does not reduce domestic investment. It is this issue, the possible crowding out of domestic investment by foreign investment, that is the empirical focus on FDI in this paper. Along with this, the closely related issue of the interaction between export growth and non-export GDP is considered. Together, these two interactive relationships, FDI and domestic investment, and exports and non-exports, represent the principal modes of transferring the dynamism of world markets to the domestic economy.

3   Analytical framework

Any serious treatment of the issue of complementarity versus substitutability of external and internal variables must be placed in an analytical context. To do this, a formal model is developed below. If an economy is characterized by full employment, then the relationships are straightforward in comparative statics, as noted above. Any increase in exports can occur only if resources dedicated to non-exports are reduced. Similarly, any inflow of foreign investment, other things equal, must replace some form of domestic expenditure. Implying as it does 100 percent crowding-out in both cases, the static full employment framework lacks interest analytically and for policy. More interesting and realistic is to consider a growing economy, in which the actual rate of growth fluctuates cyclically below a full employment ceiling.

To initiate the analysis, we define the overall rate of growth of GDP as the weighted sum of the growth rates of export and non-export value added in any period.

$$y_t = \alpha[y_{x_t}] + (1-\alpha)\,[y_{nx_t}] \tag{1}$$

where y = rate of growth of value added (VA)
  x_t = export sector
  nx_t = non-export sector
  α = ratio of export value added to GDP (Y_x/Y_{nx})

If y_{x_t} is not equal to y_{nx_t}, α changes from one period to the next, and for Y in period t, α is approximated by the ratio of the previous period $[Y_{x_{t-1}}]/[Y_{x_{t-1}} + Y_{nx_{t-1}}]$. For simplicity, we assume that the growth rate of export value added is exogenously given in the short run by the rate of growth of exports, $x*$ (that is, $y_{x_t} = x*$),[6] which assumes that the value added share of export production is constant. Let non-export GDP be determined by two factors: (1) the growth of domestic demand (a_t), and (2) spread effects from the growth of the export sector.[7] We assume in the short run that the growth of domestic demand is given $(a_t = a*)$. Therefore,

$$y_{x_t} = x^* \tag{1a}$$
$$y_{nx_t} = \lambda_1[y_{x_t}] + \lambda_2[a_t] \tag{2}$$

where λ_1 and λ_2 are the elasticities of the growth rate of the non-export sector with respect to export growth and domestic demand, respectively.

Substituting expression (2) into (1) yields:

$$y_t = \alpha[y_x*] + (1-\alpha)\{\lambda_1[y_x*] + \lambda_2[a*]\} \tag{3}$$

Combining terms, one obtains the following equation:

$$y_t = [\alpha + \lambda_1(1-\alpha)][y_x*] + \lambda_2(1-\alpha)[a*] \tag{3a}$$

Viewed at one moment in time, no problem arises from the variation in due to the difference between y_{nt_t} and y_x. The interpretation of the equation when adapted for regression analysis and estimated with logarithmic values is discussed below. The parameter λ_1 shows the effect of export growth on the non-export sector. We call this *the coefficient of export dynamism*, because it summarizes the transmission of export growth to the non-export sector. Inspecting the coefficient $[\alpha + \lambda_1(1-\alpha)]$, one can identify three cases:

1   if $\lambda_1 = 0$, export growth has a neutral impact on non-export growth, non-export growth is determined by the growth of domestic demand, and equation (3a) reduces to the original growth expression (1);
2   if $\lambda_1 > 0$, export growth increases the rate of growth of the non-export sector above the rate implied by domestic demand; and
3   if $\lambda_1 < 0$, export growth decreases the rate of growth of the non-export sector below the rate implied by domestic demand.

There would be an unambiguously positive *complementary effect* ($\lambda_1 > 0$) via the demand for inputs and consumption demand by producers of exports for the non-export sector. A trade-off effect, $\lambda_1 < 0$, would most obviously result when the expansion of export production drew resources out of the non-export sector. This would be strong when the economy was close to full employment, but could also occur if idle resources were less appropriate for export production than the resources employed in the non-export sector. A trade-off effect might also increase or decrease if the composition of exports changed over time, such that the demand for intermediate products from the non-export sector increased or decreased.

Mexico in the 1990s was an apparent example of exports involving fewer input linkages to the non-export sector. Declining linkages was pointed out by an ECLAC report, in a discussion of foreign investment in the export sector, '... these [foreign] firms, which make intensive use of capital and intra-industry trade [i.e. outside Mexico], generally create few jobs for skilled works, and their linkages with the rest of the economy are still minimal' (ECLAC 2000: 37).[8] In such a situation it is possible that the parameter λ_1 might be negative; that is, an increase in the growth rate of exports would be associated with a decline in the growth rate of the non-export sector.

A negative λ_1 by definition implies a lower overall growth rate of GDP, but this need not be the case when viewed in a dynamic context. One could imagine an exogenous rate of growth of exports so high that it generated a substantial shift of resources from non-tradables and import substitutes to exports (i.e. exports crowding out other probduciton). However, the resultant rate of growth of GDP might be greater than would be achieved were the shift not to occur. This would be the case if the export sector were characterized by higher productivity change than the non-export sector. Consider, for example, an 'Asian Miracle' rate of growth of exports of ten percent, in an economy with an initial division of the two sectors of fifty percent of GDP each. Assume further that the non-export sector's maximum growth rate, constrained by internal demand growth and productivity change, were five percent. In this case, the economy would initially grow at

7.5 percent, and could achieve a higher rate of growth only by a relative and perhaps absolute decrease in the production of the non-export sector.

Turning to investment, we use similar algebra to formulate a test for the growth effect of direct foreign investment. By definition, total investment is equal to investment by domestic agents plus investment by external agents. If i_t is total investment in time period t, and i_d and i_f are the shares of domestic and foreign investment in GDP, the following definition holds:

$$i_t = \sigma[i_{d_t}] + (1-\sigma)[i_{f_t}] \tag{4}$$

where i_{d_t} = investment by domestic agents
i_{f_t} = investment by foreign agents
σ = ratio of investment by domestic agents to total investment

Assume that foreign investment inflows are exogenous, and domestic investment is determined by a range of economic factors summarized in the term 'b', and foreign investment itself (due to crowding out or crowding in).

$$i_{d_t} = \rho_1[i_{f_t}] + \rho_2[b_t] \tag{5}$$

where ρ_1 and ρ_2 are behavioral elasticities, with the latter unambiguously positive. And total investment becomes,

$$i_t = \sigma\{\rho_1[i_{f_t}] + \rho_2[b_t]\} + (1-\sigma)[i_{f_t}] \tag{6}$$

Gathering terms, the result can be expressed as follows,

$$i_t = [1 + \sigma(\rho_1 - 1)][i_{f_t}] + \sigma\rho_2[b_t] \tag{6a}$$

As before, we consider this equation at one point in time, so that variations in the ratio of foreign to domestic investment can be ignored. The key parameter is ρ_1, the 'crowding' coefficient. As for exports, there are three possibilities:

1   $\rho_1 = 0$, foreign investment has no impact on domestic investment;
2   $\rho_1 > 0$, foreign investment 'crowds-in' domestic investment, and
3   $\rho_1 < 0$, foreign investment 'crowds out' domestic investment.

There are strong a priori arguments for crowding out (see UNCTAD 1999: 37–43). For a given rate of growth, the range of investment opportunities should be finite, and if foreign investors exploit these, fewer are left for domestic investors. However, it is also possible that some investments would only be exploited by foreign capital because of greater access to or patent-based control of the relevant technology. As for the relationship between the export and non-export sectors, whether crowding-out or crowding-in of domestic by foreign investment characterizes an economy over a given time period is an empirical question. As before, our method is to estimate the parameter ρ_1 for each Latin American country for various time periods, then to use the estimated parameters in a growth model. This procedure differs from that used by Agosin and Mayer (2000) to test for crowding-in and crowding-out, but our results for Latin America support their conclusion that crowding-in is an important phenomenon in the region.

4   Parameters by country: exports and non-exports

The analysis identifies two key parameters that affect a country's growth rate in an 'outwardly oriented' development strategy: (1) the relationship between export growth and non-export growth, and (2) the relationship between foreign and domestic investment. The central hypothesis is that one cannot generalize about these parameters across countries. Rather, they are determined by the structure of economies, world market conditions at any moment, and policies pursued by governments. For example, one would not expect the same parameter for foreign investment and domestic investment in a petroleum-based economy as in one in which exports were of manufactures. The petroleum economy would tend to generate relatively few linkages between oil and the other sectors, compared to a country exporting manufactures based on the processing of primary products.

Monetary and fiscal policies would have a major impact on both parameters. If a government follows a purposeful demand-compression programme, as many Latin American governments did in the 1980s, one would expect the stimulating effect of exports on non-export production to be quite low. Similarly, high interest rate credit rationing associated with monetary restrain would tend to foster the crowding-out of domestic investment by foreign investment.

Because of substantial differences in policies through time, therefore, our estimations are made over three time periods. The first is 1960–81, when most of the Latin American countries enjoyed high growth rates, within a so-called import substitution strategy ('industrial policy' would be the correct term). This was followed by a period during which growth for most countries was near zero, due to demand compression associated with the debt crisis (1981–89). To a great extent, the purpose of the demand compression was to reduce import levels, thus forcing a trade surplus (see De Pinies 1989). The subsequent decade was one of moderate, if unstable, recovery.

To move from our theoretical categories to empirical ones, simplifying assumptions are made. In the case of export and non-export production, it is assumed that the proportion of value added in exports remained constant over the entire period treated for each country, a standard assumption in models relating exports to growth. Thus, if Y_{x_t} is export production in constant prices, and X_t is exports, we assume for each country that $Y_{x_t} = \mu X_t$, where μ is a constant. This allows non-export production to be estimated as $(Y_t - \mu X_t)$, where Y_t is GDP. For foreign direct investment, the empirical problem is that the reported flows do not immediately become investments in the concrete, because FDI is a balance of payments

Table 6.2   Elasticity of non-export GDP with regard to exports, 1960–99

Countries	All years	1960–81	1981–90	1990–99
Argentina	0.39	0.56	−0.27	0.39
Bolivia*	nsgn	−1.81	−0.09	0.31
Brazil	0.65	0.87	0.45	0.58
Chile	0.40	0.25	0.56	0.65
Colombia	0.71	1.21	0.31	0.45
Costa Rica	0.38	0.59	0.29	−0.24
Dom Rep	0.43	1.15	0.45	nsgn
Ecuador	0.59	0.57	0.13	0.40
El Salvador	0.65	1.01	nsgn	0.24
Guatemala	0.91	0.74	0.38	0.42
Honduras	0.96	0.51	1.79	0.32
Mexico	0.41	1.02	nsgn	−0.12
Nicaragua	0.27	0.71	−0.46	nsgn
Panama	na			
Paraguay	0.61	0.93	0.15	nsgn
Peru	0.81	0.80	−0.68	nsgn
Uruguay	0.24	0.31	0.31	0.44
Venezuela	nsgn	−0.72	nsgn	nsgn
Average (nsgn = 0)	0.49	0.51	0.20	0.22
pos/neg/nsgn	15/0/2	15/2/0	10/4/3	10/2/5

*1970–99.

category and domestic investment from the national accounts.[9] Our procedure is to assume that foreign investment flows in one year translate into actual investments with a one-year time lag. This allows investment by domestic agents, as a portion of GDP, to be calculated as $(I_t - I_{f_{t-1}})$. While both of these assumptions are oversimplifications, they allow for proxy estimates of the key parameters. It should be noted that the assumption that the balance of payments flows convert to actual investments is not inconsistent with the earlier evidence that in the 1980s considerable FDI took the form of debt-equity swaps. The purpose of the investment model is to test for crowding effects manifesting them in the key parameter ρ, which would approach zero and even become negative if crowding out is important.

A few further comments are necessary before presenting the regression results and interpreting the coefficients. Since the variables are calculated as ten-year averages over three decades, and we use 'dummy' variables to identify decades, we are, in effect, assuming the variables to be constant over each decade. Thus, there is no contradiction between the annual variation in the export–GDP ratio, and treating the terms α and $(1-\alpha)$ as parameters showing weights on the growth of export and non-export value added. The same applies to the parameter σ.

Table 6.2 provides the estimates of the elasticity between exports and non-export GDP.[10] For each time period, these elasticities are calculated by a simple logarithmic regression, non-export GDP is a function of exports. If the elasticity was not significant at 0.10 or less probability, it is entered as zero. The

17 countries fall into clear categories. First, there are the *export-dynamic* countries: those for which estimated non-export GDP was consistently and positively related to exports in all periods (Brazil, Chile, Colombia, Ecuador, Guatemala, Honduras and Uruguay). Two other countries, Argentina and El Salvador, should probably be added to this category. For these, the relationship was negative (Argentina) or non-significant (El Salvador) only in the 1980s. The negative elasticity for Argentina could be explained by demand compression, which restricted growth of domestically consumed output. In the case of El Salvador, the performance of domestic output is probably explained by the Civil War that raged during the decade. For all these countries, except Uruguay, the elasticity was considerably greater during 1960–81 than during the 1990s.

Second, there are three countries with *lost export dynamism*, strongly positive elasticities in the first period, positive, but lower elasticities in the 1980s, then negative (Costa Rica) or non-significant (Dominican Republic and Paraguay) elasticities in the 1990s. It would appear for these three countries that structural changes, perhaps associated with policy changes, generated a declining tendency for exports to impart a growth dynamic to the rest of the economy. Three countries qualify as *export non-dynamic* after 1980, in which export growth was either neutral with respect to non-export growth, or negatively related (Mexico, Nicaragua and Peru). There remain two anomalous cases, Bolivia and Venezuela,[11] which show negative elasticities during 1960–81. Bolivia is the only one of the 17 in which there was a change from a negative to a positive elasticity over the three periods. Venezuela is the only country in which there is no significant positive relationship between exports and non-export GDP for any time period, perhaps due to the particular character of its petroleum-dominated export sector.

The review of countries over time periods confirms the hypothesis that one cannot generalize about the dynamism imparted by exports to the non-export economy. For some countries during some periods, the transmission of export dynamism was strikingly high (e.g. Colombia, the Dominican Republic, El Salvador and Mexico for 1960–81 and Honduras in the 1990s, all with elasticities near or above unity). For a few, it appears to have been negative to an equally striking degree (Bolivia and Venezuela, 1960–81). Even more surprising, there were countries for which the relationship changed dramatically, and cannot be easily explained by demand compression (Costa Rica and Mexico, 1960–81 compared to the 1990s). Finally, one can note that differences in elasticities cannot be explained by the size of economy (e.g. Costa Rica and Mexico), nor by the importance of petroleum in exports (again, Ecuador and Venezuela). The variation in outcomes is shown graphically for three major countries of the region in Figures 6.2–6.4: Brazil, for which the relationship was strongly positive throughout the 40 years; Mexico, positive for the 1960s and 1970s, then non-significant and negative; and, Venezuela, non-significant for the entire period.

The variations suggest that policies may matter; that is, that there may be policies which foster and undermine the dynamic transmission of growth from exports to the rest of the economy. During the 1960–81 period, when industrial policy dominated the Latin American policy agenda, 15 of the countries displayed

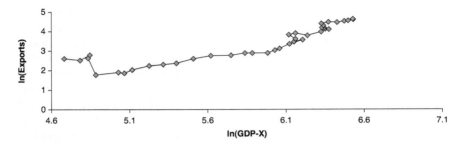

Figure 6.2   Brazil: Constant price exports and non-export GDP, 1960–99 (positive entire period).

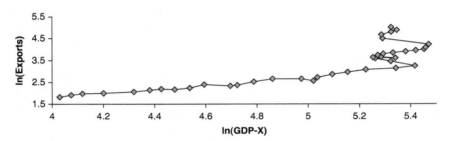

Figure 6.3   Mexico: Constant price exports and non-export GDP, 1960–99 (positive until 1980s, then negative).

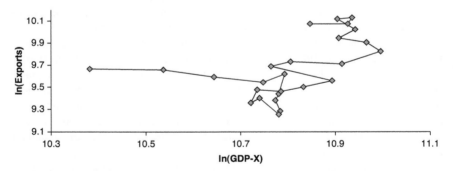

Figure 6.4   Venezuela: Constant price exports and non-export GDP, 1973–99 (negative entire period).

a positive link between exports and the non-export sector, while for the 1990s, when an 'outward-oriented' policy framework reigned, the number fell to ten. The average value of the elasticity in the 1990s was only marginally higher than during the 1980s,[12] when a lack of transmission dynamism might be explained by demand compression.

5   Parameters by country: foreign and domestic investment

As for exports and non-exports, the elasticity between foreign and domestic investment shares are calculated in a simple regression, reported in Table 6.3 for 18 countries. For these elasticities,[13] the first period covers the 1970s only because reliable statistics are not available for the earlier years. Recall that 'domestic' investment was estimated as total investment in the current year, minus foreign investment in the previous year. These calculated elasticities do not in themselves indicate direction of causality, though causality follows formally from our assumption that foreign direct investment is exogenous and domestic investment endogenous. There are strong reasons to believe that foreign investment crowds out or crowds in domestic investment and not the reverse. First, the cost of capital in the Latin American countries was higher over most of the 32 period than in the developed countries, especially in the 1980s and 1990s, in some years due to restrictive monetary policies. While in principle domestic agents could borrow in developed country money markets, once capital accounts were liberalized, in practise there were formidable barriers and high-risk premiums. Second, foreign firms typically enjoyed competitive advantages over national firms, through brand recognition and scale-economies in marketing. Mexico represented an example of the second effect in the 1990s, when foreign firms took over large shares of consumer markets (ECLAC 2000).

Turning to the statistics in Table 6.3, the most common outcome is a non-significant elasticity (34 out of 52 or 65 percent). The 18 statistically significant elasticities show strong evidence that foreign investment crowds out domestic investment, for ten are negative. This result supports the conclusion of Agosin and Mayer (2000) that crowding-out was a substantial phenomenon during the last three decades of the twentieth century (their data end in 1997).[14] For all years, 1970–97, seven countries show significant crowding-out coefficients, while for only two there is significant crowding-in. We are less interested in the statistics for all years because, again, our hypothesis is that the internal–external interaction, of investment in this case, varies over countries, and for countries over time. The elasticities by country and period support this view. Again, the variety of outcomes is shown graphically for three major countries in Figures 6.5–6.7. For Brazil the relationship is non-significant overall, and negative for Colombia. For Mexico, shown in Figure 6.7, the time pattern for exports and non-exports is repeated for foreign investment. During 1970–81, the relationship is strongly positive, non-significant in the 1980s, then negative in the 1990s.[15] Inspection of Table 6.3 shows that several other countries made a shift from positive to negative interaction.

6   External effects in a Harrod–Domar growth model

In the two previous sections, it was shown that there is considerable variation in the interaction of external and internal variables with regard to exports and investment. In this section, we investigate the impact of that variation on the growth of

Table 6.3 Elasticities between foreign direct investment and domestic fixed investment (estimated), Latin America, 1970–97

	All years	1970s	1980s	1990s
Argentina	−4.7	nsgn	nsgn	nsgn
Bolivia	na	na	nsgn	−0.6
Brazil	nsgn	nsgn	nsgn	nsgn
Chile	nsgn	nsgn	nsgn	nsgn
Colombia	−0.7	3.2	−1.3	−1.3
Costa Rica	nsgn	−1.1	nsgn	nsgn
Dom Rep	−0.4	−1.4	2.8	nsgn
Ecuador	−0.8	−1.1	nsgn	−0.8
El Salvador	3.7	6.1	nsgn	nsgn
Guatemala	nsgn	nsgn	nsgn	nsgn
Honduras	nsgn	nsgn	nsgn	nsgn
Mexico	−1.6	8.7	nsgn	−1.1
Nicaragua	nsgn	nsgn	nsgn	0.9
Panama	na	na	nsgn	3.2
Paraguay	nsgn	nsgn	nsgn	nsgn
Peru	nsgn	nsgn	nsgn	1.0
Uruguay	1.3	nsgn	3.0	−1.0
Venezuela	−2.0	nsgn	−10.4	nsgn
Average (nsgn=0)	−0.33	0.89	−0.32	−0.17
(excluding Venez.)			(0.27)	
pos/neg/nsgn	2/6/8	3/3/10	2/2/14	3/5/10

GDP, by use of a modified Harrod–Domar model.[16] As before, if the growth rate of export value added is y_x and non-export value added y_{nx}.

$$y_t = \alpha[y_{x_t}] + (1 - \alpha)[y_{nx_t}] \tag{7}$$

We assume, as above, that export growth is exogenously given, and the ratio of value added to gross output for exports is constant. Therefore, the rate of growth of export value added equals the rate of growth of exports (x).

$$y_{x_t} = x_t \tag{8}$$

The growth rate of non-export GDP is determined by the growth of effective demand. The two elements that determine the demand for the non-export sector are internal demand, approximated by aggregate investment, and the demand generated by the export sector.[17] Thus, if $(I/Y)_t = i_t$, and government expenditure (G) and taxes (R) grow at the same rate ($g_t - r_t = 0$), then the growth in non-export demand is:

$$y_{nxt} = \beta_1[i_t] + \beta_2[x_t] \tag{9a}$$

This differs from expression (8), above, in that it uses export growth instead of the growth rate of export value added. As a result, the weights will change,

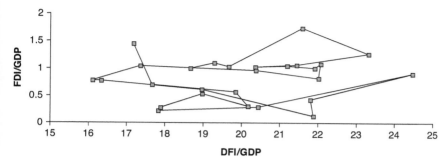

Figure 6.5 Brazil: FDI and 'domestic' fixed investment as percentages of GDP, 1970–97. (non-significant).

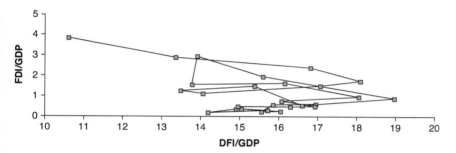

Figure 6.6 Colombia: FDI and 'domestic' fixed investment as percentages of GDP, 1970–97 (negative overall).

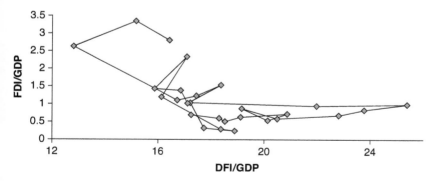

Figure 6.7 Mexico: FDI and 'domestic' fixed investment as percentages of GDP, 1970–97 (positive until 1980s, then negative).

calling for use of β in place of α (in general, $\alpha \neq \beta$). The coefficient β_2 incorporates two components. First, there is a demand effect by incomes generated in the export sector that are spent on non-export products, and the direct demand for intermediate products to produce exports. This is always positive. Second, the growth of exports may shift resources out of the non-export sector and wipe out domestic input suppliers. The combination of these effects is the overall elasticity of non-export output with respect to export output, discussed above. This elasticity, $Expt_t$, is assumed to be a structural parameter for each decade and country. This follows logically from assuming a decade as the relevant time period for estimating parameters. Investment itself is assumed to conform to a mechanism in which any period's actual investment rate reflects a partial adjustment to a desired rate. If the desired rate of investment is i_t^*, and is an adjustment-to-equilibrium φ coefficient,

$$i_t = i_{t-1} + \varphi[i_t^* - i_{t-1}] \tag{9b}$$

if $\varphi = 1$, $i_t = i_t^*$ (complete adjustment within one time period).

Desired investment is assumed to be import constrained and affected by the mix between outlays by foreign and domestic investors. Whether the latter influence is positive (crowding-in) or negative (crowding-out) is treated as an empirical question. Whether the one or the other is dominant depends on the structure of the economy and policies toward foreign investment, as discussed above.

If $Efdi_t$ is the elasticity of the share of foreign investment in GDP to the share for domestic investors (treated as a structural parameter by decade and country), and m_t is the growth rate of imports, one can write,

$$i_t^* = \sigma_1[m_t] + \sigma_2[Efdi_t] \tag{9c}$$

Import growth is assumed to be proportional to export growth in the long run, since:

1   $m > x$ implies a constant accumulation of foreign debt; and
2   $x > m$ is unsustainable, since all evidence shows that if $m > y$, implying that the share of exports in GDP would reach a limit as resources were increasingly transferred away from non-tradables and import substitutes.[18]

Thus,

$$m_t = [x_t] \tag{9d}$$

Substituting, collecting terms, and measuring the variables in logarithms, one obtains,

$$y_t = a_0 + a_1 [i_{t-1}] + a_2 [x_t] + a_3 [Efdi_t] \tag{10}$$

Table 6.4   Regression model for Latin American GDP growth data by decades, 1970–99

Variable	Coefficient	S.E	T-stat	Significance
(Constant)	0.070	0.021	3.259	0.002
[INVGDPt2]	0.025	0.012	1.974	0.055
[XPTGRWt]	0.188	0.050	3.753	0.001
D80S	−0.022	0.005	−4.226	0.000
EFDI	0.001	0.001	1.710	0.094
EXPT	0.021	0.009	2.202	0.033

R^2(adj) = 0.583 F = 14.675 @ 0.000   DF = 44
Implied reaction coefficient for DFI = 0.975

Notes
INVGDPt2 is the estimated domestic investment share in GDP, lagged two years.
XPTGRW is the real export growth.
D80S is a dummy variable for the 1980s.
EFDI is the calculated elasticity between FDI and GDI.
EXPT is the calculated elasticity between exports and non-export GDP.

The equation is estimated over three decades, with the data being averages by decade. Coefficients a_1 and a_2 are predicted to be positive. If crowding out predominates, as Table 6.2 suggests, and the benefits of a unit of foreign investment out-weigh the benefits of a unit of domestic investment, then a_3 will be positive or non-significant, and vice-versa. The same holds for coefficient a_3, with respect to exports and non-exports. The complete form taken by the estimating equation, which includes a dummy variable and the elasticity Expt as a structural parameter, is as follows:

$$y_t = a_0 + a_1[i_{t-1}] + a_2[x_t] + a_3[\text{Efdi}_t] \\ + a_4[\text{Expt}_t] + a_5 \text{D80s} + \varepsilon \qquad (11)$$

The statistical results are presented in Table 6.4. The predicted coefficients of the variables of the model are significant at 0.10 probability or less, and of the expected sign. The coefficient on the investment variable indicates that the adjustment to the desired level is almost complete for the model's lag structure (the adjustment coefficient is 0.975). Export growth is highly correlated with the GDP growth rate, and its coefficient implies that a ten percent increase in export growth (say, from 5 to 5.5 percent) increases overall growth by slightly less than 2 percent. These results were expected, and the point of the growth model is to assess the impact of possible complementarities or trade-offs between external and internal variables. Both of the elasticities are statistically significant and positive. They indicate that, for any level of investment and rate of export growth, crowding-in and the transmission of export dynamism to non-exports raises the overall growth rate.

Positive and significant coefficients for the elasticities are not an obvious outcome. Indeed it contradicts the simple outward-orientation story. With regard to exports, that story places emphasis upon export growth as such. A positive coefficient for inter-sectoral transmission indicates that the export growth rate is

Table 6.5 Decomposing difference in growth rates for Latin America, 1970s and 1990s

Growth rates	1970s	1990s
Actual	5.34	3.49
Change		−1.84
Difference due to:		
1. Export growth		0.06
2. Xpt/Nxpt elasticity		−0.61
net expt effect		−0.55
3. Investment/GDP		−0.12
4. Fdi/Dfi elasticity		−0.14
net *I/Y* effect		−0.26
Total		−0.81

subject to diminishing returns with respect to the overall growth rate. Exports in real terms cannot grow without limit. As the rate of growth rises, aggregate capacity utilization limits the extent to which the non-export sector can grow. The positive coefficient on $Expt_t$ indicates there to be an optimal rate of export growth, given the structure of an economy, in which the overall growth rate is maximized.

The statistical results tell a similar story for foreign direct investment. They indicate that stimulating foreign investment inflows will increase aggregate growth more, by increasing total investment, if there is some degree of crowding-in. In other words, the oft-listed advantages of foreign investment are not sufficient, in the Latin American case, to overcome the depressing effect of crowding-out on aggregate investment. To indicate the relative importance of the transmission of export dynamism and crowding-in, the regression model can be used to simulate counterfactuals. In 1987, we assume the aggregate investment rate and the export growth rate to be equal to the Latin American average for the 30 years (19.2 percent of GDP and 6.1 percent, respectively), and let the two elasticities vary over their observed ranges for the three decades (see Table 6.1). For convenience, the intercept term is adjusted so that the two simulations intersect when both elasticities are zero. The simulation lines indicate the gains in economic growth derivative from positive interaction between internal and external variables.

Table 6.5 provides a more specific simulation, in which the $Expt_t$ and $Efdi_t$ parameters for the 1970s are applied to the 1990s (see also Figure 6.8). The 1980s are excluded from the simulation because of the crisis nature of that decade. The exercise simulates the following counterfactual: What would have been the rate of growth of the Latin American countries in the 1990s, given the actual investment rate and export growth, if the elasticities of the 1970s had still applied between exports and non-export GDP, and between foreign and domestic investment? The first row of the table gives the cross-country average growth rate for the 1970s, when industrial policy set the framework for development policy, and

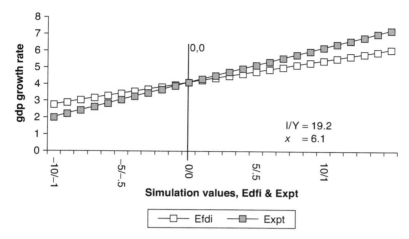

Figure 6.8 Simulated growth rates over the calculated range of elasticities between FDI & DFI, and exports & non-export GDP, Latin America, 1970–97.

the 1990s, when 'outward-orientation' was the agenda. In the subsequent rows are calculations of the difference in growth rates between the two decades attributed to the different variables in the model.[19] The relationship between exports and non-export GDP was 0.51 in the 1970s and 0.22 in the 1990s; the corresponding numbers for the interaction of foreign and domestic investment were 0.89 and −0.17, respectively. We can note that the model generates a very slight increase in growth, 0.06 percentage points, as a result of the margin rise in the growth rate of exports, and a decline in growth of 0.12 percentage points due to the fall in investment. However, because of a substantial fall in the transmission of export growth to the non-export sector, the net effect of the slightly higher export performance of the 1990s was to reduce the overall rate of growth by 0.55 percentage points. Put another way, because of the decline in the transmission of export dynamism, the same growth stimulus provided by export growth of 7.5 percent in the 1970s would have required a growth rate of 10.7 percent in the 1990s.

The aggregate investment rate was lower in the 1990s than the 1970s, and the model associated a small, 0.14 percentage point decline in growth as a result. Because of the shift from crowding-in to crowding-out, the net fall in growth associated with investment performance was 0.26 percentage points. This is the equivalent of a one percentage point 'discounting' of the aggregate investment rate; that is, an investment rate of 21.2 percent of GDP would have been required in the 1990s to achieve the same growth stimulus that the 20.2 percent rate achieved in the 1970s. In an important sense, investment in Latin America was less efficient in terms of stimulating growth in the 1990s than in the 1970s. The model implies that taken together the lost of export dynamism and the shift from crowding-in to crowding-out reduced growth across Latin American countries by three-quarters of a percentage point, 40 percent of the difference in the growth rates between the 1970s and 1990s. Overall export and investment performance in the 1990s compared to the 1970s reduced growth by slightly more, by 0.81 percentage points (last row of Table 6.4). These simulations have important policy implications, which are pursued in the concluding section.

7   Policy and outward orientation

It has become an article of faith that 'opening' a country to international trade and investment flows will improve growth performance.[20] Any change in a trade or capital account regime involves policy decisions to minimize the cost and maximize the benefits of the outcome sought, which in this case is an increase in economic growth. The conventional wisdom holds that the growth outcome will be optimized by the reduction of government regulations. This policy prescription is applied to all countries, with rare exceptions, and, by the nature of its general application it is implied that all countries should take the same path to openness. There is little theoretical justification for this generalized approach. For example, Pritchett has demonstrated that 'openness' has a variety of meanings, each measured differently, and the various measures are not, in general, correlated (Pritchett 1996).

This paper has treated the issue of openness and growth from an empirical perspective. We defined 'export dynamism' as the transmission of export growth to the non-export economy, and viewed foreign investment in terms of whether it crowds-in or crowds-out domestic investment. Using these concepts, the principal results are the following:

1   Among the Latin American countries, and for individual countries over time, great differences appear in the degree of export dynamism, and whether crowding-in or crowding-out dominates the capital market;
2   Simulation exercises indicate that the impact on growth of the degree of export dynamism and the predominance of crowding-in or crowding-out is considerable; and
3   These empirical differences do not seem explained by size of country or simple structural characteristics such as whether exports are dominated by petroleum.

Therefore, we conclude that the differences across countries and over time are, to a substantial degree, policy-driven.

Most Latin American countries in the 1990s had substantially reduced government regulations with respect to exporting and capital flows. The outcomes with regard to export dynamism and investment 'crowding' varied greatly across countries. Indeed, for only one country (Bolivia) did export dynamism improve in the 1990s compared to the 1970s, and for the region on average there was a shift towards crowding-out. An analysis of why this shift occurred is beyond the scope of this paper, though it may have in part resulted from the heavy debt burden inflicting many of the countries of the region (Borensztein 1990).

The empirical results suggest that policies matter for stimulating growth, and the deregulation path to openness was not appropriate for all countries. For some countries of the region, the structure of the economy and institutions may imply that trade and capital account deregulation would facilitate export dynamism and complementarity between domestic and foreign investments. However, it would appear that for a substantial number of the countries this is not the case, and a range of policies, consistent with multilateral rules, could be used to achieve a more growth-oriented outcome. The central issue is not whether governments should foster openness, but what policy best does so given the circumstances of each country. Equating openness with a particular policy to achieve it (deregulation) is to confuse instruments with outcomes. It would seem appropriate to look back at a literature on 'openness', where critical views could be found, that stressed costs as well as benefits.[21] The general thrust of expert opinion before the political shift that brought on the Washington Consensus was that policies towards FDI and the export sector should be part of a government's general development strategy[22] rather than derivative from abstract, *a priori* principles.

Notes

1 Net flows of foreign direct investment to Latin America continued to increase at the end of the 1990s, even though total capital flows declined (ECLAC 1999: 11–12).
2 For a detailed discussion, see UNCTAD (1998). The report observes, 'The increasing importance of [mergers and acquisitions] as a mode of entry [of FDI] give[s] rise to concerns over the loss of national control over enterprises ...' (UNCTAD 1998: 21).
3 In other words, if GDP had grown in the 1990s at the rate of the 1970s, the ratio FDI/GDP in the 1990s would have been on the trend line implied by 1970–81.
4 In a summary of the literature, a paper commissioned by the World Bank presents a generally favourable review of the impact of FDI, but comes to no general conclusion about specific benefits (Blomstrom & Kokko 1999). Hanson concludes that 'there is weak evidence that FDI generates positive spillovers for host countries' (Hanson 2001: 1). Even this minimalist statement might not apply in all cases. In a study of Morocco for the second half of the 1980s, Haddad '... reject[s] the hypothesis that foreign presences accelerated productivity growth in domestic firms' (Haddad 1992: 51).
5 For example,

> 'It remains an unanswered question whether the transnational corporations' presence is a force for reducing competition, and therefore efficiency ... or whether transnational corporations bring more efficient practices to industries that are already concentrated ...'
>
> (UNCTAD 1992: 8)

Six years later, the World Investment Report was more definitive:

> 'Worldwide cross-border [mergers and acquisitions] ... were aimed at the global restructuring or strategic positioning of firms ... One outcome is a greater industrial concentration in the hands of a few firms in each industry, usually [transnational corporations].'
>
> (UNCTAD 1998: 10)

6 Because actual export growth varies across countries, the implicit assumption is that it is determined by domestic supply conditions. This, in turn, rules out 'fallacy of competition' effects, which may be too optimistic. Faini found 'that for a representative LDC a large share, almost 60%, of the benefits of devaluation on export revenues vanish when other LDC competitors pursue similar policies'

> (Faini 1990: 1).

7   These spread affects correspond to what Kaldor called the 'super-multiplier' (Kaldor 1979).

8   Along the same line, Skott and Larudee conclude, '...liberalisation is likely to bring long-run industrialisation in the Mexican case, but...this strategy implies substantial costs to a large segment of the population in the short and medium term' (Skott and Larudee 1998: 277). Theory suggests that in the absence of policy intervention, domestic linkages would be minor in Mexico (see Rodriguez-Clare 1996: 867).

9   Though defined as direct investment in national statistics, capital inflows may not represent asset accumulation rather than investment as such. For a discussion of problems of measurement, see Agosin and Mayer (2000).

10 The elasticity of non-export GDP with respect to exports is not calculated for Panama because of the high proportion of re-exports in that country's trade statistics.

11 These are the only two countries for which there are no consistent data for the 1960s. If the elasticities for the other two countries are calculated for the 1970s only, none show negative elasticities.

12 This refers to the average when non-significant values are treated as zero.

13 Note that these elasticities are between *shares*, not (for example) dollar for dollar. This accounts for the rather high numbers for some countries in some periods.

14 Agosin and Mayer apply their model across all Latin American countries, and find that crowding out dominates in the long run (as specified in their model).

15 For a detailed discussion of Mexico, see Weeks and Dagdeviren (2000). De Mello also comes to a 'crowding-out' conclusion about FDI in Mexico: 'In the case of Mexico, the positive rend in FDI may be offsetting the negative trend in capital formation' (De Mello 1999: 148).

16 This is similar to the model used in Weeks (2000).

17 The inclusion of export growth follows Kaldor's concept of the 'super-multiplier' (Kaldor 1979).

18 If there are no re-exports, the ratio of export value added to GDP cannot exceed 100 percent. Empirical evidence shows that the practical limit is far less than this, closer to fifty per cent, because the public sector, transport, utilities and commerce produce non-tradeables for the most part.

19 The investment rate during the 1970s was 20.2 percent of GDP, compared to 19.2 per cent in the 1990s, while the rate of growth of exports rose from 7.5 to 7.8.

20 See discussion by Kozul-Wright and Rowthorn:

> Economists have, by and large...suggested that a failure to attract FDI will mean losing out on the potential benefits of globalization. Faith in these benefits has underpinned support for ... liberalizing investment.
>
> (Kozul-Wright and Rowthorn 1998: 74)

21 For example, Hymer (1976) and Hymer and Rowthorn (1970). In the same vein is the more recent article by Kozul-Wright and Rowthorn (1998: 87–89).

22 This approach is taken in Kosacoff and Ramos (1999) and Held and Szalachman (1998).

References

Agosin, M. R. and Mayer, R. (2000) 'Foreign Investment in Developing Countries: Does it Crowd in Domestic Investment?', UNCTAD Discussion Paper No. 146, Geneva: UNCTAD.

Blomstrom, M. and Kokko, A. (1999) 'How Foreign Investment Affects Host Countries' *Policy Research Working Papers*, Washington, DC: World Bank.

Borensztein, E. (1990) 'Debt Overhang, Credit Rationing and Investment,' *Journal of Development Economics,* 32(2): 315–35.

Brewer, T. and Young, S. (1995) 'Towards a Multilateral Framework for Foreign Direct Investment: Issues and Scenarios,' *Transnational Corporations,* 4(1): 69–83.

De Mello, L. R., Jr. (1999) 'Foreign Direct Investment-Led Growth: Evidence from Time Series and Panel Data,' *Oxford Economic Papers,* 51: 133–151.

De Pinies, J. (1989) 'Debt Sustainability and Overadjustment', *World Development,* 17(1).

Dollar, D. (1992) 'Outward-oriented Developing Economies Really Do Grow More Rapidly: Evidence from 95 LDCs, 1976–1985,' *Economic Development and Cultural Change,* 40(3).

ECLAC (Economic Commission for Latin America and the Caribbean) (1999) *Preliminary Overview of the Economies of Latin America and the Caribbean,* Santiago: ECLAC.

—— (2000) *Foreign Investment in Latin America and the Caribbean: 1999 Report,* Santiago: ECLAC.

Faini, R. (1990) 'The Fallacy of Composition Argument: Does Demand Matter for LDC Manufactured Exports?', Centre for Economic Policy Research Working Paper 499, London: CEPR.

Greene, J. and Villanueva, D. (1991) 'Private Investment in Developing Countries: An Empirical Analysis,' *IMF Staff Papers,* 38(1).

Haddad, M. (1992) 'Are There Positive Spillovers form from Direct Foreign Investment? Evidence from Panel Data for Morocco', *Journal of Development Economics,* 42(1): 51–74.

Hanson, G. H. (2001) 'Should Countries Promote Foreign Direct Investment?', G-24 Discussion Paper Series No. 9, Geneva: UNCTAD.

Held, G. and Szalachman, R. (1998) 'External Capital Flows in Latin America and the Caribbean in the 1990s: Experiences and Policies', *CEPAL Review,* 64: 29–47.

Hymer, S. (1976) *The International Operations of National Firms: A study of direct foreign investment,* Cambridge: MIT Press.

Hymer, S. and Rowthorn, R. (1970) 'Multinational Corporations and International Oligopoly: The Non-American Challenge,' in C. P. Kindelberger (ed.), *The International Corporation,* Cambridge: MIT Press.

Kaldor, N. (1979) 'Comment,' in F. Blackaby (ed.), *De-Industrialisation,* London: Heinemann.

Kosacoff, B. and Ramos, A. (1999) 'The Industrial Policy Debate,' *CEPAL Review,* 68: 35–60.

Kozul-Wright, R. and Rowthorn, R. (1998) 'Spoilt for Choice? Multinational Corporations and the Geography of International Production,' *Oxford Review of Economic Policy,* 14(2): 74–92.

Mallampally, P. and Sauvant, K. (1999) 'Foreign Direct Investment in Developing Countries', *Finance and Development,* 36(1).

Pritchett, L. (1996) 'Measuring Outward Orientation in LDCs: Can It be Done?', *Journal of Development Economics* 49(2): 307–35.

Rodriguez-Clare, A. (1996) 'Multinationals, Linkages and Economic Development', *American Economic Review,* 86(4): 852–73.

Skott, P. and Larudee, M. (1998) 'Uneven Development and the Liberalisation of Trade and Capital Flows: The Case of Mexico,' *Cambridge Journal of Economics,* 22: 277–95.

UNCTAD (United Nations Conference on Trade and Development) (1992) *World Investment Report: Transnational Corporations as Engines of Growth,* Geneva: UNCTAD.

—— (1998) *World Investment Report: Trends and Determinants,* Geneva: UNCTAD.

—— (1999) *World Investment Report: Foreign Direct Investment and the Challenge of Development,* Geneva: UNCTAD.

UNCTC (United Nations Centre on Transnational Corporations) (1991) *Transnational Banks and Debt-Equity Conversions,* New York: United Nations Centre on Transnational Corporations.

Weeks, J. (2000) 'Latin America and the 'High Performing Asian Economies': Growth and Debt,' *Journal of International Development,* 12: 625–54.

Weeks, J. and Dagdeviren, H. (2000) 'The State of Poverty in Mexico: The Macro Policy Context', A Report to the Department of International Development, London, UK: SOAS & DFID.

7 Real exchange rates, labor markets and manufacturing exports in a global perspective

*Massoud Karshenas**

1 Introduction

Free trade and flexible foreign exchange and labor market regimes are assumed as essential preconditions for successful integration into the global economy in much of the economics literature on globalization. The dynamics of integration of hitherto closed and regulated economies into the global economy, however, are much more complex than assumed in the literature. In this paper we examine aspects of these complex dynamic processes related to the behavior of real exchange rates and labor markets. This is attempted by studying the behavior of real exchange rates and their constituent elements in the adjustment experiences of a number of less developed economies in Asia, Latin America, Africa and the Middle East during the 1970s and the 1980s decades. These two decades were turbulent years in the international economy during which the less developed economies had to adjust to two major oil price shocks, wide primary commodity price fluctuations, increased exchange rate uncertainties and financial instability, and a general slowdown in the world economy relative to the 1960s.

The timing and the intensity of the impact of external shocks on different developing economies has been varied, and there has also been a diversity of experiences in the ability of the different economies to adjust to the new circumstances. On the whole the Asian countries were relatively more successful in adjusting to the adverse external shocks, and they achieved some of the highest rates of growth in the world economy during these two decades. Countries in Africa, the Middle East, and Latin America on the other hand faced considerable difficulties in adjusting their economies to the new external circumstances with a significant slowdown in their growth performance in this period. The relative success of Asian countries was by and large due to their ability to achieve fast rates of manufacturing export growth during this period of economic instability and slowdown in the international economy (see Karshenas 1998). The relationship between real exchange rates, manufacturing competitiveness and export performance, therefore, furnishes the entry point in this chapter into the analysis of the role of labor markets, and more specifically wage flexibility, in global economic adjustments.

In Section 2 we start by a decomposition of real exchange rate, as an index of manufacturing price competitiveness, into its constituent elements of unit labor costs and other variable and fixed costs. A distinction is also made between the manufacturing real exchange rate and the real unit value of manufacturing exports as indicators of price competitiveness. In Section 3 we examine the relationship between the two notions of real exchange rate and unit labor costs over economic cycles and in the long run across the sample countries. In Section 4 we explore the long-term relationship between manufacturing exports and real exchange rates and Section 5 examines the short-term dynamics of this relationship. Section 6 extends the analysis to the role of wage costs in manufacturing price competitiveness and conclusions are discussed in Section 7.

2   Unit labor costs and real exchange rates

The discussion of the role of labor market flexibility in manufacturing competitiveness in the literature has mainly focused on price competitiveness issues. A useful starting point in this respect would be to consider the relation between the real exchange rate and manufacturing export performance. There seems to be some consensus amongst a large number of economists on the significance of the behavior of real exchange rate for economic growth in general and for manufacturing export competitiveness in particular. Summarizing the various empirical findings on this, Helleiner (1995) concludes, "The real exchange rate may be a more reliable predictor of long-term economic performance than *any* of the variety of measures of trade policy openness" (1995: 28). Of course, as Helleiner points out, this does not say much about the direction of causality between real exchange rate and economic performance.[1] In fact, from the point of view of the manufacturing sector, the real exchange rate is nothing other than an index of price competitiveness of the sector. And as long as price competitiveness is assumed to be central to export growth, one would expect a close association between manufacturing competitiveness, the real exchange rate and export performance. There are however a number of important considerations which make the relation between the real exchange rate and manufacturing export performance more than just a truism. First, as it is recognized in the international economics literature, price competitiveness is not the only determinant of export growth. Other nonprice factors such as quality and variety changes are also important. Second, from the point of view of an economy in transition from a closed and protected state to a more open and export oriented state, it will not be of great help to reiterate that once an appropriate real exchange rate is achieved all will be well.[2] The conditions under which the appropriate exchange rate would be attained and the trajectory of the movement of the exchange rate toward that appropriate state are of crucial importance. It may be the case also that the "appropriate" exchange rate may itself be path dependent, and hence its definition, independent of the trajectory which takes us there, would be meaningless. These points become particularly important in any study of the role of labor market flexibility, and in particular wage flexibility, in the adjustment process.

We need to distinguish between three aspects of the behavior of the real exchange rate or the index of price competitiveness. The first aspect refers to the *level* of the real exchange rate; does the level of the real exchange rate properly reflect production efficiency in the manufacturing sector of the country in question? In other words, posing the same question in terms of the labor market considerations: are real wages commensurate with the level of productivity of labor and industrial skills in the country in question? The second dimension refers to the secular movements in the real exchange rate index, as well as its cyclical adjustments in response to external shocks. Has the behavior of the real exchange rate been in conformity with the requirements of adjustment to external shocks, such as adverse terms of trade movements, etc.? And if not, what has been the role of labor market (wage) rigidity in the process? The third aspect refers to the stability of the real exchange rate and the role of labor markets institutions therein. Is there a link between real exchange rate stability and export performance? And if so, what role has real wage rigidity played in such instability?

The empirical investigation of the last two sets of questions, namely, the stability and the trends in the movement of the real exchange rates in different countries over time, and their relation to manufacturing export performance are relatively straightforward. However, the first set of questions, namely, those relating to the "absolute value" of the real exchange rate and its comparison across the countries, raise vexing problems for empirical research mainly related to the choice of an appropriate base point price system which "truly" reflects competitiveness across the countries. The problem, from the point of view of manufacturing sector, is that to compare price competitiveness across countries we need to take into account the differences in product quality and technological sophistication of products in different countries.[3] Because here our main focus is on the links between wage flexibility and real exchange rate movements in the process of adjustment, we shall be mainly concerned with the last two sets of questions. As we shall observe below, however, in investigating the links between the real exchange rate movements and export performance one would be inevitably drawn into the questions pertaining to the comparison of absolute levels of real exchange rates as well.[4]

From the point of view of the manufacturing sector, the real exchange rate can be defined as an index of final product prices relative to those of the competitor countries denominated in the same currency. We shall denote this index as:

$$\text{RER} = \frac{e.P}{P^*} \tag{1}$$

where P is the domestic manufacturing price index, P^* is the composite price index of manufacturing prices in competitor countries denominated in dollars, and e is the dollar value of the domestic exchange rate. A rise in this index indicates an appreciation of the real exchange rate, or loss of price competitiveness, and a decline indicates a depreciation of the real exchange rate. To investigate the role of wage flexibility in competitiveness, we need to decompose the real exchange rate into different constituent parts reflecting wage competitiveness and other elements. For this purpose, the value of manufacturing output can be decomposed into the following elements:

Output $\equiv$ Wage Cost + Other Variable Costs + Profits

$$O.P \equiv W.L + (P_m \cdot m + R) + \pi.k.P_k$$

where O is the real value of output, W, L, P_m and m are, respectively, nominal wage rate, employment, output price, and the quantity of intermediate inputs in manufacturing. R denotes interest charges on working capital loans by the sector, and π, k, and P_k, respectively, refer to the rate of profit, real capital stock, and price index for capital stock. Assuming working capital loans are a proportion (α) of the flow of intermediate inputs, R can be written as, $R = \alpha.r.P_m.m$, where r is the interest rate. Without any prior assumptions about the interrelation between different variables, we can use the above identity to decompose the variation in prices into various elements. Dividing both sides of the equation by O and substituting for R we get:

$$P \equiv \frac{W}{O/L} + \frac{m}{O}.P_m(1 + \alpha.r) + \frac{k}{O}.\pi.P_k \tag{2}$$

Substituting P from equation (2) into (1), and denoting labor productivity as v, and the dollar price of intermediate inputs and investment goods as P_m^* and P_k^* respectively, we get:

$$\text{RER} = \frac{e.P}{P^*} \equiv \left(\frac{W.e}{v.P^*}\right) + \frac{m}{O}.\frac{P_m^*}{P^*}(1 + \alpha.r) + \frac{k}{O}.\frac{\pi.P_k^*}{P^*} \tag{3}$$

The right hand side variables in equation (3) characterize the main elements, which affect manufacturing price competitiveness. Of these, the term $(W.e / v.P^*)$ is directly relevant to the role of wage flexibility in price competitiveness. It denotes the unit cost of labor in dollars divided by the dollar index of international manufacturing prices. In what follows we shall refer to this variable as the real unit labor cost, keeping in mind that it differs from the usual definition of unit labor costs.[5] A devaluation of the nominal exchange rate, given money wages and other variables on the right hand side of equation (3) is expected to lead to a fall in real exchange rate by reducing the real unit labor costs. The same result could be achieved by a proportionate increase in labor productivity for given values of money wage rates and nominal exchange rate. In Section 6, we shall examine the behavior of the real unit labor costs for the countries in our sample.

The second term on the right hand side of equation (3) characterizes the influences of nonwage variable costs in price competitiveness. The ratio of raw materials to industrial output (m/O) is expected to change in the long run, along with changes in manufacturing technology as well as output composition in the sector. The relative price of raw materials $\frac{P_m}{P*}$ can be subject to various influences. In an economy where industrial raw materials are freely traded without any import and export restrictions, this variable indicates the international terms of trade for industrial raw materials vis-à-vis manufacturing output for the country in question.[6] An adverse terms of trade movement (e.g. resulting from an oil price shock) can lead to loss of price competitiveness unless it is neutralized by other factors, e.g. a devaluation of the exchange rate to bring about an appropriate reduction in the wage costs.[7] Some countries may also insulate their domestic manufacturing against such adverse terms of trade shocks by providing direct input subsidies to the sector (e.g. insulating the domestic agricultural raw material prices from the international price movements, or instituting a dual exchange rate regime with preferential treatment for imported manufacturing inputs). In a similar manner interest rate changes, e.g. following financial liberalization, can reduce competitiveness unless countervailing changes take place in other right hand side variables in the above equation.

The third factor in equation (3) refers to the behavior of unit profits. The relative price element of this (i.e. P^*_K/p^*) invokes the same considerations as those of P*/P* discussed above. An important influence arising from this third factor, i.e. the unit profit factor, belongs to the capital output ratio (k/O), which can have significant variations over the economic cycle, and can also vary in a significant way with other variables in the equation. For example, a devaluation of the exchange rate resulting in a reduction in real wages, can lead to an increase in capital output ratio due to its deflationary effect on the domestic economy. This, given the international terms of trade in foreign currency (that is P^*k/P^* and P^*_m/P^*) can lead to a squeeze on the rate of profit (π) or an increase in P neutralizing the original devaluation, depending on market conditions and the degree of protection afforded to the sector by the government. If domestic manufacturing prices cannot be increased because of the intensity of foreign competition following trade liberalization and the government's contractionary monetary and fiscal policy, then the deflationary effects of a devaluation would be further enhanced by a squeeze in profits and the downsizing of investment plans by the business community.

Of course, according to conventional theory such a profit squeeze is likely to be confined to the domestic oriented industries, while export oriented enterprises can benefit from an increase in export demand resulting from the original devaluation of the exchange rate. Such relative profitability change is in fact the mechanism through which economic liberalization combined with exchange rate devaluation is meant to redirect resources to more profitable export oriented industries. In a growing economy with high rates of growth of investment and productivity improvements, and where the manufacturing sector is already well integrated in the international economy with reasonable levels of production efficiency, this mechanism is expected to work effectively. In such economies, marginal changes in the real exchange rate may be sufficient to reinstate profitability and encourage exports in the face of an adverse external or internal shock, e.g. adverse external terms of trade shocks or adverse internal productivity shocks. The main mechanism is to maintain the final product prices at a competitive level while maintaining profitability by creating a wedge between the real exchange rate ($P.e/P^*$) and the product wages ($W.e/v.P^*$), sufficient to compensate for the adverse terms of trade shock.

However, in hitherto closed economies where the manufacturing sector has been mainly geared to production for the domestic market, the reorientation of production toward export markets is a much more complicated and drawn out process. Old production equipment needs to be renovated or scrapped, new export oriented lines need to be established through new investment, new contacts need to be established in the international market, new institutions need to be devised to alleviate the enhanced business risk resulting from operation in the international market, etc. Such structural changes, however, are of a relatively longer term nature, with a totally different time profile from the responses of the other variables discussed above. In the meantime the impact of the devaluation and liberalization program, especially if it is of the "shock therapy" type administered to some of the Eastern European economies, would be to plunge the economy into a deep recession. Although the foreign currency value of manufacturing prices relative to world prices can fall significantly in this process, unless this is combined by large scale scrapping of old capital and lay-off of labor, whereby undue squeeze on profit rates is prevented, this would not mean a genuine improvement in competitiveness. The same can happen without a devaluation of the nominal exchange rate, in countries that resort to import compression combined with protection of inefficient industries, where real wages and hence dollar unit labor costs can be falling without a commensurate improvement in the price competitiveness.[8] In such economies profitability is maintained entirely at the expense of real wages in the short-run, without the long run beneficial effects that the conventional adjustment measures can bring about.

The above analysis points to an important issue in assessing the role of devaluations in the process of adjustment; that is, devaluations are most effective when they create a wedge between the real exchange rate and the unit labor costs rather than reducing the real exchange rate *per se*. Because, as seen above, real devaluations which do not increase this gap can lead to a squeeze in profits and hence do not constitute a genuine improvement in competitiveness. In dynamic economies which are well integrated into the international economy and resort to devaluations to neutralize an adverse terms of trade shock, this gap is generated by growth of wages lagging behind the growth of labor productivity. In protected economies which resort to devaluations, at a time of economic crisis, as a part of the adjustment mechanism to open up to the international economy and become more competitive, this would initially take the form of a combination of a decline in real wages and improved productivity resulting from other necessary measures taken to gradually renovate and improve production efficiency of the existing equipment, as well as those resulting from investment in new equipment. In the latter type economies, if the other necessary restructuring measures are not introduced, the main burden of the real devaluation will be carried by wage earners. This could easily lead to a spiral of lower wages, lower labor productivity, and lower profits (due to the rise in capital output ratio as well as adverse productivity effects of wages falling below efficiency wages), which despite a substantial apparent real devaluation (i.e. lower dollar prices relative to international prices) does not improve competitiveness and export performance. A typical example is the situation of the Russian economy in the 1990s and some other developing economies during similar "shock therapy" episodes, e.g. Chile in the 1970s.

At this stage it may appear that the above analysis is contrary to the empirical evidence which exists on price responsiveness of manufacturing exports from the less developed countries. This is not so. To clarify this point, we need to introduce a further notion of the real exchange rate which has been the focal point of empirical studies on price responsiveness of exports; that is, *the relative price of manufactured exports denominated in foreign currency over the prevailing prices in competitor countries.* We shall refer to this concept of real exchange rate, which is normally used in the export demand functions in estimating price responsiveness of exports, as the *relative unit value of exports.* There is a crucial difference between the concept of real exchange rate discussed above and its relation to export performance, and the price responsiveness of exports in relation to changes in the relative unit value of exports. The former, which has been the main issue of our discussion so far, is expected to influence exports by changing the profitability of exporting relative to the production for the domestic market. And this they will achieve if other necessary policies to promote exports are already in place. This process, as discussed above, involves a restructuring of the domestic industry which could be costly and takes time. The price index used in measuring this definition of the real exchange rate refers to the entire manufacturing sector. The relative unit value of exports, on the other hand, is based on the price index of existing exports. Exports may be highly responsive to relative unit value changes, but the dollar prices of exports may not necessarily respond to exchange rate devaluations (we shall discuss the empirical evidence on this below). The way devaluations lead to improved export performance is not mainly through increased quantities of the same exports through price reductions but rather through a greater variety of products becoming more profitable to export. This is not because the demand for exports is price inelastic, but because the supply price may not be sensitive to exchange rate changes in the short to medium run.[9] In the long run, the relative movement of the two real exchange rates, namely the one defined from the export side as compared to the one defined from the manufacturing sector side, also depends on the relative productivity improvements in export industries vis-à-vis the manufacturing sector as a whole, as well as the changes in the composition of exports and quality improvements which affect the export unit values.[10]

Any realistic analysis of the role of wage flexibility in price competitiveness and export performance needs to distinguish between these two notions of real exchange rate and the various determinants of real exchange rate discussed above. In Section 3, we shall focus on the empirical evidence regarding the behavior of the real exchange rate in relation to the movements in labor costs as well as the relative export unit values.

3   Unit labor costs, real exchange rates, and export prices

The movement of the real exchange rate index for 26 countries in Asia, Africa, the Middle East, and Latin America are shown in Figures 7.1, 7.2, and 7.3, respectively. The domestic price index in each case was calculated as the manufacturing price index denominated in domestic currency, and the world price index (P^*) was measured as a weighted index of manufacturing prices in 33 countries in U.S. dollar denomination[11]. In addition to the real exchange rate index, the diagrams also show the index of the real unit labor costs as defined above,[12] as well as the relative price of manufacturing exports. The relative price of exports is measured as the ratio of export unit values over the world price index (P^*) as defined above.[13]

The movements of the three variables for each country have specificities of their own which need to be studied in the context of the economic structures and policies in the country in question. Here, we will be mainly concerned with possible similarities within and across the regions which could be observed in the general behavior of the series and their co-movement. The main aim is to see whether the more successful Asian economies as a group show any distinct characteristics compared with other regions.

The first observation is that, as expected, the co-movements in the real exchange rate and the unit labor costs are much more closely synchronized than the movement of the relative export prices in relation to any of these two variables. What is particularly remarkable is that relative export prices remain stable during periods of wild cyclical fluctuations in real exchange rate and unit labor costs. In this respect, there are no noticeable differences between the Asian economies and other economies in the sample.

The second noticeable feature is the relatively large depreciation of the real exchange rates and unit labor costs in most countries during the 1980s. As the figures show, with the clear exception of Korea and Singapore, in almost all the sample countries across the regions there has been a substantial devaluation of the real exchange rate during the 1980s. In this respect also there does not seem to be major differences between the high performing countries in Asia, with the exception of Korea and Singapore, and the countries in other regions. The real exchange rate in Korea has remained remarkably stable as compared to other sample countries, only starting what appears to be an upward trend led by unit labor costs from the late 1980s.[14] Singapore is distinct in following a continuous upward trend both in the real exchange rate and unit labor costs throughout the period. Other countries in Asia do not seem to have experienced real exchange rate movements which, either in their cyclical variations or in their secular movements, are not shared by various other countries in other regions.

An important question that follows from the discussion of the previous section, relates to the behavior of the real exchange rate during the primary commodity price boom of the early 1970s and the oil price boom of the early 1980s, and its implications for export performance. Is there a systematic difference in the real exchange rate variations during the two oil price shocks between the successful

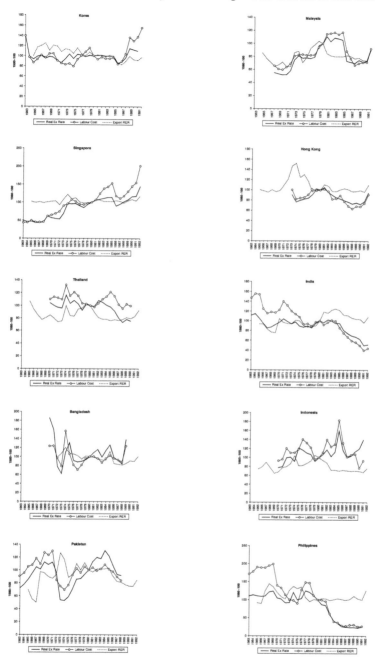

Figure 7.1 Real exchange rates, unit labor costs and relative export unit values in Asia, 1963–92.

Source: Based on UNIDO (1995) and World Bank (1995).

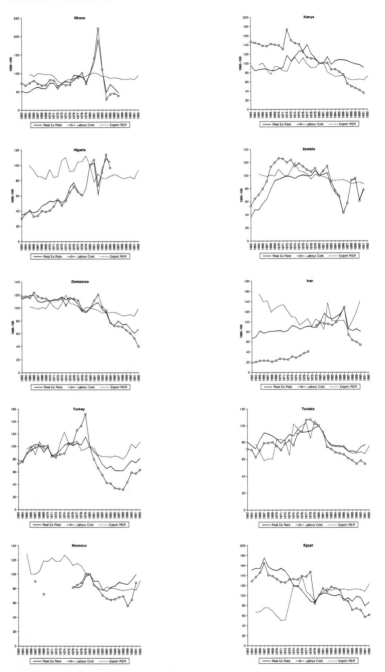

Figure 7.2 Real exchange rates, unit labour costs and relative export unit values in Africa and the Middle East, 1963–92.
Source: Based on UNIDO (1995) and World Bank (1995).

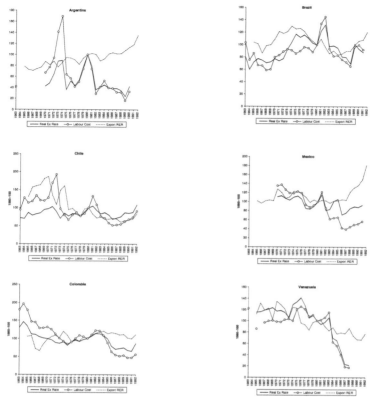

Figure 7.3 Real exchange rates, unit labor costs and relative export unit values in Latin America, 1963–92.

Source: Based on UNIDO (1995) and World Bank (1995).

adjusters and other countries? And how is this related to manufacturing export performance? To address this question we have divided the 1963–92 period into five subperiods separated by the two oil price shock periods of 1971–75 and 1979–81, as shown in Table 7.1. The table shows the average annual changes in real exchange rates and real unit labor costs during the five subperiods in different sample countries. As can be seen, the pattern of real exchange rate behavior across the countries during the first oil price boom (1971–75) does not indicate any distinct differences between the Asian countries and others in the sample. Oil economies such as Malaysia and Indonesia in Asia exhibit the same pattern of real exchange rate revaluation as oil economies in other regions. With the exception of India, Pakistan, and to some extent Bangladesh, the revaluation of the real exchange rate in the rest of the Asian countries during 1971–75 was higher than any other subperiod, and also surpassed those of many other countries in the rest of the regions during 1971–75. Similar observations can be also made about the

Table 7.1 Average annual changes in real exchange rates, real product wages, and relative export unit values, 1965–92

	1 Real exchange rate					2 Dollar unit labour costs (W.e/vP*)					3 Relative export unit values (export RER)				
	1965–71	1971–75	1975–79	1979–81	1980–92	1965–71	1971–75	1975–79	1979–81	1980–92	1965–71	1971–75	1975–79	1979–81	1980–92
Asia															
Korea	-2.9	2.8	0.8	-0.1	0.8	-1.8	-2.7	9.0	-10.7	3.1	1.8	-2.2	-0.9	-2.6	-1.1
Malaysia	-2.2	11.4	4.6	6.7	-3.5	-1.2	7.2	2.5	9.8	-4.3	-3.8	5.0	9.9	-10.0	-1.0
Singapore	2.6	16.9	-1.5	5.8	1.4	5.7	11.5	-3.0	4.9	3.2	0.4	3.8	-3.4	4.7	0.5
Hong Kong	na	na	5.8	1.9	-2.1	na	na	5.0	1.2	-2.7	1.0	-8.2	-6.8	3.5	-0.2
Thailand	na	2.5	-1.8	-1.7	-3.8	na	2.0	-3.9	-2.4	-0.2	-4.0	4.1	5.6	-7.2	-1.6
India	-1.9	-3.2	1.1	0.7	-6.2	-2.5	-6.6	-2.4	-3.2	-8.1	0.9	1.5	-2.4	14.1	-1.1
Bangladesh	na	-0.6	-7.0	8.0	0.0	na	1.7	-2.0	2.2	0.8	na	3.8	-2.2	-1.5	-2.1
Indonesia	na	7.7	-6.5	7.7	1.3	na	3.4	-5.6	7.3	-2.7	-1.9	3.7	6.2	-5.8	-3.1
Pakistan	5.6	-19.0	11.4	9.7	-1.8	4.4	-12.5	6.7	-0.6	-2.0	8.2	2.6	5.3	-6.9	-2.6
Philippines	-0.3	2.3	3.9	-12.7	-15.1	-2.7	-9.1	5.7	-5.9	-13.9	4.3	6.7	-8.7	1.2	0.2
Africa															
Ghana	4.9	3.6	-0.2	25.9	-15.4	1.1	-2.7	2.6	33.4	-21.8	-0.3	-1.7	2.4	4.7	-2.5
Kenya	-0.2	6.4	-3.0	-5.5	-0.8	-1.0	-0.3	-6.3	-4.3	-10.1	-1.9	6.5	-4.0	5.8	-4.1
Nigeria	5.6	6.3	-3.0	19.3	2.3	3.6	6.5	-0.1	21.3	0.6	-1.9	4.4	5.2	-18.5	-1.9
Zambia	12.8	0.0	1.6	-2.9	-2.9	11.5	-1.7	-2.0	-1.9	-3.6	0.7	3.0	-2.2	-1.5	-1.1
Zimbabwe	-0.7	0.5	-6.1	6.3	-4.6	-0.8	-0.4	-5.4	8.3	-7.7	0.7	3.0	-2.2	-1.5	-0.7
MENA															
Iran	2.1	2.2	0.8	14.0	-3.1	3.2	6.1	23.7	2.0	-5.9	-2.3	-8.3	1.5	-10.5	1.5
Turkey	2.0	5.7	1.8	-11.4	-1.6	2.9	4.5	10.2	-32.3	-3.5	-0.8	8.0	-3.1	0.4	0.7
Tunisia	1.1	4.3	0.6	-3.2	-2.4	1.2	4.6	4.0	-5.3	-5.0	2.3	5.2	0.2	-6.9	-3.3
Morocco	na	na	5.0	-3.5	0.3	na	na	6.4	-8.1	-2.3	1.3	0.4	-3.3	-8.9	-1.3
Egypt	-0.2	-7.5	-8.7	9.8	-1.7	-0.7	1.3	-8.5	15.4	-5.9	-4.4	25.4	-8.9	10.1	0.7
Latin America															
Argentina	na	-2.4	15.6	0.7	-8.6	na	2.1	1.7	0.0	-11.0	2.1	2.7	-1.6	4.4	1.2
Brazil	0.5	12.3	-2.9	8.8	-2.9	-2.6	0.9	1.1	20.9	-3.0	2.7	1.7	-4.7	1.6	0.4
Chile	4.5	-6.4	1.8	8.5	-0.6	4.1	-27.5	4.3	22.7	-3.6	2.1	-3.2	-2.1	-8.1	-1.5
Mexico	na	0.2	-6.8	12.3	-1.3	na	-2.9	-8.8	13.9	-7.5	3.9	1.7	-5.0	-0.4	3.5
Colombia	-5.0	-3.3	3.7	4.6	-4.2	-5.8	-9.8	6.1	2.4	-8.7	-0.3	1.6	-0.7	2.3	-0.3
Venezuela	0.5	3.7	-7.0	-7.8	-20.5	2.2	3.9	-3.2	-4.1	-24.6	1.1	-0.7	-6.0	1.5	-2.7

Sources: Based on UNIDO (1995), and World Bank (1995).

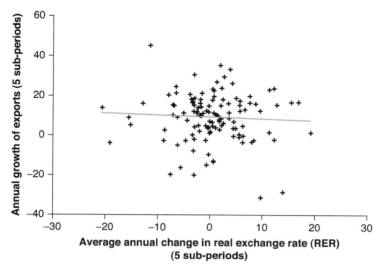

Figure 7.4 Growth of exports vs. real exchange rate.
Source: Based on UNIDO (1995) and World Bank (1995).
Note: Five sub-periods as in Table 7.10.

1979–81 oil price shock. Most Latin American countries witnessed substantial revaluations of their exchange rates, but again this was not dissimilar to the experience of most countries in Asia. Setting aside the question of regional patterns in real exchange rate behavior, however, a comparison of the experiences of individual countries across the sample as a whole could convey further useful information regarding the links between the real exchange rate and manufacturing exports in general.

To study the relationship between real exchange rate changes and manufacturing export growth we examined the correlation between the two variables during each subperiod across the 26 countries. We also examined the correlation between exchange rate changes during the oil price boom periods and export growth performance in the subsequent periods. None of the tests showed any significant relationship between the two variables, and in only one or two subperiods the direction of correlation was in accordance to that expected by theory. For economy of space we do not reproduce all these results here. The scatter plot in Figure 7.4, which shows the relation between the exchange rate changes and export growth for the pooled sample of the five subperiods, is representative of the picture we get in individual subperiods as well.

To have a better understanding of the relationship between the real exchange rate and manufacturing export performance we need a more detailed multivariate analysis which can take into account the effect of other factors that influence export performance. We will begin with a cross-section regression analysis of the long-run behavior of export performance across the sample countries, and follow this with a panel study of the short-term response of manufacturing exports.

4   A cross-section study of the long-term behavior of manufacturing exports

The cross section study is conducted in relation to growth rates over two long periods, namely 1970–92 and 1980–90. The regression results are shown in Tables 7.2 and 7.3, respectively, for the two periods. In each period, the average annual growth of manufacturing exports is regressed on the average annual percentage changes in the real exchange rate (RER) as well as a number of other variables.[15] These other variables are the following:

RERX, is the average annual change in the relative unit export values. In a cross section analysis of this type, where it may be assumed that the shifts in world demand for manufactures affects the sample countries more or less uniformly, relative changes in this variable across the countries can be attributed by and large to changing supply conditions in individual countries. Hence, following standard demand analysis, this variable is expected to have a negative relation with export performance.

RERDIV, is a measure of instability of the real exchange rate (RER), estimated as the standard deviation of the fluctuations of the real exchange rate around a deterministic time trend.[16] This variable is expected to capture the effect of stability and hence credibility of incentives on export performance. The greater the instability of real exchange rate, *ceteris paribus* the lower would be export performance, and hence one would expect a negative correlation between this variable and export growth.

INVST, depicts the average annual rate of growth of gross investment in the economy as a whole. This variable captures the effect of nonprice factors in export performance. High investment growth rates are associated with technological dynamism, flexibility of production structure, and the facility with which price incentives are translated into improved export performance. The causality could of course run from greater export performance to higher investment growth rates. On these grounds, this variable is expected to have a positive association with export growth. On the other hand, when the substitution element between the exportables and nontraded goods is dominant, as advocated in conventional trade theory, this variable is expected to either have a negative or no significant relationship with export growth.

ULABDIF, is the difference between the growth of real exchange rate (RER) and real unit labor costs. As discussed above, the growing wedge between these two variables would allow price competitiveness and profitability to be maintained simultaneously when the manufacturing sector is faced with adverse terms of trade shocks, or during the deflationary phase of the adjustment process when the manufacturing sector faces a profit squeeze and rising capital output ratios. On these grounds, in the short to medium term the correlation between this variable and export performance is expected to be positive.

WAGE, is the wage rate in 1974, measured in current dollars and adjusted for overall labor productivity across the countries. This variable is meant to capture the effect of the overvaluation of the exchange rate in the initial period from the

Table 7.2 Regression of manufacturing export growth on real exchange rate and other variables, 1970–92

Dependent variable = annual growth of manufacturing exports, 1970–92
No. of observations = 26

Variable	(1)		(2)		(3)		(4)	
	Coefficient	T-statistic	Coefficient	T-statistic	Coefficient	T-statistic	Coefficient	T-statistic
Constant	8.93	5.52	6.68	1.84	9.79	2.27	2.18	1.24
RER	0.12	0.22	−0.66	−1.61	−0.52	−1.12		
RERX			−1.76	−2.11	−2.02	−2.33	−2.37	−2.92
RERDIV			−0.28	−1.79	−0.23	−1.45		
INVST			1.01	3.98	0.85	2.88	1.04	4.19
ULABDIF					−0.22	−0.08		
WAGE					−0.02	−1.31		
R-squared	0.00		0.60		0.63		0.50	
Adjusted R-squared	−0.04		0.52		0.52		0.46	
Log likelihood	−89.45		−77.46		−76.20		−80.22	

RER = Average annual growth of manufacturing real exchange rate (e.P/P*), 1970–92
RERX = Average annual growth of relative export unit values (e.Px/P*), 1970–92
RERDIV = Index of instability of real exchange rate (RER), 1970–92 (as defined in the text)
INVST = Average annual growth of investment, 1970–92
ULABDIF = Annual average growth of RER minus growth of relative unit labour costs (e.W/v.P*), 1970–92
WAGE = Index of relative efficiency wages (as defined in the text)

Source: Based on data provided in World Bank (1995) and UNIDO (1995).

Table 7.3 Regression of Manufacturing Export Growth on Real Exchange Rate and other variables, 1980–92

Dependent Variable = annual growth of manufacturing exports, 1980–92
No. of Observations = 26

Variable	(1)		(2)		(3)	
	Coefficient	*T-Statistic*	*Coefficient*	*T-Statistic*	*Coefficient*	*T-Statistic*
Constant	8.98	5.13	5.80	1.16	7.85	1.60
RER80	0.10	0.38	-0.10	-0.32		
RER70					-0.17	-0.34
RERX80			-1.56	-1.96	-1.63	-1.99
RERDIV			-0.02	-0.10	0.01	0.03
INVST			0.78	2.12	0.68	2.13
ULABDIF80			-0.08	-0.42		
ULABDIF70					0.09	0.23
WAGE			-0.01	-0.80	-0.02	-1.26
R-squared	0.01		0.47		0.46	
Adjusted R-squared	-0.04		0.30		0.28	
Log likelihood	-87.69		-79.59		-79.86	

RER80 = Average annual growth of manufacturing real exchange rate ($e.P/P*$), 1980–92
RER70 = Average annual growth of manufacturing real exchange rate ($e.P/P*$), 1970–80
RERX80 = Average annual growth of relative export unit values ($e.Px/P*$), 1980–92
RERDIV = Index of instability of real exchange rate (RER), 1970–92 (as defined in the text)
INVST = Average annual growth of investment, 1970–92
ULABDIF80 = Annual average growth of RER minus growth of relative unit labour costs ($e.W/x.P*$), 1980–92
ULABDIF70 = Annual average growth of RER minus growth of relative unit labour costs ($e.W/x.P*$), 1970–80
WAGE = Index of relative efficiency wages (as defined in the text)

Source: Based on data provided in World Bank (1995) and UNIDO (1995).

point of view of the manufacturing sector in a protected economy. It allows a comparison of real exchange rate levels across the countries in the initial period. In countries with a protected manufacturing sector and an overvalued exchange rate, the wage rate in the initial period, after making adjustments for productivity differentials, is expected to be relatively higher than other sample countries. The adjustment factor adopted here is per capita income in 1974 measured at purchasing power parity exchange rate. The dollar wages in 1974 for each country is divided by per capita income at purchasing power parity exchange rate to arrive at the *WAGE* variable. The association of this variable with manufacturing export performance is expected to be negative.

As can be seen from Table 7.2, over the 1970–92 period as a whole only investment and relative export unit values (RERX) have significant coefficients with expected signs. The changes in real exchange rate (RER) do not either on their own or in combination with other variables, have a statistically significant effect on export performance. The variable representing the instability of the real exchange rate (RERDIV) has a negative, though statistically insignificant, coefficient. The coefficients of WAGE and ULABDIF variables also, though having the correct sign, are not statistically significant. As a comparison of equations (3) and (4) shows, the exclusion of all the variables other than investment and unit export values does not significantly affect the goodness of fit of the regression. These regression results should be interpreted as summarizing long-term association between export growth and other variables, bearing in mind that in the long run the causality can run from export performance to the right hand side variables. The varied cyclical behavior across the sample countries in the real exchange rate and other variables over the 1970–92 period also introduces additional problems in interpreting the regression results. To reduce the effect of these latter influences, we have repeated the exercise for the 1980–92 period, with the results shown in Table 7.3.

The results for the 1980s decade, as shown in Table 7.3, are remarkably similar to those of the 1970–92 period as a whole. Investment growth and changes in relative unit export values remain the only variables that appear to significantly influence manufacturing export growth. The changes in real exchange rate and the gap between the real exchange rate and real unit labor costs do not seem to play an important role in distinguishing between the high export performers and other countries in the sample. It would be interesting to examine whether the behavior of these two variables over the 1970s decade has had any bearing on export performance during the 1980s. As the regression results in equation (3) in Table 7.3 show, the inclusion of the real exchange rate and the exchange rate gap (ULABDIF) for the 1970s does not change the results of the earlier equations.

The cross section regression results seem to confirm our earlier observations that the behavior of the real exchange rate does not seem to be a major distinguishing feature of the high performing economies in Asia compared the rest of sample countries in the long run. The regression results for the 1980s also suggest that the high rates of growth of manufacturing exports by successful adjusters during that period could not be explained by the changes in the real exchange rate either during the 1980s or the 1970s. Such long-term tendencies, however, do not provide a useful guide for economic policy. In the long run real exchange rates are subject to various determinations outside and control of policy makers, and they are themselves highly influenced by export performance and the growth of the economy in general. We therefore need to examine the short-term influence of the real exchange rate and other variables on export performance through a panel analysis in the next section.

5   A panel study of the short-term behavior of manufacturing exports

The data on 26 sample countries over a 30-year period provides 780 observations for a time series/cross section study of the determinants of export performance. To avoid the complications arising from varied dynamic behavior of the variables in different sample countries and possible nonstationarity of the variables, we shall conduct our analysis in terms of growth rates rather than levels of variables. However, in contrast to the cross section study above where the growth rates referred to long term trend rates of growth, in the panel regressions the individual annual growth rates for the sample period are utilized. The results of the panel analysis therefore refer to short-term determinants of export performance.

We start with a fixed effect panel regression model of the following type:

$$y_{it} = \alpha_0 + \alpha_i + \lambda_t + \beta'x_{it} + \varepsilon_{it} \qquad\qquad i=1,\dots, N \text{ and } t = 1, \dots, T$$

where, y is the dependent variable (i.e. export growth rate), α and λ_t are fixed effects for each country and each time period, respectively, and x is the vector of explanatory variables. The results are shown in equations (1) and (2) in Table 7.4.[17] All the variables are defined as in the cross section exercise above, with the difference that here they refer to annual growth rates for all the years rather than average period growth rates. The only new variable is OUTPUT, which represents the rate of growth of manufacturing output. This variable is meant to capture the substitution effect between exports and hitherto non-traded manufacturing products. According to conventional theory, where during the adjustment period the substitution effect is expected to be strong, one would expect either a negative or a weak effect of output growth on export performance in the short run. In a more dynamic context, however, where output growth can lead to productivity improvement, higher manufacturing profitability, and increased variety of manufacturing output, one would expect a positive influence from higher output growth on manufacturing exports.

As can be seen from both equations (1) and (2), real exchange rate changes (i.e. RER and its lagged value RER(−1)) do not seem to have any association with export growth. Relative unit export values, however, have a highly significant negative effect on manufacturing exports. These results are remarkably similar to the cross section results pertaining to the long term behavior of manufacturing exports discussed above.

The difference in the rate of growth of the real exchange rate and the relative unit labor costs (i.e. variable ULABDIF), has a significant positive effect on export growth, both contemporaneously and with a one-year time lag. As discussed above, it is the change in the gap between the real exchange rate and relative unit labor costs, rather than the changes in the real exchange rate *per se*, which is expected to have a significant effect on export performance during the adjustment period. The OUTPUT variable also has a positive and significant effect on manufacturing exports, indicating that the substitution effect in the adjustment process is overshadowed by more dynamic influences in export performance.

The equation was also estimated by a random effects model, where the fixed country and time effect variables, namely α_i and λ_t, are assumed to be random realizations of two stochastic variables from two independent distributions with mean zero, and independent of the regression error term ε_{it}. One advantage of this method of estimation is that we can also include time invariant, country specific variables, such as the WAGE and RERDIV, and INVST, used in the cross section exercise above. The results which are shown in equation (3) in Table 7.4, are very similar to those of equation (2). Instability of the real exchange rate (measured by RERDIV) appears to have a negative, though not statistically significant, effect on export growth. The long term trends in investment growth rates (the variable INVST) also has a positive, though not significant effect on export growth. The variable WAGE, which is meant to reflect the effect of industrial protection and exchange rate overvaluation in the initial period, has a significant and negative influence on export growth.

The empirical results shed light on some of the analytical questions raised at the beginning of this section in a number of ways. Though the initial level of protection of manufacturing production and the resulting overvaluation of the exchange rate seem to have a negative effect on export growth and economic adjustment, this type of overvaluation, as far as export competitiveness is concerned, does not seem to be amenable to correction by a mere devaluation of the real exchange rate. This is not because exports are price inelastic. On the contrary, as we have observed, both in the short run and in the long run, manufacturing exports seem to be highly responsive to relative unit export values. The problem is that relative unit export values do not seem to be responsive to the changes in real exchange rate (defined from the viewpoint of the manufacturing sector as a whole). This could be observed from the following random effects panel regression, estimated by regressing the growth of relative unit export values on the changes in real exchange rate and its lag values:

$$\text{RERX} = 0.18 - 0.001 \text{ RER} + 0.013 \text{ RER}(-1) + 0.035 \text{ RER}(-2) - 0.077\text{RER}(-3)$$
$$\quad (0.139) \quad (-0.04) \quad (0.41) \quad (1.13) \quad (-0.87)$$

Numbers in parentheses show the value of estimated coefficients divided by their standard error (the number of observations = 555). It may be argued that though relative export prices may not be responsive to real exchange rate devaluations,

Table 7.4 Regression of manufacturing export growth on real exchange rate and other variables, 1963–92

Dependent variable = Growth of manufacturing exports
No. of observations = 567

| | Fixed effects model with group and time dummy variables | | | | Random effects model | |
| | (1) | | (2) | | (3) | |
Variable	Coefficient	Standard Error	Coefficient	Standard Error	Coefficient	Standard Error
Constant	13.300	1.180	11.007	1.663	15.320	4.780
RER	0.006	0.088	-0.019	-0.085	0.038	0.082
RER(-1)	-0.071	0.091	-0.043	-0.088	-0.068	0.085
RERX**			-1.078	0.121	-0.978	0.111
RERX(-1)			0.005	0.118	-0.135	0.110
ULABDIF**			0.452	0.117	0.449	0.118
ULABDIF(-1)**			0.338	0.117	0.247	0.117
ULABDIF(-2)			0.059	0.118	0.017	0.117
DLO**			0.426	0.173	0.608	0.166
DLO(-1)			-0.147	0.177	-0.122	0.171
RERDIV					-0.106	0.158
WAGE**					-0.026	0.013
I-TREND					0.368	0.321
R-squared	0.166		0.316		–	
Autocorrelation-Coefficient	-0.002		-0.052		-0.046	
Log likelihood	-2816.868		-2626.610		–	

RER = Growth of manufacturing real exchange rate ($e.P/P*$)
RERX = Growth of relative export unit values ($e.Px/P*$)
DLO = Growth of manufacturing output
ULABDIF = Growth of RER minus growth of relative unit labour costs ($e.W/v.P*$)
RERDIV = Index of instability of real exchange rate (RER), 1970–92 (as defined in the text)
I-TREND = Average Annual Growth of Investment, 1970–92
WAGE = Index of relative Efficiency Wages (as defined in the text)

Source: Based on data provided in World Bank (1995) and UNIDO (1995).

Notes:

such devaluations through their deflationary impact may release production capacities which could be redirected toward export markets. As we have observed, however, the positive and significant relationship between investment growth, or manufacturing output growth, and exports indicates that such substitution effects do not appear to be significant.

In none of the estimated regression equations do real exchange rate changes seem to have a significant direct effect on manufacturing export growth. As we have observed, however, when exchange rate devaluations lead to a growing wedge between the real exchange rate and the real unit labor costs (i.e. an increase in variable ULABDIF), they exert a statistically significant effect on export performance in the short run. Such a change is equivalent to a fall in the share of wages in manufacturing output. To see this more clearly we can write the real unit labor costs as:

$$\frac{W.e}{v.P^*} = \frac{W}{v.P} \cdot \frac{e.P}{P^*} = \frac{W.L}{O.P} \cdot \frac{e.P}{P^*}$$

or:

$$UL = WSH.RER$$

where UL stands for real unit labor costs, WSH is the share of wages in output and RER is the real exchange rate. This could be written as:

$$\dot{U}L = \dot{W}SH + \dot{R}ER$$

or,

$$ULABDIF = \dot{R}ER - \dot{U}L = -\dot{W}SH \tag{4}$$

where dots above the variables indicate rate of change. In other words, real devaluations seem to be only effective in promoting exports to the extent that they lead to a decline in the share of wages in output during the process of adjustment. This is not only an empirical finding supported by our panel regression analysis, but also, as discussed in Section 2, it follows from the logic of the role of the real exchange devaluations in the adjustment process. As argued before, the fall in the share of wages in the adjustment process is either to compensate for an adverse terms of trade shock or to maintain profitability in the face of increased price competition in economies opening up to the global economy. Though in the long run there does not appear to be any significant relationship between the change in wage shares and export performance, in the short to medium term falling wage shares seems to be associated with higher export growth in the adjusting countries. This distributional conflict in the process of adjustment seems to be the main link between exchange rate devaluations, wage flexibility and price competitiveness. Of course, as seen above, changes in the manufacturing wage shares is only one element in the list of variables influencing export performance during the adjustment process, and furthermore, the variables examined in the above regressions explain only a small part of the variations in export performance across the countries and over time. However, our purpose in this section has been to identify the links between wage flexibility and price competitiveness rather than a full explanation of export performance *per se*. In Section 6 we shall examine the extent to which the behavior of wage shares has varied between the successful adjusters in Asia and other countries and the underlying determinants of wage competitiveness across the sample countries.

6   Wage flexibility, labor productivity, and adjustment

As observed in the previous section, a fall in wage shares can help maintain manufacturing price competitiveness and profitability in the face of an adverse external terms of trade shock, or in liberalizing economies where the manufacturing sector faces increased price competition from abroad. To see this more succinctly, we may start with the following mark-up pricing rule:

$$P.O = (1 + \eta)(W.L + P_m.m)$$

where η is the mark-up over wages and other variable costs, and other variables are as defined in the previous section. The share of wages in output can thus be written as:

$$\frac{W.L}{P.O} = \frac{W.L}{(1 + \eta)(W.L + P_m.m)} = \frac{1}{(1 + \eta)(1 + k)}$$

where k is the ratio of raw material costs to the wage bill. Given the technology of production and labor productivity in the short run, and assuming that in a liberalized economy output prices are constrained by international competition, any increase in the price of raw materials (an adverse terms of trade shock to manufacturing) needs to be compensated by a decline in the wage shares to maintain industrial profitability. The extent to which this process is inhibited by wage setting institutions in a particular country, lack of wage flexibility could be said to be an obstacle in the adjustment process. As a first step toward examining the role of labor market flexibility in the process of adjustment, we may therefore start with examining the behavior of wage shares in the countries under study.

   The trends in wages shares and mark-ups for sample countries in Asia, Africa, and the Middle East, and Latin America are shown respectively in Figures 7.5, 7.6 and 7.7. The behavior of these variables in each country has specificities of its own which needs a close country specific examination. Here we shall be mainly concerned with general patterns, particularly those which may distinguish the successful adjusters in Asia from the rest of the sample. As can be seen, the mark-ups across all the countries in the sample are relatively much more stable than the wage shares, indicating that short-term fluctuations in the raw material costs are by and large mirrored in the behavior of wage shares. In this respect, the experience

Table 7.5 Correlation between wage shares, mark-ups and variable input costs, 1963–95

	Correlation coefficient between annual percentage changes in:	
	Wage share and input costs (1+k)	*Mark-up (1+h) and input costs (1+k)*
Asia		
Korea	−0.94	−0.48
Malaysia	−0.96	−0.28
Singapore	−0.97	−0.33
Hong Kong	−0.96	0.21
Thailand	−0.99	−0.85
India	−0.92	0.20
Bangladesh	−0.94	−0.37
Indonesia	−0.92	−0.58
Pakistan	−0.93	−0.23
Philippines	−0.85	−0.08
Africa		
Ghana	−0.86	−0.51
Kenya	−0.98	−0.43
Nigeria	−0.58	−0.55
Zambia	−0.77	−0.48
Zimbabwe	−0.79	−0.29
MENA		
Iran	−0.86	−0.07
Turkey	−0.93	−0.14
Tunisia	−0.96	−0.17
Morroco	−0.40	0.06
Egypt	−0.90	0.14
Latin America		
Argentina	−0.78	−0.25
Brazil	−0.96	0.38
Chile	−0.81	−0.05
Mexico	−0.99	0.85
Colombia	−0.94	0.02
Venezuela	−0.83	−0.04

Source: Based on data provided in UNIDO (1995).

of the Asian countries does not seem to be different from the countries in other regions. This is further reflected in the co-variation of the annual wage shares and raw material costs, and mark-ups and raw material costs, as shown in Table 7.5. As the table shows, the correlation coefficient of annual changes in wage shares and variable input costs in most of the sample countries is close to −1, and much higher than the correlation between mark-ups and variable input costs. In this respect, the experience of Asian countries does not seem to be much different from the rest of the sample.

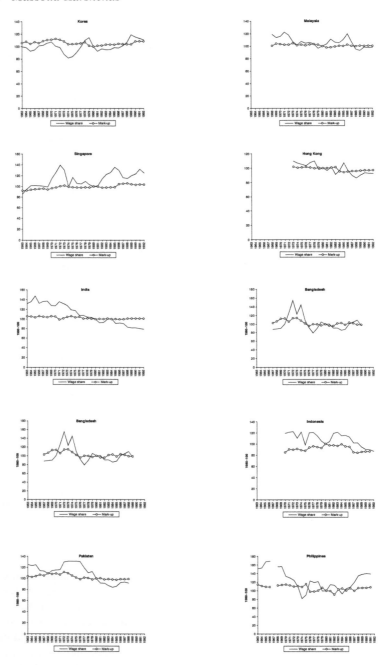

Figure 7.5 Wage shares and Mark-ups in Asian manufacturing, 1963–92.
Source: Based on UNIDO (1995).

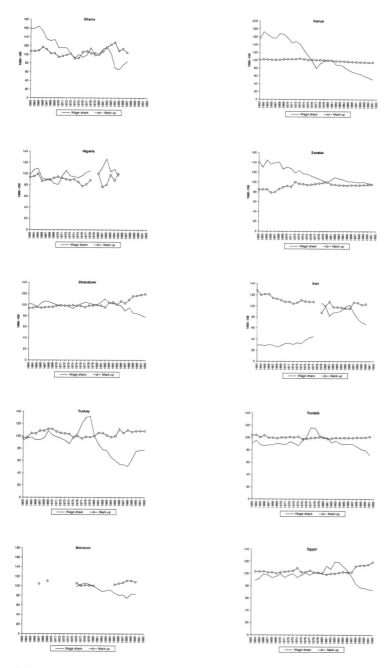

Figure 7.6 Wage Shares and Mark-ups in African and middle eastern manufacturing, 1963–92.
Source: Based on UNIDO (1995).

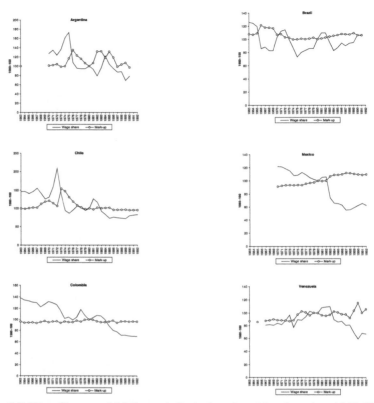

Figure 7.7 Wage Shares and Mark-ups in Latin American Manufacturing, 1963–92.
Source: Based on UNIDO (1995).

During the 1980s period, however, distinct differences can be observed in the behavior of wage shares in Asia as compared to the rest of the regions. During this period, the Asian sample countries with the exception of the two oil economies, i.e. Malaysia and Indonesia, all either witnessed a rising trend in wage shares or followed the historical trends of the 1970s. In contrast, the majority of countries in Africa, Middle East, and Latin America have witnessed sharp declines in the trend growth rates of manufacturing wage shares during the 1980s. Amongst the countries in Africa and the Middle East, the two oil economies of Nigeria and Iran are noted for a relatively belated but nevertheless noticeable downward adjustment in wage shares in the late 1980s, and in Latin America, Brazil, and Chile show a more moderate decline with a cyclical pattern in wage shares. On balance, however, the non-Asian economies exhibit a much sharper downward adjustment in wage shares during the 1980s as compared to the successful adjusters in Asia.

On the basis of the behavior of wage shares it may be concluded that lack of wage flexibility has not been a stumbling block for adjustment in general, and export competitiveness in particular, in non-Asian economies. Wage shares can of course vary due to variations in labor productivity, wages, and prices, and hence to examine wage flexibility from the point of view of both the employers and workers we need to further decompose the determinants of wage shares in different sample countries. From the point of view of employers, given labor productivity and raw material prices, it is the real product wages which affect profitability, and from the point of view of workers what matters is the real consumption wage. The changes in wage shares can be written as:

$$\text{WSHR} = \frac{\dot{W}}{P} - \dot{v} = \frac{\dot{W}}{P_c} - \left(\dot{v} - \frac{\dot{P}_c}{P}\right)$$

where P_c is the consumer price index and other variables are as defined earlier, and dots above the variables denote rate of change. The trends in labor productivity, real product wages and real consumption wages for the three broad regions, namely, Asia, Africa and the Middle East, and Latin America are shown in Figures 7.8, 7.9, and 7.10, respectively. As can be seen a remarkable feature of the wage behavior in Asia is that real consumption wages have had a continuous upward trend in all the countries, particularly accelerating during the 1980s. In one or two countries in Asia in the 1980s, such as India and Indonesia, where there has been a declining trend in wage shares, this has not been brought about by a fall in real wages, but rather by product wages lagging behind productivity growth. In most other countries in Asia, in fact real product wages grew faster than the relatively high rates of productivity growth during the 1980s, giving rise to the rising wage shares observed above. This contrasts sharply to the picture for other regions where in a number of countries, despite the increasing trend in labor productivity during the 1980s, one can observe a declining trend in both consumption wages and product wages. Countries such as, Kenya, Iran, Turkey, Tunisia, Egypt, Zimbabwe, Mexico, Colombia, Argentina, Venezuela, and to some extent Ghana, are notable examples of this pattern during the 1980s. In a few other non-Asian countries, where real wages have not been declining during the 1980s, the rate of productivity growth has been well above real wage increases, thus giving rise to the declining wage shares that we have already observed.

The overall trend growth rates in wage share, labor productivity and real wages, along with a measure of the annual rate of depreciation of the nominal exchange rate and the rate of inflation for the sample countries are shown in Table 7.6. Though such trend growth rates obscure the wide fluctuations in the behavior of some of the variables, particularly in regions outside Asia, the contrast between the trends in different regions is sharp enough to convey a general picture. As shown in the table, in all the Asian countries, regardless of the rate of productivity growth, real consumption wages registered positive growth rates during the

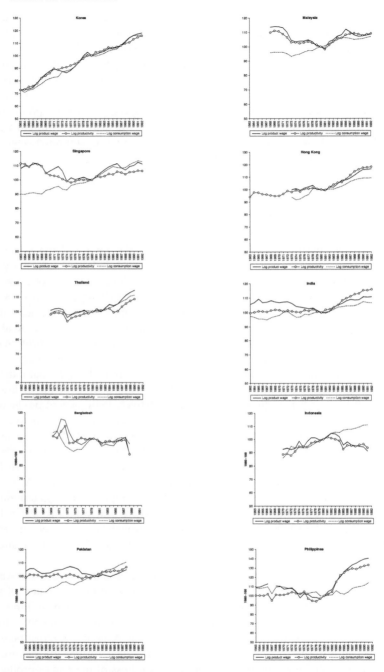

Figure 7.8 Real wages and labor productivity in Asian manufacturing, 1963–92.
Source: Based on UNIDO (1995) and World Bank (1995).

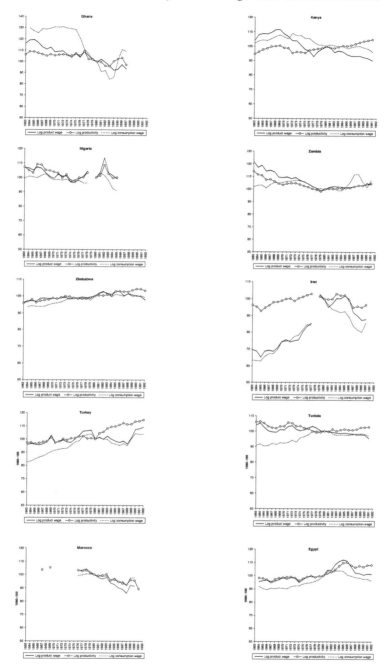

Figure 7.9 Real wages and labor productivity in African and middle eastern manufacturing, 1963–92.
Source: Based on UNIDO (1995) and World Bank (1995).

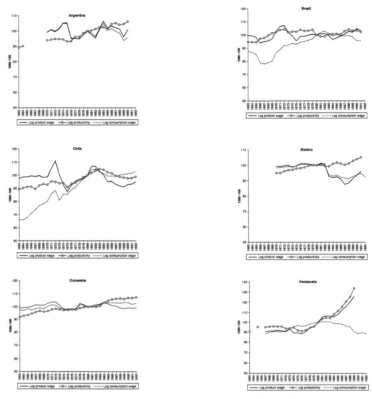

Figure 7.10 Real wages and labor productivity in Latin American manufacturing, 1963–92.
Source: Based on UNIDO (1995) and World Bank (1995).

1980s. Product wages also registered positive trend growth rates in all the Asian countries, with the exception of Bangladesh and Indonesia, where productivity growth was negative. In the non-Asian countries, however, irrespective of the rate of productivity growth, real wages in general followed a declining trend. This applies to both product wages and real consumption wages. In a few cases, where product wages registered a positive trend growth rate, this rate was well below the rate of productivity growth, thus leading to the decline in wage shares across all the countries outside Asia.

The above evidence lends support to our earlier observation that downward wage flexibility is not a distinguishing feature of the successful adjusting countries in Asia *vis-à-vis* other countries. This, however, does not necessarily mean that labor markets in Asia are less flexible than those of other regions. In economies with fast rates of labor productivity growth, as in most Asian countries, one would expect real wages to grow more or less in tandem with labor productivity. Whether the rate of growth of product wages surpasses that of labor productivity in such economies, depends on the tightness of the labor market, the

Table 7.6 Growth of real wages, labor productivity, nominal exchange rate and inflation, 1980–91

	Wage share	Real product wages	Labour productivity	Consumption wages	Nominal exchange rate	Rate of inflation
	1980–91	1980–91	1980–91	1980–91	1980–91	1980–91
Asia						
Korea	1.8	7.4	5.6	7.5	0.6	5.4
Malaysia	-0.9	3.2	4.0	2.3	1.7	1.8
Singapore	1.4	3.5	2.1	4.6	-2.0	2.9
Hong Kong	-0.8	7.4	8.2	4.5	3.0	4.5
Thailand	3.6	7.0	3.4	5.8	1.6	2.3
India	-2.0	4.6	6.6	2.9	9.5	6.9
Bangladesh	0.8	-1.8	-2.6	0.1	7.0	12.0
Indonesia	-1.9	-4.9	-3.1	4.2	11.1	17.1
Pakistan	-0.5	2.6	3.0	6.4	7.9	9.7
Philippines	3.1	18.0	14.8	5.7	11.2	1.1
Africa						
Ghana	-6.3	-5.0	1.3	10.7	31.6	53.3
Kenya	-6.2	-3.7	2.5	-1.2	10.5	13.4
Nigeria	-1.4	-2.7	-1.3	-10.8	31.3	10.4
Zambia	-0.7	1.2	1.9	3.5	43.9	41.5
Zimbabwe	-2.6	-0.9	1.7	-0.5	15.4	14.4
MENA						
Iran	-2.7	-5.5	-2.8	-8.2	16.9	13.9
Turkey	-1.9	2.7	4.6	1.3	36.4	38.3
Tunisia	-2.5	-1.4	1.1	-0.8	5.8	8.2
Morocco	-1.4	-5.0	-3.6	-2.0	4.8	9.7
Egypt	-4.1	-1.6	2.5	-2.6	13.3	15.2
Latin America						
Argentina	-2.3	0.3	2.7	-1.3	155.0	157.4
Brazil	-0.2	1.7	1.9	-2.3	150.9	142.6
Chile	-3.2	-5.3	-2.1	-0.5	20.5	23.5
Mexico	-5.4	-3.4	1.9	-2.7	46.7	53.2
Colombia	-4.3	-1.1	3.2	1.0	24.1	23.5
Venezuela	-25.2	-11.3	14.0	-5.4	26.1	25.1

Sources: Based on UNIDO (1995) aand World Bank (1995).

Notes
Growth rates refer to trend % growth rates derived by regressing ln (x) on a time trend variable.

general growth of the economy and demand for labor from the other sectors of the economy. The impact of labor institutions would be most pronounced during adjustment episodes when real wage growth may have to be checked or a reduction in real wages may be required. What the above analysis establishes is that lack of downward flexibility in real wages does not appear to be connected to the comparative adjustment performance across the countries in our sample.

7   Concluding remarks

A large body of the literature on the role of labor market institutions in the adjustment process has been preoccupied with the question of lack of downward flexibility of real wages arising from government legislation or strong trade unions protecting the wages of organized labor. It appears, however, from the foregoing that, (1) there has been a considerable downward flexibility of wages in our sample countries, and (2) the apparent downward flexibility in wages bears little relation to successful adjustment and export performance in the long run. These findings, however, do not reduce the significance of labor market institutions in the adjustment process. If anything, the considerable fluctuations in wage shares in each sample country and the significant variation of the wage shares across the countries are indicative of the crucial role that labor market institutions play in the adjustment process. The empirical findings in this paper set the ground work for further research on the role of labor institutions in the adjustment process. The following are some of the links between the foregoing analysis and the role of labor market institutions in the adjustment process which need further research.

The behavior of real wages examined in the previous section is the outcome of relative movements of money wages and prices in the economy, and any particular real wage movement could be consistent with a wide range of money wage or price configurations. As shown in Table 7.6, one can observe extreme variations in rates of inflation and nominal devaluations across various sample countries which at the same time exhibit real wage reductions or a fall in wage shares of more or less similar orders of magnitude. For example, Tunisia and Argentina have had a fall in real consumption wages and wage shares on a similar scale, while the rates of nominal devaluations and inflation in the former country are in single digit range and in the latter are above 150 percent. It is likely that labor market institutions play a critical role in explaining the variations in the inflationary wage or price spirals as well as the final real wage outcome. Of course, the extent to which labor market institutions can play a part in such inflationary processes is largely conditioned by fiscal, monetary, and trade policies of the country in question. However, these policies can be themselves strongly influenced by the nature of the labor market institutions in the country in question. To address these issues we need to supplement the information analyzed in this paper, with a typology of labor institutions in different sample countries.

A second but related set of issues concerns the impact of labor market institutions on the timing of the real wage response in the process of adjustment. As we observed in the econometric results in Section 5, variations in wage shares seem to have a significant impact on export performance in the short run, but in the long run there does not seem to be a significant relation between wage shares and export performance or success in structural adjustment in general. This suggests a possibly critical role for the timing of real wage response in the process of adjustment. Countries which due to real wage resistance may not be able to implement a fast enough response to adverse external shocks, can lose their competitive edge in the international markets and may find it difficult to catch up in later years even by introducing more sever real wage cuts in the long run. The existence of strong dynamic economies in manufacturing exports enhances the significance of this factor. The question of role of labor institutions on the timing of adjustment is another area for future research.

Finally, the very notion of wage flexibility, and labor market flexibility in general, need further rigorous examination. The observed degree of real wage reduction, or reduction in wage shares, in different countries is not an appropriate indicator of labor market flexibility, or even wage flexibility for that matter. As we have seen above, in many sample countries in Africa and the Middle East, in the absence of free wage bargaining between the workers unions and employers, the governments have managed to bring about sharp real wage reductions, with little apparent success in export competitiveness or economic adjustment. Labor market flexibility can be only defined in terms of an appropriate set of labor institutions which are conducive to appropriate wage or employment outcomes in the process of adjustment, taking into account the available information at the sectoral and microeconomic level which cannot be mustered by authoritarian governments, or "free" markets, or outside lending agencies for that matter. To investigate these issues further, we need to supplement the information on various wage or employment outcomes in the process of adjustment in the countries studied above, with an appropriate categorization of the prevailing labor market institutions in different countries in terms of their organizational structures, the degree of centralization of collective bargaining, trade union politicization, etc.

Notes

* I am grateful to Ben Fine, Hashem Pesaran, Mehdi Shafaeddin, John Sender, Anwar Shaikh, and Andrew Glyn, for comments on an earlier draft. I am responsible for all the remaining errors and omissions.
1 For example, in countries where rapid rate of productivity growth leads to fast rates of growth of exports, it would be easier to maintain external and internal balance with fiscal and monetary stability, and hence a stable and "appropriate" real exchange rate.
2 As Keynes (1971: 65) put it aptly, "Economists set themselves too easy, too useless a task if in tempestuous seasons they can only tell us that when the storm is long past the ocean is flat again."
3 From the point of view of the economy as a whole, productivity differences between the traded and nontraded goods sectors presents additional problems of comparison which are by now well known in the literature. For an early discussion of this see e.g. Balassa (1964).
4 Of course, technological and product quality changes also affect the *movement* of the real exchange rate indexes in long-period comparisons across the countries.

5 In the literature, it is usually the dollar value of unit labour cost (i.e. *W.e/v*) which is considered (see, e.g. Kaldor 1978; Mazumdar 1994). In comparative country studies where it is assumed that the different countries compete in the same market and hence face the same international price indexes, the two definitions produce the same results.

6 There may be of course other nontradable intermediate inputs such as electricity and other services. These, however, are not explicitly shown in the equation, because they are subject to the same influences as the wage cost element already discussed.

7 It should be noted that here we are concerned with terms of trade effects for specific countries. A general increase in raw material prices which affects all the countries in a similar manner would create a proportionate increase in P^*, and hence no adverse terms of trade effects for any specific country.

8 Of course, in such economies the productivity of labour is also likely to be falling and hence the fall in the unit labour costs will be somewhat less than that implied by the fall in real wages.

9 This point is being increasingly recognized in the applied international trade literature. See, e.g. Dornbusch (1987), Menon (1995) and Koujianou and Knetter (1997) for a survey of this literature.

10 Another factor which can affect the export unit values in a significant way over short time intervals is the change in exchange regulations and trade controls which could lead to under-invoicing or over-invoicing of exports by traders trying to evade official exchange controls.

11 The 33 countries included in the measurement of world industrial prices were selected from a sample of 50 countries on the basis of the availability of price data for the whole of the 1963–92 period. The sample includes 17 industrial countries and 16 developing countries.

12 Real unit labour costs are defined as $W.e/v.P^*$, and are measured in following way. W is the total remuneration of labour divided by the number of persons employed, e is the market exchange rate defined as dollars per unit of domestic currency, v is the index of output per employed worker, and P^* is the dollar price index of world industrial output.

13 For testing export price responsiveness it is more appropriate to use an international price index relevant to the prices of the trading partners of the country in question. For comparability to the real exchange rate variable, however, we have used the same international price index for both variables.

14 It should be noted that because the world industrial price index (P^* in the denominator of equation (1)) is dominated by the prices in OECD countries, the movement in the real exchange rate by and large reflects the price movements relative to the OECD average.

15 The average annual growth rates are trend growth rates estimated by regressing the log of the variable on a time trend. For some countries due to missing data for the end years, the periods may be one or more years shorter than indicated in the tables. But for each country the growth rates in all the variables refer to the same subperiod.

16 These are estimated as the standard error of the regression of RER on a quadratic time trend function for each individual country during the period concerned. Other measures of exchange rate instability, such as the deviations from linear time trend and the average of the absolute value of annual growth rates, were also used in the regressions, but the results were not significantly different.

17 As a result of missing values for the beginning and end years for some countries the number of observations has been reduced from 780 to 567.

References

Balassa, B. (1964) 'The Purchasing-Power Parity Doctrine: A Reappraisal', *Journal of Political Economy*, 72: 584–96.

Dornbusch, R. (1987) 'Exchange Rates and Prices', *American Economic Review*, 77(1): 93–106.

Helleiner, G. K. (1995) 'Trade, Trade Policy and Industrialization Reconsidered', World Development Studies 6, Helsinki: The United Nations University, WIDER.

Kaldor, N. (1978) 'The Effects of Devaluations on Trade in Manufactures' in *Further Essays on Applied Economics*, ch. 7, pp. 99–118, London: Duckworth.

Karshenas, M. (1998) 'Labour Markets and the Diversity of Adjustment Experiences', Working Paper Series, No.78, London: Department of Economics, SOAS.

Keynes, J. M. (1971) *A Tract on Monetary Reform*, London: Macmillan.

Koujiannou, G. P. and Knetter, M. M. (1997) 'Goods Prices and Exchange Rates: What Have We Learned?', *Journal of Economic Literature*, 35: 1243–72.

Mazumdar, D. (1994) 'The Republic of Korea', in S. Horton, R. Kanbur, and D. Mazumdar (eds.), *Labour Markets in an Era of Adjustment*, vol. 2, ch. 12, pp. 535–83, Washington, DC: The World Bank.

Menon, J. (1995) 'The Degree and Determinants of Exchange Rate Pass-through: Market Structure, Non-tariff Barriers and Multinational Corporations', *The Economic Journal*, 106(435): 434–44.

UNIDO (1995) *Industrial Statistics Database* (INDTAT), Vienna: UNIDO.

World Bank (1995) *Socio-economic Time Series Access and Retrieval System (STARS)*, Washington DC: World Bank.

Part III

Globalization, gender, and inequality

8   The great equalizer?: Globalization effects on gender equality in Latin America and the Caribbean[1]

Stephanie Seguino

1   Introduction

Globally, gender gaps in well-being remain pervasive. Proponents of globalization have argued that economic growth, facilitated by policies to liberalize investment, trade, and financial flows as well as to privatize industry and reduce public sector deficits, will have a differentially beneficial effect on gender equality. Competitive pressures in a globalized economy, it is argued, make women an attractive source of labor, given their relatively lower wages. In the Latin America and Caribbean (LAC) region where there is greater gender equity in education relative to many other developing countries (World Bank 2001), globalization *cum* liberalization of markets then should bode well for women.

Critics of globalization have argued that women are often disadvantaged in an economic process founded on liberalized trade, investment, and financial flows. This is related to the fact that the state's role is often attenuated under such a policy regime, in part because the mobility of capital puts downward pressure on public spending, making it difficult to fund social spending and safety nets. Further, there is evidence that employment is increasingly insecure, and women are often slotted for the jobs with the least security. Finally, investment mobility is greatest in labor-intensive industries, where women are concentrated. Women are disadvantaged in efforts to bargain for higher wages, because firms can credibly threaten to relocate in such cases.

To evaluate these competing hypotheses, I consider the case of Latin America and the Caribbean. Economic performance in the region has varied widely over the last 30 years. Most countries have taken significant steps to liberalize their economies, either voluntarily or due to pressure from international financial institutions in the context of structural adjustment. A consequent shift in economic structure is evident throughout the region, with growth of export demand contributing to an increase in manufacturing as a share of GDP in most countries. These industries tend to be female-intensive in employment.

On the supply side, women in the region, already by 1970, ranked substantially above women from other developing regions in well-being, measured in terms of health and education (although they had less education than men). They did not, however, have equitable opportunities to earn income, and faced exclusion from positions of power in political and economic institutions. This region then is an interesting one in which to consider the effects of globalization, both because the moves toward liberalization have been substantial and because women had many of the prerequisites to participate in the paid economy as workers.

To consider these issues, I begin first by reviewing the literature on gender and economic growth. I then develop a set of well-being indictors, using a Borda ranking methodology that facilitates comparisons across countries. Trends in well-being are assessed, and the effects of growth since 1970 on these trends are evaluated. Panel data analysis is also used to measure the impact of four categories of variables on trends in gender gaps in well-being – female bargaining power, structure of production, macroeconomic conditions, and government spending.

2   Growth and gender equity

Gender inequality in developing countries may be linked to the inadequacy of societies' material resources. Females, it is often argued, are placed at the back of the queue, whether for food, health care, education or jobs, given that all of these are in short supply. We might therefore expect per capita income to be positively correlated with gender inequality, and indeed, several studies provide evidence to support this hypothesis (Dollar and Gatti 1999; World Bank 2001).[2] As a result, economic growth is argued to be a key factor in promoting gender equity in well-being. If this holds, the thorny question of *how* to stimulate economic growth still remains. The debate can broadly be characterized as between those who argue for market liberalization against the view that the state plays an important role in moving economies up the industrial ladder to higher value-added production and in insuring a fair distribution of resources.[3]

Proponents of trade, investment, and financial liberalization, and privatization – or succinctly, globalization – have argued that women, in particular, should benefit from a strategy that relies on economic openness and, in particular, exports as the engine of growth. This is because women are the preferred source of labor, owing to competitive pressures firms face to keep unit labor costs low. Sustained demand for female labor should drive up female wages relative to those of men as labor markets tighten. Increased access to jobs and higher relative wages raise women's incomes absolutely and indirectly, by increasing their bargaining power within the household to leverage a more equitable distribution of resources.

Moreover, rapid growth, signaling rising per capita incomes, should generate more revenue for households to invest in female family members, closing the gender gap in well-being. This "income effect," in the view of some, is not necessarily gender-biased, because females' lower future earnings make it rational to direct household investments to men when income is limited. By implication, this view suggests that economic growth will overcome the structural bias against females. Furthermore, it is conceivable that economic growth generates increases in state-level resources that can be differentially allocated to females, thus improving their relative well-being during the process of growth.

There is ample research, however, showing that the benefits of economic growth under the recent regime of globalization are not necessarily broadly shared – across class, ethnic, or gender groups (Milanovic 2002; Benería 2003). Numerous authors, for example, state that Latin America grew more slowly than Asia over the last three decades because the benefits of growth were not broadly shared, leading to political conflict that resulted in dysfunctional macroeconomic policy and ultimately, slower growth (Larraín and Vergara 1998).

Using a human development approach, Ranis and Stewart (2002) find little evidence of beneficial effects of economic growth in LAC over the past four decades. They attribute the failure of growth to improve human development in the region to the disruptive effects of debt crisis and harsh structural adjustment programs that relied on excessive cuts in social expenditures. They find evidence, however, that growth combined with high social expenditures did promote growth in some countries in the region. It is precisely this latter component, however, which is compromised in the globalization process as state-level mechanisms to provide a safety net are inhibited through declining tax revenues, privatization of public sector social services, and slow growth induced by financial mobility effects on domestic interest rates.

Research in the area of gender and macroeconomics reveals that the effects of economic growth on women's relative well-being differ, depending on how women's labor and unpaid labor are affected by a country's growth path, and by implication, the shifting economic structure. One thread of that work explores the ways in which the process of capital accumulation can lead firms to exploit women's gender role, with women channeled into the most insecure jobs (Benería and Sen 1981; Elson and Pearson 1981; Standing 1989; Hsiung 1996). For example, in Latin America, informal sector employment as a share of total nonagricultural employment has been rising since 1980, with 57 percent of jobs characterized as informal in the 1990s (Gatti and Kucera 2004). Almost half of all women work in the informal sector, and they are more likely than men to be in informal sector work (Charmes 2000).

Although informal sector work is sometimes residual employment, in the Latin America region, Benería (2003) argues that the informal and formal sectors are linked through subcontracting. This strategy is compatible with gender norms, reflecting as it does, the "male breadwinner" bias in job allocation (Elson and Cagatay 2000). While this strategy enhances profits, it also undermines the benefits of increased demand for female labor because of the lack of a job ladder and the tenuousness of these jobs, which hold down female wages. There is evidence that these tendencies have worsened during the recent period of globalization, which shifts economies from a wage-led to profit-led growth path.[4]

The degree to which women benefit from liberalization-induced growth is also influenced by how the structure of the economy changes, coupled with patterns of job segregation. Years ago, Boserup (1970) argued that women are marginalized in this structural shift, due to technological change that favors men's access to resources. While she referred primarily to the shift from agriculture to industrial production, her arguments continue to hold currency. Female labor absorption under insecure conditions of work is notable in semi-industrialized economies where labor-intensive manufacturing growth has been strong, and, to a lesser but growing extent, services (Standing 1989). In some countries, the growth of the services sector is a result of worsened conditions in the industrial sector, and its increase as a share of GDP reflects the growth of residual employment in the informal sector as workers are sloughed off from the industrial sector with trade liberalization (Kempadoo 1999; Benería 2001; Charmes 2000). In other cases, the expansion of the services sector is based on increased export demand for informatics services, reflecting a structural shift away from manufacturing or agriculture.[5]

Whatever the determinants of services and manufacturing expansion as a share of GDP, these are female-intensive sectors (Standing 1989). This contrasts with country experiences in which resource- or capital-intensive manufacturing growth has provided a significant demand-side stimulus. In those cases, labor demand tends to be male-dominated. Examples of the latter are Trinidad and Tobago, where the petroleum industry dominates, and Taiwan, where the move up the industrial ladder has led to the loss of female employment in the manufacturing sector (Berik 2000). Most developing economies fall into the former category, where liberalization and other policies have led to the expansion of labor-intensive manufacturing and services.

Do these structural shifts lead to improvements in women's well-being? Some have argued that they are likely to because women's access to employment increases, which can improve their bargaining power in the home. Lim (1990) and Kabeer (2000) emphasize this aspect of liberalization and export-oriented growth, arguing that women gain on net, while others (including Kabeer herself), note that women's access to insecure work may have little effect on women's "voice" within the household (see also Benería 2003). The net effect on female relative well-being remains, however, an empirical question.

Trade expansion has also been argued to be female labor intensive, although again the effects on well-being are ambiguous. Although not focused specifically on gender, Winters *et al.* (2004) conclude from their review of the empirical evidence that trade liberalization can and often does reduce income poverty, due to falling prices and expanded employment opportunities. Given that women are considered to be over-represented among the poor, it might be expected that trade liberalization in the region over the last 30 years has contributed to greater gender equity in well-being.

Several studies note, however, that the employment benefits of trade liberalization differentially affect women and men due to job segregation that slots women for less desirable jobs (Fontana *et al.* 1998; Cagatay 2001). The positive effect of female access to paid work is offset by women's relatively weaker bargaining power to negotiate with employers for higher wages. In research on Mexican *maquila* workers, Fussell (2000) finds, for example, that as export manufacturing has become more competitive internationally, wages have declined steadily. She notes that although export manufacturing "may provide employment to the least-skilled women who have few other options in the local labor market ... overall, it reflects a race to the bottom in manufacturing wages resulting from globalization of production" (Fussell 2000: 77). This is because women tend to be concentrated in "mobile" industries – industries for which it is relatively easier to relocate to lower wage sites, should wages rise, as compared to men who are more concentrated in nontradable, capital-intensive industries (Brofenbrenner 2000; Seguino 2000c, 2003a).

Furthermore, women's access to paid work may increase total labor time, if men do not contribute to the performance of unpaid tasks (Floro 1995). Female unpaid labor time may also increase if liberalization results in male out-migration in search of work, as in the case of Mexican corn farmers post-NAFTA (Winters *et al.* 2004). Insofar as increased workload compromises women's health (or leads to excessive demands on girl children), female relative well-being may be negatively affected. Moreover, while import tariff reductions can reduce the cost of basic goods, which benefits women in their role as family caretakers, they may be costly if this leads to disproportionate female loss of employment. Trade liberalization is also often associated with currency devaluation, which raises the cost of imported goods, and in those cases, household budgets are squeezed, placing greater pressure on women to find alternative resources to support their families.

Finally, economic growth increases resources available for government investment in public goods that improve well-being. But two problems exist, making the link between growth, public spending, and equity tenuous. First, there has been a marked increase in pressure from international financial institutions and financial markets for governments to privatize social services and to reduce public sector spending. Second, there is no guarantee that public expenditures will be gender-enabling. Gender-sensitive budget analysis reveals government spending as a source of inequality in gender well-being.[6]

We can summarize this discussion by describing the potential effects of growth on women's relative well-being as occurring along three pathways. As per capita income rises, more resources can be shared with women: (1) at the household level, because higher incomes leave more resources for female members of the family, who previously received a smaller share; (2) due to higher levels of government spending, insofar as these increase female access to education and health care; (3) because job creation disproportionately benefits women, and as a result, women have more bargaining power in the household and are seen as more economically valuable.

An alternative viewpoint is that women's ability to achieve parity in quality of life with men is likely to depend on the type of growth process and development strategy, with equity dependent on strategies that favorably affect, for example, the distribution of jobs by sex, and state-level expenditure patterns that are female-enabling. Indeed, it can be argued that growth is not necessary for (2) and (3) to occur since, regardless of the growth rate of the economy, government could choose to reallocate expenditures to social spending that benefits women, or could increase women's relative access to jobs, by such policies as affirmative action.[7] In this view, economic growth, as pursued in the recent period of globalization, is not sufficient to improve relative well-being.

3   Conceptualizing well-being

This paper considers the question of whether growth in the recent period of globalization has promoted gender equity in well-being in LAC. I focus on relative indicators of female well-being rather than absolute, because improved female bargaining power (which relative improvements in female well-being implies) is an essential means to leverage change in otherwise discriminatory norms and institutions.

Numerous efforts have been made in recent years to develop adequate indicators of gender differences in well-being. Recent research argues that gender relative well-being can be conceptualized as operating along three dimensions: (1) *capabilities gaps* refers to basic human abilities as measured through education, health, and nutrition; (2) differences in *access to resources and opportunities* refers primarily to equality in the opportunity to generate income, measured with wage and employment data; and (3) *empowerment* reflects women's ability to participate in deliberative bodies in key social, economic, and political institutions (Grown *et al.* 2003; Malhotra *et al.* 2002). The latter are often represented using female share of parliamentary seats and women's share of professional and technical positions as well as their share of managerial and administrative jobs.

It should be noted that there are likely feedback effects between the three categories of well-being. For example, an improvement in capabilities can establish the preconditions for participation in income-generating activities. The recent bargaining power literature, however, emphasizes that women's lesser well-being relative to men's is often due to unequal power in the household. Improvements in women's fallback position or outside options, as indicated by relative access to income, can improve their ability within the household to negotiate for an equitable distribution of resources and unpaid labor burden. The shift in power may have a positive effect on capabilities, particularly those of the young. It may also leverage women's increased access to deliberative bodies and to positions of economic power.

This study focuses on the capabilities and opportunities dimensions of well-being, although the specific indicators in each category differ somewhat from those used in other studies. (For a detailed discussion of all indicators, see Appendix A.) In the capabilities category, three *health indicators*[8] are used: the ratio of females to males in the population, the ratio of female to male mortality rates relative to a representative developed country (Sweden), and the fertility rate. In addition, there are three *education variables*: the ratio of female to male gross secondary school enrollment rates, the ratio of male to female illiteracy rates, and the ratio of female to male educational attainment for those over 15. Indicators of *women's relative access to material resources* are: the female share of the labor force, female share of total employment, and the ratio of male to female unemployment rates. This amounts to a 2/3 weighting for capabilities variables and 1/3 weighting of variables measuring access to resources and opportunities. Political and economic empowerment variables, though important, had to be omitted due to data deficiencies.

There have also been efforts to develop composite measures of gender equity in well-being. These are useful because there are divergences in gender equity across indicators even within the same country. Thus, a country might have comparatively high relative female educational attainment but score poorly on health indicators. The most well-known of these, the UNDP's Gender Development Index (GDI) and Gender Empowerment Measure (GEM), are problematic due to income components, which confound absolute with relative well-being.[9] Cross-country comparisons of trends in well-being require that another method to aggregate the indicators be found. In this paper, I use a very simple method of rank order scoring, the Borda Rule.

4 Relative female well-being in Latin America and the Caribbean

Data on the nine indicators discussed in the previous section were amassed for 21 Latin American and Caribbean countries for the period 1970–2000, or the closest year, where noted (see Table B.1 in Appendix B for a list of countries in the sample, and Table B.2 for a list of variables, definitions, and sources). This section provides an analysis of those data, evaluating cross-country differences in well-being in 2000 as well as secular trends in gender equity in well-being for the period 1970–2000. Countries with more than three missing variables were dropped from the sample, and unfortunately, this included a number of the small Caribbean island economies, making that region disproportionately under-represented in the sample.

4.1 Data on well-being

A summary of gendered differences in well-being indicators for 21 Latin America and Caribbean economies in 2000 is given in Table 8.1. The cross-country comparisons show substantial variation in well-being across indicators. Some variables are correlated, as shown in Table 8.2, although in a number of cases, correlations are weak, arguing for the relevance of a composite index rather than relying on a single indicator. Notable is the strong positive correlation between female share of the labor force and the ratio of females to males in the population. Although this does not provide any information on causality, it is consistent with the argument that female bargaining power evidenced by participation in labor markets can influence gender well-being in other categories.

Data on total years of educational attainment were missing for two countries – Bahamas and Belize. To retain as many countries as possible in the sample, missing data values were predicted by regressing the variable with missing values on the remaining well-being indicators.[10] The resulting parameter estimates were used to predict the missing observations. (Those values that are predicted are shown in bold type in Table 8.1).

It is useful to discuss for a moment the issue of ratios of female to male educational attainment that exceed 1, which gives the impression of male disadvantage. This occurs in several countries in our sample, particularly in Anglophone Caribbean countries. A consequence of this state of affairs has been the proliferation of the thesis of the marginalization of the Caribbean male, with the ensuing debate reflecting confusion as to the legitimacy of continuing to focus on women, given male underachievement in education (Barriteau 2006).[11] From

Table 8.1 Gender well-being indicators for Latin America and the Caribbean, 2000

Country	F/M population	F/M mortality (rel. to Sweden)	Fertility	F/M secondary school enrollment rates	F/M youth illiteracy rate	F/M total avg. yrs. education	Female share of labor force	Female share of total employment	Ratio F/M unemployment rates
Argentina	1.04	0.81	2.51	1.08	0.71	1.02	32.7	40.0	1.16
Bahamas	1.03	0.70	2.19	1.00	0.45	1.10	47.2	48.4	1.61
Barbados	1.07	0.93	1.75	1.05	0.87	0.98	46.2	46.5	1.71
Belize	0.98	1.03	3.13	1.15	0.48	0.90	23.9	31.0	1.87
Bolivia	1.01	1.35	3.93	0.87	3.15	0.85	37.7	44.0	1.37
Brazil	1.02	0.88	2.20	1.17	0.61	0.82	35.4	40.3	1.61
Chile	1.02	0.88	2.16	1.02	0.64	0.99	33.2	33.3	1.26
Colombia	1.02	0.91	2.55	1.11	0.65	1.17	38.4	44.7	1.35
Costa Rica	1.00	0.98	2.50	1.12	0.70	0.99	30.8	32.3	1.67
Dominican Republic	0.97	1.03	2.71	1.19	0.84	1.03	30.4	28.7	3.01
Ecuador	0.99	1.08	3.03	1.04	1.20	1.00	27.7	38.7	1.81
El Salvador	1.04	0.94	3.10	0.99	1.15	0.98	36.0	40.7	0.54
Honduras	0.99	1.01	3.92	1.23	0.87	0.71	31.4	36.0	1.03
Jamaica	1.02	1.09	2.46	1.04	0.27	1.15	46.2	42.0	2.23
Mexico	1.05	0.99	2.59	1.03	1.35	0.91	32.9	33.3	1.47
Panama	0.98	0.99	2.50	1.07	1.29	0.99	35.0	33.6	1.90
Paraguay	0.98	1.05	2.50	1.05	1.03	0.97	29.8	42.5	1.10
Peru	1.02	1.11	2.78	0.94	2.61	0.88	31.0	44.8	1.15
Trinidad & Tobago	1.00	1.19	1.75	1.08	1.22	1.06	34.0	36.6	1.54
Uruguay	1.06	0.72	2.23	1.33	0.56	1.09	41.5	42.4	1.68
Venezuela	0.99	0.92	2.82	1.41	0.48	1.04	34.5	35.4	1.35

Source: See Appendix Table B.2.

Table 8.2 Correlation matrix, gender well-being measurers for LAC, 2000

	F/M population	Relative F/M mortality	Fertility	F/M secondary school enrollment rates	F/M youth illiteracy rate	F/M total avg. yrs. education	Female share of labor force	Female share of total employment	Ratio F/M unemployment rates
F/M population	1.00	-0.44	-0.41	-0.19	-0.04	0.19	0.64	0.57	-0.30
Relative F/M mortality		1.00	0.44	-0.42	0.69	-0.31	-0.32	-0.14	0.08
Fertility			1.00	-0.07	0.44	-0.56	-0.39	-0.14	-0.22
F/M secondary school enrollment rates				1.00	-0.60	-0.09	-0.11	-0.36	0.20
F/M youth illiteracy Rate					1.00	-0.43	-0.16	0.21	0.24
F/M total avg. yrs. education						1.00	0.45	0.20	0.30
Female share of labor force							1.00	0.66	0.06
Female share of total employment								1.00	-0.36
Ratio F/M unemployment rates									1.00

Source: See Appendix Table B.2.

this perspective, it could be argued that if our concern is gender equity, male disadvantage should also be penalized in our assessments of a country's progress. Mathematically devising a formula to do so in these analyses does not pose a problem. Rather, of deeper concern are the conceptual issues. Should a country be considered male disadvantaged in some areas, for example, education, if male well-being exceeds that of females in several others? Given the gender inequities in most other categories, for this analysis, I forgo use of a ranking strategy that penalizes male inequality.

Focusing on how women's relative well-being has changed over time, Table 8.3 summarizes changes in gendered measures of well-being for the period 1970–2000. In many cases, the direction of change is toward improvement in well-being, but there are a number of cases in which female relative well-being has worsened.

Several categories are of particular interest. The ratio of females to males in the population fell in 10 out of 21 countries. In other contexts, low F/M population ratios are attributed to female disadvantage in access to food, nutrition, or infanticide and sex selective abortion (Sen 1990). In the Caribbean, the cause may be more strongly related to female out-migration, which occurs at a slightly higher rate than for males. In seven countries, the ratio of female to male unemployment rates fell, indicating women's decreasing ability to obtain work relative to men. Women's relative access to secondary schooling also fell in six countries, while the ratio of female to male unemployment rates rose in eight countries, indicating an increased burden of joblessness borne by women. Note also that in four countries, female to male educational attainment fell.

Average changes (weighted and unweighted by population) are shown in the last two lines of the table. On average, the unweighted change is toward improved well-being (the improvement is statistically significant for all but F/M population ratios and unemployment rates). With regard to weighted changes in well-being, the single dimension along which women fare worse is access to work, as indicated by the increase in the female to male unemployment rate ratio. This is driven by declines in women's relative access to work in Brazil, the largest country in the sample. The decline is statistically significant.

These average data allow us to make some comparisons between flow and stock variables, the former representing current levels of female disadvantage and the latter cumulative disadvantage. We might anticipate that if female disadvantage were waning, the average change in secondary school enrollment rates (a flow) would be larger than change in total educational attainment (a stock). It is larger, a difference that is statistically significant.

On the other hand, while the weighted average change in female share of the labor force was 11.64 percentage points for this sample, women's share of employment increased only 5.73 percentage points. This is indicative of women's greater difficulty in finding employment, and is also consistent with the view of numerous observers that female labor force participation in LAC in the past two decades is related to distress sales of labor as male incomes have declined and public services decreased, rather than an emancipatory reallocation of labor time.

Table 8.3 Change in gender well-being in LAC, 1970–2000

	F/M population	Relative F/M mortality	Fertility	F/M secondary school enrollment rates	F/M youth illiteracy rate	F/M total avg. yrs. education	Female share of labor force	Female share of total employment	Ratio F/M unemployment rate
Argentina	0.05	-0.10	0.60	-0.06	-0.20	0.06	7.84	6.25	-0.30
Bahamas	0.01	-0.30	1.26	-0.10	-0.26	0.10	7.16	6.24	-0.90
Barbados	-0.06	-0.12	1.27	0.03	0.11	-0.04	6.02	2.28	0.06
Belize	-0.03	-0.08	3.76	-0.08	-0.72	-0.08	3.16	-0.24	0.29
Bolivia	-0.02	0.13	2.59	0.15	0.43	0.18	5.90	1.58	0.35
Brazil	0.02	-0.38	2.79	0.14	-0.49	-0.08	11.74	9.04	0.66
Chile	-0.01	-0.11	1.79	-0.13	-0.41	0.03	10.84	3.87	-0.17
Colombia	0.01	-0.42	2.92	0.14	-0.38	0.28	14.24	6.41	-0.06
Costa Rica	0.01	-0.24	2.44	0.05	-0.27	0.00	12.70	8.00	-0.45
Dominican Rep.	0.00	-0.28	3.34	-0.11	-0.20	0.08	8.24	0.10	0.36
Ecuador	0.00	-0.27	3.17	0.19	-0.30	0.09	9.18	1.23	-0.19
El Salvador	0.05	-0.31	3.21	0.08	-0.20	0.32	15.42	7.51	-1.42
Honduras	0.00	-0.31	3.28	0.33	-0.19	-0.20	9.10	-6.28	-0.14
Jamaica	-0.03	-0.11	2.85	0.05	-0.30	0.04	3.20	2.78	-0.53
Mexico	0.05	-0.29	4.05	0.39	-0.21	0.27	13.80	2.32	-0.33
Panama	0.02	-0.40	2.70	-0.05	0.13	0.00	9.82	4.77	0.48
Paraguay	-0.04	-0.20	3.41	0.02	-0.37	0.10	3.40	2.13	-0.51
Peru	0.03	-0.25	3.44	0.17	-0.34	0.16	8.66	3.89	-0.09
Trinidad & Tobago	-0.02	-0.12	1.84	0.01	-0.61	0.11	4.50	6.29	-0.26
Uruguay	0.05	-0.18	0.69	0.15	-0.05	0.04	15.24	3.45	0.04
Venezuela	0.01	-0.22	2.50	0.35	-0.65	0.04	13.96	7.48	0.49
Average Change									
Unweighted	0.005	*-0.22*	*2.57*	*0.08*	*-0.26*	*0.07*	*9.24*	*3.77*	-0.12
Weighted	*0.024*	*-0.30*	*2.89*	*0.18*	*-0.35*	*0.08*	*11.64*	*5.73*	*0.13*

Source: See Appendix Table B.2.

Note: Fertility is measured as declines. Thus, for Argentina, female fertility fell 0.60. *Average change* refers to sample average changes in well-being. *Bold italicized* print in the last two rows indicates categories for which average change is statistically significant at the 5% level.

4.2   *Ranking ordering using the Borda Rule*

A cross-country comparison of trends in well-being requires that we find a method to aggregate the set of indicators. To do this, I use a very simple method of rank-order scoring, the Borda Rule. The basis of the rule is as follows. To rank countries according to an aggregate measure, we give equal weight to each indicator. A country is awarded a point equal to its rank for each criterion (or indicator). I then sum the points for each indicator to obtain an aggregate score and that score is used to rank countries.[12] Table 8.4 gives the ranking for the greatest change in gender equity in well-being from 1970 to 2000.

No country does uniformly well in all categories. For example, in the case of Anglophone Caribbean, males are significantly less likely be unemployed than females, despite lower average levels of educational attainment.[13] There also is little uniformity in rankings within categories (i.e. health, education, and labor market variables), although rankings are most similar across health categories. (Thus, a country that ranks low in gender equity in one of those categories has a similarly low ranking in the remaining two health categories as well.)

El Salvador ranks highest in improvement in women's relative well-being, a notable feat since per capita GDP growth over this 30-year period averaged −0.25 percent a year, whereas Colombia is second. The performance of El Salvador and Colombia is surprising, given the long period of conflict these countries have undergone. War is often associated with declines in male share of the population and labor force, suggesting that these improvements may be due to downward harmonization rather than improvement in female well-being. On the other hand, war and conflict have been shown to have severely negative consequences for women in terms of violence, resulting in part from norms of hypermasculinity that surge during such times (UNIFEM 2002). There are, however, indications that the driving force in the improved rankings of El Salvador and Colombia is improvements in female well-being. For example, in both countries, fertility declined by half and substantial improvements in female education absolutely as well as relatively were registered. Mexico ranks third, and this performance fits with the predictions of globalization proponents that liberalization is good for women.

The two countries with the highest per capita growth over this period – Chile and Dominican Republic – ranked among the lowest. Trinidad and Tobago, with a petroleum-based economy and therefore substantial government revenues for public investment, nevertheless ranks very low also. Some countries might rank low for change in gender gaps if they started at a very high level of gender equity, and thus had little distance to go to close gender gaps. Such is the case of Barbados, which ranks second for gender equity in well-being in 2000, and last in change in gender equity in well-being from 1970 to 2000.

I consider more formally the relationship between growth and well-being in the next section of the paper. Here, for illustrative purposes, I estimate the effect of growth on well-being, using a methodology similar to one used by the World Bank (2001), albeit with a more restricted sample. The Bank analysis is based on

Table 8.4 Ranking for change in gender equity in well-being, LAC 1970–2000

Borda ranking (1=greatest positive change in gender well-being)	Country	F/M population	Relative F/M mortality	Fertility	F/M secondary school enrollment rates	F/M youth illiteracy rate	F/M total avg. yrs. education	Female share of labour force	Female share of total employment	RatioF/M unemployment rates	Total borda points
1	El Salvador	20	16	15	12	6	21	21	19	21	151
2	Colombia	11	20	13	14	15	20	19	17	9	138
3	Mexico	19	15	21	15	5	19	17	8	17	136
4	Venezuela	12	13	8	20	19	10	18	18	2	120
5	Peru	17	9	19	17	4	17	10	12	11	116
6	Brazil	15	19	11	13	18	2	15	21	1	115
7	Costa Rica	14	11	7	10	14	5	16	20	16	113
8	Uruguay	21	17	2	16	8	8	20	10	8	110
9	Bahamas	13	13	3	3	17	14	7	14	19	103
10	Ecuador	10	10	14	18	7	13	12	4	10	98
11	Argentina	18	7	1	5	13	11	8	15	18	96
12	Honduras	8	14	16	19	9	1	11	1	15	94
13	Paraguay	2	8	18	8	11	15	3	6	20	91
14	Panama	16	18	10	6	2	6	13	13	4	88
15	Jamaica	3	4	12	11	21	9	2	9	12	83
16	Trinidad & Tobago	5	3	6	7	12	16	4	16	13	82
17	Chile	7	5	5	1	16	7	14	11	14	80
17	Dominican Rep.	9	12	17	2	10	12	9	3	6	80
19	Bolivia	6	1	9	15	3	18	5	5	3	65
20	Belize	4	2	20	4	20	3	1	2	5	61
21	Barbados	1	6	4	9	1	4	6	7	7	45

Source: See Appendix Table B.2.

regressions of single indicators of well-being in 1995 (rather than a composite index) on the natural log of per capita GDP in 1995.[14] They find that per capita GDP has a positive effect on gender equity in well-being. The Bank argues, on the basis of these results, that promotion of economic growth is a critical component of any program to reduce gender inequality. By using per capita GDP in the end year of the analysis, the Bank's method fails to isolate the effects of the macroeconomic policies associated with globalization on well-being over the last 25 years. Those are precisely the policies of which many gender experts have been so critical for their negative effects on women's well-being.

To evaluate the impact of globalization policies, it would be necessary to isolate the effect of changes in per capita income during the relevant period. I do this by regressing Borda rankings for change in equity on total growth of per capita GDP for the period 1970–2000, controlling for initial per capita income (in 1970).[15] Initial income has a positive effect on equity in well-being, implying that those countries with the largest gains in gender equity already had the highest per capita income by 1970. But, as the scatter plot in Figure 8.1 shows there is a negative association between GDP growth from 1970 to 2000 and equity. (That figure shows the partial correlation of equity with total per capita income growth from 1970 to 2000, with the trend line given by a LOESS fit). The coefficient on the growth variable is significant at the 5 percent level, suggesting that improvements in women's well-being during this period, where they did occur, were due to factors other than globalization-induced growth. These results may not be surprising because five out of the ten highest ranked countries in Table 8.4 peaked in terms of per capita GDP during the 1970s or earlier.

In reality and in contrast to the Bank's claims, economic growth in the current environment of liberalization can produce contradictory gender effects. Structural change induced by growth may generate employment, thus increasing women's access to private sources of income. But state-distributed resources may decline with pressure on public sector budgets. Women's increased employment, even if due to distress sales of labor and despite the insecurity of work, may improve their status within the household. This might occur if they are perceived to have a more important role in providing household income, whether because their access to work has increased or because men's has declined. But the shift in bargaining power within the household may also stimulate a backlash against females that shows up in other ways, such as family dissolution or violence against women. While micro-level analyses are needed to assess the household level effects of such policies, in the next section, I attempt to disentangle these various macro-level factors that influence well-being.

5   Panel data results

In this section, I assess the determinants of gender equity in well-being across countries over time. I use individual indicators as dependent variables for the panel data analysis for several reasons. While a composite index is useful for ranking countries according to well-being, the variance of the dependent variable

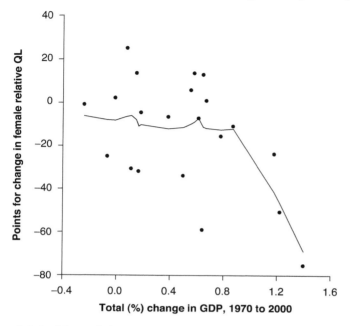

Figure 8.1 Partial correlation between change in female relative well-being and growth
GDP, 1970–2000.
Note: Nearest neighbor (LOESS) fit (degree = 1.0, span = 0.4).

is artificially constrained by the range of ranks. Second, independent variables
may operate on individual measures of well-being differently (see e.g. Richards
et al. 2002; Mason and Smith 2003). Finally, missing data makes computation of
a time-series composite index unreliable.

5.1   Variables

The dependent variables used in the regressions are: female to male population
ratio, ratio of female to male secondary school enrollment, and relative female to
male mortality rates. The choice of these individual measures can be explained as
follows. If we were to choose a single measure of gendered differences in quality
of life, a good proxy is the female to male population ratio. Decisions to invest in
female children's nutrition, health care, and even seeing a pregnancy through
when the fetus is known to be female, reflects society's valuation of females.
Social perceptions aside, improvements in women's access to power and material resources enable them to invest more in their daughters' health and nutrition,
and to avoid sex-selective abortions or infanticide that favors males. In LAC, a
decline in F/M population ratios can also be due to female-intensive out-migration,
rather than a reduction in life chances. The lack of employment opportunities
to sustain self and families that this implies, however, is in itself an important

Table 8.5 Regression variable codes and definitions

Regression variable codes	Description of variable
DEBTX	Total debt service as % of exports
FMPOP	Ratio of females to males in population
FSHLF	Female share of labor force
GR	Growth rate of per capita GDP in $1995
GRGOV	Growth rate of total (real) government expenditures
INVGR	Growth rate of gross fixed capital formation
MFGVA	Manufacturing value-added as % of GDP (Annual growth rate for manufacturing value added based on constant local currency)
RELMORT	Male to female mortality rates, relative to reference population (Sweden)
RSENROLL	Ratio of female to male gross secondary school enrollment rates
SERVVA	Services value-added as % of GDP (Annual growth rate for services value added based on constant local currency)
TRADE	Sum of exports and imports of goods and services measured as a share of GDP
XGR	Annual growth rate of exports of goods and services based on constant local currency

indicator of female relative well-being. More generally, then the F/M population ratio can be seen as a proxy measure of gender well-being but does not reveal the precise processes that contribute to changes in gender gaps.

I explore growth effects on gross secondary school enrollment rates, a measure that can be considered a flow variable, as noted – it reflects current gender norms and stereotypes as well as bargaining power, in contrast to measures of total educational attainment, which summarizes current and past discrimination. Finally, I test for determinants of relative female to male mortality rates (relative, i.e. to the ratio in the reference country, Sweden; see Appendix A for more details on this variable). This variable may capture differences in women's and men's access to income and other resources that can sustain health. The gap could also vary across countries and over time, in response to changes in the adequacy of a country's health care system and infrastructure that insure, for example, clean water and protection from infectious diseases. It may thus also be influenced by a country's stage of development, in addition to gender gaps in income and empowerment.

From the previous discussion, right-hand side variables fall into four categories: (1) economic growth, (2) economic structure, (3) government spending, and (4) women's empowerment. I turn first to a discussion of the independent variables. (All regression variables and codes are listed in Table 8.5.)[16]

5.1.1 Economic growth

Economic growth is measured as average annual GDP growth from 1970 to 2000. There may be reason to be concerned that economic growth is not truly exogenous, if equity influences growth. I, therefore, also run regressions with investment growth and export growth, two variables causally linked to growth in the literature.

5.1.2   Economic structure

I test for the effects of economic structure by including as regressor manufacturing value-added as a percentage of GDP. The expansion of manufacturing as a share of GDP, particularly light-manufacturing, is linked to improvement in women's job access. Countries specializing in manufactured exports for which terms of trade are declining, however, may find that specialization in this area yields few if any benefits for well-being. This is an especially salient issue for developing countries, because there is evidence that light-manufacturing expansion among semi-industrialized economies has also led to a process of immiserizing growth (Erturk 2001–02). Whether this differentially impacts women depends on how the effects of declining terms of trade are distributed. If it leads to greater stresses on females as a result of deterioration of work conditions due to competitive pressures, then gender effects may be apparent. Services value-added as a share of GDP is also used to capture structural change. Finally, trade as a share of GDP is used as an additional economic structure variable. Gender effects are ambiguous. Women are the target labor supply for labor-intensive industries, but mobility of firms holds down compensation.

5.1.3   Government expenditures

Government spending can act as a redistributive mechanism such that women's relative well-being is enhanced by increases in social expenditures. Whether such spending is gender-equitable is an empirical question, because governments may allocate spending in such a way that reinforces rather than rectifies gender imbalances in well-being. To capture this effect, I use the growth rate of government consumption, adjusted for inflation. The government consumption variable is imprecise because it includes a variety of other expenditures unrelated to well-being. Data on measures such as public health and education spending are incomplete, however, and thus I am forced to rely on government spending in the aggregate. In addition, I include measures of debt as a percentage of exports which may affect expenditures on public goods that can affect women's relative well-being and may thus also attenuate the benefits of export earnings for the domestic economy.

5.1.4   Empowerment

Finally, as an empowerment variable, I use female share of the labor force. This variable represents a means to well-being as well as an end (insofar as access to work may improve the quality of life intrinsically), because it reflects female access to income that can increase household bargaining power. As noted, even unpaid work may improve women's value to the household and thus status, allowing them to leverage more resources for female family members. Female share of employment would have been preferred as a variable here, but it could not be used due to a large number of missing values.

These categories of right-hand side variables listed above represent the diverse avenues through which female well-being may improve. The growth variable reflects the effect of total expansion of resources, whereas economic structure, government resources, and female empowerment may have redistributive effects. Of the three redistributive effects, the first occurs as a result of the interaction of economic structural change with labor markets, mediated by gendered job access. The second reflects government policy. (While government policy is itself likely to be influenced by female political representation, political empowerment measures are not available for time-series analysis.) Finally, the third represents the impact of greater female bargaining power that results from the effect of labor market access on distribution within the household.

5.2   *Data and estimation*

Regressions are estimated using a two-way error components model. The basic model can be summarized as:

$$Y_{it} = \alpha + X_{it}\,\beta + \upsilon_{it}$$

where the error term υ_{it} has three components:

$$\upsilon_{it} = \mu_i + \lambda_t + \varepsilon_{it}$$

Here, μ_i captures the country specific-effects while λ_t represents time-varying effects. Country (fixed) effects control for unobserved time-invariant differences that might affect the gender well-being variable.

Various econometric issues need to be considered. First, one may expect measurement errors due to inaccuracies in schooling, labor force participation, as well as in some macroeconomic variables, leading to large standard errors, and thus a downward bias on t-statistics. This may not necessarily lead to misleading econometric results, provided that the biases are constant over time and the errors are random. In addition, the use of pooled time-series data, which yields a large number of observations, permits behavioral relationships to be detected, even though nontrivial random errors in the data may exist.

Second, data must be stationary for standard inference procedures to apply in time-series analysis. To check for stationarity, unit root tests were conducted. Those variables that were found to be nonstationary were first-differenced, resulting in stationary series. Variables so-adjusted are preceded by a difference operator in the reported regression results.

Heteroskedasticity problems are frequently encountered with cross-sectional data, and therefore regressions use GLS, with cross-sectional weights derived from the residual cross-sectional standard deviations. While this procedure corrects for heteroskedasticity across countries, a more general form is necessary to allow variances within a cross section to vary over time. This was done by obtaining standard errors in accordance with White's variance–covariance matrix in all regressions. I also corrected for autocorrelation, where necessary, using an autoregressive process modeled as an AR(1) with a common country coefficient.

Some right-hand side variables are potentially endogenous. In particular, the growth rate of GDP may be simultaneously determined by the gender variables.[17] This is less likely to be an issue with the schooling measure used here, but it may be relevant for the population ratio and mortality ratio. To check for this, Hausmann tests were run with the results indicating no evidence of endogeneity for per capita GDP growth.[18] In addition, I ran a set of regressions, proxying for GDP growth with the growth rate of gross fixed capital formation and export growth. The literature suggests that these variables are correlated with GDP growth, but not with the dependent variables. There is, however, some dispute about the effect of exports on growth (see, e.g. Rodríguez and Rodrik 2001).

Finally, these regressions use unbalanced panels, due to the variations in data availability. Thus, the inclusion or exclusion of certain variables causes the sample size to change. This does not present any econometric problems, and may be viewed as a test of robustness of the independent variables. In this analysis, however, some variables have missing data for all countries for the 1970s and 1980s, for example, and thus inclusion of those variables causes the period of analysis to change. In those cases, the results are not strictly comparable to regressions where variables span the entire period of 1970–2000.

5.3   Results

Regression results from estimating the determinants of the female to male population ratio (*FMPOP*) are given in Table 8.6. The lagged value of *d* (*FMPOP*) is used to capture prior differences across countries, with the coefficient measuring adjustments to the *FMPOP*, assuming no differences in the remaining independent variables, and $d(\cdot)$ is the difference operator. Equation (1) shows that economic growth (GR) *h*as a significant negative effect on *FMPOP*. Structural change variables – manufacturing and service value-added as share of GDP (*MFGVA* and *SERVVA*) – are significant, and suggest a positive effect on gender equity. Trade as a share of GDP (*TRADE*) and debt as a percentage of exports (*DEBTX*) are insignificant, however. The female share of the labor force (*FSHLF*) is positive but insignificant, and this may suggest that female-intensive employment effects of structural change are captured by *MFGVA* and *SERVVA*. The coefficient on growth rate of government consumption (*GRGOV*) is positive and significant. (We should not read much into the high R^2 because the lagged dependent variable is likely the cause.)

Equation (2) proxies for economic growth with the growth rate of gross fixed capital formation (*INVGR*) and the growth rate of exports of goods and services (*XGR*). Neither of these variables is significant, and they have opposite signs. *MFGVA* continues to be positive and significant, along with the growth rate of government consumption, while the positive coefficient on female share of the labor force becomes significant in this regression.

Table 8.6 Panel data results, LAC, 1970–2000 Fixed effects, GLS, dependent variable: d(F/M population ratio)

	Eq. 1	*Eq. 2*
d(FMPOP(−1))	0.958	0.962
	(59.54)***	(55.66)***
GR	−0.001	
	(2.585)***	
INVGR		0.001
		(0.87)
XGR		−0.001
		(0.67)
d(MFGVA)	0.051	0.023
	(2.50)**	(2.51)***
d(SERVVA)	0.022	0.011
	(1.92)**	(1.04)
d(TRADE)	0.003	−0.001
	(0.27)	(0.26)
d(DEBTX)	−0.002	−0.02
	(0.43)	(0.28)
d(FSHLF)	0.441	0.470
	(1.57)	(1.68)*
GRGOV	0.034	0.034
	(6.45)***	(6.42)***
N	332	319
Adj. R^2	0.953	0.950
Breusch–Godfrey	0.854	1.392
	(p = .43)	(p = .25)

Note
Absolute values of *T*-statistics are in parentheses. A triple asterisk (***) indicates $p < 0.01$, a double asterisk (**) $p < 0.05$, and a single asterisk (*) $p < 0.10$.

Table 8.7 presents the results of regressing the change in the ratio of female to male gross secondary school enrollment rates on the same set of independent variables. Here, in Equation 1, the coefficient on economic growth is insignificant, while *MFGVA* is positive and significant. Trade as a share of GDP is negative and significant, while the remaining variables are insignificant. The adjusted R^2 of these regressions falls dramatically. These results suggest multiple contradictory processes are at work. Interestingly, the growth of government expenditures has no effect on gender equity in education, suggesting that public spending on education has not contributed to a closure of gender gaps. But the shift to manufacturing has had a positive effect, and may well be related to incentives to invest in female education as a result of women's expanded work opportunities. (It could also signify that when women gain access to employment, they are able to leverage more gender equitable education spending.) On the other hand, trade has a negative effect on education. The pathway by which trade negatively affects

Table 8.7 Panel data results, LAC, 1970–2000 Fixed effects, GLS, dependent variable: d(F/M Gross Secondary School Enrollment Rates)

	Eq. 1	*Eq. 2*
d(RSENROLL(−1))	0.081	0.079
	(0.47)	(0.69)
GR	0.0002	
	(0.97)	
INVGR		0.0003
		(2.84)***
XGR		−0.0007
		(2.12)**
d(MFGVA)	0.081	0.072
	(4.34)***	(3.15)***
d(SERVVA)	0.018	0.034
	(0.14)	(2.26)**
d(TRADE)	−0.001	−0.0001
	(3.14)***	(1.61)*
d(DEBTX)	−0.010	−0.011
	(1.06)	(1.30)
d(FSHLF)	0.013	0.005
	(0.03)	(0.12)
GRGOV	−0.001	0.002
	(0.59)	(0.65)
N	313	299
Adj. R^2	0.106	0.166
Breusch–Godfrey	1.006	1.169
	(p = .37)	(p = .31)

Note:
Absolute values of *T*-statistics are in parentheses. A triple asterisk (***) indicates $p < 0.01$, a double asterisk (**) $p < 0.05$, and a single asterisk (*) $p < 0.10$.

female education is not revealed in this analysis, and requires country-level case studies to answer that question. As the gender and trade literature suggests, however, it could be related to the effect of higher cost imports (from devaluation) that reduces household income available for education expenditures, with girls more disadvantaged than boys.

Equation 2 shows that investment growth has a positive effect on female relative education, while export growth exerts a negative significant effect. It is not clear why these variables would operate in opposite directions, unless in fact declining terms of trade or instability of export earnings produce negative gender effects. Nevertheless, the sum of these coefficients is roughly zero, suggesting that the net effect on education is small (a Wald test confirms that the sum of these coefficient is not significantly different from zero). The structural change variables retain their significance in this equation, again with the exception that *SERVVA* becomes positive and significant.

Table 8.8 presents results on the determinants of relative female to male mortality. A positive sign on coefficients indicates that increases in the independent

Table 8.8 Panel data results, LAC, 1970–2000 Fixed effects, GLS Dependent variable: (F/M adult mortality rates relative to Swedish ratio)

	Eq. 1	*Eq. 2*
d(RELMORT(−1))	0.763	0.749
	(14.46)***	(12.12)***
GR	0.0001	
	(6.64)***	
INVGR		0.001
		(0.98)
XGR		0.001
		(0.90)
d(MFGVA)	−0.011	0.004
	(1.59)	(0.74)
d(SERVVA)	0.005	0.017
	(0.38)	(3.32)***
d(TRADE)	0.001	−0.0002
	(0.26)	(0.07)
d(DEBTX)	0.003	0.003
	(4.84)***	(2.74)***
d(FSHLF)	−0.126	−0.180
	(1.99)**	(2.47)**
GRGOV	−0.002	−0.002
	(2.91)***	(2.29)**
N	335	321
Adj. R^2	0.792	0.766
Breusch–Godfrey	2.561	0.764
	($p = .04$)	($p = .57$)

Note:
Absolute values of *T*-statistics are in parentheses. A triple asterisk (***) indicates $p < 0.01$, a double asterisk (**) $p < 0.05$, and a single asterisk (*) $p < 0.10$.

variables contribute to higher female mortality relative to males – thus a deterioration of gender equity in well-being. The first equation shows a positive significant effect of growth on women's relative mortality (relative to men's and relative to the reference country ratio). Increases in the debt ratio raise female relative mortality rates, while female share of the labor force and the growth rate of government expenditures have significant negative effects. These results should be viewed with some caution because, as the Breusch–Godfrey test shows, autocorrelation is present, and could not be eliminated with standard techniques. Equation 2 results show that the growth variables have an insignificant effect, while *SERVVA* and *DEBTX* exhibit positive effects which are significant. At the same time, *FSHLF* and *GRGOV* retain their negative significant effect.

The contradictory effect of *SERVVA* as compared to *FSHLF* is difficult to explain, but may be due to collinearity of these variables if indeed structural shift partially induces female entrance into paid labor force. (Re-estimation of these equations with *MFGVA SERVVA*, dropping *FSHLF*, results in positive but insignificant coefficients on these variables.)

Table 8.9 Summary of regression results

	FMPOP		RSENROLL		F/M RELMORT	
	Eq.1	*Eq.2*	*Eq.1*	*Eq.2*	*Eq.1*	*Eq.2*
GR	—*		+		+*	
INVGR		+		+*		+
XGR		—		—*		+
MFGVA	+*	+*	+*	+*	—	+
SERVVA	+*	+	+	+*	—	+*
TRADE	+	—	—	—*	—	—
DEBTX	—	—	—	—	+*	+*
FSHLF	+	+*	+	+	—*	—*
GRGOV	+*	+*	—	+	—*	—*

Note:
*indicates significance at the 10 percent level or better.

6 Discussion of results

Table 8.9 summarizes results from the panel data estimations. Four variables have positive effects on gender equity in well-being (with varying degrees of robustness): manufacturing and service value-added as a share of GDP, female share of the labor force, and the growth rate of government consumption. The positive effect of the shift to manufacturing is noteworthy, and this may occur via the impact on the relative demand for female labor. Despite the fact that female share of the labor force includes both employed and unemployed women, as well as paid and unpaid work, it is clear from these results that women's economic activity improves their well-being. Whether due to the bargaining power that this confers on women to negotiate with male members of the family, or because women directly generate income, the effect is positive and significant in most cases.

The remaining variables do not have a consistently positive or negative effect on gender equity in well-being, with the exception of economic growth to which I now turn. These results show a negative effect of economic growth on F/M population ratios and a positive effect on F/M mortality (and no effect on gender gaps in education). These results are consistent with those for several Asian economies, where growth was also found to have a negative (but statistically insignificant) effect on female relative population ratios (Seguino 2002). Some research has shown that inequality is lower among poorer income households in that region (Murthi *et al.* 1995), while higher *FMPOP* ratios go hand-in-hand with higher levels of poverty (Drèze and Sen 1995). One reason advanced to explain why female relative well-being may decline as incomes rise is the "emulation" effect, explained as follows. In low-income households, women's labor is crucial for family survival, especially in agricultural households. But as incomes rise, poor classes seek to emulate wealthier ones that limit women's economic activity (despite women's high levels of education). The practise of circumscribing women's activities enhances the patriarch's social status because it acts as an indicator of the male head of household's wealth. The result for women, however, is that their bargaining power decreases.

Latin America and the Caribbean, however, are influenced not only by differing economic structures but also by diverse sets of gender norms and stereotypes. In Anglophone Caribbean, women have more freedom to participate in labor markets, although this is less the case in Central America (see, e.g. Fleck 1996). Nevertheless, seclusion is not practiced in the Americas and thus higher income is less likely to induce this "emulation effect." If not, a different explanation has to be sought for why growth does not improve gender equity in well-being.

The answer may be found in the type of growth, or the characteristics of the growth process. If growth results in increased economic insecurity and job "flexibility," due to the process of globalization that makes capital more mobile, women may differentially bear the costs of economic insecurity, which may be driving the results found here for population ratios. In the Caribbean, for example, one result of economic insecurity has been out-migration, with women more likely to emigrate than men. Further, if women are more likely to get the insecure jobs or bear the burden of government expenditures that reduce social services, then improvements in female relative well-being are likely to be stymied, even with growth.

The inability for growth to improve women's relative well-being may also be due to a "backlash" against women of downward harmonization as a result of a deterioration of men's economic status. Much of the research on this region in recent years indicates that women have entered the labor force at least in part in response to declining incomes and employment of male household members. The erosion of men's well-being and income generating opportunities may contribute to higher rates of domestic violence, as men's traditional role as breadwinner is compromised, leading to a "crisis of masculinity" (Chant 2000). Thus, men's inability to fulfill norms of masculinity may have produced negative reactions to women that have redounded negatively on F/M population ratios and relative mortality rates.

There is some evidence consistent with this explanation. For example, Larraín (1999) notes that Latin America and the Caribbean, the part of the world with the least equitable distribution of wealth, is also one of the areas with the highest rates of violence in the home.[19] Larraín (1999) argues that unequal income distribution is one of the chief factors fuelling the rise in domestic violence in Latin America and the Caribbean.[20] Her research findings indicate that women who work outside of their homes and earn their own incomes are less likely to be beaten, and have greater possibilities of escaping the situation by separating from their partners.[21] Of course, one of the problems observed is that the jobs that many women can get in export industries or informal sector jobs make it difficult to bargain for higher wages, and thus, their employment may both put them in danger of backlash at home, and leave them unable to escape due to low wages.[22]

Negative effects of men's declining economic fortunes may also put pressure on family structures in a way that increases women's labor burdens. Based on research in rural Costa Rica, Chant (2000) finds that men's declining economic opportunities lead to family dissolution, as echoed by Martín, a 30-year old bricklayer, who participated in a focus group session: "*La mujer que tiene su propia plata pierde el cariño para el esposo. Muchos matrimonios han fracasado por eso"* ("A woman who has her own money loses affection for her husband. Many marriages have been ruined because of this"). According to Chant, men's inability to provide can set in motion a vicious circle whereby men abandon their responsibilities and women increase labor effort to fill the gap.

7 Conclusion

In this paper, I develop a set of indicators to track trends in gender equity in well-being over the period 1970–2000 for Latin America and the Caribbean. Using a composite index based on these indicators, I rank countries according to equity in well-being in 2000 and change in gender equity over the past 30 years. The data show that gender equity in well-being has improved but not unambiguously so. Several countries have experienced declines in individual indicators of well-being, and there is a significant worsening of women's experience of unemployment relative to men's. Growth since 1970 is not shown to improve gender equity, measured using a composite index.

In panel data estimations, economic growth exhibits a negative effect on female to male population ratios and a positive effect on relative female to male mortality rates. Manufacturing and service value-added as a share of GDP are positively correlated with improvements in women's relative well-being as are government consumption growth and to a lesser extent, female share of the labor force.

Economic growth under liberalized conditions appears to have contradictory, and in some cases, worryingly negative gender effects. Unraveling those contradictions is a complex task, and country-specific conditions probably play an important role, making it impossible to generalize about the precise dynamics at play. That said, it appears that macroeconomic, trade, and finance policies in the last 30 years have contributed to the growth of insecure employment. Men have also been negatively affected, and women have responded by trying to cushion adverse effects on household income by increasing paid labor time. Many who have gained access to employment have done so primarily in insecure positions and frequently in the informal economy. The social insurance necessary to cushion that increased vulnerability in markets is not forthcoming, due to limits on the ability of the state to provide a social safety net.

While this paper attempts to provide a panoramic view of progress in achieving equity in well-being, there are limitations to this exercise that must be acknowledged. Gender-disaggregated data are still in short supply, and many of our measures are only proxies. Second, the most serious weakness of this paper, in my view, is the lack of detail on the effect of ethnicity on gender equity. In fact, it is possible that gender inequity varies by ethnicity, with subaltern women bearing the greatest burden of inequality. I am, however, constrained by lack of country-level data to assess this, and it thus remains the object of future work.

This brings me to my last point, which is that a study such as this allows us to see broad trends and consider the role of macroeconomic policy, but a deeper understanding of causality and connections is usefully gained at the country level.

A case-study approach could give us some insight into why growth, for example, appears to have no discernible effect on secondary schooling equity, but has a negative effect on female to male population ratios. Such studies would also be able to illuminate more fully the types of government expenditures that are gender-enabling and the processes that have led to such redistributive policies. Finally, the connective tissue in these relationships is political, economic, and social institutions which vary across countries, and to fully understand trends, we also need to know how they are supporting or impeding change.

Appendix A

1 Indicators of gender equity in well-being

In the selection of these indicators, I make a distinction between flow variables and stock variables. The former represents a snapshot at a moment in time of gender relative well-being, while the stock variables are measures that represent the cumulative effect of gender bias in well-being. (All indicators are measured so that a positive value indicates an increase in gender equity.)

2 Health indicators

2.1 *The ratio of females to males in the population*

I rely on the number of females per 100 males in the population as an indicator of health as well as female social status, following Saith and Harriss-White (1999) and others.[23] This can be considered a stock variable (rather than a flow) since it summarizes cumulative gender inequality as it has operated over a long period of time. In 2000, the ratio of females to males globally ranged from a low of 52 (United Arab Emirates) to a high of 117 (Latvia), with a global unweighted mean of 101.2.[24] The causes for this variation are complex and include both biological and social determinants. In general, women's natural advantage in longevity is offset to varying degrees by their lower social status.

The ratio varies over the life cycle. Male birth rates exceed those of females by roughly five percent at birth due to biological factors, but female survival is higher from the fetal stage forward, if females and males are given similar care. This is explained by female resistance to diseases in infancy and differences in sex hormones in adolescence, which leads to higher mortality rates for males up to the age of 30. At that point, the ratio becomes balanced. But beyond this stage, if females are not severely disadvantaged, their survival rates exceed males' up to menopause, causing the population ratio to favor females. As fertility rates decline and populations live longer, female relative ratios would likely lead to a higher share of women than men in the population because women usually outlive men. Operating in the opposite direction, there are a growing number of female abortions, as sex-selective abortion becomes more commonplace (Clarke 2000). Falling ratios may also be due to excess female mortality, gender inequities in access to resources for female children, including health care and nutrition, female-intensive out-migration, and female-intensive violence (see Clarke 2000 on spatial geographic distribution of men and women as mobility of women changes).

In societies where males are seen as socially and economically more valuable, or women are unable to exert sufficient power to protect female children on an equal basis with male children, we would expect a lower ratio than where greater equity is evident. A movement toward a higher ratio can be interpreted as a higher female quality of life or greater equity in well-being, though the exact chain of causality is not revealed in the indicator. In this sense, the variable is a rough proxy for the complex social dimensions of gender inequality. One of the challenges of using this variable is that a rising ratio, beyond a threshold ratio, may be due to male disadvantage, resulting from violence, war, or greater male use of alcohol and drugs, for example. That threshold ratio is not easy to determine since factors that influence mortality and life expectancy vary over time. This problem exists with a variety of the variables used in this analysis, such as education ratios, where female education exceeds male education for some countries. Theoretically, we might want to develop a method of calculating indicators so that female well-being that exceeds males' is not counted as a social "good." In practise, only one of the countries in our sample has a female to male population ratio that is noticeably high (Barbados at 107), and it is about equivalent to the European average of 106, where life expectancies are very high.

2.2 *Ratio of adult male to female mortality rates*

Adult male mortality rates (measured per 1000 persons) generally exceed female rates due to a variety of factors, including a higher incidence for males of such behaviors such as alcohol and tobacco consumption and violence. The gap between male and female mortality rates will be smaller, however, if women have less access to healthcare or food, if maternal healthcare provision is lacking, and if mortality from domestic violence is severe. In contrast to the population ratio, which captures differences in treatment of the young, this measure focuses on the adult population, although in some sense, it reflects cumulative discrimination since women's health status in adulthood may be more compromised than men's if treated unequally in earlier years. Gender bias is inferred by contrasting the male to female mortality rate with that of a reference developed country population. Following Svedberg (1996), I use Sweden as the reference population.[25] This method is used as a way to sort out the biological factors that lead to gender differences in mortality rates from those that are behavioral. A ratio below 1 indicates country-specific gender bias relative to the reference population.

2.3 *Fertility*

Measures of female fertility (average number of live births per adult female) are an indirect measure of women's well-being. Excess fertility frequently points to women's lack of control over reproductive decisions, and reflects stress on women's health, both through the physical cost of child-bearing and nurturing in early years, as well as in the labor time required to care for additional children. In the latter regard, this can also therefore be considered a variable that measures access to resources. As women spend more time in the care of children, there is less time available for activities that generate income. A decline in fertility is considered to be an indicator of improvement in women's quality of life, reflecting improvements in their agency.

3   Education

There is intrinsic benefit to women's education beyond income-earning possibilities, in that it leads to women's enhanced understanding of the array of choices they may face, as well as their agency to change inequitable situations. I use three measures of relative educational attainment – secondary enrollment rates, youth illiteracy, and total educational attainment. These are discussed in further detail below.

3.1   *Ratio of female to male gross secondary school enrollment rates*

The gross ratio of female to male secondary enrollment rates is a flow variable. It tells us, at a given point in time, what percentage of female children of secondary school age are enrolled relative to the male rate in the same age group. This variable reflects treatment of females relative to males, indicated by society's relative willingness to invest resources in their education in the current period. There are limitations on the ability of this variable to reflect gender inequality since these data do not take account of past discrimination against women in access to education. Further, because this is a gross (not net) ratio, it does not account for gender differences in drop-out rates.[26]

3.2   *Ratio of male to female youth Illiteracy rates*

The ratio of male to female illiteracy rates for those aged 15–24 is used in this analysis to capture gender differences in well-being. The literacy rate, defined as the ability of a person to read and write, with understanding, a short simple statement on everyday life, is often frowned on as an indicator. This is because, frequently, the characteristic is self-reported and, there are cross-country differences in the literacy criterion. While that weakness is difficult to overcome, it is attenuated in this case, since we are measuring ratios of male to female rates, rather than absolute levels of attainment. I use this variable in addition to the variable on secondary school enrollment because it captures a threshold of empowerment that can lead to improvement in status and bargaining power. This is also a flow variable.

3.3   *Ratio of female to male total average years of educational attainment*

Another measure of education used here is the ratio of women's to men's total educational attainment of those over 15. This is a stock variable in that it gives information about older members of the population and summarizes past discrimination. It provides further breadth in our understanding of gender equity, since it includes measures of schooling beyond basic levels. One might argue that in increasingly industrialized societies, higher levels of educational attainment are necessary not only as a means to develop the mental skills to make choices but also to provide access to labor markets.

4   Access to resources

Access to resources is influenced by a person's ability and agency to engage in productive activity. That access may occur directly, via the generation of earnings, or indirectly, if outside work options influence a woman's bargaining power within the household, leading to a gender-enabling redistribution of household resources. Education does not insure access to material resources. Therefore, a separate set of indicators is required to capture this aspect of well-being.

The gap between education and access to resources is in part explained by pervasive job discrimination, with women paid significantly less than men on average, after accounting for gender differentials in productivity. This may be the result of employer behavior in noncompetitive markets (Black and Brainerd 2002). There is also evidence that the effect of job segregation, with women over-represented in "mobile" industries or flexible jobs, is low bargaining power vis-à-vis employers relative to men, with the result that wage gaps remain wide, even as educational gaps close (Bhattacharya and Rahman 1999; Seguino 2000c; Berik *et al.* 2002).

Measuring access to resources, while necessary, is complex. Data on job segregation and pay differentials would have been preferred, but these are sparse. I therefore rely on labor market data, which provides a proxy for access to income, although in an imprecise way. There is no single measure that can capture labor market outcomes, in part due to the complexity of gender differences in labor market outcomes. It is also dangerous to rely on a single indicator since across countries, variables may be collected or measured differently[27] and thus I include three measures of access to resources, all related to labor and labor market outcomes.

4.1   Female share of the labor force

Labor force comprises all people who furnish labor for the production of goods and services at any time during a specified time period, and thus includes both the employed and unemployed. It covers work that is for pay and not for pay (e.g. subsistence agriculture). Even if providing unpaid labor, women's contribution to economic well-being of the household via their productive labor can improve their status within the family and society. Berik and Bilginsoy (2000), for example, provide convincing evidence for Turkey that women's participation rate in unpaid labor activities is a good measure of their economic value, perhaps related to the importance of female labor in agriculturally based economies. This then is a broad measure of women's ability to engage in productive activities, but it may overstate their well-being for several reasons. First, the status conveyed by productive activity may differ from country to country. Second, countries differ in the criteria adopted to determine whether workers, particularly unpaid family workers on farms, are to be counted among the economically active. Also, the lower bound on age of workers to be considered economically active differs from country to country.

4.2 Female share of employment

Female share of employment should be closely related to female share of the labor force, but this variable differs in some important respects. The data on employment refer to labor in paid employment or self-employment, for one or more hours a week. The employed include workers who (1) are temporarily laid off, (2) are not at work due to illness or other contingency, and (3) are on leave, with or without pay, but who nevertheless retain a formal attachment to their job. Because this variable reflects gender differences in unemployment, which can reduce household bargaining power, it captures an aspect of well-being not captured in the female share of the labor force. It is, though, not a precise measure of unemployment or access to income due to differences in measurement.

4.3 Ratio of male to female unemployment rates

Sen (1990) and others focus on women's paid labor as a measure both of their value and their bargaining power. Specifically, access to income is assumed to improve women's bargaining power since the cost of leaving a job or a relationship is reduced as they gain access to independent sources of income. Moreover, women's access to income can have important effects on the ability to provide material resources for themselves and their children that male members may not provide with their income. This can lead to an increase in women's ability to affect the distribution of resources within the family, and also the distribution of unpaid labor time between women and men. Unfortunately, I lack sufficient time-series data to differentiate between paid and unpaid labor, or on relative female to male wages. I therefore use the ratio of male to female unemployment rates, which generally refers to paid employment. There are differences in the way that countries measure this variable as well, with Anglophone Caribbean economies, for example, including discouraged workers among the unemployed (Seguino 2003b). This is a more accurate measure of unemployment since it counts persons who might otherwise be recorded as nonlabor force participants if they do not have a job and have given up looking for work – even if they desire a job.

Appendix B

Table B.1 Sample countries

Argentina, Bahamas, Barbados, Belize, Bolivia, Brazil, Chile, Colombia, Costa Rica, Dominican Republic, Ecuador, El Salvador, Honduras, Jamaica, Mexico, Panama, Paraguay, Peru, Trinidad and Tobago, Uruguay, Venezuela

Table B.2 List of gender well-being variables, definitions, and sources

Variable category	Variable	Description of variable	Source
Health	F/M population	Ratio of females to males in population	World Bank (2003)
	Relative F/M mortality	Ratio of adult female to male mortality rates per 1000 (probability of dying between the ages of 15 and 60), relative to reference population (Sweden)	World Bank (2003)
	Fertility	Female fertility rate	World Bank (2003)
Education	F/M secondary school enrollment rate	Ratio of female to male gross Secondary school enrollment	World Bank (2003)
	F/M youth illiteracy rate	Ratio of female to male youth illiteracy rate (15–24)	United Nations Common Database (from UNESCO)
	F/M total average years education	Ratio of female to male average years of total education	Barro and Lee (2000)
Labor market access and income	Female share of labor force	Female share of labor force	World Bank (2003)
	Female share of total employment	Female share of employment	ILO (2003)
	Ratio F/M unemployment rate	Ratio of female to male unemployment rates	ILO (2003)

Notes

1 I am grateful to Ramya Vijaya, Caren Grown, and Anwar Shaikh for helpful comments on earlier drafts of this paper.

2 Gender well-being is measured as gross secondary school enrollment ratios in both studies and society's resources are measured as per capita income. Additional control variables are incorporated into the analyses, including measures of civil freedoms and culture (e.g. religious preference).

3 See, for example, Amsden (1998) and Chang (2002) on the role of the state, and Seguino and Grown (2006) on these issues as regards gender equality.

4 On the gender effects, see, for example Benería (2001), Sayeed and Balakrishnan, (2004) and Balakrishnan (2002). On wage-led and profit-led growth, see Bhaduri and Marglin (1990), and for the relationship between income distribution, gender and growth, see Blecker and Seguino (2002).

5 An example of this is the expansion of data processing in Jamaica and Barbados, as well as the growth of call centers in India.

6 In LAC, Barbados has been in the forefront of these initiatives, and St Kitts and Nevis and Trinidad and Tobago have also begun or are beginning to develop the methodologies to conduct such audits.

7 It could be argued, in response, that growth can enlarge the economic pie, making redistributive policies less gender-conflictive. The importance of that would depend on country-specific institutional arrangements that mediate conflict. In some cases, where such arrangements do not exist, male backlash in response to redistributive policies that favor women can be socially disruptive.

8 Measures of HIV/AIDs incidence and maternal mortality are also useful indicators. They are not part of the analysis presented here, because accuracy of data on AIDs is questionable. I nevertheless did include these variables in well-being ranking for 2000 (results not reported here), and the rankings were similar to those without the additional indicators.

9 For critiques of the GDI and GEM, see Bardhan and Klasen (1999), Oudhof (2001), Dijkstra (2002), and Elson (2002).

10 Alternatively, one could simply substitute missing values with the mean for the nonmissing observations. That method, however, has several limitations, including underestimation of the variance, and distortion of the shape of the distribution. In this case, the missing data estimation is more efficient because there are very few missing variables and a greater amount of available information is used.

11 In the case of the Caribbean, men's lower educational achievement appears to be related to higher male drop-out rates, as men leave school to engage lucrative income-earning (sometimes illegal) activities that do not require higher education. I cannot explain the relative higher female educational attainment in several of the Spanish-speaking countries in the sample.

12 Thus, in our case, with 9 indicators and 21 countries, country A is awarded points between 1 (lowest achievement) and 21 (highest achievement) for each of 9 criteria. These are summed to provide the aggregate score (maximum = 189, minimum = 9), which is then used to rank countries on gender equality in well-being.

13 Note that the Borda ranks on youth illiteracy are also low for these countries. Given very low illiteracy rates in these countries (1–4 percent), the male to female ratios of illiteracy rates may not provide a great deal of information on gender equity.

14 The World Bank study uses several measures of well-being that differ from those used here – for example, life expectancy and primary school enrollment.

15 The Bank's analysis also controls for gender equality in rights, using the Humana Index. That index is, however, outdated and is also very obscure in how gender equality is being measured, and so I do not include it here.

16 See Table B.2 for sources of gender well-being data. All macroeconomic data listed in Table 8.5 are from World Development Indicators.
17 Several studies make this link including Hill and King (1995), Dollar and Gatti (1999), and Seguino (2000a and 2000b), although using varying gender equity measures.
18 This was done by regressing the gender variable on all independent variables (the "constrained" model). The "suspect" variable (GDP growth) was then regressed on all exogenous variables. The resulting fitted values were then added to the constrained model. *t*-tests of the significance of that variable did not support the hypothesis of endogeneity of the growth variable.
19 There is also evidence of a dramatic increase in other forms of violence in the region since the 1970s, including homicides (Buvinic *et al.* 1999).
20 Violence against women may not be exclusively domestic. For example, the spate of unsolved murders of approximately 370 women – many of whom were workers in the *maquila* industry – in Ciudad Juarez, Mexico over the past decade points to the insecurity of women's lives (Amnesty International 2004). These deaths may reflect a broader male hostility towards women (also evident in the failure of the police to take meaningful steps to solve the murders), possibly attributable to women's increased visibility in the work arena that is perceived to be in competition with men's job opportunities.
21 Research also shows that the incidence of domestic violence is high: one out of every four Latin American and Caribbean women have been the victims of physical abuse at home, while 60–85 percent had been subjected to some degree of psychological violence (Buvinic, *et al.* 1999).
22 There is evidence of this behavior from other parts of the world as well. For example, Pepall (1998) found that, among female borrowers in Bangladesh, a majority reported an increase in verbal and physical aggression from male relatives after taking out loans.
23 This measure is used in place of life expectancy data, which are based on model life tables rather than real data. A weakness of the latter approach is that the tables are estimated from data that are often difficult to verify, given the underreported number of infant deaths (Bardhan and Klasen 1999). Moreover, that variable does not capture age-specific differences in mortality due to gender discrimination.
24 Author's calculations from World Bank's *World Development Indicators*, 2002. The mean is unweighted and is not significantly different from the unweighted median. Clarke (2000), using data from the United Nations *Demographic Yearbook* (1997), found for 1995 an average ratio of females to 100 males of 106 for developed economies, 107 for the Europe region, and 111 for Eastern Europe (the latter the highest globally).
25 For a more in-depth discussion of this issue, see Agnihotri (1999).
26 Data on net enrollment rates would have been preferable but the large number of missing observations for the set of countries studied here made this infeasible.
27 For example, some data are obtained from workers 15 and older, while others count workers 12 and over. Data may be drawn from establishments with differing minimum sizes (e.g. 5 vs. 10 workers). Some countries include only civilians, while others include military in employment data.

References

Agnihotri, S. (1999) 'Inferring Gender Bias from Mortality Data: A Discussion Note' *Journal of Development Studies,* 35(4): 175–200.
Amnesty International (2004) *Intolerable Killings: Ten years of Abductions and Murders in Ciudad Juárez and Chihuahua.* Online. Available HTTP: <http://www.ammestyusa. org/women/juarez/> (accessed 27 May 2004).

Amsden, A. (1998) 'A Theory of Government Intervention in Late Industrialization' in L. Putterman and D. Rueschemeyer (eds.), *State and Market in Development: Synergy or Rivalry?* Boulder, CO: Lynne Rienner Publishers.

Balakrishnan, R. (ed.) (2002) *The Hidden Assembly Line: Gender Dynamics of Subcontracted Work in a Global Economy,* Bloomfield, CN: Kumarian Press.

Bardhan, K. and Klasen, S. (1999) 'UNDP's Gender-Related Indices: A Critical Review' *World Development,* 27 (6): 985–1010.

Barriteau, V. E. (2006) 'Engendering Development or Gender Main-streaming? A Critical Assessment From the Commonwealth Caribbean' in E. Kupier and Barker, D. (eds.) *Feminist Perspectives on Gender and the World Bank.* London and New York: Routledge.

Barro, R. and Lee, J.-W. (2000) 'International Data on Educational Attainment: Updates and Implications', CID Working Paper No. 42, Cambridge, MA: Harvard University.

Benería, L. (2001) 'Shifting the Risk: New Employment Patterns, Informalization, and Women's Work', *mimeo,* Cornell University.

Benería, L. (2003) *Gender, Development and Globalization: Economics as If All People Mattered,* New York and London: Routledge.

Benería, L. and Sen, G. (1981) 'Accumulation, Reproduction, and Women's Role in Economic Development Revisited', *Signs* 3(2).

Berik, G. (2000) 'Mature Export-Led Growth and Gender Wage Inequality in Taiwan', *Feminist Economics* 6(3): 1–26.

Berik, G. and Bilginsoy, C. (2000) 'Type of Work Matters: Women's Labor Force Participation and the Child Sex Ratio in Turkey', *World Development,* 28(5): 861–78.

Berik, G., van der M. Rodgers, Y., and Zveglich, J. Jr. (2002) 'Does Trade Promote Gender Wage Equity? Evidence from East Asia', CEPA Working Paper 2002–14, New School University, New York.

Bhaduri, A. and Marglin, S. (1990) 'Unemployment and the Real Wage: The Economic Basis for Contesting Political Ideologies', *Cambridge Journal of Economics,* 14(4): 375–93.

Bhattacharya, D. and Rahman, M. (1999) 'Female Employment Under Export Propelled Industrialization: Prospects for Internalizing Global Opportunities in the Apparel Sector in Bangladesh.' UNRISD Occasional Paper No. 10, Geneva: United Nations Research Institute for Social Development (UNRISD).

Black, S. and Brainerd, E. (2002) 'Importing Inequality? The Effects of Increased Competition on the Gender Wage Gap', NBER Working Paper No. W 9110, Cambridge, MA: National Bureau of Economic Research.

Blecker, R. and Seguino, S. (2002) 'Macroeconomic Effects of Reducing Gender Inequality in Export-Oriented, Semi-Industrialized Economies', *Review of Development Economics,* 6(1): 103–19.

Boserup, E. (1970) *Women's Role in Economic Development,* London: Allen & Unwin.

Brofenbrenner, K. (2000) 'Uneasy Terrain: The Impact of Capital Mobility on Workers, Wages, and Union Organizing', submitted to the U.S. Trade Deficit Review Commission.

Buvinic, M., Morrison, A., and Shifter, M. (1999) 'Violence in Latin America and the Caribbean: A Framework for Action', in A. R. Morrision and M. L. Biehl (eds.) *Too Close to Home: Domestic Violence in the Americas,* Washington, DC: Inter-American Development Bank.

Cagatay, N. (2001) 'Trade, Gender, and Poverty', UNDP Background Paper, New York: UNDP.

Chang, H.-J. (2002) *Kicking Away the Ladder,* London: Anthem Press.

Chant, S. (2000) 'Men in Crisis?: Reflections on Masculinities, Work, and Family in Northwest Costa Rica', *The European Journal of Development Research,* 12 (2).

Charmes, J. (2000) 'Size, Trends, and Productivity of Women's Work in the Informal Sector', Paper Presented at the Annual IAFFE Conference, Istanbul, August 15–17.

Clarke, J. (2000) *The Human Dichotomy: The Changing Numbers of Males and Females,* Amsterdam: Pergamon.

Dijkstra, A. G. (2002) 'Revising the UNDP's GDI and GEM: Towards an Alternative', *Social Indicators Research,* 57: 301–38.

Dollar, D. and Gatti, R. (1999) 'Gender Inequality, Income, and Growth: Are Good Times Good for Women Are Good Times Good for Women?', Policy Research Report on Gender and Development, World Bank Working Paper Series No. 1, Washington, DC: World Bank.

Drèze, J. and Sen, A. (1995) *India: Economic Development, and Social Opportunity.* Oxford: Oxford University Press.

Elson, D. (2002) 'Gender Justice, Human Rights, and Neo-Liberal Economic Policy' in M. Molyneux and S. Razavi (eds.), *Gender Justice, Development and Human Rights,* pp. 78–114, Oxford: Oxford University Press.

Elson, D. and Pearson, R. (1981) 'The Subordination of Women and the Internationalisation of Factory Production' in K. Young, C. Wolkowitz, and R. McCullah (eds.) *Of Marriage and the Market,* pp. 144–66, London: CSE.

Elson, D. and Cagatay, N. (2000) 'The Social Content of Macroeconomic Policies', *World Development,* 28(7): 1347–64.

Erturk, K. (2001–02) 'Overcapacity and the East Asian Crisis', *Journal of Post Keynesian Economics,* 24 (2): 253–75.

Fleck, S. (1996) 'Non-Cooperative Bargaining and Power in the Household: Evidence from Honduras', Paper Presented at Annual IAFFE Meeting, Washington, DC, June 21–23.

Floro, M. (1995) 'Economic Restructuring, Gender, and the Allocation of Time', *World Development,* 23(11): 1913–29.

Fontana, M., Joekes, S., and R. Masika. (1998) 'Global Trade Expansion and Liberalization: Gender Issues and Impacts', IDS BRIDGE Report No. 42, Brighton, UK: IDS.

Fussell, E. (2000) 'Making Labor Flexible: The Recomposition of Tijuana's Maquiladora Female Labor Force', *Feminist Economics,* 6(3): 59–81.

Gatti, R. and Kucera, D. (2004) 'Labor Standards and Informal Employment in Latin America', *World Development,* 32(5): 809–28.

Grown, C., Gupta, G. R., and Khan, A. (2003) *Promises to Keep: Achieving Gender Equality and the Empowerment of Women,* Washington, DC: International Center for Research on Women.

Hill, M. A. and King, E. M. (1995) 'Women's Education and Economic Well-Being', *Feminist Economics,* 1(2): 1–26.

Hsiung, P.-C. (1996) *Living Rooms as Factories: Class, Gender, and the Satellite Factor System in Taiwan,* Philadelphia, PA: Temple University Press.

ILO (International Labour Organization) (2003) *Yearbook of Labour Statistics.* Geneva: Author.

Kabeer, N. (2000) *The Power to Choose: Bangladeshi Women and Labour Market Conditions in London and Dhaka,* London and New York: Verso.

Kempadoo, K. (ed.) (1999) *Sun, Sex and Gold: Tourism and Sex Work in the Caribbean,* Lanham, MD: Rowman and Littlefield.

Larraín, S. (1999) 'Curbing Domestic Violence: Two Decades of Activism', in A. R. Morrision and M. L. Biehl (eds.) *Too Close to Home: Domestic Violence in the Americas,* pp. 105–30, Washington, DC: Inter-American Development Bank.

Larraín, F. and Vergara, R. M. (1998) 'Income Distribution, Investment and Growth' in A. Solimano (ed.), *Social Inequality: Values, Growth, and the State*, pp.120–39, Ann Arbor, MI: University of Michigan Press.

Lim, L. (1990) 'Women's Work in Export Factories: The Politics of a Cause' in I. Tinker (ed.), *Persistent Inequalities: Women and World Development*, pp. 101–19, New York: Oxford University Press.

Malhotra, A., Schuler, S., and Boender, C. (2002) 'Measuring Women's Empowerment as a Variable in International Development', Working Paper, International Center for Research on Women, Washington, DC: ICRW.

Mason, K. and Smith, H. L. (2003) 'Women's Empowerment and Social Context: Results from Five Asian Countries', *mimeo*, World Bank and University of Pennsylvania.

Milanovic, B. (2002) 'Two Faces of Globalization: Against Globalization as We Know It', World Bank Research Department Working Paper, Washington DC: World Bank.

Murthi, M., Guio, A.-C., and Drèze, J. (1995) 'Mortality, Fertility, and Gender Bias in India: A District Level Analysis', *Population and Development Review*, 21(4): 745–82.

Oudhof, K. (2001) 'The GDI as a Measurement Instrument on Gender Aspects of Development in the ECE Region', *Statistical Journal of the United Nations Economic Commission for Europe*, 18(1): 1–25.

Pepall, J. (1998) 'Bangladeshi Women and the Grameen Bank'. Online. Available HTTP: <http://www/idrc.ca/reports/prn_report.cfm?article_num=264> (accessed May 1, 04).

Ranis, G. and Stewart, F. (2002) 'Economic Growth and Human Development in Latin America', *CEPAL Review*, 78: 7–24.

Richards, D., Delleny, R., and Sweeney, S. (2002) 'Economic Globalization and Women's Agency: Oppression or Opportunity?', Paper Presented at the 2001 Annual Meeting of the American Political Science Association, San Francisco, CA, Aug. 29–Sept. 3.

Rodríguez, F. and Rodrik, D. (2001). 'Trade Policy and Economic Growth: A Skeptic's Guide to the Cross-National Evidence', in B. Bernanke and K. S. Rogoff (eds), *Macroeconomics Annual 2000*, Cambridge, MA: MIT Press for NBER.

Saith, R. and Harriss-White, B. (1999) 'The Gender Sensitivity of Well-Being Indicators', *Development and Change*, 30: 465–97.

Sayeed, A. and Balakrishnan, R. (2004) 'Why Do Firms Disintegrate? Towards an Understanding of the Firm Level Decision to Sub-Contract and Its Impact on Labor' in W. Milberg (ed.), *Labor and the Globalization of Production: Causes and Consequences of Industrial Upgrading*, pp. 104–19, New York: Palgrave MacMillan.

Seguino, S. (2000a) 'Gender Inequality and Economic Growth: A Cross-Country Analysis', *World Development*, 28 (7): 1211–30.

—— (2000b) 'Accounting for Gender in Asian Growth', *Feminist Economics*, 6(3): 27–58.

—— (2000c) 'The Effects of Structural Change and Economic Liberalization on Gender Wage Differentials in South Korea and Taiwan', *Cambridge Journal of Economics*, 24(4): 437–59.

—— (2002) 'Gender, Quality of Life, and Growth in Asia 1970 to 1990', *The Pacific Review*, 15(2): 245–77.

—— (2003a) 'Is More Mobility Good?: Mobile Capital and the Low-Wage Low-Productivity Trap', University of Vermontt Working Paper, Burlington: University of Vermont.

—— (2003b). 'Why are Women in the Caribbean So Much More Likely Than Men to be Unemployed?' *Social and Economic Studies*, 52(4): 83–120.

Seguino, S. and Grown, C. (2006) 'Gender Equity and Globalization: Macroeconomic Policy for Developing Countries', *Journal of International Development*, 18: 1–24.

Sen, A. (1990) 'More Than 100 Million Missing Women', *New York Review of Books*, 37 (December 20).

Sen, A. (2000) *Development as Freedom,* New York: Anchor Books.

Standing, G. (1989) 'Global Feminization Through Flexible Labor', *World Development*, 17(7): 1077–95.

Svedberg, P. (1996) 'Gender biases in Sub-Saharan Africa', *Journal of Development Studies,* 32(6): 933–43.

UNIFEM (United Nations Development Fund for Women) (2002) *Progress of the World's Women,* New York: Author.

Winters, L. A., McCulloch, N., and McKay, A. (2004) 'Trade Liberalization and Poverty: The Evidence So Far', *Journal of Economic Literature,* 42(1): 72–115.

World Bank (2001) *Engendering Development,* Oxford and New York: Oxford University Press.

—— (2003) World Development Indicators, Washington DC: World Bank.

9   Poverty and growth in least developed countries: some measurement and conceptual issues

Massoud Karshenas *

1   Introduction

Poverty reduction has become a central global policy objective. Some international aid institutions have proposed to make aid disbursements contingent upon poverty reduction performance. Little attention, however, has been paid to the fact that we do not as yet have reliable and consistent measures of poverty suitable for intercountry comparisons for low-income countries. International poverty comparisons pose vexing conceptual and measurement problems, and have been extensively discussed in the literature. Three basic conceptual and methodological issues are involved in measuring absolute poverty in low-income countries: (1) the choice of an appropriate poverty index, (2) the choice of an absolute poverty line, and (3) the choice of a metric and the measurement of its distribution. In this paper we are mainly concerned with the last issue. We focus here on money metric measures of poverty, or what is known as income or consumption poverty, and adopt the $1 a day and $2 a day poverty lines advocated by the World Bank. These choices are not of course free from controversy, but our aim here is to highlight the measurement and methodological problems associated with the prevailing practises regarding the third set of issues.

The purpose of the paper is twofold. First, it provides poverty estimates for low-income countries, consistent with national accounts statistics and hence comparable over time and across countries. We argue that such consistent estimates are essential for the study of long-term trends in poverty as well as the analysis of the relationship between poverty and other macroeconomic variables in cross-country empirical studies. The existing data on poverty published by the World Bank fail to satisfy the required consistency tests. For example, as we shall show in this paper, the existing estimates, compared to the national accounts consistent estimates, appear to systematically underestimate poverty in the poorest of Least Developed Countries (LDCs).

The second task of the paper is to provide estimates of poverty in LDCs where reliable data on income distribution do not exist. The method used is to decompose the variations in absolute poverty into mean expenditure and distributional components, and to extrapolate expected poverty for the LDCs on the basis of their mean per capita consumption expenditure. We also provide confidence intervals for our poverty estimates. The precision of the poverty estimates is measured by the standard error of the mean predicted value, which also indicates the significance of independent variations in income distribution across the countries and over time for poverty. We focus on poverty gap and headcount measures of poverty, and consider the one-dollar and two-dollar per day (in 1985 purchasing power parity (PPP)) absolute poverty lines advocated by the World Bank.

The two tasks set out in the above paragraphs are quite distinct. The first task relates to the adoption of appropriate estimation methods for poverty – appropriate from the point of view of cross-country comparisons and time consistency – in the case of countries where income distribution data are available. The second task is to inquire into the possibility of estimating poverty measures, with an acceptable degree of precision, for low-income countries where distribution data are not available. This is clearly predicated upon the availability of a consistent data set for a reasonably large sample of countries. Nevertheless, the two tasks are based on distinct estimation methods and rationales, and their results should stand or fall on their own merits.

Because the first task can best be treated in the context of the discussion of data in later sections, in the next section we shall start with examining some of the underlying assumptions for the possibility of decomposing poverty measures. This is followed by a discussion of data and estimation methods in Section 3. In Sections 4 and 5 we present new national accounts consistent estimates of headcount poverty and poverty gap for the LDCs. Section 6 deals with the validation of the results and compares the properties of the new estimates with the existing estimates. Section 7 examines the implications of our estimates for the recent debate on poverty and economic growth; and concluding remarks are made in Section 8.

2   Location and distributional elements in poverty change

To get a better understanding of the underlying assumptions of the estimation method adopted here, it would be helpful to consider the two polar cases of poverty reduction shown in Figure 9.1. In this figure it is assumed that income distribution takes a parametric form, with u the mean of the distribution, and S, a vector representing shape parameters of the density function. Panel (a) in the figure depicts a situation where, for a given poverty line z, absolute poverty reduction is taking place purely due to location effects. The polar opposite is shown in panel (b), where the mean of the distribution remains constant and poverty reduction takes a purely redistributional form. Of course these two polar cases are only theoretical possibilities – in reality poverty differences across countries, or their changes over time, are generated by combined and often interdependent effects of the two. It should also be noted that in many theoretical distribution functions, for example, Pareto distribution, the location and distribution effects are not separable.

An important assumption, necessary for our decomposition exercise, is therefore that the distribution function can be written as a function of the mean and a set of shape parameters. This is satisfied in a number of popular distributions such

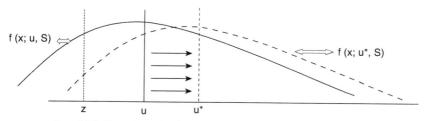

Panel (a)- Poverty reduction through distribution-neutral growth

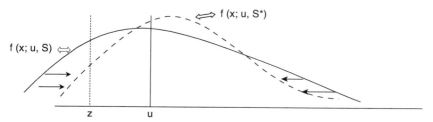

Panel (b)- Poverty reduction through growth-neutral redistribution

Figure 9.1 Absolute poverty, growth, and income distribution.

as the normal, the log-normal, and logistic distributions. In other words, for poverty line z, the cumulative density function for country i can be written as:

$$F_i(z) = F(u_i, S_i; \Sigma, z) \tag{1}$$

where u_i is the mean of the distribution, S_i is a shape parameter that captures the distributional influences on absolute poverty, and Σ is a vector of other shape parameters, which are either common across the countries or, if different, do not affect the poverty measure. As u_i and S_i vary across countries or over time, therefore, this generates a family of S-shaped curves which, for given poverty line z, produce the poverty measure for different countries or times.

$F_i(z)$ in Equation (1) is the headcount poverty measure for country i with mean and shape parameters u_i and S_i. In empirical work, this is approximated by P_i, the proportion of population with income below poverty line z, and hence $F_i(z) = P_i + \omega_i$, where ω_i is a white noise error term. Hence:

$$P_i + \omega_i = F(u_i, S_i; \Sigma, z) \tag{2}$$

The next set of assumptions is regarding the nature of the shape parameter S, and its relation to the mean of distribution u.[1] One of the most celebrated hypotheses in the literature, that related to the Kuznets curve, maintains an inverted-U shape relationship between income distribution and per capita income (Kuznets 1955).[2] Kuznets' hypothesis, however, refers to income distribution in general and may not necessarily apply to the relationship between u_i and S_i, which is only concerned with the shape parameter at the lower tail of the distribution. Furthermore, because we are focusing on a limited range of very low-income countries, any possible Kuznets effects are likely to be monotonic rather than U shaped. In any event, to account for possible Kuznets effects for our set of low income countries we assume the following general functional form for S_i:

$$S_i = h(u_i) + \varepsilon_i$$

where ε_i is a white noise error term, assumed to be independent of u_i. Substituting in Equation (2) we get:

$$P_i + \omega_i = F(u_i, h(u_i) + \varepsilon_i ; \Sigma, z) = F(g(u_i, \varepsilon_i))$$

where the fixed parameters such as z and ε are absorbed in the function g. Applying the inverse function F^{-1} to both sides of this equation we get:

$$F^{-1}(P_i + \omega_i) = g(u_i, \varepsilon_i) \tag{3}$$

Expanding both sides of Equation (3) by Taylor series expansion around P_i for the left and 0 for the right hand side, and taking all the terms with ω_i and ε_i to the right hand side, the equation can be approximated by a polynomial in u_i as:

$$F^{-1}(P_i) = \alpha + \beta_1 u_i + \beta_2 u_i^2 + \beta_3 u_i^3 + \dots + v_i \tag{4}$$

where v_i is a composite error term with mean zero and variance, which is a function of u_i. Assuming an appropriate S shaped functional form F, the parameters of this equation can be consistently estimated by OLS, and standard errors can be adjusted for possible heteroskedasticity in v_i. The appropriate functional form for F, the length of the polynomial in u_i, and the structure of the variance of v_i, can, of course, only be decided by the data. We applied various popular functional forms such as cumulative normal, log-normal, and logistic distributions, and the best fit was achieved by the logistic function. In the case of the logistic function the above simplifies to:

$$\log(P_i/(1-P_i)) = \alpha + \beta_1 u_i + \beta_2 u_i^2 + \beta_3 u_i^3 + \dots + v_I \tag{5}$$

3   Data and estimation

To measure poverty we need data on distribution of income or consumption, as well as a location factor, namely the mean income or consumption. The World Bank provides two relatively large data sets based on household expenditure and income surveys on its web site. One is the data set used by Chen and Ravallion (2000), largely based on World Bank's Living Standard Measurement Surveys

(LSMS), which is available on the World Bank's web site. The second data set is the Deininger and Squire (1996) data set, which is also available on the World Bank's web site.[3] Our main data source is the former source of data, but we have complemented this data with a few extra observations from the Deininger and Squire dataset (mainly for the 1960s and 1970s decades). The list of sample countries and observations is shown in Table 9.1. The 92 observations listed in the table are chosen according to the following criteria.

First we have only chosen countries for which data on the distribution of expenditure are available, excluding countries with only income distribution data. Household consumption is arguably a better indicator of long term well-being as compared with income. It is also known that the data on household income distribution in developing countries are much less reliable than the consumption data. Furthermore, the mixing of income and consumption data, which is the normal practice in World Bank estimates of poverty, can lead to incompatible estimates for inter-country comparisons (see e.g. Atkinson and Brandolini 2001). The exclusion of countries where data on distribution of consumption are not available leaves out most of the Latin American countries. Because most of the low-income countries which constitute the LDCs are located in Africa and Asia, we have altogether omitted the Latin American countries. This increases the homogeneity of our sample countries, which is essential for our analysis.[4]

The World Bank databank also provides estimates of headcount poverty (for $1 and $2 poverty lines) for our sample countries. The poverty measures supplied by the World Bank, however, suffer from certain deficiencies which make them inappropriate for our estimation purposes. First, as already pointed out, the World Bank measures are based on a mix of consumption and income distribution data for different countries which raises questions regarding comparability of the poverty measures for different countries. More importantly, however, the World Bank estimates are based on average consumption or income from national surveys, which are often highly inconsistent with the national accounts data, both in level terms and in relation to trends.

This can be seen from data on per capita consumption in 1985 PPP exchange rates, based on national accounts and survey means for sample observations shown in Table 9.1. For example in countries such as Tanzania (1991), Ethiopia (1981, 1995) and Mali (1989), average consumption figures according to the World Bank's household budget surveys are two to nearly three times higher than the national accounts estimates. On the other hand, in countries such as Bangladesh, India, Indonesia, Pakistan, and Thailand, the household survey estimates are between 50 and over 100 percent lower than the national accounts consumption data. The same glaring inconsistency is shown in consumption trends over time. For example, according to the household survey data average consumption increased by over 17 percent in Ethiopia between 1981 and 1995. According to the national accounts data, however, this variable fell by over 13 percent between these two years. In Bangladesh between 1984 and 1991, according to household surveys average consumption fell by close to 7 percent, but the national accounts data indicate a growth of average consumption of over 13 percent in the same period.

Table 9.1 Survey based and National Accounts (NA) based per capita consumption for sample observations

| Obs. | Country | Year of survey | Per capita consumption | | Obs. | Country | Year of survey | Per capita consumption | |
			N.A. based	Survey based				N.A. based	Survey based
1	Algeria	1988	1384.5	1875.4	26	India	1997	837.0	500.1
2	Algeria	1995	1295.4	1754.8	27	India*	1965	440.8	..
3	Bangladesh	1984	729.6	535.1	28	India*	1970	504.6	..
4	Bangladesh	1985	753.9	586.0	29	Indonesia	1984	965.4	559.4
5	Bangladesh	1988	765.8	518.7	30	Indonesia	1987	970.7	618.6
6	Bangladesh	1991	796.0	498.7	31	Indonesia	1990	1085.2	689.2
7	Bangladesh	1995	885.8	613.3	32	Indonesia	1993	1243.6	761.6
8	Burkina Faso	1994	401.7	477.9	33	Indonesia	1996	1561.6	962.4
9	Egypt	1991	1243.5	984.8	34	Indonesia	1998	1591.3	679.9
10	Ethiopia	1981	231.8	558.4	35	Indonesia*	1976	598.4	..
11	Ethiopia	1995	228.8	657.8	36	Cote d'Ivoire	1985	1050.6	1632.1
12	Gambia	1992	623.0	504.7	37	Cote d'Ivoire	1986	1059.4	1485.6
13	Ghana	1987	630.2	854.4	38	Cote d'Ivoire	1987	1065.4	1458.1
14	Ghana	1989	607.5	887.2	39	Cote d'Ivoire	1988	969.0	1159.9
15	Ghana*	1992	793.5	..	40	Cote d'Ivoire	1993	881.8	1016.9
16	Guinea–Bissau*	1991	347.5	..	41	Cote d'Ivoire	1995	823.1	947.7
17	India	1983	591.6	427.9	42	Kenya	1992	640.5	996.8
18	India	1986	622.4	466.1	43	Kenya	1994	546.8	819.3
19	India	1987	617.7	456.8	44	Lesotho	1986	696.0	1132.6
20	India	1988	674.2	464.4	45	Lesotho	1993	599.7	890.7
21	India	1989	679.3	454.1	46	Madagascar	1993	528.7	..
22	India	1990	681.5	462.7	47	Madagascar	1980	856.1	557.1
23	India	1992	744.7	461.7	48	Mali	1989	426.6	852.8
24	India	1995	781.2	473.7	49	Mali	1994	353.9	360.8
25	India	1996	819.7	491.6	50	Mauritania	1988	567.4	534.4

Table 9.1 Continued

Obs.	Country	Year of survey	Per capita consumption N.A. based	Per capita consumption Survey based	Obs.	Country	Year of survey	Per capita consumption N.A. based	Per capita consumption Survey based
51	Mauritania	1993	680.0	605.9	72	Philippines	1991	1190.0	975.0
52	Mauritania	1995	642.3	661.1	73	Philippines	1994	1260.5	990.0
53	Morocco	1985	1330.1	1708.9	74	Philippines	1997	1342.3	1224.3
54	Morocco	1990	1526.5	2352.4	75	Rwanda	1984	592.1	518.1
55	Mozambique	1996	589.9	588.7	76	Senegal	1991	851.2	707.8
56	Nepal	1985	393.1	491.9	77	Senegal	1994	801.7	754.1
57	Nepal	1995	489.1	584.4	78	Sri Lanka	1985	1472.4	875.2
58	Niger	1992	312.7	523.0	79	Sri Lanka	1995	1884.1	981.4
59	Niger	1995	331.1	401.9	80	Tanzania	1991	303.6	735.8
60	Nigeria*	1986	564.3	..	81	Tanzania	1993	291.3	..
61	Nigeria*	1992	674.8	..	82	Thailand	1992	2275.9	1005.1
62	Nigeria*	1993	425.3	..	83	Thailand	1998	2564.6	1543.1
63	Nigeria*	1996	414.5	..	84	Tunisia	1985	1958.2	2107.0
64	Pakistan	1987	942.5	456.1	85	Tunisia	1990	2065.4	2266.7
65	Pakistan	1990	989.7	462.9	86	Turkey	1987	2305.5	2006.6
66	Pakistan	1993	1053.0	572.9	87	Turkey	1994	2174.6	1892.7
67	Pakistan	1996	1167.4	558.0	88	Uganda	1989	465.8	639.7
68	Pakistan*	1969	748.1	..	89	Uganda	1992	443.1	598.4
69	Pakistan*	1979	865.1	..	90	Zambia	1991	348.0	434.3
70	Philippines	1985	1110.2	833.1	91	Zambia	1993	269.5	318.9
71	Philippines	1988	1205.3	919.9	92	Zambia	1996	279.0	345.7

Sources: Penn World Tables 5.6, World Bank 2001, Deininger and Squire 1996, and World Bank 2001b.

Notes
1- Data for countries with * are based on Deininger and Squire dataset.
2- Per capita consumption data are in 1985 PPP exchange rates.
The World Bank consumption data has been converted from 1993 ppp to 1985 ppp base by using 1.08 factor given by the World Bank. Beyond 1992, the Penn World Tables data are extrapolated using real per capita growth of consumption in constant dollars given in WDI (World Development Indicators).

The inconsistency between the household survey results and the national accounts has been discussed in the literature (see for e.g. Hamner *et al.* 1997; Bhalla 2002; Pyatt 2000, Ravallion 2000b, 2001; Deaton 2000). The implications of the large discrepancies between the two sources for empirical work, however, have not been often fully recognized in the wider literature. For example, the results of econometric work on poverty and growth, where poverty estimates are based on household survey measurements and growth figures are based on national accounts, estimates can be misleading. Growth elasticity of poverty estimates based on this type of mixing data are also highly suspect – as, relative to national accounts the average consumption in household surveys seem to systematically overestimate consumption in poor African countries, and underestimate it in relatively richer Asian countries (e.g. Thailand, Pakistan, India, Bangladesh, etc.). Because of this discrepancy between the different regions or income groups, the usual explanations put forward in the literature to account for the lack of consistency between the two data-sources are also incomplete.[5]

The difference between average consumption figures based on household surveys and national accounts is not of course unexpected. The two figures are indeed even conceptually different. For example, the national accounts consumption data include current spending by unincorporated businesses and nonprofit organizations, which are excluded from the household survey means. The question is whether such differences exert significant and systematic effects in cross-country comparisons of poverty. In a recent paper, Ravallion (2000a) has compared the national accounts and survey estimates of average consumption and income for a large sample of countries and has concluded that the estimates of average consumption expenditure in the two sources are not significantly different. Ravallion's test is based on the null hypothesis that the ratio of survey average consumption to the national accounts (NA) averages has a mean that is not significantly different from 1. He uses a standard *t*-test for this purpose. Though Ravallion (2000a) does not specify the names of the sample countries used in this test, we have managed to replicate the test by using a sample of 84 observations on which the World Bank databank provides average consumption expenditure from household surveys. In row I of Table 9.2 we have replicated the *t*-test conducted by Ravallion for the null hypothesis of the mean of the survey/NA consumption ratio being equal to 1. The table also shows the *t*-statistic for a range of possible alternatives ranging from 0.0 to 1.5. As pointed out by Ravallion (2000a), this test does not reject the hypothesis of mean ratio being equal 1 and seems to have a high power against the alternatives listed in the table.

This test, however, is very sensitive to the order in which the two variables are considered as well as the implicit assumptions about the statistical dependence of the two series. To see this more clearly, we have inverted the consumption ratio reported by Ravallion – that is, we have calculated the NA/survey consumption ratio – and applied the same *t*-test to the inverted series. The results are reported in row II of Table 9.2. As can be seen, for the inverted series the hypothesis of the mean ratio being equal to 1 is strongly rejected.[6] Because there is no a priori reason why we should choose one series rather than its inverse to conduct the test,

Table 9.2 *t*-tests for the household survey and the national accounts estimates average consumption

I- The ratio of survey to NA estimat's (Ravallion's test):

Null hypothesis, $\mu\ (c^1/c^2) =$	0.5	0.6	0.7	0.8	0.9	**1**	1.1	1.2	1.3	1.4	1.5
t-statistic	9.96	8.02	6.08	4.14	2.20	**0.26**	−1.68	−3.62	−5.56	−7.50	−9.44

II- The ratio of NA to survey estimates (Ravallion's test reversed):

Null hypothesis, $\mu\ (c^2/c^1)=$	0.5	0.6	0.7	0.8	0.9	**1**	1.1	1.2	1.3	1.4	1.5
t-statistic	13.01	11.07	9.14	7.20	5.26	**3.33**	1.39	−0.55	−2.48	−4.42	−6.36

III- Tests of the difference between the average consumption means:

Null hypothesis, $\mu\ (c^2-c^1)=$	−40	−20	**0**	20	40	80	120	140	160	180	200
(a)- *t*-statistic (pooled sample)	3.15	2.67	**2.19**	1.71	1.23	0.28	−0.68	−1.16	−1.64	−2.12	−2.60
(b)- *t*-statistic (non-independent samples)	4.08	3.46	**2.84**	2.22	1.60	0.36	−0.88	−1.50	−2.12	−2.74	−3.36
(c)- *t*-statistic (independent samples)	2.23	1.89	**1.55**	1.21	0.87	0.20	−0.48	−0.82	−1.16	−1.50	−1.84
(null as % of mean consumption)	−4.6	−2.3	**0.0**	2.3	4.6	9.2	13.8	16.1	18.4	20.7	23.1
(null as % of minimum consumption)	−12.5	−6.3	**0.0**	6.3	12.5	25.1	37.6	43.9	50.2	56.4	62.7

our results cannot support the hypothesis that the two series have the same mean. Under these circumstances the correct procedure would be to test the difference between the means of the two series, which is neutral to the order adopted. This also allows taking into account the possible lack of statistical independence between the two series. This is done in row III of Table 9.2, under three separate assumptions; namely, (1) pooled sample, (2) nonindependent samples, and (3) independent samples. As can be seen, under the first two assumptions the hypothesis of equality between the two means is rejected, and only under option (3), that is, independent samples, the null hypothesis of mean difference being zero is not rejected. The power of this test, particularly under assumption (3) however, is extremely low. As shown in the row IV of Table 9.2, the possible mean difference between the two series, which cannot be rejected by the *t*-test, ranges from −6.3% to 62.7% of per capita consumption in the country with lowest consumption in the sample.

The discrepancy in average consumption between the household survey and national accounts data, apart from definitional discrepancies between the two concepts, is due to possible errors in both sources of data.[7] Which of the two sources is more appropriate for poverty measurement depends on the nature of study concerned. If the purpose of the study is to compare poverty in a number of countries and time periods, then clearly the household survey data on average consumption is less reliable. What crucially matters for such comparative work is the consistency of data compilation methods across countries and over time. Household consumption surveys conducted at distant points in time and across countries, with possibly different methodologies, sample designs, and responses are not particularly reliable indicators of means or trends, especially when they exhibit average consumption or incomes that are highly divergent from national account estimates. Unless calibrated by external information, averages or location factors are unlikely to be comparable across the different household expenditure surveys – even when they are reliable information sources regarding the distribution of income or consumption. Household expenditure surveys are at best good indicators of distribution of income or expenditure, but can be highly unreliable with regard to averages.[8] Under these circumstances average income or consumption in national accounts estimates, despite their shortcomings, furnish a more consistent and comparable set of location variables than those generated by the household surveys.[9]

In this paper we have therefore based our poverty estimates on national accounts location variables. This generates poverty estimates that are consistent with the national accounts. To estimate national accounts consistent poverty measures we still need to combine the distribution information provided in household surveys with the location variables from the national accounts. The extent to which the location errors in household surveys affect the accuracy of distribution data as well, depends on whether the location errors arise because of under- (over-) reporting of income in particular deciles or they uniformly affect all income groups, or whether they are due to the problems with survey sample design.[10] In any event, because the location effects are likely to be more important than distribution effects in cross-country and time comparisons of poverty (particularly as we are mainly concerned with the lower end of the distribution), the likely errors involved in using the distribution data from household surveys may not be as significant as those arising from location effects. Using the national accounts information for the location effects and the household budgets for the distribution effects is the only available option for deriving national accounts consistent poverty estimates, while at the same time being least sensitive to the measurement errors in household budget data. We have adopted this method also because one of the aims of the paper is to estimate expected poverty for countries where household budget surveys do not exist. As pointed out above, data consistency is of utmost importance for this type of exercise. We shall compare the properties of our poverty estimates with the World Bank estimates based on household survey averages.

Figure 9.2 (panels (a) and (b)) plots the new national accounts consistent poverty estimates against average consumption for all the countries and years for the $1-a-day and $2-a-day poverty lines. Countries included in the $1 poverty line graph have per capita income below $1,000 a year (in 1985 PPP dollars). Above this per capita income level headcount poverty becomes negligible. The number of observations for the $1 poverty line are, therefore, less than those estimated for $2 poverty line.[11] A logistic curve is fitted to the observations in both panels. The estimation method for this curve, which we may refer to it as the poverty curve, is discussed below. The variation of the poverty measures around the "poverty curves" is remarkably low – indicating that independent variations in income distribution explain a small part of variations in poverty across our sample of low income countries and over time.[12] To compare the new poverty estimates with the World Bank poverty measures based on household survey location factors, we have plotted the two series against per capita consumption in Figure 9.3.[13] The same sample of countries and the same years are included in both series in this figure.[14] As can be seen, the World Bank estimates show much higher variations around the trend, and show much lower slopes in the case of both the $1 and $2 poverty measures (panels (a) and (b)). The much larger variation of the World Bank series is not unexpected, because those series are generated by using a different location factor from that depicted on the horizontal axis of Figure 9.3. The figure, however, helps to highlight the dangers of mixing incompatible data sources in measuring poverty trends – which is not uncommon in the literature (see e.g. Chen *et al.* 1994; Ravallion and Chen 1997; Chen and Ravallion 2000).[15] What is also clear is that, at least for the low income countries considered here, the World Bank estimates systematically underestimate poverty in poorer countries and overestimate it for the richer ones. The substantial differences between the new results and the World Bank results are of course solely due to the differences in the location factors used, as both series use the same distributions.

4   Headcount poverty estimates in the LDCs

The low standard errors of the fitted curves to the new poverty measures indicate that one may be able to estimate, with a high degree of precision, the expected

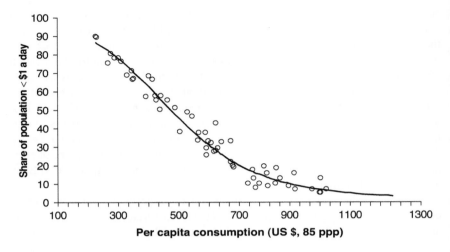

Figure 9.2a Headcount poverty versus per capita private consumption.

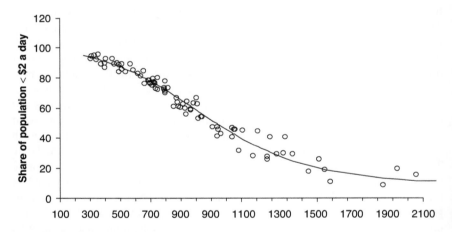

Figure 9.2b Headcount poverty versus per capita private consumption.

value of poverty in low income LDCs for which income distribution data are not available. Before attempting this, we need to further explore the possibility of introducing additional explanatory factors which may further reduce the standard errors of the fitted curves. For example, because of structural changes and different policy regimes over time, the relationship between poverty and average consumption may have changed. To cater for this, we have introduced a time-dummy variable D90 which distinguishes the 1990s decade from the earlier decades.[16] Similar structural differences may affect the relationship between poverty and

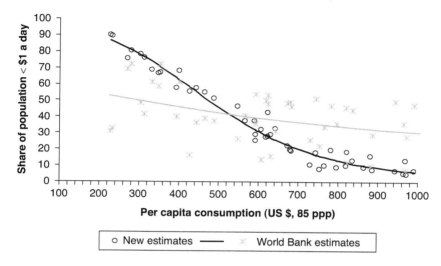

Figure 9.3a Headcount poverty versus per capita private consumption.

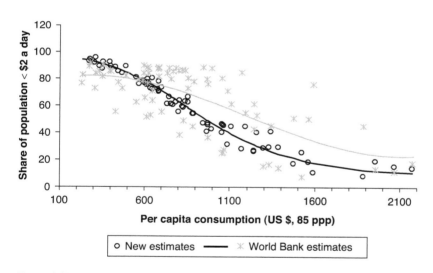

Figure 9.3b Headcount poverty versus per capita private consumption.

average consumption across regions as diverse as Asia and sub-Saharan Africa. For this reason we have also added a REGION dummy variable to the regression lines. Regression results are shown in Tables 9.3 and 9.4. The dependent variable is the logistic transformation of the new headcount poverty measure for the $1 and $2 poverty lines, discussed earlier. Various other functional forms were tried, but only the preferred logistic model results are shown in the tables.

Table 9.3 Estimated regression of poverty (below $1 a day) on average consumption and other variables

Variable	(I) Coeff.	SE	t-statistic	(II) Coeff.	SE	t-statistic	(III) Coeff.	SE	t-statistic	(IV) Coeff.	SE	t-statistic
Constant	2.9376	0.14	21.29	3.93	0.309	12.71	3.63	0.31	11.61	3.66	0.288	12.71
C (consumption)	-0.006	0.00	-24.3	-0.00974	0.001	-8.48	-0.0084	0.00	-7.83	-0.0087	0.001	-8.70
C2 (consumption sq.)				3.09E-06	0.000	3.19	2.47E-06	0.00	2.90	2.68E-06	0.000	3.41
REGION							-0.388	0.09	-4.29	-0.435	0.081	-5.39
D90							-0.138	0.08	-1.69			
No. of observations	58			58			58			58		
R-squared	0.934			0.946			0.967			0.965		
Adjusted R-squared	0.933			0.944			0.964			0.963		
SE of regression	0.342			0.315			0.250			0.256		
Mean dependent var.	-0.665			-0.665			-0.66459			-0.66459		
SD dependent var.	1.326			1.326			1.326024			1.326024		

Notes
D90 is dummy variable for the 1990 decade. REGION is an Africa(0)/Asia(1) dummy variable.
Consumption (C) is per capita private consumption expenditure in 1985 PPP dollars.
Standard errors are White Heteroskedasticity–Consistent Standard Errors.

Table 9.4 Estimated regression of poverty (below $2 a day) on average consumption and other variables

Variable	(I)			(II)			(III)			(IV)		
	Coeff.	SE	t-statistic	Coeff.	SE	t-statistic	Coeff.	SE	t-statistic	Coeff.	SE	t-statistic
Constant	2.7362	0.13	20.27	4.07	0.15	27.31	4.05	0.15	26.31	4.05	0.15	26.42
C (consumption)	-0.003	0.00	-15.2	-0.00537	0.00	-16.68	-0.00529	0.00	-15.63	-0.00529	0.00	-15.77
C^2 (consumption sq.)				1.17E-06	0.00	8.07	1.15E-06	0.00	7.72	1.15E-06	0.00	7.79
REGION							-0.062	0.05	-1.17	-0.060	0.05	-1.16
D90							0.010	0.05	0.19			
No. of observations	90			90			90			90		
R-squared	0.878			0.962			0.962			0.962		
Adjusted R-squared	0.877			0.961			0.960			0.961		
SE of regression	0.466			0.262			0.264			0.263		
Mean dependent var.	0.533			0.533			0.533			0.533		
SD dependent var.	1.328			1.328			1.328			1.328		

Notes

D90 is dummy variable for the 1990 decade. REGION is an Africa(0)/Asia(1) dummy variable.
Consumption (C) is per capita private consumption expenditure in 1985 PPP dollars.
Standard errors are White Heteroskedasticity-Consistent Standard Errors.

Table 9.3 shows the results for the $1 poverty line for various specifications. In addition to the REGION and time dummy variables we included various powers of consumption to determine the most appropriate form of the polynomial function specified in Equation (9.5). Only the first and second powers were significant and the best fit was a polynomial of degree two as shown in Table 9.3. Regression II in Table 9.3 corresponds to the fitted line in Figure 9.3a. The R^2 of close to 0.95 reflects the close fit of this curve as observed in the figure. With the addition of the time and region dummies in regression III, adjusted R^2 increases to over 0.96. The negative and significant regional dummy variable indicates the adverse structural features of the sub-Saharan African countries, which imply a more unequal distribution of income than in Asia. The time-dummy in regression model III is not statistically significant. We have used equation IV in Table 9.3 for predicting the expected value of poverty ($1 line) in the LDCs.

Table 9.4 shows the regression results for the $2 poverty line. As in the $1 case, the best fit was achieved by the logistic function, as compared with the cumulative normal and log-normal functions. Similarly, a polynomial of power two in per capita consumption turned out to be most appropriate. As shown in models III and IV in Table 9.4, the addition of the regional and time dummies does not improve the fit of the model. This is not an unexpected result, as in most low income countries in our sample the majority of the population fall below the $2 line, and hence distributional changes over a wide range of the incomes (below the poverty line) do not affect the headcount poverty measure. We have therefore used equation II in Table 9.4 for predicting the expected value of absolute poverty (below $2) for the LDCs.

The close fit of the logistic regression lines implies that we may be able to predict the expected value of poverty for countries where income distribution data are not available, with a fair degree of accuracy. We have used the average figures for per capita private consumption for 1995–99 to estimate headcount poverty for the LDCs for this period based on the above regressions. Real consumption figures in international dollars (1985 PPP) are based on Penn World Tables for the 1965–92 period, and on World Bank (2001b) for the rest of the period.[17] The results are shown in Table 9.5, which also shows the 95 percent confidence interval for the poverty estimates. It is significant to note that for the majority of the LDCs, per capita consumption for the major part of the population falls below the $1-and $2-a-day poverty lines. We may refer to this as a situation "generalized poverty," which is quite distinct from normal poverty observed in more developed countries. Indeed, it is unlikely that the close fit of the poverty curve to the observations can also apply to situations other than the generalized poverty situation (see Section 7).

5 Poverty gap and the average consumption of the poor

The same decomposition procedure applied to the headcount poverty measure above, can also be applied to other poverty measures such as the poverty gap. Poverty gap is defined as the difference between the mean income (consumption)

Table 9.5 Expected headcount poverty in least developed countries, 1995–99

	% population living below 1$ a day			% population living below 2$ a day		
	Estimate	*95 % confidence interval*		*Estimate*	*95 % confidence interval*	
Angola	73.3	73.1 ,	73.5	91.5	91.4 ,	91.7
Benin	17.7	17.4 ,	18.0	64.4	64.2 ,	64.5
Burkina Faso	61.6	61.4 ,	61.8	88.4	88.3 ,	88.4
Burundi	70.8	70.6 ,	71.0	90.9	90.8 ,	91.0
Central Afr. Rep.	67.2	67.0 ,	67.3	89.9	89.8 ,	90.0
Chad	81.7	81.3 ,	82.1	93.7	93.6 ,	93.8
Congo Dem. Rep.	90.6	89.9 ,	91.2	96.0	95.9 ,	96.2
Djibouti	56.3	56.1 ,	56.5	86.8	86.7 ,	86.8
Ethiopia	85.4	84.9 ,	85.9	94.7	94.5 ,	94.8
Gambia	35.5	35.2 ,	35.9	78.4	78.3 ,	78.5
Guinea	64.9	64.8 ,	65.1	89.3	89.2 ,	89.4
Guinea-Bissau	79.1	78.8 ,	79.4	93.0	92.9 ,	93.2
Haiti	39.2	38.9 ,	39.5	80.2	80.2 ,	80.3
Lesotho	45.3	45.1 ,	45.6	82.9	82.8 ,	82.9
Liberia	46.7	46.5 ,	47.0	83.4	83.4 ,	83.5
Madagascar	47.6	47.3 ,	47.8	83.7	83.7 ,	83.8
Malawi	58.9	58.7 ,	59.1	87.6	87.5 ,	87.6
Mali	71.6	71.4 ,	71.8	91.1	91.0 ,	91.2
Mauritania	30.9	30.6 ,	31.2	75.8	75.7 ,	75.8
Mozambique	40.1	39.8 ,	40.3	80.6	80.6 ,	80.7
Niger	74.4	74.2 ,	74.7	91.8	91.7 ,	92.0
Rwanda	60.5	60.3 ,	60.6	88.0	87.9 ,	88.1
Senegal	15.0	14.7 ,	15.3	60.7	60.5 ,	60.8
Sierra Leone	60.5	60.3 ,	60.7	88.0	87.9 ,	88.1
Somalia	71.7	71.5 ,	72.0	91.1	91.0 ,	91.2
Sudan	23.3	23.0 ,	23.6	70.1	70.0 ,	70.2
Tanzania	79.2	78.9 ,	79.5	93.1	92.9 ,	93.2
Togo	66.5	66.4 ,	66.7	89.8	89.7 ,	89.8
Uganda	42.8	42.5 ,	43.1	81.8	81.8 ,	81.9
Zambia	80.0	79.6 ,	80.3	93.3	93.1 ,	93.4
Bangladesh	10.3	10.1 ,	10.4	59.3	59.1 ,	59.4
Bhutan	24.8	24.5 ,	25.1	76.4	76.2 ,	76.5
Laos	2.2	0.9 ,	5.2	19.0	18.7 ,	19.2
Myanmar	52.3	51.7 ,	52.9	88.1	87.9 ,	88.3
Nepal	40.0	39.5 ,	40.4	84.1	83.9 ,	84.3

Note
Estimates are for average 1995–99 period.

of the poor and poverty line, expressed as percentage of the poverty line. It is a simple indicator of income distribution among the poor. However, as soon as one fixes the value of the absolute poverty line, changes in poverty gap can take place as a result of the combination of variations in income distribution and the overall mean income. It can be shown that, similar to the headcount measure, poverty gap can also be approximated by a polynomial function of mean consumption (of total population) and distributional components as set out in Equation (4) in Section 2. As the poverty gap index varies between 0 and 1, an S shaped curve, similar to the one fitted to the headcount measure would be appropriate. Again, depending on the goodness of fit of the model to the data, one may be able to estimate more or less precise measures of poverty gap for countries where income distribution data are not available on the basis of the regression results.

Because we have fixed absolute poverty lines at $1 and $2, it may be more informative if we report estimates of average consumption of the poor rather than the poverty gap. Having estimates of the average consumption of the poor, one can calculate poverty gap by a simple transformation of the average consumption figures. The information on the average consumption of the poor can also serve a useful purpose by making it possible to estimate the amount of income transfers necessary to raise the consumption of the poor above the poverty line. We have therefore estimated the following regression equation:

$$F^1(CP_i) = \alpha + \beta_1 u_i + \beta_2 u_i^2 + \beta_3 u_i^3 + \ldots + v_i \tag{6}$$

where CP is average consumption of the poor, u is average consumption of total population, and F is an appropriate S shaped functional form. As before, the polynomial in u characterizes the location effect on the average consumption of the poor, and the residual v the independent distributional effects. We have calculated the average consumption of the poor for the same number of countries and years as above, using World Bank's distribution data and the POVCAL program used by the World Bank. The only difference between our measures of poverty gap and the World Bank's is that we use overall per capita consumption data which are consistent with national accounts in contrast to average survey results. The mean annual consumption of the poor for the observations in our sample is plotted against average annual per capita consumption of the whole population (both measured in 1985 PPP) in Figure 9.4a for the $1 poverty line and Figure 9.4b for the $2 line. The figures also show the fitted logistic curve to the two sets of data. The regression results for Equation (6) are shown in Table 9.6 (for the $1 line) and Table 9.7 (for the $2 line). As for the headcount regressions, in addition to the polynomial in overall consumption, we have also tried the time and region dummies discussed above. Among the various S-shaped curves, such as cumulative normal, logistic, and lognormal, the cumulative logistic curve attained the best fit for both regressions.

As shown in Tables 9.6 and 9.7, the time dummy variable was not significant in any of the regressions, but the regional dummy had a positive and significant coefficient in both, indicating that for given level of overall per capita consumption, the average consumption of the poor in Asian countries is higher than in Africa. In the case of the $1 regression line a first-degree polynomial in consumption achieves the best fit, and in the case of the $2 line a second-degree polynomial fits best. In both equations more than 90 percent of the variations in the consumption of the poor is explained by the variations in average consumption and the regional dummy variable. Hence, except for the distributional effects

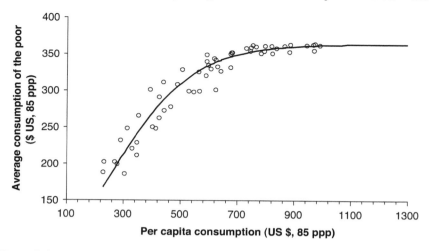

Figure 9.4a   Average annual consumption of the poor vs. per capita national consumption ($1 poverty line).

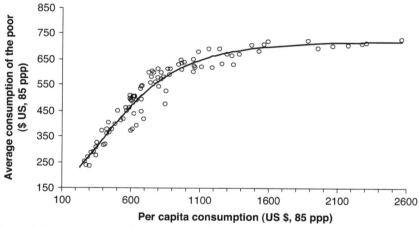

Figure 9.4b   Average annual consumption of the poor vs. per capita national consumption ($2 poverty line).

associated with the regional dummy variable and those associated with the variations in mean consumption, income distribution plays a relatively small independent role in explaining the variations in poverty gap for the sample countries and years. This of course does not mean that the distribution of income or assets do not matter for the consumption of the poor. They can and do matter critically through their influence on growth.

We next compare our poverty gap measures with those of the World Bank. Figures 9.5a and 9.5b show the scatter plot of the new estimates of the average

Table 9.6 Estimated regression of average consumption of the poor (below $1 a day) on per capita consumption and other variables

Variable	(I)			(II)			(III)			(IV)		
	Coeff.	SE	t-statistic	Coeff.	SE	t-statistic	Coeff.	SE	t-statistic	Coeff.	SE	t-statistic
Constant	-1.75	0.17	-10.07	-1.63	0.45	-3.64	-1.53	0.14	-10.85	-1.49	0.13	-11.42
C (consumption)	0.0070	0.00	20.55	0.0065	0.00	3.58	0.005884	0.00	20.24	0.0059	0.00	21.41
C² (consumption sq.)				3.54E-07	0.00	0.22						
REGION							7.79E-01	0.15	5.27	8.44E-01	0.12	6.88
D90							0.182	0.12	1.50			
No. of observations	58			58			58			58		
R-squared	0.893			0.893			0.948			0.945		
Adjusted R-squared	0.891			0.890			0.945			0.943		
SE of regression	0.518			0.522			0.369			0.376		
Mean dependent var.	2.429			2.429			2.429			2.429		
SD dependent var.	1.573			1.573			1.573			1.573		

Notes
D90 is dummy variable for the 1990 decade. REGION is an Africa(0)/Asia(1) dummy variable.
Consumption (C) is per capita private consumption expenditure in 1985 PPP dollars.
Standard Errors are White Heteroskedasticity-Consistent Standard Errors.

Table 9.7 Estimated regression of average consumption of the poor (below $2 a day) on per capita consumption and other variables

Variable	(I) Coeff.	(I) SE	(I) t-statistic	(II) Coeff.	(II) SE	(II) t-statistic	(III) Coeff.	(III) SE	(III) t-statistic	(IV) Coeff.	(IV) SE	(IV) t-statistic
Constant	-0.849	0.12	-7.31	-1.72	0.18	-9.43	-1.58	0.18	-9.03	-1.58	0.18	-8.88
C (consumption)	0.0024	0.00	15.63	0.0043	0.00	9.78	0.0037	0.00	8.43	0.0037	0.00	8.58
C^2 (consumption sq.)				-7.59E-07	0.00	-3.69	-0.00	0.00	-3.00	-6.17E-07	0.00	-3.05
REGION							0.385	0.06	6.46	0.385	0.06	6.92
D90							0.004	0.08	0.05			
No. of observations	90			90			90			90		
R-squared	0.870			0.908			0.922			0.922		
Adjusted R-squared	0.869			0.905			0.919			0.920		
SE of regression	0.466			0.395			0.366			0.364		
Mean dependent var.	1.273			1.273			1.273			1.273		
SD dependent var.	1.285			1.285			1.285			1.285		

Notes
D90 is dummy variable for the 1990 decade. REGION is an Africa(0)/Asia(1) dummy variable.
Consumption (C) is per capita private consumption expenditure in 1985 PPP dollars.
Standard Errors are White Heteroskedasticity-Consistent Standard Errors.

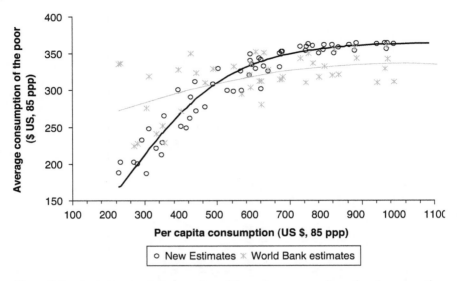

Figure 9.5a   Average annual consumption of the poor vs. per capita national consumption ($1 poverty line).

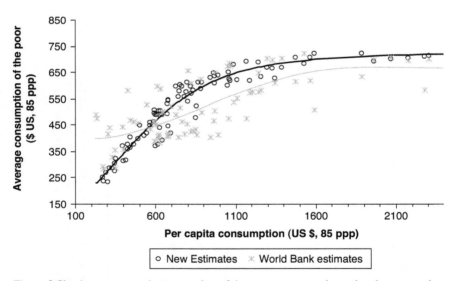

Figure 9.5b   Average annual consumption of the poor vs. per capita national consumption ($2 poverty line).

consumption of the poor against per capita consumption, compared with the consumption figures calculated on the basis of the World Bank's poverty gap estimates for the two poverty lines. As can be seen, the World Bank estimates seem to systematically overestimate average consumption of the poor in poorer countries, and underestimate it in the case of the richer ones. As pointed out before, the only difference between the new estimates and the World Bank ones is that they use different location variables, but the income distribution data for the two are the same. In particular in the case of the $1 poverty line, World Bank's estimates of the average consumption of the poor for a number of lower income countries is on average the same as for countries that have per capita overall consumption of two to three times higher than the former (Figure 9.5a). This is of course purely because of the difference between the survey and national accounts consumption averages.

Given the relatively close fit of the data in the regressions in Tables 9.6 and 9.7, we may be able to estimate relatively reliable measures of expected consumption of the poor in LDCs where income distribution data are not available. We have used regression IV in both Tables to estimate expected consumption of the poor for a number of LDCs for the $1 and $2 poverty lines. The average per capita consumption for 1995–99 is used to calculate expected consumption of the poor in that period. The results for daily consumption of the poor measured in 1985 PPP dollars are shown in Table 9.8 for the $1 and $2 poverty lines. The Table also shows the 95 percent confidence intervals for the expected consumption of the poor for 1995.

6 Validation of the results

The choice of national accounts estimates of average consumption in this paper has been based on the argument that the average income or consumption figures based on national accounts data furnish a better set of location variables for cross-country comparison of poverty, as compared to the survey averages. In Section 7 we shall discuss in what sense the term poverty should be used in this context. In this section we shall report a number of validation tests for our results and further compare the properties of the new estimates with the World Bank estimates based on survey averages. Given the two tasks of this paper mentioned at the outset, our validation tests are accordingly grouped into two types. The first one is to consider how realistic our estimation results are for countries where distribution data are not available. The second task is to consider how valid our poverty estimates are as compared to the World Bank estimates for countries where distribution data are available. We start with the first validation test.

To check the plausibility of our poverty estimates for countries where income distribution data are not available, it would be instructive to examine the accuracy of the estimates for countries where such data are available, so that estimates can be compared with actual figures. This is done by the following procedure: we drop individual observations from the sample one at a time, estimate our regressions with the reduced sample, and then compare the estimated poverty from the regression for the missing observation against the actual poverty measure. For each observation we get one such prediction error on the basis of which we can judge the precision of our estimates. This is done for the four regressions that have formed the basis of our four expected poverty measures reported above. We

Table 9.8 Expected average daily consumption of the poor in LDCs, 1995–99
(dollar per day, 1985 PPP)

	% population living below 1$ a day			% population living below 2$ a day		
	Estimate	*95 % confidence interval*		*Estimate*	*95 % confidence interval*	
Angola	0.63	0.63 ,	0.64	0.81	0.80 ,	0.81
Benin	0.96	0.96 ,	0.96	1.45	1.45 ,	1.45
Burkina Faso	0.73	0.73 ,	0.73	0.94	0.94 ,	0.94
Burundi	0.66	0.66 ,	0.66	0.84	0.83 ,	0.84
Central Afr. Rep.	0.69	0.68 ,	0.69	0.88	0.88 ,	0.88
Chad	0.55	0.54 ,	0.55	0.70	0.69 ,	0.71
Congo Dem. Rep.	0.42	0.41 ,	0.44	0.55	0.54 ,	0.56
Djibouti	0.76	0.76 ,	0.77	0.99	0.99 ,	0.99
Ethiopia	0.50	0.50 ,	0.51	0.64	0.63 ,	0.65
Gambia	0.88	0.88 ,	0.88	1.21	1.21 ,	1.21
Guinea	0.70	0.70 ,	0.71	0.90	0.90 ,	0.91
Guinea–Bissau	0.58	0.57 ,	0.58	0.74	0.73 ,	0.74
Haiti	0.86	0.86 ,	0.86	1.17	1.17 ,	1.17
Lesotho	0.83	0.83 ,	0.83	1.11	1.10 ,	1.11
Liberia	0.82	0.82 ,	0.82	1.09	1.09 ,	1.09
Madagascar	0.82	0.81 ,	0.82	1.08	1.08 ,	1.08
Malawi	0.75	0.74 ,	0.75	0.97	0.96 ,	0.97
Mali	0.65	0.65 ,	0.65	0.83	0.82 ,	0.83
Mauritania	0.90	0.90 ,	0.91	1.27	1.26 ,	1.27
Mozambique	0.86	0.86 ,	0.86	1.16	1.16 ,	1.16
Niger	0.62	0.62 ,	0.63	0.80	0.79 ,	0.80
Rwanda	0.74	0.73 ,	0.74	0.95	0.95 ,	0.95
Senegal	0.97	0.97 ,	0.97	1.50	1.49 ,	1.50
Sierra Leone	0.74	0.73 ,	0.74	0.95	0.95 ,	0.95
Somalia	0.65	0.65 ,	0.65	0.83	0.82 ,	0.83
Sudan	0.94	0.93 ,	0.94	1.36	1.36 ,	1.37
Tanzania	0.58	0.57 ,	0.58	0.74	0.73 ,	0.74
Togo	0.69	0.69 ,	0.69	0.89	0.88 ,	0.89
Uganda	0.84	0.84 ,	0.85	1.13	1.13 ,	1.13
Zambia	0.57	0.56 ,	0.57	0.72	0.72 ,	0.73
Bangladesh	0.99	0.99 ,	0.99	1.63	1.63 ,	1.63
Bhutan	0.95	0.95 ,	0.95	1.40	1.40 ,	1.41
Laos	1.00	1.00 ,	1.00	1.91	1.91 ,	1.92
Myanmar	0.86	0.85 ,	0.86	1.12	1.11 ,	1.12
Nepal	0.90	0.90 ,	0.91	1.24	1.24 ,	1.24

Note
Estimates are for average 1995–99 period.

have plotted the prediction errors calculated in this way in Figure 9.6, for headcount poverty, and Figure 9.7, for the average consumption of the poor. We have also reported the mean absolute error of our estimates in Table 9.9. As can be seen, the observations are clustered very close to the 45 degree lines in all the figures, indicating that the errors are reasonably small – a fact that is also supported by

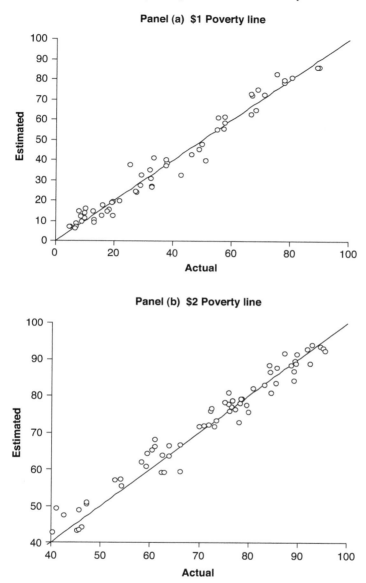

Figure 9.6   Estimated versus Actual Headcount Poverty.

relatively small mean absolute errors in Table 9.9. Table 9.9 also reports mean absolute error of the World Bank estimates, compared to our new (actual) estimates. The substantially larger size of the mean absolute error for the World Bank estimates in all the cases is worthy of note. It means that, under the maintained hypothesis that the new estimates are the preferred ones, the World Bank estimates

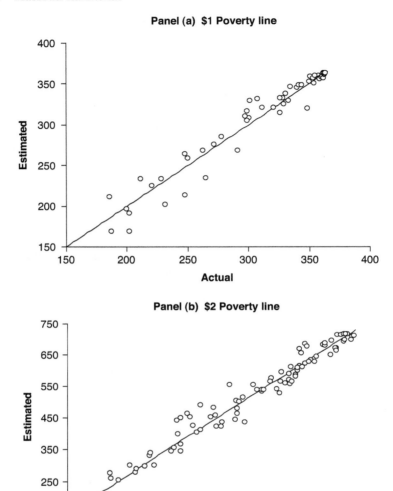

Figure 9.7   Average Annual Consumption of the Poor, Estimated vs. Actual (in $ at 1985 PPP).

of poverty in the case of countries where distribution data are available, are even less reliable than our regression estimates for countries where distribution data are not available. We have not yet, however, formally validated the assumption that the new national accounts consistent estimates are preferred to the World Bank estimates. This is the task of our next validation exercise. Our next validation test, therefore, is to see how the national accounts consistent measures compare to the World Bank estimates in countries where distribution data are available.

Table 9.9 Validation of estimated poverty measures

	Headcount measure of poverty		Average consumption of the poor	
	Below $1	*Below $2*	*Below $1*	*Below $2*
Actual (mean)	39.4	57.1	309.9	526.3
Estimated (mean)	40.0	59.9	310.2	529.3
Mean absolute error	3.0	3.5	10.0	16.9
(% of mean poverty)	(7.5)	(6.2)	(3.2)	(3.2)
Mean absolute error of World Bank estimates	19.1	17.6	39.5	123.1
(% of mean poverty)	(48.5)	(30.9)	(12.7)	(23.4)

Note
Mean absolute errors of World Bank estimates are measured in relation to the new actual estimates.

There has been a growing literature comparing the merits of national accounts and survey consumption and income averages in measuring poverty (see for e.g. Deaton 2000; Ravallion 2001). In none of this literature, however, has there been an attempt to test the properties of the poverty measures estimated on the basis of the two location variables. Our second validation test aims to do this. Our argument so far, in preferring the national accounts location factors, has been based on the fact that unless survey averages are calibrated by external information (e.g. national accounts data), they do not generate reliable averages, even when they contain reliable distribution information. However, if this argument is correct we should be able to test this on the basis of the available external information on poverty that is derived independent of the two poverty estimates being compared (e.g. information on malnutrition, etc.). One such external information is the data on the percentage of undernourished population produced by the FAO. The second external indicator is the UNDP's human development indicator (HDI). As both the FAO and the UNDP data are available for a relatively large number of sample countries, we shall attempt to test the new estimates against the World Bank estimates using these two indicators.

The test consists of comparing the explanatory power of the two poverty measures in relation to the FAO measures of undernourished population, and the UNDP measure of HDI. We have regressed the FAO series (percentage of undernourished population) on our new poverty measures and the World Bank measures, with the results reported in Table 9.10. A similar regression is run using the HDI measure of the UNDP, with the results reported in Table 9.11. Two sets of results are reported in each table, corresponding to the two measures of headcount poverty reported above.[18] The number of observations in the sample varies between different equations depending on the availability of data common to the three sources of data. As can be seen from Tables 9.10 and 9.11, when both poverty measures are included in the regression, in all the four models, the new estimates show highly significant coefficients with the correct sign, but the World Bank poverty measures have insignificant coefficients in all the cases except one.

Once we drop the World Bank measures from the regression the adjusted R^2 in fact improves in three equations out of four, and with the exclusion of the new estimates the explanatory power of the regression is drastically reduced. Any of the standard statistical tests of variable selection applied to these regressions will clearly reject the World Bank estimates in favor of the new estimates. These results indicate that the new estimates contain almost all the useful information that the World Bank estimates may contain, but the information content of the World Bank estimates of poverty are rather low.[19] Because we can also show that in most regressions reported in Tables 9.10 and 9.11 the coefficient of the World Bank poverty variable is significantly different from those of the new estimates, the use of the World Bank data in cross-country analysis, when it does generate significant results, can be misleading.

In the light of the regression results in Tables 9.10 and 9.11, we can further examine the implications of the mean absolute errors reported in Table 9.9. The fact that the mean absolute error of the World Bank estimates is many times larger than the mean absolute error of our expected poverty measures based on regression results, can mean that the information content of the World Bank data on poverty is even less than our estimates for countries where distribution data are not available. To test this more directly, we have re-run the above regressions, this time using our poverty measures based on logistic regressions (used in our first validation test reported above) rather than the actual new poverty estimates. The results, reported in Tables 9.12 and 9.13, indicate that even our expected poverty estimates that do not utilize the actual income distribution information for the sample countries can be better indicators of poverty than the World Bank estimates.[20]

7   The relationship between poverty and growth

The relationship between economic growth and poverty reduction has been subject to a good deal of controversy and debate in recent years. The issues have been hotly contested amongst academics, policy makers, the NGOs, and the popular presses of various hues. A recent summing up of this debate has tried to explain the apparent lack of understanding between the incumbents on the basis of differences in perspectives, between on the one hand economists and responsible policy makers (referred to as the finance ministry tendency), and on the other hand the NGOs and the interested members of the public (the civil society tendencies) (Kanbur 2001). The reality, however, is much more complex. There seems to be some degree of confusion on this issue even amongst the academic and policy-making community.

A related issue, which highlights some of the underlying problems in the growth or poverty debate is what in the policy literature, mostly those emanating from the World Bank's research department, is referred to as the growth elasticity of poverty reduction. The term growth elasticity of poverty reduction implicitly assumes that there is a stable relationship between growth of per capita income and poverty reduction. Most of the elasticity estimates are based on cross-country regressions of the percentage change in some measure of poverty (e.g. the

Table 9.10 Validation of the new poverty estimates against the World Bank estimates

Dependent variable: % population undernourished

Variable	(1) Combined regression			(2) New estimates			(3) World Bank estimates		
	Coeff.	SE	t-statistic	Coeff.	SE	t-statistic	Coeff.	SE	t-statistic
Model I: Headcount poverty (below $1 a day)									
Constant	21.24	4.11	5.17	22.14	2.66	8.33	23.33	4.33	5.39
P1 (New estimates)	0.20	0.07	2.94	0.20	0.06	3.43			
P1 (World Bank estimates)	0.03	0.10	0.29				0.16	0.10	1.61
No. of observations	55			55			55		
R-squared	0.183			0.181			0.047		
Adjusted R-squared	0.151			0.166			0.029		
Log likelihood	-205.94			-205.98			-210.16		
White Heter. Test:	$F_{(5, 49)}$ 1.442			$F_{(2, 52)}$ 0.363			$F_{(2, 52)}$ 1.426		
Model II: Headcount poverty (below $2 a day)									
Constant	4.57	3.56	1.28	8.81	2.95	2.98	7.24	3.73	1.94
P2 (New estimates)	0.21	0.06	3.56	0.28	0.05	6.12			
P2 (World Bank estimates)	0.13	0.06	2.04				0.27	0.05	5.14
No. of observations	80			80			80		
R-squared	0.359			0.324			0.253		
Adjusted R-squared	0.342			0.315			0.244		
Log likelihood	-297.07			-299.16			-303.15		
White Heter. Test:	$F_{(5, 74)}$ 1.049			$F_{(2, 77)}$ 0.268			$F_{(2, 77)}$ 1.679		

Note
P1 refers to headcount measure of poverty (below $1 a day). P2 refers to headcount measure of poverty (below $2 a day).

Table 9.11 Validation of the new poverty estimates against the World Bank estimates

Dependent variable: Human development indicator index

Variable	(1) Combined regression			(2) New estimates			(3) World Bank estimates		
	Coeff.	SE	t-statistic	Coeff.	SE	t-statistic	Coeff.	SE	t-statistic
Model I: Headcount poverty (below $1 a day)									
Constant	0.470	0.030	15.75	0.490	0.019	25.45	0.451	0.032	13.908
P1 (New estimates)	-0.002	0.0005	-3.58	-0.001	0.0004	-3.55			
P1 (World Bank estimates)	0.001	0.001	0.87				-0.0004	0.001	-0.608
No. of observations	56			56			56		
R-squared	0.200			0.189			0.007		
Adjusted R-squared	0.170			0.174			-0.012		
Log likelihood	65.43			65.04			59.37		
White Heter. Test:	F(5, 50) 2.745			F(2, 53) 1.473			F(2, 53) 6.864		
Model II: Headcount poverty (below $2 a day)									
Constant	0.712	0.028	25.15	0.699	0.023	30.05	0.68	0.03	19.92
P2 (New estimates)	-0.003	0.000	-6.45	-0.003	0.000	-9.28			
P2 (World Bank estimates)	0.000	0.001	-0.81				-0.003	0.0005	-5.48
No. of observations	84			84			84		
R-squared	0.516			0.512			0.268		
Adjusted R-squared	0.504			0.506			0.259		
Log likelihood	84.92			84.58			67.50		
White Heter. Test:	F(5, 78) 3.71			F(2, 81) 3.032			F(2, 81) 11.177		

Note

P1 refers to headcount measure of poverty (below $1 a day). P2 refers to headcount measure of poverty (below $2 a day).

Table 9.12 Validation of the new expected poverty measures against the World Bank estimates

Dependent variable: % population undernourished

Variable	(1) Combined regression			(2) New estimates			(3) World Bank estimates		
	Coeff.	*SE*	*t-statistic*	*Coeff.*	*SE*	*t-statistic*	*Coeff.*	*SE*	*t-statistic*
Model I: Headcount poverty (below $1 a day)									
Constant	21.08	4.03	5.23	21.97	2.54	8.65	23.33	4.33	5.39
P1 (New estimates)	0.21	0.06	3.28	0.21	0.06	3.69			
P1 (World Bank estimates)	0.02	0.10	0.21				0.16	0.10	1.61
No. of observations	55			55			55		
R-squared	0.211			0.202			0.047		
Adjusted R-squared	0.180			0.187			0.029		
Log likelihood	−204.98			−208.52			−210.16		
White Heter. Test:	$F_{(5, 49)}$ 2.10			$F_{(2, 52)}$ 0.441			$F_{(2, 52)}$ 1.426		
Model II: Headcount poverty (below $2 a day)									
Constant	1.92	3.58	0.54	6.12	3.01	2.03	7.24	3.73	1.94
P2 (New estimates)	0.22	0.06	3.68	0.32	0.05	6.95			
P2 (World Bank estimates)	0.13	0.06	2.04				0.27	0.05	5.14
No. of observations	77			77			77		
R-squared	0.410			0.385			0.253		
Adjusted R-squared	0.394			0.377			0.244		
Log likelihood	−282.81			−292.71			−303.15		
White Heter. Test:	$F_{(5, 71)}$ 3.41			$F_{(2, 74)}$ 0.363			$F_{(2, 74)}$ 1.679		

Note

P1 refers to headcount measure of poverty (below $1 a day). P2 refers to headcount measure of poverty (below $2 a day).

Table 9.13 Validation of the new expected poverty measures against the World Bank estimates

Dependent Variable: Human Development Indicator Index

Variable	(1) Combined regression			(2) New estimates			(3) World Bank estimates		
	Coeff.	SE	t-statistic	Coeff.	SE	t-statistic	Coeff.	SE	t-statistic
Model I: Headcount Poverty (below $1 a day)									
Constant	0.470	0.030	15.89	0.489	0.019	26.182	0.451	0.032	13.91
P1 (New estimates)	-0.002	0.000	-3.726	-0.001	0.000	-3.634			
P1 (World Bank estimates)	0.001	0.001	0.898				-0.0004	0.001	-0.608
No. of observations	56			56			56		
R-squared	0.213			0.194			0.007		
Adjusted R-squared	0.183			0.179			-0.012		
Log likelihood	65.88			66.87			59.37		
White Heter. Test:	$F_{(5, 50)}$ 2.10			$F_{(2, 53)}$ 0.441			$F_{(2, 53)}$ 6.864		
Model II: Headcount Poverty (below $2 a day)									
Constant	0.696	0.027	26.26	0.712	0.022	32.063	0.68	0.03	19.92
P2 (New estimates)	-0.004	0.001	-7.961	-0.004	0.000	-10.891			
P2 (World Bank estimates)	0.001	0.001	0.982				-0.003	0.000	-5.48
No. of observations	80			80			80		
R-squared	0.582			0.594			0.268		
Adjusted R-squared	0.571			0.589			0.259		
Log likelihood	88.76			91.91			67.50		
White Heter. Test:	$F_{(5, 74)}$ 3.41			$F_{(2, 77)}$ 0.363			$F_{(2, 77)}$ 11.177		

Note P1 refers to headcount measure of poverty (below $1 a day). P2 refers to headcount measure of poverty (below $2 a day).

headcount measure) against the percentage change of per capita consumption or GDP, with possibly some trend variables. Thus the results are generally presented as a fixed or single valued elasticity for a large heterogeneous sample of countries for which income distribution data are available at different points of time. These results, however, vary substantially, depending on the particular sample of countries chosen, and the poverty lines and poverty measures adopted.

For example Ravallion and Chen (1997) provide headcount poverty elasticities ranging from –0.53 to –3.12, for various poverty lines and samples, based on consumption averages from household surveys. With similar methodologies UNECA (1999) provide measures of income growth elasticity of headcount poverty for Africa of –0.92 and –0.85. Ravallion *et al.* (1991) on the other hand calculate headcount elasticities of –2.2 for the developing countries and –1.5 for sub-Saharan Africa, based on per capita consumption growth. And the list goes on. The question that arises is what meaning can one give to these aggregate elasticity estimates? Under what conditions can one assume stable poverty reduction elasticities and what are the reasons for the clearly unstable elasticity measures? In answering these questions one also touches on some the important issues in the growth or poverty reduction debate.

To examine the conditions under which it may be plausible to assume a stable relationship between growth and poverty reduction, it would be helpful to distinguish between a situation of generalized poverty and what one may refer to as the "normal" poverty situation. The difference between the two is depicted in Figure 9.8, which shows two economies A and B with the same distribution of income but considerably different average per capita incomes. The same international poverty line, Z (say $1-a-day), generates totally different estimates of headcount poverty in the two cases. Case A in the figure, that is, the normal poverty situation, is where poverty is confined to the tail of the distribution. In Case B, the generalized poverty situation, the majority of the population fall below the poverty line. As shown in the previous section, Case B is typical of the LDC economies with reference to the $1 and $2 a day international poverty lines.

In case A, economic growth is neither necessary nor sufficient for poverty reduction. It is not necessary because the economy already has sufficient resources to introduce poverty alleviation program. It is not sufficient, because no matter how high an economy's per capita income level may be, there will always be individuals or households who, because of their own special circumstances or because of sectoral shifts or cyclical fluctuations in the economy, fall below the poverty line. Poverty reduction in these circumstances depends on social and political processes and necessarily involves a redistribution of income. The introduction of different types of social welfare system in the European countries after the Second World War is an example this type of poverty reduction. The differences in observed rates of extreme poverty in different European countries in the postwar period is explained more by their social and political institutions than their per capita income levels. High rates of economic growth may ease the acceptance of redistribution policies, but there is no empirical relationship linking high

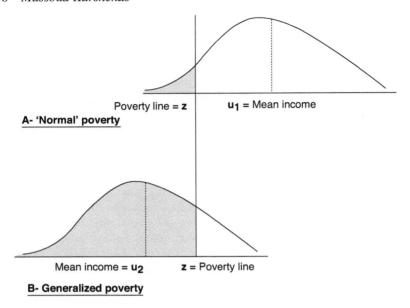

Figure 9.8   Generalized poverty and normal poverty.

growth rates to the introduction of more adequate welfare systems in these countries.

In Case A, or in a "normal" poverty situation, therefore, the term growth elasticity of poverty reduction is not a very meaningful concept – at least for the case of absolute poverty which is the main concern here. In Case B, the generalized poverty case, however, the situation is very different. Because majority of the population in this case fall below the poverty line, growth and poverty reduction are necessarily linked. Redistribution can play some direct role in alleviating the worst aspects of poverty even in such economies, but reduction of poverty of the type characterized by the absolute poverty line Z can be achieved on a non-negligible scale only through economic growth. This does not mean that redistribution of income and assets in such economies do not play an important role in poverty reduction, but that such a role, to be significant under the conditions of generalized poverty, has to be mediated through economic growth. Efficiency enhancing redistribution of assets and incomes are indeed essential for poverty alleviation when there is extreme generalized poverty.

Under the conditions of generalized poverty, economic growth is not only necessary for poverty alleviation on a major scale, but under "normal" conditions, it can be also sufficient. We shall shortly examine what constitutes "normal" conditions, but it should be clear that it is only with the existence of such normal conditions or normal patterns that the term growth elasticity of poverty reduction becomes meaningful. Growth elasticity of poverty reduction, therefore, is a plausible concept only under the conditions of generalized poverty and when economies can be assumed to follow similar "normal" historical patterns of development.

The next question is what are the empirical regularities or historical patterns of growth and poverty reduction, and under what conditions can they justify the notion of growth elasticity of poverty at an aggregate level? To address this question we have plotted the $1 and $2 headcount poverty measures for our sample observations against per capita consumption at 1985 PPP exchange rates in Figure 9.9. The data refer to more than 34 countries over three decades, and if there are any regular pattern between headcount poverty at the two international poverty lines and per capita consumption it should be reflected in this figure. To observe the normal pattern in the historical relationship between the two variables we have dropped some of the clearly outlying countries such as South Africa, Zimbabwe, and Namibia, and as pointed out above have confined the sample to only Asian and African developing countries. As can be seen there seems to be a clear relationship between the level of per capita consumption and headcount poverty. The relationship, however, is a highly nonlinear one, and very different from the linear or log-linear relationship often assumed in aggregate elasticity estimates.

A number of points need to be emphasized about the relationships between per capita consumption and poverty depicted in Figure 9.9. One point is that, as the observations are mainly cross-country, with some countries having more than one observation, the pattern should be regarded as a long-term "normal" relationship between growth and poverty. It is a normal relationship in the sense that according to observed patterns countries emerging out of a situation of generalized poverty are expected to follow these paths in the long-run. For example, an average African LDC where close to 89 percent of the population live below $2 a day and where per capita consumption is on average $1.13 a day at 1985 PPP rates, would be expected to increase its per capita consumption to over $4 a day to achieve headcount poverty of about 20 percent.[21] This is the, so to speak, necessary condition. The sufficiency condition on the other hand maintains that if an economy with generalized poverty, with close to 89 percent of the population living below $2 a day, and with an overall per capita consumption of $1.13 can grow so that its overall per capita consumption reaches $4 a day, then this economy is likely to attain poverty rates of about 20 percent. This is what the "normal" patterns of economic development according to Figure 9.9 indicate. However, there are exceptions such as South Africa and Zimbabwe (excluded from the figure), indicating that economic growth may not be sufficient for poverty reduction. But the exceptional historical experiences of countries such as South Africa and Zimbabwe, and the lack of political and economic sustainability of these experiences, also indicates that these may be exceptions that indeed prove the rule. Though there is no guarantee that the future trajectories of growth and poverty reduction will follow the past, it is highly likely that there will be always a strong relationship between the two under the conditions of generalized poverty.

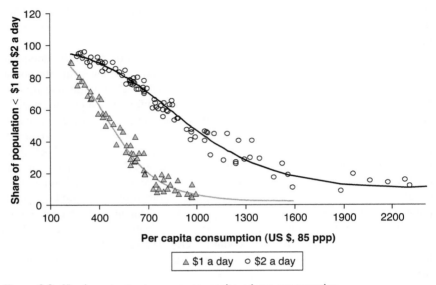

Figure 9.9 Headcount poverty versus per capita private consumption.

Even though Figure 9.9 shows a close association between growth and poverty reduction in LDC type economies suffering from generalized poverty, it nevertheless does not support the validity and usefulness of the aggregate elasticity concept often used in the studies of poverty in the LDCs. The highly nonlinear shape of the apparent relationships between poverty reduction and growth indicates that one should be wary of the pitfalls of such aggregate measures. Figures 9.10 and 9.11 show the growth elasticities of poverty implicit in the nonlinear relationship in Figure 9.9, for the headcount poverty and the average consumption of the poor respectively, for both the $1 and $2 poverty lines. As can be seen both the marginal response of poverty to growth as well as its elasticity is critically dependent on the poverty line chosen as well as on the level of per capita income or consumption in the country concerned. Considering the point made above about the relevance of growth elasticities for countries with generalized poverty, Figure 9.10 indicates that for the $1 poverty line such growth elasticities can range from −0.5 to about −3.0, and for the $2 poverty line it can vary between −0.5 and over −2.0, for the range of per capita incomes that fall into the generalized poverty category. Similarly, Figure 9.11 indicates that the elasticity of the consumption of the poor with respect to the growth of overall per capita consumption can vary between 0.5 and close to 0.75 for both the $1 and $2 poverty lines, for different levels of per capita consumption within the LDC range. This is incidentally in conformity with Kuznet's hypothesis that at the early stages of development, income inequalities tend to increase. Economic growth, nevertheless, reduces poverty in countries suffering from generalized poverty.

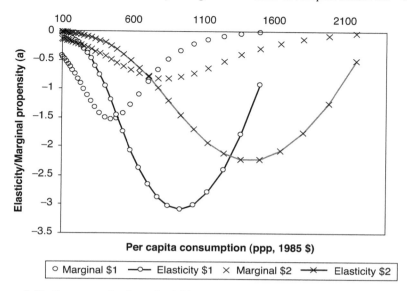

Figure 9.10 Poverty reduction elasticities and marginal propensities for headcount poverty ($1 and $2 poverty lines).

Notes: (a) Per cent for elasticities, and change per $10 increase in annual per capita consumption for the marginal.

8 Concluding remarks

In this concluding section it may be appropriate to start with spelling out some of the caveats and reservations about the concepts, data, and methods used in this paper. First, one should be careful not to extrapolate poverty on the basis of the above results for consumption ranges beyond the sample. The nonlinear relationship between poverty and average consumption makes such extrapolation particularly hazardous. It is also very likely that at higher income levels the statistical models applied would become less precise, as the residuals or the independent income distribution effects can become more prominent.

Second, our results should not convey the impression that only growth matters for poverty alleviation and that income distribution plays a minor role. Such an impression results only from a mechanistic and superficial interpretation of the results. As we have emphasized at various places in the paper, under the conditions of generalized poverty income distribution can play a crucial role in poverty alleviation through its growth effects. For example, consider a redistribution of assets and incomes in the agricultural sector, for example, following a land-reform, that may at the same time result in a rapid growth of productivity and incomes in that sector and in the economy as a whole.[22] The growth of the other sectors of the economy in this process can lead to income distribution outcomes, which may be very different from the initial effect of the land reform. This, however, does not mean that the original redistribution has not played any role in

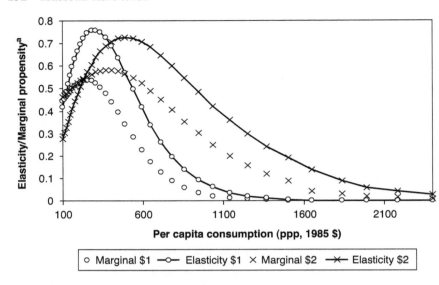

Figure 9.11   Poverty reduction elasticities and marginal propensities (average consumption of the poor, below $1 and $2 a day).

Notes: (a) Per cent for elasticities, and change per $1 increase in annual per capita consumption for the marginal.

poverty alleviation. Such dynamic effects, however, are too complex to be picked up by statistical analysis of this nature or through simplistic cross-country econometrics exercises based on aggregate ex-post observations. Recent debates on the respective roles of growth and income distribution on poverty alleviation based on this type of exercise, therefore, are likely to remain sterile and unproductive.

Third, despite the fact that in parlance with the existing literature we have referred to the new estimates as poverty indicators, one should be aware of the differences between these measures and the conventional national measures of poverty. The headcount measure of the population living below $1 or $2 a day can differ from national poverty measures based on poverty lines defined on the basis of appropriate consumption baskets and prices facing different groups of the population.[23] The $1 and $2 poverty lines also may not reflect the intensity of poverty in different countries. This is not just because of the differences in institutions, customs, and the available goods and services, or the differences in the distribution of consumption among the poor in different countries. It is also, and possibly more importantly, because of the errors involved in measuring PPP exchange rates relevant to the consumption basket of the poor in each country. As they are, the consumption PPP exchange rates for many poor countries are extrapolated on the basis of available information on other "similar" countries and hence are not very accurate. Furthermore, even when accurately estimated, they do not reflect the appropriate exchange rates for the consumption basket of the poor.

The real value of the $1 and $2 headcount poverty measures is that they provide reasonably comparable information across countries on resources available to the poorest part of the population to sustain their lives. One cannot remain faithful to both this type of internationally comparable notion of poverty, and the nationally defined measures of poverty. The problems associated with the World Bank's measures of poverty highlighted in this paper, may have arisen because of their attempt to strike a balance between these two essentially different notions of poverty. However, once one defines internationally comparable poverty lines like the $1 and $2 a day lines, one should be more concerned about the comparability of the measured poverty across countries rather than being close to nationally defined measures of poverty. It is not unlikely that in the case of some countries the new poverty measures estimated in this paper are different from the national measures of poverty. As long as our measures are internationally comparable and consistent, however, this should not be a cause of concern, because internationally comparable absolute poverty measures are meant to serve a different purpose from the national definitions of poverty. An important contribution of internationally comparable poverty measures based on the $1 and $2 poverty lines is to identify low-income countries suffering from extreme "generalized" poverty. Economic policies for growth and poverty alleviation in such economies are likely to be very different from policies that appear to be effective in the context of economies with a more "normal" poverty situation.[24]

In this context two issues which can greatly benefit from further research, and are indeed in need of such research, stand out. First is the estimation of more accurate PPP exchange rates for the low-income countries, appropriate for inter-country poverty comparisons. The existing estimates are clearly unsatisfactory. Another area of research which needs serious attention is the reconciliation of the national accounts and survey data on average income and consumption. With poverty alleviation becoming a central international goal for low-income countries, these tasks become particularly urgent as the existing data and methodologies inhibit effective policy and analytical research.

Notes

* I am grateful to Ben Fine, Charles Gore, Farhad Mehran, Noman Majid, Hashem Pesaran, Graham Pyatt, John Sender, Rob Vos, and Marc Wuyts for comments on an earlier draft. I am responsible for all the remaining errors and omissions.
1 For ease of exposition here we assume a single shape parameter, but what follows also applies to the cases where S is assumed to be a vector of shape parameters.
2 For a review of the empirical literature on Kuznets hypothesis see, for example, Fields (1989, 1991) and Anand and Kanbur (1993).
3 See World Bank (2001a) and Deininger and Squire, (1996).
4 We have also excluded South Africa, Zimbabwe, and Namibia from the sample, though for these countries data on distribution of consumption expenditure are available. The reason for excluding these countries is that they are clear outliers, that is, poverty and income distribution in these countries is clearly very different from other countries in the sample.
5 In the literature (e.g. Ravallion 2001) it is mainly attempted to explain the likely reasons why in a country such as India household survey data may underestimate the level

and growth of consumption relative to national accounts estimates. As seen above, however, there are countries where the reverse is true.

6   The reason for this phenomenon could be lack of independence of the two series. Plotting the consumption ratio variable against per capita private consumption one can clearly observe a systematic trend. Because the mean of trended variables is very sensitive to the particular observations chosen, one difference between the above test and that conducted by Ravallion (2000) can be due to the difference in samples. Another difference between the two tests may be that we use national accounts consumption data, based on Penn World Tables, while Ravallion (2000) may be based on new PPP estimates by the World Bank.

7   One potentially important source of discrepancy between the two consumption series, which came to my attention only after completing this work, can be the difference in the PPP exchange rates used. The World Bank has recently changed the base year from 1985 to 1993, and according to them the $1 and $2 poverty lines have correspondingly changed to $1.08 and $2.15 in 1993 prices. However, the change of the base year, if correctly done, should not make any difference to the measurements. As the final year of the Summers and Heston's dataset on PPP exchange rates is 1992, it is difficult to check the consistency of the new World Bank figures with the old ones. It appears, however, that apart from changing the base year, the World Bank 1993 PPP rates are also re-estimates of some of the earlier measures in Penn World Tables version 5.6 (see, e.g. Chen and Ravallion 2000). Because there is no official documentation on this and the data are not available publicly, we have used the original Penn World Tables version 5.6 estimates to calculate per capita consumption in 1985 PPP exchange rates.

8   Ravallion (2003) has argued that the discrepancy between the two series is likely to be due to the noncompliance of the rich households in household budget surveys, with the implication that poverty estimates based on household mean surveys would be still accurate, even when they are underestimates of the true distribution mean. This hypothesis, however, does not seem to be supported by evidence on the nature of discrepancy between the survey and national accounts means. As noted above, survey means in many instances are higher than national accounts means (see also, Karshenas 2004).

9   This of course does not mean that national accounts estimates are very accurate. Indeed the errors involved in national accounts estimates of consumption, particularly in LDCs, can be very substantial, as these are usually estimated as residuals. Nevertheless the methods of measurement of national accounts are likely to be more consistent over time and across countries than the survey averages.

10   See, Atkinson and Brandolini (2001) on the problems associated with intercountry comparison of distribution data based on secondary sources.

11   There are 58 observations for the $1 line and 90 observations for the $2 line. The number of observations for the $2 poverty line is less than the number of observations in Table 9.1 because per capita income in Ethiopia is too low to estimate precise headcount poverty the two observations listed in the table for Ethiopia. These two observations have therefore been dropped.

12   This of course does not imply that income distribution has no significant effect on poverty. Such effects are however likely to be mediated via location or growth effects, and are too complex to be identified in statistical models of this type.

13   In order to be consistent with the World Bank estimates we have used World Bank's POVCAL program to estimate the new poverty measures.

14   There are fewer observations in Figure 9.4 as compared with Figure 9.3, because the former only contains observations for which both World Bank estimates and national accounts based estimates of poverty are available.

15   For example, according to Chen and Ravallion (2000: 8),

   If there is only one survey for a country, then we estimate measures for each reference year by applying the growth rate in real private consumption per person from the national accounts to the survey mean – assuming in other words that the Lorenz curve for that country does not change.

The problem here is not the assumption of constancy of the Lorenz curve, which is a permissible assumption given the lack of data. The main problem is the mixing of poverty measures and trends with totally different and incompatible location variables.

16 The number of observations for the 1960s and the 1970s decades are too few to distinguish the four decades separately.
17 Post-1992 figures are estimated by applying growth rates of real per capita consumption from the World Bank WDI databank to the Penn World Table PPP figures.
18 The same tests were applied to the other two poverty measures, namely, the average consumption of the poor for the $1 and $2 poverty lines. But because the results are not different from the headcount poverty results, they are not reported here.
19 This is of course in relation to the HDI and the FAO poverty measures, which themselves can be subject to serious errors. For a critique of the FAO's nutrition measure see for example, Svedberg (1999).
20 The above of course depends on the assumption that the FAO and UNDP data are generated independent of the two poverty measures being examined. These results need to be further examined using other independent sources of information on poverty.
21 Though this statement can be also made in terms of the "growth elasticity of poverty reduction" terminology, it is important to note that this elasticity depends on the initial level of per capita income as well as on the poverty line chosen, which differs from the fixed elasticity figures normally used in the literature. This point is further elaborated in the text that follows.
22 The point here is not whether asset redistribution will lead to growth or not. Even if it has negative growth effects the above argument still holds.
23 Ravallion *et al.* (1991) show that the one-dollar poverty line is relatively close to the average of official poverty lines in a number of low income countries. The variations around this average are nevertheless still quite substantial.
24 On this point see UNCTAD (2000 and 2001).

References

Anand, S. and Kanbur, S. M. R. (1993) 'Inequality and Development: A Critique', *Journal of Development Economics*, 41(1): 19–43.

Atkinson, A. B. and Brandolini, A. (2001) 'Promise and Pitfalls in the Use of 'Secondary' Data-Sets: Income Inequality in OECD Countries as a Case Study', *Journal of Economic Literature*, September, 39: 771–99.

Bhalla, S. S. (2002) *Imagine There is No Country: Poverty, Inequality, and Growth in the Era of Globalization*, Washington, DC: Institute for International Economics.

Chen, S. and Ravallion, M. (2000) 'How Did the World's Poorest Fare in the 1990s?', *mimeo*, Washington, DC: World Bank.

Chen, S., Datt, G., and Ravallion, M. (1994) 'Is Poverty Increasing or Decreasing in the Developing World?', *Review of Income and Wealth*, 40: 359–76.

Deaton, A. (2000) 'Counting the World's Poor: Problems and Possible Solutions', *mimeo*, Princeton, NJ: Research Program in Development Studies, Princeton University.

Deininger, K. and Squire, L. (1996) 'A New Data Set Measuring Income Inequality', *World Bank Economic Review*, 10(3): 565–91. Online Available HTTP <http:www.worldbank.org/research/growth/dddeisqu.htm>.

Fields, G. S. (1989) 'Changes in Poverty and Inequality in Developing Countries', *World Bank Economic Observer*, 4(2): 167–85.

Fields, G. S. (1991) 'Growth and Income Distribution', in G. Psacharopoulos (ed.), *Essays on Poverty, Equity and Growth*, Oxford: Pergamon Press.

Hamner, L., Pyatt, G., and White, H. (1997) 'Poverty in sub-Saharan Africa: What Can We Learn from The World Bank's Poverty Assessments?', *mimeo*, The Hague: Institute of Social Studies.

Kanbur, S.M.R. (2001) 'Economic Policy, Distribution and Poverty: The Nature of Disagreements', *World Development* 29(6).

Karshenas, M. (2004) 'Global Poverty Estimates and the Millennium Goals: Towards a Unified Framework', *Employment Strategy Papers*, No. 5, Geneva: International Labour Office.

Kuznets, S. (1955) 'Economic Growth and Income Inequality', *American Economic Review*, 45(1): 1–28.

Pyatt, G. (2000) 'The Distribution of Living Standards Within Countries: Some Reflections on an Evolving International Data Base', *mimeo*, The Hague: Institute of Social Studies.

Ravallion, M. (2000a) 'Do National Accounts Provide Unbiased Estimates of Survey-based Measures of Living Standards?', *mimeo*, Washington, DC: World Bank.

—— (2000b) 'Should Poverty Measures be Anchored in National Accounts?', *Economic and Political Weekly*, August 26–September 2, pp. 3245–52.

—— (2001) 'Growth, Inequality and Poverty: Looking Beyond Averages', *mimeo*, Washington, DC: World Bank.

—— (2003) 'The Debate on Globalization, Poverty and Inequality: Why Measurement Matters', Washington, DC: World Bank.

Ravallion, M. and Chen, S. (1997) 'What can New Survey Data Tell Us about Recent Changes in Distribution and Poverty?', *World Bank Economic Review*, 11(2): 358–82, Washington, DC: World Bank.

Ravallion, M., Datt, G., and van de Walle, D. (1991) 'Quantifying Absolute Poverty in the Developing World', *Review of Income and Wealth*, 37: 345–61.

Svedberg, P. (1999) "841 Million Undernourished?" *World Development* 27(12): 2081–98.

UNCTAD (2000) *Least Developed Countries Report 2000*, Geneva: UNCTAD.

UNCTAD (2001) *Least Developed Countries Report 2001*, Geneva: UNCTAD.

UNECA (1999) *Economic Report on Africa, 1999*, E/ECA/CM.24/3, Addis Ababa: Economic Commission for Africa.

World Bank (2001a) POVCALNet. Online. Available HTTP <www.worldbank.org/research/povmonitor/index.htm> Washington, DC: World Bank

World Bank (2001b) *World Development Indicators,* Washington, DC: World Bank.

Part IV

Globalization, capital mobility, and competition

10 Capital account liberalization, free long-term capital flows, financial crises, and economic development[1*]

Ajit Singh

1 Introduction: Main issues and the international policy context

The main objective of this paper is to review the theoretical issues and available empirical evidence on capital account liberalization, which in addition to being of interest in their own right are of importance to present multilateral discussions in two international policy contexts. First, they are a concern in the debate on the New International Financial Architecture (NIFA). Second, they are part of the post-Doha agenda in the WTO, in relation to FDI flows. The focus of this paper is on developing countries and it considers policy from the perspective of (1) economic development and (2) the global rules of the game rather than the economic policy within individual countries. The paper essentially examines the question: What kind of global economic order in relation to capital flows can best serve the interests of developing countries?

Capital account liberalization is the area where there is the greatest disconnection between economic theory and actual events in the real world. In analyzing liberalization of capital flows, it is customary to distinguish between short-term (e.g. portfolio flows and short-term bank loans) and long-term flows (e.g. FDI). Neoclassical theory suggests that free flows of external capital (including short-term capital) should be equilibrating and help smooth a country's consumption or production paths. However, in the real world, exactly the opposite appears to happen. Liberalization of the short-term capital account has invariably been associated with serious economic and financial crises in Asia and Latin America in the 1990s. The proponents of neoclassical theory argue that the case for free capital flows is no different from that for free trade – the former could simply be regarded as a form of intertemporal trade. The first part of the paper (Sections 2–4) will address this central controversy in relation to developing countries and specifically ask the following questions:

- To what extent, if any, are trade liberalization and free capital flows analogous in their effects on social welfare? What are the conditions necessary to maximize their potential net benefits?

- What is the nature of the relationship between capital account liberalization and economic crises?
- Why do such crises occur far more in developing than in advanced countries?
- Do free capital flows lead to faster long-term economic growth, which may compensate for the crisis and the economic instability associated with capital account liberalization?
- What kind of multilateral framework, if any, would be most appropriate for regulating international capital flows that would best serve the interests of developing countries?

In the light of the recent deep economic and financial crises in Asia, Latin America, and Russia many (but by no means all) economists will today accept that free short-term capital flows could have seriously adverse consequences for developing countries, as these flows are often volatile and subject to surges and sudden withdrawals. However, long-term capital flows, particularly FDI, are regarded as being much more stable and therefore for this and other reasons are thought to have a positive influence on long-term economic development. It is therefore suggested that developing countries, in liberalizing their capital account, may wish in the short- to medium-term to liberalize only long-term capital flows such as FDI, while still controlling, partially or wholly, short-term flows.

Even Joseph Stiglitz who has been a fierce critic of precipitate capital account liberalization in developing countries appears to favor free FDI flows. Thus Stiglitz (2000) finds striking

> the zeal with which the International Monetary Fund (IMF) had requested an extension of its mandate to include capital market liberalization a short two years earlier at the Annual Meetings in Hong Kong. It should have been clear then, and it is certainly clear now, that the position was maintained either as a matter of ideology or of special interests, and not on the basis of careful analysis of theory, historical experience or a wealth of econometric studies. Indeed, it has become increasingly clear that there is not only no case for capital market liberalization, but that there is a fairly compelling case against full liberalization
>
> (p. 1076)

Stiglitz, however, emphasizes that his general strictures against capital account liberalization are primarily directed against short-term speculative flows. He writes,

> The argument for foreign direct investment, for instance, is compelling. Such investment brings with it not only resources, but also technology, access to markets, and (hopefully) valuable training, an improvement in human capital. Foreign direct investment is also not as volatile – and therefore as disruptive – as the short-term flows that can rush into a country and, just as precipitously, rush out.
>
> (p. 1076)

This paper will take major issue, with the orthodox *laissez-faire* position (see for e.g. Summers 2000; Fischer 1999), of the desirability of speedy capital account liberalization in developing countries. It will however also part company with Stiglitz in important respects. It will be argued here that although Stiglitz is right in suggesting that free trade in capital is not the same thing as free trade in goods, he implicitly assigns too much virtue to the latter. This argument will be made here more in global economic terms rather than in those of the traditional concepts, such as infant industry protection. It will further be suggested that not only do developing countries need controls against short-term capital flows for many of the reasons Stiglitz puts forward, but they also require discretion to regulate FDI flows if it is thought to be desirable. Later in this paper it will be argued that even free movements of FDI may contribute to financial fragility in developing economies and also may not serve the cause of economic development in a number of other ways.

These issues of capital account liberalization are of course not only of academic interest but also clearly of serious policy concern for developing countries. With respect to the latter, it is important to emphasize, the present paper concentrates exclusively on the international dimension of the policy debate on the subject. The goal of capital account liberalization for all countries, together with an orderly and fast progress towards it, has been at the heart of the proposals by G7 countries for NIFA. Similarly, the European Union and Japan have raised the question of the free movements of FDI as an important subject for study and eventual negotiations at the WTO. Unlike the aborted OECD Multilateral Agreement on Investment, these new proposals wholly exclude short-term capital flows and focus entirely on FDI. To date, these proposals have received little academic or public attention. Now, following the Doha WTO Ministerial Declaration, these issues are on the international agenda and merit urgent scrutiny. There is already a large literature on the NIFA.[2] However, the advanced countries proposal for the free movement of FDI has not been much studied. The second half of the paper redresses this imbalance by focusing on FDI flows, specifically on the proposed new multilateral agreement on such flows.

To sum up, the main contribution of this paper lies first in bringing together the relevant theory and empirical evidence from diverse areas (theory of international trade, of international factor movements, of industrial organization, of finance, and of economic development) to bear on important international economic policy issues with respect to both short-term and long-term capital flows to developing countries. Second, the paper contributes by examining these multilateral arrangements entirely from a developing country perspective. Third, it contributes by providing analysis and evidence to suggest that even unfettered FDI, a capital inflow favored by most economists, may not serve the developmental needs of many countries. Fourth, the paper contributes by providing a critical analysis of the proposed new multilateral agreement (PMAI) being put forward at the WTO by some advanced countries. As mentioned above, very little work has been done on this subject before.

2   Free trade versus free capital movements: Are they analogous?[3]

2.1   Free trade and economic openness: analytical considerations

The traditional case for free trade can best be put in terms of the two fundamental theorems of welfare economics. According to the first welfare theorem, a competitive equilibrium in the absence of externalities and nonsatiation constitutes a Pareto optimum. The second theorem, which is more relevant for present purposes, states that any Pareto optimum can be realized as a competitive equilibrium in the presence of all-around convexity, provided suitable lump-sum transfers can be arranged among the participants. Most of these assumptions are erroneous or are not easily met in the real world. Nevertheless, neoclassical economists suggest that such considerations do not destroy the case for free trade but only change the nature of the argument. Thus, Krugman (1987) concludes his classic defense of free trade in terms of modern theory as follows: "this is not the argument that free trade is optimal because markets are efficient. Instead it is a sadder but wiser argument for free trade as a rule of thumb in a world whose politics are as imperfect as its markets."

However, as Chakravarty and Singh (1988) suggest, the politics of a world of increasing returns to scale are more likely to gravitate toward "managed" rather than free trade. Instead of either free trade or autarchy, this would be a world in between – one in which there were trade restrictions, government assistance to favored industries and a plethora of special arrangements between countries, in other words, the messy real world. In place of all-around convexity, this real world is characterized by learning by doing (Arrow 1962), dynamic economies, and cumulative causation (Young 1928; Kaldor 1978). This is, therefore, the world of second best and of multiple equilibria and the purpose of policy is to move from a bad to a good equilibrium. The gains from such policy intervention have, however, to be balanced against the losses from government failure and appropriate policy can therefore be prescribed only on a case-by-case basis (Ocampo and Taylor 2000; Gomory and Baumol 2000). Provided there is a mechanism for ensuring full employment of each nation's resources, and if we abstract, for the moment, from the possibility of government failure, a policy of selective economic openness would be a source of great advantage for an economy for any one of the following reasons:[4]

1   it may enable a country to concentrate its relatively specialized resources in areas of production where the world demand is highly income and price elastic;
2   it may lead to diffusion of knowledge of a nature which can lead to considerable upgradation of the *quality* of local factors of production;
3   it may lead to sufficient competitive pressure to eliminate X-inefficiency;

4 trade may lead to changes in the distribution of income which can lead to a greater share of accumulation in national income;
5 trade may facilitate what Schumpeter stressed so much: an accelerated process of creative destruction.

In general, trade openness works positively if the phenomenon of "learning" from contacts with the rest of the world is institutionalized through suitable adaptations on the policy side involving appropriate government interventions, which make the domestic economy more responsive to change. This is a main lesson that emerges from the outstanding industrial success of East Asian economies during the second half of the twentieth century.[5] Countries such as Japan and Korea established comprehensive technology and industrial policies to institutionalize such learning. It is important to appreciate that although Japan and Korea were "trade open" in the sense of being export or outward oriented, they were not so open on the side of imports. Both countries maintained, formally or informally, selective import controls for long periods during the course of their industrialization. The strategic interests of the U.S. hegemon permitted such selective openness without threatening retaliation.[6] To pursue these policies of selective economic openness, it is necessary for developing countries to have not only appropriate institutions to minimize the incidence of government failure but also a world conjuncture which permits them to pursue commercial and industrial policies, on a nonreciprocal basis, which best suit their developmental requirements. Chakravarty and Singh (1988) point out that in such a world, selective economic openness may be a superior strategy than either free trade or autarchy. They also suggest that at a theoretical level, *learning over time* is a more relevant paradigm for developmental gains from trade than the neoclassical story that emphasizes the exploitation of arbitrage opportunities (see Pasinetti 1981, for a detailed discussion of the learning approach to this issue).

To sum up, while the classical and neoclassical arguments for "free trade" suffer from serious conceptual and operational difficulties, there are indeed substantive benefits from selective trade or economic openness, which are more robust than the traditional neoclassical theory suggests. However, such benefits can be realized only in a world conjuncture in which full employment and other structural conditions outlined above are met, coupled with an appropriate set of domestic policies which go considerably beyond the limits of commercial policy as traditionally defined.

2.2 The case for capital account liberalization

The case for capital account liberalization was authoritatively put forward by Stanley Fischer, the former Deputy Managing Director of the International Monetary Fund, in the following terms:

- that the benefits of liberalizing the capital account outweigh the potential costs;
- that countries need to prepare well for capital account liberalization: economic policies and institutions, particularly the financial system, need to be adapted to operate in a world of liberalized capital markets; and
- that an amendment of the IMF's Articles of Agreement is the best way of ensuring that capital account liberalization is carried out in an orderly, nondisruptive way, that minimizes the risks that premature liberalization could pose for an economy and its policy makers (Fischer 1997).

Fischer suggests that, at a theoretical level, capital account liberalization would lead to global economic efficiency, allocation of world savings to those who are able to use them most productively, and would thereby increase social welfare. Citizens of countries with free capital movements would be able to diversify their portfolios and thereby increase their risk-adjusted rates of return. It would enable corporations in these countries to raise capital in international markets at a lower cost. It is suggested, moreover, that such liberalization leads to further development of a country's financial system which in turn is thought to enhance productivity in the real economy by facilitating transactions and by better allocation of resources. Some argue that free capital movements will help increase world welfare through another channel, namely transferring resources from ageing populations and lower rates of return in advanced countries to younger populations and higher rates of return in newly industrializing economies. Such resource transfers will be Pareto optimal as both rich and poor countries would gain.

Summers (2000) succinctly sums up the core point of the orthodox perspective as follows: "... the abstract argument for a competitive financial system parallels the argument for competitive markets in general ... Just as trade in goods across jurisdictions has benefits, so too will intertemporal trade and trade that shares risks across jurisdictions have benefits."

Orthodox economists recognize that there are risks attached to capital account liberalization. Markets sometimes overreact or react late or react too fast. However, Fischer argues that "... capital movements are mostly appropriate: currency crises do not blow up out of a clear blue sky, but rather start as rational reactions to policy mistakes or external shocks. The problem is that once started, they may sometimes go too far." (Fischer 1997: 4–5) In general, Fischer believes that capital markets serve as an important discipline on government macroeconomic and other policies "which improves overall economic performance by rewarding good policies and penalizing bad" (Fischer 1997: 4).

Two initial observations may be made with respect to this orthodox case for capital account liberalization. The first is that not all orthodox economists favor such liberalization. Bhagwati (1998) for example, a leading theorist and advocate of free trade in goods and services regards capital account liberalization as inappropriate for developing countries. Second, it is important to note that as in the case of the neoclassical argument for free trade, the maintenance of full employment and macroeconomic stability constitute an important prerequisite for reaping the benefits of a globalized capital market. Specifically, as Rakshit (2001) suggests, the theoretical model of the beneficial effects of free capital movements makes the following assumptions:

1 resources are fully employed everywhere;
2 capital flows themselves do not stand in the way of attaining full employment or macroeconomic stability; and
3 the transfer of capital from one country to another is governed by long-term returns on investment in different countries.

The question whether these assumptions are likely to be valid under the current global economic regime is examined below.

2.3 The analytical case against free capital flows

The theoretical case against the view that unfettered capital movements are essential for maximizing the gains from trade and world economic welfare has been made by a number of economists from different schools of thought. First within the neoclassical tradition itself, Stiglitz (2000) argues that the concept of free movements of capital is fundamentally different from that of free trade in goods. Capital flows are subject to asymmetric information, agency problems, adverse selection, and moral hazard. Although such problems may occur also in trade in goods and services, they are intrinsic to financial flows and are far more important.

Importantly, there are also diverging views about the price formation process in asset markets such as the stock market and the currency markets. Orthodox economists subscribe to the theory of efficient markets. In this view, prices are a collective outcome of actions of a multitude of individual economic agents whose behaviors are assumed to be based on utility maximization and rational expectations. This price formation process is thought to lead to efficient prices in these markets. A powerful counterview is that put forward by John Maynard Keynes (1936) in Chapter 12 of the General Theory and which is encapsulated in his well known "beauty contest" analogy which highlights the role of speculation in determining prices.

Thus, in Keynesian analysis, which has been formalized in recent theoretical contributions, price formation in asset markets may often be dominated by speculators or noise traders in modern parlance. Moreover, theoretical work on Darwinian selection mechanisms indicate that the Friedman (1953) assertion that rational investors will always wipe out speculators is far from being valid in all situations.[7]

Furthermore, the critical school emphasizes that financial markets are particularly prone to coordination failures and often generate multiple equilibria, some good, and some bad. In the absence of appropriate coordination by the government or international authorities, an economy may languish in a low-level equilibrium, producing suboptimal output and employment levels.

The post-Keynesian economists (see for e.g. Davidson 2001) take a more radical stance. They put forward analyses and evidence in favor of Keynes' thesis "that flexible exchange rates and free international capital mobility are incompatible with global full employment and rapid economic growth in an era of multilateral free trade." These economists also challenge the orthodox presumption that transparency and availability of more information would make the financial markets less prone to crisis. They point out that the crises are fundamentally due to the fact that the future is uncertain and people have different perceptions about it.

Keynes was very skeptical about the ability of the world economy under free trade and free capital movements to maintain balance of payments equilibrium between countries at full employment levels of output. In a famous passage he observed,

> ... the problem of maintaining equilibrium in the balance of payments between countries has never been solved ... the failure to solve the problem has been a major cause of impoverishment and social discontent and even of wars and revolutions ... to suppose that there exists some smoothly functioning automatic mechanism of adjustment which preserves equilibrium only if we trust to matters of laissez faire is a doctrinaire delusion which disregards the lessons of historical experience without having behind it the support of sound theory.
>
> (Moggridge 1980: 21–22)

Consequently the Keynesian design for the postwar international financial system did not envisage free capital movements.

In summary, the orthodox theory that financial liberalization leads to global economic efficiency based on the analogy with free trade is flawed on several counts including some within the neoclassical tradition itself.

3 Empirical research on financial liberalization and economic crisis

3.1 Banking and currency crises and the real economy

The theoretical expectation of free capital movements leading to smoother income and consumption trajectories for individuals and countries following economic shocks than would otherwise be the case, has been confounded by the experience of developing countries. There now exists substantial empirical evidence suggesting a close link between the liberalization of the financial system and economic and financial crises particularly in developing countries. Developed countries, including the US, the UK and Scandinavian countries, have also been subject to such crises, but compared with developing countries, the incidence has been relatively low and the social costs correspondingly smaller. However, developing countries have suffered not only more but also deeper crises and virtual financial meltdowns.

As against this impressionistic evidence, the results of detailed econometric studies are more mixed. The empirical literature on this subject is vast and still growing at a fast rate. There are at least four kinds of studies which are relevant. First contributions to the financial literature support the orthodox case that financial liberalization in emerging markets reduces the cost of equity capital and has a positive impact on domestic investments (see for e.g. Bekaert, *et al.* 2001; Henry 2000; Chari and Henry 2002). Second, studies on financial liberalization, banking and currency crisis find that there is a close causal relationship between these variables, thus providing support for the antiliberalization camp. Some of these studies will be reviewed below. A third strand of this literature concerns financial crashes and suggest that financial liberalization is much more risky in this respect for developing than for advance countries. Leading contributions in this area are Martin and Rey (2002), Wyplosz (2001), Mendoza (2001), and McKinnon and Pill (1999). The fourth part of this literature considers the relationship between capital account liberalization and long-term economic growth.

It is not our purpose here to systematically review this whole body of literature but rather to draw relevant conclusions for a multilateral global framework for short- and long-term capital flows from a developing country perspective. However, to indicate the nature and the kind of evidence produced by these studies a few of them will be briefly examined below.

Kaminsky and Reinhart's (1999) paper explored the links between banking crises, exchange rate crises, and financial liberalization. The sample consisted of 20 countries, of which 14 were developing ones and it covered the period 1970–95. The authors found that there was a sharp increase in both types of crises since 1980. The average number per year of banking crises in their sample rose from 0.3 during 1970–79 to 1.4 in 1980–95. The two authors found that the banking crises and the currency crises are closely related and that the banking crises are often preceded by financial liberalization.

In their influential study Demirguc-Kunt and Detragiache (1998) examined banking crises during the period 1980–84 for a sample of 53 developed and developing countries. They found that banking crisis is more likely to occur where the financial system has been liberalized. They also found a two-way interaction between banking and currency crisis. Where the banking systems are not sufficiently developed, with capital account liberalization, banks become vulnerable to external economic shocks. The authors' findings suggest that vulnerability is reduced with institutional development and strengthening of the banking system through prudential regulation. They also found that financial liberalization leads to an intensification of competition among banks and hence to greater moral hazard and risk-taking than before.[8]

The recent Asian crisis provides almost a laboratory experiment for examining the role of capital account liberalization in causing or exacerbating that region's severe economic downturn. Williamson and Drabek (1999) provide evidence to suggest that countries which did or did not have economic crisis were differentiated only by whether or not they had liberalized their capital accounts. Most economists would now agree that even if premature financial liberalization without adequate prudential regulation was not the root cause of the crises in countries such as Thailand, Korea, and Indonesia, it greatly contributed to the occurrence of the crisis and to its depth. Indeed, the economic fundamentals prior to the crisis of the affected countries were better than those of India, but the latter country was spared the crisis because of its control over the capital account.

Similarly, China managed to avoid the crisis and continued to have fast economic growth. China also had not liberalized its capital account.[9]

It is argued by some that even with the acute economic crisis of 1998–99, over the long run Korea with its economic openness was a much more successful economy than India. This argument has some plausibility but it overlooks the crucial fact that Korea's outstanding industrialization record over the previous three decades was not accomplished by a liberalized financial system but rather by a highly controlled one. However, when the system was liberalized in the 1990s it was followed by an unprecedented crisis (see also Demetriades and Luintel 2001).

3.2   Social and economic costs of the crisis

The Asian crisis was extremely important in terms of its economic and social impact on the populations of the affected countries. The World Bank (2001: 73) notes: "In terms of lost output and the implications for poverty and unemployment, the Asian crisis represents one of the most acute periods of financial instability in this century". The crisis greatly increased poverty, reduced employment and real wages, and caused enormous social distress. Indeed the economic downturn was so enormous that in a country like Indonesia it led to a virtual disintegration of the social fabric of the country. This is why the Asian crisis is aptly termed, not just an ordinary slowing of GDP growth due to an economic shock, or a normal cyclical recession but an enormous meltdown. It is important to appreciate, however, that even if there is no meltdown, economic slowdowns or recessions have bigger social costs in developing than developed countries because of the lack of publicly provided social security in the former group. There is evidence that in both country groups the effects of a downturn fall disproportionately on the poor and on women (see further Singh and Zammit 2000; Stiglitz 1999; World Bank 1999).

Turning to an investigation of costs purely in economic terms, there are good analytical reasons to believe that economic crises would negatively affect both investment and long-term growth.[10] In addition, recessions and meltdowns also have fiscal and redistributive implications which may affect the economy for a long period of time. Caprio and Klingebiel (1996) estimates indicate that the costs of a banking crisis are typically quite large; their research indicated that these ranged from 3.2 percent of GDP in the U.S. savings and loans crisis of 1984–91 to 55.3 percent for the banking crisis in Argentina from 1980 to 1982 (Table 10.1). On the basis of more recent evidence, Aizenman (2002) estimates the average cost of currency crisis to be 8 percent of the precrisis GDP and the average cost of a simultaneous crisis banking and currency crisis is 18 percent of precrisis GDP. He also reports that "the twin crises are mainly concentrated in financially liberalized emerging market economies" (2002: 5).

In a pioneering study Easterley *et al.* (2000) have investigated economic instability for a large cross-section of developed and developing countries over the period 1960–90. As Table 10.2 indicates, developing countries typically suffer greater instability than developed countries with respect to output, employment, real wages, capital flows, and terms of trade changes.[11] In neoclassical analysis it

Table 10.1 Fiscal costs of banking crisis in selected countries (percentage of GDP)

Country	(Date)	Cost (percentage of GDP)
Argentina	(1980–82)	55.3
Chile	(1981–3)	41.2
Uruguay	(1981–4)	31.2
Israel	(1977–83)	30.0
Cote d'Ivoire	(1988–91)	25.0
Senegal	(1988–91)	17.0
Spain	(1977–85)	16.8
Bulgaria	(1990s)	14.0
Mexico	(1995)	13.5
Hungary	(1991–5)	10.0
Finland	(1991–3)	8.0
Sweden	(1991)	6.4
Sri Lanka	(1989–93)	5.0
Malaysia	(1985–8)	4.7
Norway	(1987–9)	4.0
United States	(1984–91)	3.2

Source: Caprio and Klingebiel (1996) quoted in Chang (2001).

is customary to attribute instability to the lack of flexibility in labor markets, particularly to wage rigidity. However, Easterly *et al.* find that despite greater labor market flexibility (measured by changes in real wages) in developing countries they exhibit greater volatility than developed countries (Table 10.2). The authors' results suggest that the characteristics of the financial system rather than the labor market are the more important causes of economic instability. Their econometric analysis shows that financial variables are statistically significant in explaining both volatility of GDP growth and the likelihood of a downturn. They find that openness and policy volatility also have a significant influence on growth volatility. In general, Easterly *et al.*'s findings suggest that countries with weak financial systems display greater instability in GDP growth in part because these institutional shortcomings amplify the effects of the volatility of capital flows.

3.3 Capital account liberalization and proximate causes of instability

The fundamental theoretical reasons why capital account liberalization may lead to economic instability were analyzed in Section 2. The present subsection briefly reviews some of the proximate reasons for this instability, namely:

1 self-fulfilling expectations;
2 volatility in capital flows;
3 increased competition among banks following liberalization as mentioned above; and
4 the changes in the global financial system and the short-termism of the leading players.

Table 10.2 Economic instability and related variables: differences between developing and high-income OECD countries

| Variable | Developing countries | | High income OECD countries | | t-statistic for difference in mean | p-value |
	Mean	Number of observations	Mean	Number of observations		
Growth	0.007	163	0.027	23	−5.659	0.000
Standard deviation of growth	0.061	163	0.026	23	9.779	0.000
(Median standard deviation of growth)	0.052		0.022			
Standard deviation of employment	0.098	83	0.035	21	6.652	0.000
Standard deviation of real wage index	2.119	90	1.883	21	0.833	0.410
Standard deviation of real wage changes	1.197	85	0.321	21	8.116	0.000
Private capital flows/ GDP	1.722	146	0.372	22	2.743	0.009
Standard deviation of private capital flows/GDP	2.662	138	2.311	22	0.808	0.420
Standard deviation of terms of trade changes	0.123	117	0.041	23	9.688	0.000
Standard deviation of money growth	0.219	148	0.077	20	6.757	0.000

Source: Easterly, Islam, and Stiglitz (2000).

3.3.1 Self-fulfilling expectations

There is a large literature based on the self-fulfilling expectations which suggests that capital account liberalization is much more likely to lead to financial crisis in emerging markets than in developed countries. This literature points to the role of factors such as moral hazard, credit constrains, and over-borrowing syndrome for these different outcomes between the two groups of countries. Martin and Rey (2002), is an important contribution to these studies. It provides empirical evidence that there is a negative relationship between the probability of a financial crisis and per capita income after liberalization, whereas before liberalization there is little relationship between these variables. The authors report that the results are robust to alternative definitions of financial crash. Their model of self-fulfilling expectations does not require any appeal to special factors mentioned above to explain these empirical facts. Rather in their model, for intermediate levels of international financial transactions costs, pessimistic expectations can be self-fulfilling leading to a financial crash. The crash is accompanied by capital flight, a drop in income below the financial autarky level and market incompleteness.

3.3.2 Volatility

The volatility and the procyclicality of the private capital flows to developing countries are well-attested features of international capital movements during the last two decades.[12] Such in-flows come in surges, often bearing no relationship to the economic fundamentals of the country and leave the country when they are most needed, that is, in a downturn. As Williamson and Drabek (1999) note, even in a country such as Chile which was deeply integrated with the world financial markets, private foreign capital suddenly withdrew in the event of a fall in copper prices. There is however an important debate on the comparative volatility of the different components of capital flows, which will be reviewed in the following sections.

As to the effects of the volatility of capital flows, Ramey and Ramey (1995) found that it was positively related to volatility of GDP growth, a result confirmed by Easterly *et al.* (2000). The former two authors also reported a negative relationship between long-run economic growth and the volatility of GDP growth, a result again confirmed by Easterly *et al.* (2000), and also by World Bank (2001), among others. Table 10.3, from the latter publication, presents regression results of the effects of capital flows and their volatility on growth per capita, for a large sample of developing countries over successive decades, covering the period 1970–98. The table also contains the normal control variables used in such cross-section analyses (e.g. initial GDP per capita, initial schooling, population growth rate, investment rates, and a measure of policy). Volatility of capital flows is measured by the standard deviation of the flows. The dependant variable is the rate of growth of GDP per capita. The table suggests an economically important and statistically significant negative relationship between capital flow volatility and GDP growth per capita for the period as a whole 1970–98.[13] It is however interesting that the negative relationship becomes weaker over time, with the value of the relevant

Table 10.3   Effects of capital flows and their volatility on growth per capita, by decade

| Independent variable | Dependent variable: rate of GDP growth per capital | | | |
	1970–98	1970–79	1980–89	1990–98
Capital flows	0.287**	−0.149	0.133	0.275**
Capital flows volatility	−0.344**	−0.322**	−0.188	−0.124
Initial GDP per capital	−0.508**	−0.345	−0.940**	0.159
Initial schooling	1.429	−1.749	3.640*	−0.446
Population growth rate	−0.513**	−0.438	−0.573**	0.869**
Investment	0.182**	0.309**	0.164**	0.094**
Policy	0.008**	0.007**	0.011**	0.013**
Inflation rate	−0.002**	−0.008	−0.001**	−0.004**
Openness of the economy	0.001	0.006	0.001	−0.024**
Adjusted R^2	0.75	0.59	0.57	0.38
No. of Countries.	72	56	74	100

*denotes significance at the 10 percent level, and ** at the 5 percent level.

Source: World Bank (2001).

coefficient rising from a statistically significant −0.322 during 1970–79 to −0.124 in 1990–98 when the coefficient was also statistically insignificant. Other results from Table 10.3 will be commented on in the following section.

The next issue is why are the capital flows to developing countries so volatile? Analysis and evidence suggests that both internal (e.g. weak domestic financial systems, frequent economic shocks) and external factors, particularly the animal spirits of foreign investors, are involved in making these flows volatile.

Kindleberger (1984) has observed that financial markets are subject to frequent crises, which he ascribes to periodic and alternating bouts of irrational exuberance and pessimism of investors largely unrelated to fundamentals. Importantly, Kindleberger's historical analysis is implicitly endorsed by Alan Greenspan, the Chairman of the U.S. Federal Reserve himself, who recently commented as follows on the 1987 U.S. stock market crash and the Asian financial meltdown of the 1990s:

> At one point the economic system appears stable, the next it behaves as though a dam has reached a breaking point, and water (read, confidence) evacuates its reservoir. The United States experienced such a sudden change with the decline in stock prices of more than 20 percent on October 19, 1987. There is no credible scenario that can readily explain so abrupt a change in the fundamentals of long-term valuation on that one day ... but why do these events seem to erupt without some readily evident precursors? Certainly, the more extended the risk-taking, or more generally, the lower the discount factors applied to future outcomes, the more vulnerable are markets to a shock that abruptly triggers a revision in expectations and sets off a vicious cycle

of contraction. ... Episodes of vicious cycles cannot easily be forecast, as our recent experience with Asia has demonstrated.

Greenspan (1998)

This mirrors the Keynesian view of investor behavior and the significance of mass psychology in price formation in the financial markets, as discussed earlier. Keynes's insights on this subject have been formalized in current theoretical literature, which is able to provide a "rational" explanation for the herd-like behavior, contagion, and other irrational manifestations of economic agents in financial markets.[14]

It is also important to emphasize another major factor in causing the volatility of external capital flows to developing countries. Kaufman (2000) and Williamson (2002) have stressed the significance of changes in the nature and character of the financial markets in enhancing capital flow volatility. The intense competition in the world fund management industry together with the nature of rewards offered to fund managers have helped to make the latter short-termist in their investment decisions.[15] As Kaufman notes:

(In the new global financial system) most prominent banks, securities firms, and even a few insurance companies possess departments that emulate the trading and investment approach of the hedge funds. Even the corporate treasuries of a number of non-financial corporations are engaged in this activity. Once arcane and exotic, the hedge fund approach to investment has been mainstreamed.

Kaufman (2000:61)

Finally, analysis and evidence for increased competition among banks following liberalization is provided by Furman and Stiglitz (1999) and Stiglitz (2000) among others.

4 Evidence on capital account liberalization and long-term economic growth

In principle it is possible for the instability caused by capital account liberalization to be more than compensated for by faster long-term economic growth arising from the greater availability of capital inflows. This is the promise held by the proponents of this policy regime (see for e.g. Fischer 1997; Summers 2000, referred to earlier). It will therefore be useful to review the available empirical evidence on this issue.

A good starting point is the broad-brush approach adopted by Singh (1997a) in analyzing this issue. He considers the case of advanced countries whose experience, he suggests, is relevant for developing economies. This is because the former have operated under a regime of relatively free trade and capital movements for nearly two decades – a period long enough to make at least a preliminary assessment of the effects of this economic regime on performance. Evidence suggests that the record has been less than impressive despite the fact that the world economy during this period has not been subject to any abnormal negative shocks like the oil price increases of 1973 and 1979. Indeed, the economic performance of industrial countries during this later period has been much worse than in the earlier period of the 1950s and 1960s when they functioned under a myriad of capital controls.

- GDP growth in the 1980s and 1990s under a liberal regime regarding private capital flows was much lower than that achieved in the "illiberal" and regulated "golden age" of the 1950s and 1960s;
- Productivity growth in the last 15 years has been half of what it was in the "golden age;"
- The critical failure is, however, with respect to employment: eight million people were unemployed in the OECD countries in 1970, but by the mid-1990s 35 million were unemployed, that is, 10 percent of the labor force.

Singh's analysis also shows that the poor performance of industrial countries during the 1980s and 1990s cannot alternatively be ascribed to exogenous factors such as the exhaustion of technological opportunities, or to labor market imperfections. Industrial economies have more flexible markets today than they did in the golden age. In addition they have the benefit of a new technological paradigm of information and communication technology which many economic historians regard as on a par with the most important technological revolutions of the last two centuries. In view of all these factors – a new technological paradigm, more flexible markets, absence of economic shocks such as the oil shocks of 1973 and 1975 – orthodox analyses would suggest that OECD economies should be growing today at a much faster rate than in the golden age. But as we see the opposite has been true.

Eatwell's (1996) and Singh's (1997a) analyses indicate that the poor performance of industrial countries in the recent period is closely linked to intrinsic features of the liberal financial regime. Coordination failures have led to suboptimal levels of the OECD and world aggregate demand, output, and employment. When capital flows were regulated in the 1950s and 1960s, and there was successful coordination under the hegemony of the United States, payments balance between countries was achieved at much higher levels of output and employment than has subsequently been the case under financial liberalization.

In contrast with the above broad-brush approach, there exist numerous econometric studies of the effects of capital account liberalization on economic growth with definitely mixed results. Prakash Loungani (2002) has recently reviewed the IMF contributions on the subject, he reached the following conclusion:

> ... What impact do capital flows have on growth? The evidence is decidedly mixed and appears to depend, somewhat, on the particular flow studied (or the measure of capital market openness used), the sample period, the set of countries, and whether cross-section or panel data is used. Recent IMF work provides an illustration of mixed findings. In a much-cited study, Borensztein,

De Gregorio, and Lee (1998) find that FDI increases economic growth when the level of education in the host country a measure of its absorptive capacity–is high. Mody and Murshid (2002) find that capital inflows boost domestic investment almost one–to–one, but the strength of this relationship appears to be weakening over time. In contrast, Edison, Levine, Ricci, and Slok (*forthcoming*), using the new measures of openness, do not find evidence of a robust link between international financial integration and economic growth.

Two main conclusions emerge from the above review of empirical evidence on capital account liberalization, financial crisis, and GDP growth. First, there is strong evidence of a close relationship between liberalization and economic and financial crises in developing countries. This relationship is robust and in the circumstances of these countries there are also strong analytical arguments for both its existence and robustness. Second, available evidence for the view that free capital flows promote faster long-term economic growth in developing countries, is much weaker. Aizenman (2002) reaches a broadly similar conclusion: "… there is solid evidence that financial opening increases the chance of financial crisis. There is more tenuous evidence that financial opening contributes positively to long-run growth." However, from the perspective of economic policy an important consideration is how to proceed from the short to the long-term. The economic crises and the instability which capital account liberalization is seen to generate, may compromise a country's future economic development by inducing capital flight and lowering domestic investment and long-term economic growth. In summary, in view of these facts and analyses, Stiglitz (2000) is fully justified in castigating the IMF for its promotion of universal capital account liberalization when most developing countries were not ready for such policies. Fortunately, in the wake of the Asian crisis the IMF has in the most recent period moderated its stance in this respect.

5   Capital account liberalization and FDI[16]

As explained in the Introduction that while finding a "compelling" case against any general liberalization of the capital account, Stiglitz (2000) also suggest that there is a "compelling" case in favor of FDI. In view of the fickleness of the short-term capital flows and the gyrations of the markets, he comprehensively rejects the argument that capital account liberalization is desirable because it imposes discipline on countries forcing them to follow good economic policy. However, he states that "far more relevant for the long run success of the economy is the foreign direct investment and the desire to acquire and sustain FDI provide strong discipline on the economy and the political process" (2000: 1080). Although, he does not specifically address this issue, Stiglitz comes close to accepting here the principles of the new proposal which is being put forward at the WTO by EU and Japan for a multilateral agreement on investment (hereafter PMAI), covering only FDI. The background to this proposal is as follows. It will be recalled that three years ago the OECD countries failed to negotiate a Multilateral Agreement on

Investment (MAI) amongst themselves, which was intended to be later acceded to by developing countries. PMAI is similar to MAI with a critical difference that unlike the latter the former will only be confined to FDI. This clearly represents a significant concession to developing countries. The advanced countries' preference would seem to be to establish a binding treaty at the WTO which would create for FDI a regime similar to that of (free) trade in goods. As this agreement would be based on WTO's basic concepts, previous history suggests that it is likely to include the following kinds of elements:

- the right of establishment for foreign investors (the concept of market access);
- the principle of "most-favored nation" treatment;
- the principle of "national treatment;"
- investment protection, including matters relating to expropriation and the transfer of capital;
- additional disciplines relating to, among other matters, entry, stay, and work of key personnel;
- prohibition of performance requirements on foreign investors;
- rules on investment incentives;
- binding rules for settling disputes through the WTO dispute settlements mechanism.[17]

In favoring FDI Stiglitz seems to be a part of a general consensus among economists, which suggests that compared with debt and portfolio investment, FDI, apart from its other merits, is the safest source of funds for developing countries. It is thought to neither add to a country's debt, nor (being bricks and mortar) can it be quickly withdrawn from the country. Furthermore, in view of the other virtues of FDI in bringing new technology, organizational methods, etc. and importantly spillovers to domestic industry, the proponents claim that the case for PMAI becomes overwhelming.

Those propositions will be contested below and it will be argued that unfettered FDI is not in the best interests of developing countries. As in the case of short-term flows, FDI also requires appropriate regulation by these countries to enhance social welfare. As such measures would be denied to them by PMAI it is suggested here that poor countries should resist the proposed agreement.

It will be useful to begin this analysis by noting that there has also been a sea change in developing countries' perspective on, and attitude toward, FDI. In the 1950s and 1960s, developing countries were often hostile toward multinational investment and sought to control multinational companies' activities through domestic and international regulations. However, during the last two decades emerging countries have been falling over themselves to attract as much multinational investment as they can.

This enormous shift in developing countries stance toward multinational investment is associated with the major changes which have occurred in the pattern of international capital flows to developing counties. The former may be regarded as both a cause and the consequence of the latter. The most important change in capital flows for the purpose of this paper is the emergence of FDI as a predominant source of external finance for developing countries during the 1990s. Between 1996 and 1998 FDI inflows to developing countries constituted about 10 percent of their gross capital formation. (Singh 2001; UNCTAD 2001). It is also important to note that alongside these changes in the pattern of external finance, analysis and evidence suggest that developing countries' need for external finance has greatly increased. This is in part due to the liberalization of trade and capital flows in the international economy. UNCTAD (2000) suggests that because of these structural factors, developing countries have become more balance of payments constrained than before: the constraint begins to bite at a much slower growth rate than was the case previously in the 1970s and 1980s. In these circumstances it is not surprising that developing countries have radically changed their attitude toward FDI. There has also, therefore, been intense competition among these counties for attracting FDI.

This competition has resulted in a shift in the balance of power toward multinationals in their dealings with developing countries. An important objection to PMAI is that if it were approved it would, instead of redressing this imbalance, make it worse than before. This is because the Agreement would essentially give the multinationals a license to (or not to) invest wherever or whenever they like regardless of the circumstance and needs of developing countries.

6   FDI and financial fragility

Leaving aside other characteristics of FDI (to be discussed later), we will consider it first simply as a source of finance, and examine its implications for balance of payments and for macroeconomic management of the economy. In contrast to portfolio investments, FDI by definition is supposed to reflect a long-term commitment as it involves normally a stake of 10 percent or more in a host country enterprise together with managerial control.[18] In view of the latter element, the presumption is that the inflow of foreign capital in this form will be more stable than portfolio investments. The latter are easier to liquidate and following an internal or external shock, investors may quickly withdraw such funds from the host country.

There are, however, important arguments to suggest that the presumption of stability in net FDI inflows may not be correct. First, the distinction between FDI and portfolio investment has become very much weaker with the growth of derivatives and hedge funds. As Claessens *et al.* (1995) observe, even at an elementary level it is easy to see how a long-term "bricks and mortar" investment can be converted into a readily liquid asset. They note that a direct investor can use his or her immovable assets to borrow to export capital and thereby generate rapid capital outflows.

Another reason why FDI may be volatile is because a large part of a country's measured FDI according to the IMF balance of payments conventions usually consists of retained profits. As profits are affected by the business cycle, they display considerable volatility. This also prevents FDI from being anticyclical and stabilizing unless the host and home county economic cycles are out of phase with each other. That may or may not happen.

Furthermore, there is evidence that like other sources of finance FDI flows can also at times come in surges. Apart from their contribution to volatility, these FDI surges, as those for example of portfolio investment can lead to equally undesirable consequences such as exchange rate appreciation and reduced competitiveness of a country's tradable sector.

Claessens *et al.* (1995) concluded that there were no statistically significant differences in the time series properties of the different forms of capital flows including FDI and that long-term flows were often as volatile as short- term flows. Williamson (2002) has suggested that this study may have failed to find differences between flows because it measured volatility in terms of the second moments of the time series instead of the ones of a higher order. The latter are relevant with respect to occasional "meltdowns" which occurred for example in the Asian crisis. UNCTAD's 1998 study of the stability of capital flows between 1992 and 1997 found that FDI was relatively more stable than portfolio flows, but there were important exceptions. The latter included Brazil, South Korea, and Taiwan.[19] Lipsey (2001) also concluded that the FDI flows were relatively more stable overall.

It has been argued in favor of the FDI-stability thesis that during the Asian crisis and its aftermath, while bank lending and portfolio flows were sharply reversed, FDI continued much as before. However the motivation for this could have been what Krugman called the "fire-sale" of devalued assets as a result of the crisis. Evidence, however, seems to suggest that it is more likely that the relative stability of FDI is due in part to the fact that the governments abolished regulations preventing or limiting FDI in domestic enterprises (albeit under IMF conditionality in the affected countries). Multinationals have used this opportunity to increase their holdings in local firms at cheap prices (World Bank 2001).

Even if FDI is somewhat less volatile than other flows there are other important implications of FDI for a host country's balance of payments which need to be considered. These derive from the fact that an FDI investment creates foreign exchange liabilities not only now but also into the future. This characteristic leads to the danger that unfettered FDI may create a time profile of foreign exchange outflows (in the form of dividend payments or profits repatriation) and inflows (e.g. fresh FDI) which may be time inconsistent. Experience shows that such incompatibility, even in the short run may easily produce a liquidity crisis. The evidence from the Asian crisis countries with the latter suggests that it could in turn degenerate into a solvency crisis with serious adverse consequences for economic development (see further Kregel 1996; Singh 2001, on these points).

These considerations suggest that to avoid financial fragility the government would need to monitor and regulate the amount and timing of FDI. Because the nature of large FDI projects (whether or not for example these would produce exportable products or how large their imports would be) can also significantly affect the time profile of aggregate foreign exchange inflows and outflows, both in the short- and long-term, the government may also need to regulate such investments. To the extent that the PMAI would not permit this kind of regulation of FDI, it would subject developing economies to much greater financial fragility than would otherwise be the case.

It could in principle, be argued that even if the financial fragility point is conceded, a PMAI may still benefit developing countries by generating greater overall FDI which could compensate for the increased financial fragility. However, this proposition is of doubtful validity. We saw earlier that there has been a huge increase in FDI in the 1990s. This occurred without any MAI and was clearly a product of a number of other factors.[20] Similarly, there does not seems to be any connection between regulatory constraints on FDI and the total amount of FDI which a country may be able to attract. Malaysia (see further US, 1996) and China, (see Braunstein and Epstein 1999), to illustrate, are large recipients of FDI despite having significant control and regulation over FDI projects.

7 FDI and real economy, technology transfer, spillovers, investment and savings

Apart from FDI as a source of finance two of the most important ways in which a developing country may benefit from such investments is through (1) transfer of technology and (2) from spillovers. The latter refer to the effects of FDI on raising productivity in local firms. These firms may be helped by foreign investment in a variety of ways, including the demonstration effect of the new technology and the enhancement of the quality of inputs which such investment may promote. On the other hand, there may be few positive or even negative spillovers, if FDI leads to local firms being forced out of the market because of greater competition.

Both issues of technology transfer and spillovers have been widely studied and there exists on these subjects a large and controversial literature. The main lesson which however comes from these writings in relation to the question of technology transfer is that a country is more likely to benefit from multinational investment if the latter is integrated into its national development and technological plans (see further Dunning 1994; Freeman 1989; Milberg 1999; South Center 2000). This is the reason why, other than Hong Kong, most successful Asian countries (including China and Malaysia as seen above) have not allowed unfettered FDI but have extensively regulated it.

On the issue of spillovers, early studies were quite optimistic about the positive externalities from FDI on domestic industries. However, these studies suffered from severe methodological difficulties particularly in relation to the question of causation. More recent research which uses more up-to-date methodology as well as large microeconomic data sets arrives at much more pessimistic conclusions. Thus, in an influential study, Aitken and Harrison (1999) found that in Venezuela multinational investment had a negative effect on productivity of domestic plants in the industry. Such results are quite common from microlevel data (Hanson 2001). Similarly, World Bank (2001) reaches the following conclusion from its comprehensive survey of the empirical studies of the effects of FDI on productivity growth in developing countries:

The productivity benefits of capital flows – through the transfer of technology and management techniques and the stimulation of financial sector development – are significant in countries where a developed physical infrastructure, a strong business environment, and open trade regimes have facilitated the absorption of those flows, *but not otherwise.* (Italics added).

World Bank (2001:59)

A critical issue in evaluating the effects of FDI on the real economy is its impact on domestic savings and investments. Economic theory does not yield any unambiguous predictions about how domestic investment may be affected by foreign capital inflows. In general, this would depend on the level of development of the economy, its degree of integration with international economy, and its absorptive capacity. Table 10.4 shows the results of World Bank's analysis of the impact of various types of capital flows on investments and savings for a large cross-section of developing countries for the period 1972–98. The results show that although FDI is positively associated with the investment, there is little relationship with savings. The long-term bank lending has a more important influence on investment than does FDI. Portfolio investment is, on the other hand, associated more with savings than with investments.

A more interesting analysis of this issue is reported in the recent study by Agosin and Mayer (2000). This study is able to examine the regional variations in the effects of FDI on the "crowding" in and out of domestic investment. The two authors' research covered the period 1970–96 and included host countries from all three developing regions, Africa, Asia, and Latin America. The results of the econometric exercise suggest that over this long period there was a strong "crowding in" in Asia, "crowding out" in Latin America and more or less neutral effects in Africa. Agosin and Mayer conclude:

… the most far-reaching liberalizations of FDI regimes in the 1990s took place in Latin America, and that FDI regimes in Asia have remained the least liberal in the developing world … Nonetheless, it is in these countries that there is strongest evidence of CI (crowding in). In Latin America, on the other hand, … liberalization does not appear to have led to CI.

Agosin and Mayer (2000:14)

Turning finally, but for reasons of space, extremely briefly, to the relationship between FDI and long-term economic growth, Lipsey's (2001) comprehensive survey succinctly sums up the evidence on this issue as follows:

… As with the studies of wage and productivity spillovers, those of the effects of FDI inflows on economic growth are inconclusive. Almost all find positive effects in some periods, or among some group of countries, in some specifications, but one cannot say from these studies that there are universal effects. There are periods, industries, and countries where FDI seems to have

Table 10.4 Marginal impact of various types of capital flows on investment and saving

Independent Variable	Dependent variables											
	Investment	Saving	Investment	Saving	Investment	Saving	Investment	Saving	Investment	Saving	Investment	Saving
	(1A)	(1B)	(2A)	(2B)	(3A)	(3B)	(4A)	(4B)	(5A)	(5B)	(6A)	(6B)
Aggregate Capital flows	0.72**	0.03										
Long-term capital			0.88**	0.10								
Bank lending					1.45**	-0.17						
FDI							0.84**	-0.03				
Portfolio investment									0.50	0.84*		
Short-term debt											0.23**	0.05
All other flows	0.33**	0.33**	0.22	-0.16	0.53**	-0.03	0.58**	-0.23	0.52**	-0.27	0.62	0.06
Growth rate, lagged	0.33**	0.33**	0.31**	0.36**	0.33**	0.46**	0.36**	0.45**	0.49**	0.48**	0.32**	0.39**
Change in terms of trade	0.01	0.04**	0.01	0.04**	0.01	0.05**	0.02**	0.05**	-0.00	0.04**	0.01**	0.05**
Inflation, lagged	-0.00	– 0.00**	-0.00	– 0.00**	0.00	– 0.00**	-0.00	– 0.00**	-0.00	-0.00*	-0.00	-0.00
Adjusted R^2	0.70	0.70	0.70	0.70	0.71	0.72	0.72	0.71	0.72	0.73	0.73	0.73

*denotes significance at the 10 percent level, ** at the 5 percent level.

Source: World Bank (2001).

Note
Fixed-effects regressions of investment (or saving) ratios against capital flows based on an unbalanced sample, consisting of a maximum of 118 countries, spanning the period 1972–98. The method of estimation was two-stage least squares, when a good instrument could be found; otherwise simple ordinary least squares results are reported.

little relation to growth, especially when other factors, mostly related to FDI also are included as explanations.

Lipsey (2001)

What can be concluded for PMAI from the above analysis of various aspects of FDI? The main implication would appear to be that a global regime of unfettered FDI would not be Pareto-optimal for all nations. Countries have different (1) levels of economic development, (2) previous history, (3) endowments, (4) path trajectories, and (5) public and private sector capabilities of making effective use of FDI. Some may benefit from unrestricted FDI inflows and may have the absorptive capacity to cope with FDI surges and famines. Others may benefit more from its purposive regulation so as to avoid coordination or other market failures arising from unfettered FDI, as outlined above. A regime of unrestricted capital flows as envisaged in PMAI would deprive countries of policy autonomy in this sphere. In some cases, for example countries with ineffective or weak governments, this may not matter. However, there are other countries where regulation of FDI would bring net benefit because the correction of market failures would easily outweigh government failures. The so-called "developmental states" in Asia have been obvious examples of this. The PMAI would not serve the developmental needs of these countries. The main message of this paper is, therefore, that in the real world of second best, a case by case approach and selectivity is called for rather than a one-size-fits-all universal rules of the kind contained in PMAI.

8 Conclusion

The first part of the paper examined the theoretical and empirical case for short-term capital account liberalization in developing countries and found it wanting. Indeed, as Stiglitz suggests, there is arguably a compelling case against it. The second part considered the question of long-term capital account liberalization specifically, that of FDI. Most economists, including Stiglitz, favor such capital flows into developing countries. On closer analysis, however, it is shown here than even FDI, if unregulated, may do more harm than good to many countries. It is therefore suggested that developing countries should resist the new multilateral agreement on investment, which Japan and the EU are proposing at the WTO, even though it will cover only FDI.

Notes

* The author and editor would like to thank the editors of the Eastern Economic Journal (with special appreciation to the late Professor Ken Koford, who, until his untimely death in 2005, was the editor of the Eastern Economic Journal), for their kind permission to allow this paper to be reprinted in this volume.
1 I am grateful for helpful comments from Philip Arestis as well as from session participants at the EEA meeting in Boston in March 2002. As I could not attend the meeting Philip kindly presented there an earlier version of this paper on my behalf. That I am also indebted to Joseph Stiglitz's writings on the subject, despite important disagreements, will be clear from the paper. It is also a pleasure to record my gratitude to the

Editor and the four referees of Eastern Economic Journal, whose sometimes fierce comments greatly helped to improve the paper. This work was carried out at the Centre for Business Research at Cambridge University. The Center's contributions are gratefully acknowledged. The usual caveat applies.

2 For a comprehensive and recent contribution, see for example Feldstein (2002).

3 This section of the paper draws on Chakravarty and Singh (1988).

4 Such a mechanism, for example, existed in the "Golden Age" of the post-Second World War era when, under the aegis of a single hegemonic economic power, namely the U.S., European economies were able to maintain high levels of aggregate demand to ensure full employment (Glyn *et al.* 1990; Singh 1995a).

5 See further Freeman (1989), Singh (1995b), and Amsden (2001).

6 The US was willing to open its own markets to East Asian manufacturers without insisting on reciprocal opening of East Asian market. See further, Glyn *et al.* (1990), Singh (2005).

7 On this set of issues, see for example, Stiglitz (1994), Allen and Gale (2000), Singh (2003), and Glen and Singh (2005)

8 A referee has objected that because Kaminsky and Reinhart (1999) and Demirguc-Kunt and Detragiache (1998) include both developing countries (DCs) and advanced countries (ACs), it is not legitimate to draw conclusions about DCs alone from this evidence. However, as argued in the text below, DCs are more prone to financial crises following liberalization than ACs. Considering the two groups of countries together will underestimate the strength of the relationship between financial liberalization, banking and currency crisis and underdevelopment rather than to overstate it.

9 For fuller discussion of these issues see Singh (2002), Glen and Singh (2005), Jomo (2001), Singh and Weisse (1999) and Rodrik (2000).

10 See further Pindyck (1991), World Bank (2001), Easterly *et al.* (2000).

11 IMF (2002; see Box 3.4, P126), broadly supports these conclusions.

12 See further Williamson (2002), Ocampo (2001), Singh and Zammit (2000), Stiglitz (2000), Glen and Singh (2005).

13 Similar results are reported in IMF (2002).

14 See further, Shiller (2000), Singh and Weisse (1999), Singh (1999).

15 For a fuller discussion of the issues involved in this argument see Cosh *et al.* (1990) and Singh (2000).

16 This and the following sections are based on Singh (2001).

17 See further Singh and Zammit (1998).

18 This is the empirical definition of FDI adopted by many countries to distinguish it from portfolio flows.

19 A referee has pointed out that the problems of FDI volatility are not just a problem for developing countries but also for the US where there has been a substantial drop in FDI recently.

20 See further Singh (1997a, 1997b), Singh and Weisse (1999).

References

Agosin, M. R. and Mayer, R. (2000) 'Foreign Investment in Developing Countries: Does it Crowd in Domestic Investment?', Discussion Paper No. 146, Geneva: UNCTAD.

Aitken, B. J. and Harrison, A. E. (1999) 'Do Domestic Firms Benefit from Direct Foreign Investment? Evidence from Venezuela', *American Economic Review,* 89(3): 605–18.

Aizenman, J. (2002) 'Financial Opening: Evidence and Policy Options', NBER Working Paper 8900, Cambridge, MA: National Bureau of Economic Research.

Allen, F. and Gale, D. (2000) *Comparing Financial Systems,* Cambridge, MA: MIT Press.

Amsden, A. H. (2001) *The Rise of "The Rest": Challenges to the West from Late-Industrializing Economies,* New York: Oxford University Press.

Arrow, K. (1962) 'The Economic Implications of Learning by Doing', *Review of Economic Studies*, 29(3): 155–73.

Bekaert, G., Harvey, C., and Lundblad, C. (2001) 'Does Financial Liberalization Spur Growth?', NBER Working Paper No. 8245, Cambridge, MA: National Bureau of Economic Research.

Bhagwati, J. (1998) 'The Capital Myth: The Difference Between Trade in Widgets and Trade in Dollars', *Foreign Affairs*, 77: 7–12.

Borensztein, E., Giorgio, J. De., and Lee, J.-W. (1998) 'How does Foreign Investment Affect Growth?', *Journal of International Economics*, June, 115–35.

Braunstein, E. and Epstein, G. (1999) 'Towards a New MAI' in J. Michie and J. G. Smith (eds.) *Global Instability and World Economic Governance,* New York: Routledge.

Caprio, G. and Klingebiel, D. (1996) 'Bank Insolvencies: Cross-Country Experience', World Bank Policy Research Working Paper 1620, Washington, DC: The World Bank.

Chakravarty, S. and Singh, A. (1988) *The Desirable Forms of Economic Openness in the South'*, WIDER Discussion Paper, Helsinki: World Institute for Development Economics Research.

Chang, H.-J. (ed.) (2001) *Joseph Stiglitz and the World Bank: The Rebel Within,* London, UK: Anthem Press, Wimbledon Publishing Company.

Chari, A. and Henry, P. (2002) 'Capital Account Liberalization: Allocative Efficiency or Animal Spirits?', NBER Working Paper 8908, Cambridge, MA: National Bureau of Economic Research.

Claessens, S., Dooley, M., and Warner, A. (1995) 'Portfolio Capital Flows: Hot or Cool?', *World Bank Economic Review,* 9 (1): 153–174.

Cosh, A. D., Hughes, A., and Singh, A. (1990) 'Takeovers and Short Termism: Analytical and Policy Issues in the UK Economy', in A. Cosh, A. Hughes, A. Singh, J. Carty, and J. Plender, (1990) 'Takeovers and Short Termism in the UK', Industrial Policy Paper No. 3, London: Institute for Public Policy Research.

Davidson, P. (2001) 'If Markets are Efficient, Why Have There Been So Many International Financial Market Crises Since the 1970s?', in P. Arestis, M. Baddeley, and J. McCombie (eds.), *What Global Economic Crisis?*, NY and UK: Palgrave, Hampshire.

Demetriades, P. O. and Luintel, K. B. (2001) 'Financial Restraints in the South Korean Miracle', *Journal of Development Economics*, April, 64(2): 459–79.

Demirguc-Kunt, A. and Detragiache, E. (1998) 'Financial Liberalization and Financial Fragility' in Proceedings of Annual Bank Conference on Development Economics, pp. 20–1, Washington, DC, April.

Dunning, J. (1994) Re-evaluating the Benefits of Foreign Direct Investment, *Transnational Corporations,* 9(1): 23–52.

Easterly, W., Islam, R., and Stiglitz, J. E. (2000) 'Shaken and Stirred: Explaining Growth Volatility', in B. Pleskovic and N. Stern (eds.) *Annual World Bank Conference on Development Economics, The International Bank for Reconstruction and Development* pp. 191–211, Washington, DC: The World Bank.

Eatwell, J. (1996) 'International Financial Liberalization: The Impact on World Development', ODS Discussion Paper Series No. 12, New York: UNDP.

Edison, H., Levine, R., Ricci, L., and Slok, T. (*forthcoming*) 'International Financial Integration and Economic Growth', *Journal of International Money and Finance*.

Feldstein, M. (2002) 'Economic and Financial Crises in Emerging Market Economies: Overview of Prevention and Management', NBER Working Paper Series No. 8837, Cambridge, MA: National Bureau of Economic Research.

Fischer, S. (1997) 'Capital Account Liberalization and the Role of the IMF, Paper Presented at The Seminar Asia and the IMF', Hong Kong, China, September 19.

Fischer, S. (1999) 'On the Need for an International Lender of Last Resort', *Journal of Economic Perspectives,* 13: 85–104.

Freeman, C. (1989) 'New Technology and Catching Up', *European Journal of Development Research,* 1(1).

Friedman, M. (1953) *Essays in Positive Economics,* Chicago, IL: University of Chicago Press.

Furman, J. and Stiglitz, J. E. (1999) 'Economic Crises: Evidence and Insights from East Asia', Brookings Papers on Economic Activity No. 2, Washington, DC: Brookings Institution.

Glen, J. and Singh, A. (2005) 'Corporate Governance, Competition and Finance: Re-thinking Lessons from the Asian Crisis', *Eastern Economic Journal,* 31(2): 219–244.

Glyn, A., Hughes, A., Lipietz, A., and Singh, A. (1990) 'The Rise and Fall of the Golden Age', in S. A. Marglin and J. B. Schor (eds.) *The Golden Age of Capitalism,* Oxford: Oxford University Press.

Gomory, R. E. and Baumol, W. J. (2000) *Global Trade and Conflicting National Interest,* Cambridge, MA: MIT Press.

Greenspan, A. (1998) Testimony of the Chairman, Alan Greenspan, before the Committee on Banking and Financial Services, U.S. House of Representatives, Washington, DC, 30 January.

Hanson, G. H. (2001) 'Should Countries Promote Foreign Direct Investment?', G-24 Discussion Paper Series No. 9, New York: UNCTAD.

Henry, P. B. (2000) 'Do Stock Market Liberalizations Cause Investment Booms?', *Journal of Financial Economics,* 58(1–2): 301–34.

IMF (2002) *World Economic Outlook,* Washington, DC: International Monetary Fund.

Jomo, K. S. (2001) 'Growth After the Asian Crisis: What Remains of the East Asian Model?', G-24 Discussion Paper Series No. 10, New York and Geneva: United Nations and Center for International Development, Harvard University and UNCTAD.

Kaldor, N. (1978) *Further Essays on Economic Theory,* London: Duckworth.

Kaminsky, G. L. and Reinhart, C. L. (1999) 'The Twin Crises: The Causes of Banking and Balance-of-Payments Problems', *American Economic Review,* 89(3): 473–500.

Kaufman, H. (2000) *On Money and Markets: A Wall Street Memoir,* New York: McGraw Hill.

Keynes, J. M. (1936) *The General Theory of Employment Interest and Money,* New York: Harcourt, Brace & Company.

Kindleberger, C. P. (1984) *A Financial History of Western Europe,* London: George Allen & Unwin.

Kregel, J. A. (1996) 'Some Risks and Implications of Financial Globalization for National Policy Autonomy', UNCTAD Review, Geneva: United Nations.

Krugman, P. R. (1987) 'Is Free Trade Passé?', *Journal of Economics Perspectives,* 1(2): 1–43.

Lipsey, R. E. (2001) 'Foreign Direct Investors in Three Financial Crises', NBER Working Paper 8084, Cambridge, MA: National Bureau of Economic Research.

Loungani, P. (2002) 'Capital Flows', *IMF Research Bulletin,* September 2002, 1–3.

Martin, P. and Rey, H. (2002) 'Financial Globalization and Emerging Markets: With or Without Crash?', NBER Working Paper No. 9288, Cambridge, MA: National Bureau of Economic Research.

McKinnon, R. and Pill, H. (1999) 'Exchange-Rate Regimes for Emerging Markets: Moral Hazard and International Over-borrowing', *Oxford Review of Economic Policy* 15(3).

Mendoza, E. (2001) 'Credit, Prices and Crashes: Business Cycles with a Sudden Stop', NBER Working Paper No. 8338, Cambridge, MA: National Bureau of Economic Research.

Milberg, W. (1999) 'Foreign Direct Investment and Development: Balancing Costs and Benefits'. *International Monetary and Financial Issues for the 1990s*, 11: 99–115, Geneva: UNCTAD.

Mody, A. and Murshid, A. P. (2002) 'Growing Up with Capital Flows', IMF Working Paper 02/75, Washington, DC: IMF.

Moggridge, D. (1980) *The Collected Writings of John Maynard Keynes.* Vol. XXV, Cambridge, MA: Cambridge University Press.

Ocampo, J. A. (2001) 'Rethinking the Development Agenda'. *Economic Commission for Latin America and the Caribbean.* Santiago: ECLAC.

Ocampo J. A. and Taylor L. (2000) 'Trade Liberalization in Developing Economies: Modest Benefits But Problems With Productivity Growth, Macro Prices, And Income Distribution', in H. D. Dixon (ed.) *Controversies in Macroeconomics Growth, Trade and Policy.* Oxford: Blackwell.

Pasinetti, L. L. (1981) *Structural Change and Economic Growth*, Chapter 11, Cambridge, MA: Cambridge University Press.

Pindyck, R. S. (1991) 'Irreversibility, Uncertainty and Cyclical Investment', *Journal of Economic Literature,* 29(3): 1110–48.

Rakshit, M. K. (2001) 'Globalization of Capital Markets: Some Analytical and Policy Issues', in S. Storm and C. W. M. Naastepad (eds.) *Globalization and Economic Development, Essays in Honour of Waardenburg,* UK/Massachusetts, USA: Edward Elgar.

Ramey, G. and Ramey, V. (1995) 'Volatility and Growth', *American Economic Review,* 85(3): 559–86.

Rodrik, D. (2000) 'Development Strategies for the 21st Century', in B. Pleskovic and N. Stern (eds.) *Annual World Bank Conference on Development Economics* 2000, Washington, DC: World Bank, pp. 85–124.

Sakakibara, E. (2001) 'The East Asian Crisis – Two Years Later', in B. Pleskovic and N. Stern (eds.) *Annual World Bank Conference on Development Economics 2000,* pp. 243–55, Washington, DC: World Bank.

Shiller, R. J. (2000) *Irrational Exuberance.* Princeton, NJ: Princeton University Press.

Singh, A. (1995a) 'The Causes of Fast Economic Growth in East Asia', *UNCTAD Review,* Geneva: United Nations, pp. 91–127.

—— (1995b) 'Institutional Requirements for Full Employment in Advance Economies', *International Labour Review,* 134(4–5): 471–96.

—— (1997a) 'Liberalization and Globalization: An Unhealthy Euphoria', in J. Michie and J. G. Smith (eds.) *Employment and Economic Performance: Jobs, Inflation and Growth,* pp. 11–35, New York: Oxford University Press.

—— (1997b) 'Financial Liberalization, Stockmarkets and Economic Development', *The Economic Journal,* 107: 771–82.

—— (1999) 'Should Africa Promote Stock Market Capitalism?', *Journal of International Development,* 11: 343–65.

—— (2001) 'Foreign Direct Investment and International Agreements a South Perspective', Occasional Paper No. 6, Trade-Related Agenda, Development and Equity (T.R.A.D.E), South Centre, Geneva: South Centre.

—— (2002) 'Asian Capitalism and the Financial Crisis', in J. Eatwell and L. Taylor (eds.) *International Capital Markets: Systems in Transition,* Oxford: Oxford University Press, pp. 339–67.

—— (2003) 'Competition, Corporate Governance and Selection in Emerging Markets', *The Economic Journal,* 113(491): F443–63.

—— (2005) 'Special and Differential Treatment: The Multilateral Trading System and Economic Development in the Twenty-first Century', in P. Gallagher (ed.) *Putting Development First,* London and New York: Zed Books, pp. 233–63.

Singh, A. and Weisse, B. A. (1999) 'The Asian Model: A Crisis Foretold', *International Social Science Journal,* 51(160): 203–15.

Singh, A. and Zammit, A. (2000) 'International Capital Flows: Identifying the Gender Dimension', *World Development,* 28(7): 1249–68.

South Centre (2000) *Foreign Direct Investment, Development and the New Global Economic Order: A Policy Brief for the South,* Geneva: South Centre.

Stiglitz, J. E. (1994) 'The Role of the State in Financial Markets', *Proceedings of the World Bank Annual Conference on Development Economics,* Washington, DC: The World Bank.

—— (1999) 'Reforming the Global Economic Architecture: Lessons from Recent Crises', *The Journal of Finance,* 54(4): 1508–21.

—— (2000)) 'Capital Market Liberalization, Economic Growth, and Instability', *World Development,* 28(6): 1075–86.

Summers, L. (2000) 'International Financial Crises: Causes, Prevention and Cures', *American Economic Review,* Papers and Proceedings, 90: 1–16.

UNCTAD (2000) *Trade and Development Report,* Geneva: UNCTAD.

—— (2001) *Trade and Development Report,* Geneva: UNCTAD.

Williamson, J. (2002) 'Proposals for Curbing the Boom-Bust Cycle in the Supply of Capital to Emerging Markets', Discussion Paper No. 2002/3, United Nations University, Helsinki: WIDER.

Williamson, J. and Drabek, Z. (1999) 'Whether and When to Liberalize Capital Account and Financial Services', Staff Working Paper ERAD-99-03, World Trade Organization, Economic Research and Analysis Division, Geneva: WTO.

World Bank (1999) *World Development Report: Knowledge for Development* (1998/99) Washington, DC: The World Bank.

—— (2001) *Global Development Finance: Building Coalitions for Effective Development Finance,* Washington, DC: The World Bank.

Wyplosz, C. (2001) 'How Risky is Financial Liberalization in the Developing Countries?' CEPR Discussion Paper 2724, London: Centre for Economic Policy Research.

Young, A. A. (1928) 'Increasing returns and economic progress', *Economic Journal,* 38: 527–42.

11 Globalization and profitability since 1950: a tale of two phases?

Andrew Glyn

1 Introduction

This paper returns to an old issue – the behavior of profitability – but with a contemporary spin – the impact of globalization. The focus is mostly on the advanced capitalist countries (ACCs) for data reasons. This partial picture is slightly broadened in the final section. Section 1 examines the long-term behavior of the profit rate in the USA, Japan, and Germany (the so-called G3) plus the UK. Has the profit rate in the most important blocks converged over the past 50 years as might be expected from other indicators of convergence? An obvious route for globalization to have affected profitability trends is through greater international competition in the manufacturing sector and so we examine the relation of manufacturing to overall profitability. As well as affecting overall profitability trends through erosion of monopoly positions, international competition also affects the share-out of aggregate profits between countries through fluctuations in the real exchange rate. Section 3 examines the extent to which volatility in real exchange rates has increased the volatility of manufacturing profits, a potentially important factor inhibiting the manufacturing sector.

2 Long-run trends in the postwar profit rate

Figure 11.1 presents data on the profit rate for nonfinancial companies for G3 plus the UK from 1950 to 2001. This is probably the best economy-wide measure of underlying trends in profitability. A few features of the series should be highlighted:

1   The profit rate is the nonfinancial corporations' pretax net profit rate (i.e. net of capital consumption) as a percentage of the net stock of fixed assets (at replacement cost) plus the value of inventories. The inclusion of inventories as part of capital advanced is uncontroversial conceptually, but is not always followed in empirical studies. It makes some difference to profit rate levels and also to trends. In Japan, USA, and Germany inventories were about 12 –15 percent of the net fixed capital by the end of the 1990s for the nonfinancial sector; in Japan the ratio had been nearly 40 percent in 1970, in

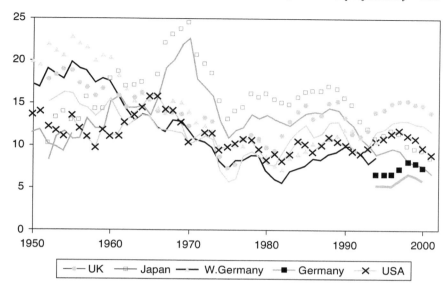

Figure 11.1 Rate of profit: non-financial companies (% pre-tax return on net fixed assets and inventories).

Germany nearly 25 percent, and in USA about 18 percent. Omitting inventories would exaggerate the fall in profitability in Japan relative to that in the USA. In manufacturing trends in inventories are more important still.

2   Data for corporations alone are not available for Germany and we constructed a series for nonagricultural, nonfinancial business that includes unincorporated enterprises (with appropriate adjustment for self-employment incomes). There is also a break in the German series in 1994 reflecting both the inclusion of the former GDR (which reduced the profit rate by less than 1 percent point) and for the introduction of the new system of national accounts (which reduced it by more than 2 percent points for reasons that are obscure).

The profit rate began to fall in Europe at the end of the 1950s. The US decline followed the peak in the mid-1960s, whereas in Japan the fall after 1970 was sharp and concentrated but still left profitability at a comparatively high level until the second collapse in the early 1990s. Outside Japan the profit rate shows some upward trend after the early 1980s most sharply the UK under Thatcher. The rise of the US profit rate, before and during the boom of the later 1990s, was mild and profitability slipped before the end of the boom as Brenner (2002) has emphasized.

Across the four countries profit rates look less dispersed in 2001 than they were in the 1950s. Bearing in mind the measurement problems, the German, US, and UK profit rates have been close to each other since 1960 and Japan joined them in the early 1990s. If the US profit rate is regarded as the center of gravity for the ACCs, as the discussion of postwar "catch-up" suggests, then that center of

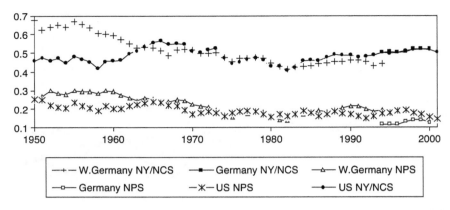

Figure 11.2 Profit shares (NPS) and output capital ratios (NY/NCS): Non-financial corporations.

gravity has slipped a little as compared to the 1950s and especially the 1960s. The very high profit rates achieved in Germany and Japan during their years of peak growth are long gone. If we make some plausible adjustments to the UK and German figures to improve comparability in 2000/2001 profit rates were around the range 7–10 percent in all countries – rather close![1]

It is possible to split the profit rate movements for the USA and Germany into shifts in the net profit share and shifts in the output capital ratio (Figure 11.2). The downward movements in the profit rate up to the early 1980s reflected both influences (rising organic composition and profit squeeze if you will), with if anything the influence of the profit squeeze being the stronger.[2] In the USA there was quite a strong recovery in the output capital ratio after 1980 and little trend in the profit share, whereas in Germany there was some rebound in both (discounting the 1994 breaks in the series).

Discussion about the impact of globalization on the ACCs has been focused on the manufacturing sector as most susceptible to international competition, initially coming from within the OECD and increasingly from low-wage producers in the South. The manufacturing profit rate, for the same four countries analyzed above, is shown in Figure 11.3. Japan presents the most dramatic pattern with profitability storming up in the 1950s, held at a very high rate in the 1960s, declining precipitously in the early 1970s and then stable till a further lurch down in the early 1990s.[3] A slide in manufacturing profitability began much earlier in Europe, in the 1950s, and continued through the 1970s so that by 1980 it was a fraction of the 1950s level. The USA presents a muted version of the same pattern, interrupted by the mid-1960s boom. The US manufacturing profit rate has fluctuated around the 6–13 percent mark in the 1980s and first half of the 1990s, as compared to 3–10 percent in Germany and the UK, with Japan tipping into the latter group in the early 1990s. US manufacturing profitability showed a rather strong recovery after the mid-1980s. In the UK also the Thatcher effect was

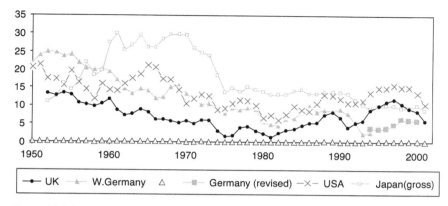

Figure 11.3 Rate of profit: manufacturing (% pre-tax return on net fixed assets and inventories).

stronger in pushing up profits in manufacturing than in the economy as a whole, which is quite consistent with the sharp improvement in productivity and the weakening of the unions being concentrated there. By contrast the recovery in German manufacturing profitability was reversed by the early 1990s recession and subsequent stagnation.

There is a strong case for attributing a role to international competition in the decline in manufacturing profitability before 1980. The growth of intra-OECD trade, especially in manufacturing, was a strong feature of the 1960s and 1970s and it is plausible that monopolistic positions within domestic markets and even some export markets were eroded over this period. Just how far increasing competition was from overseas rather than domestic sources is hard to determine. However, it should be recognized that the decline in manufacturing profitability was not reflected in rising profitability in the rest of the economy as should have happened if the process was simply an equalization of the profit rate without other distributional consequences. The failure of the rest of the economy to gain in profits what manufacturing lost implies that part of the benefit from increased competition and thus lower relative prices in manufacturing were absorbed in rising real wages. If the process of profit squeeze derived only from rising product market competition then it would be accompanied by a squeeze on relative wages in manufacturing declining union mark-ups on nonunion wages and the like. This is not the pattern of the 1960s and 1970s. Thus it is hard to see how the labor market can be denied a central role in this process.[4]

Adrian Wood (1994) underlined the decline of manufacturing profitability by comparing average manufacturing and nonmanufacturing profit rates (1994: Figure 5.5). Figure 11.4 updates his picture, confined to the four countries analyzed above but using the broader measure of capital stock including inventories.[5] The pattern Wood described, of the erosion of the super-profit in manufacturing

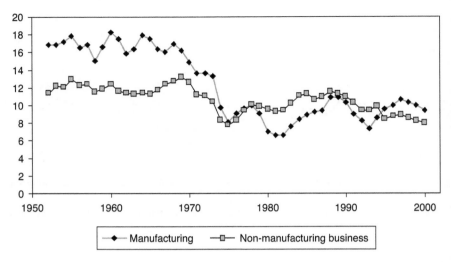

Figure 11.4 Net profit rates (%): manufacturing and non-manufacturing (average of USA, Japan, Germany, UK).

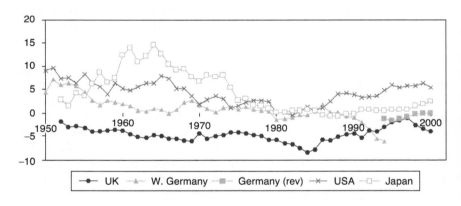

Figure 11.5 Profit rate differentials (% points) manufacturing less whole economy.

from the late 1960s, is fully confirmed. By the end of the 1970s profitability was very similar within and outside manufacturing and so it has stayed.[6]

Figure 11.4 refers to the (simple) average of four countries. The comparative pattern of manufacturing and the rest within individual countries is telling as well (see Figure 11.5). Germany in the 1950s and Japan in the 1960s had large profit rate differentials in favor of manufacturing, but these were fully eroded at the end of the 1950s and early 1970s, respectively. Consistent with the long history of UK failure in manufacturing, its profitability appears always to have been lower than the rest of the economy – even in the relatively protected 1950s. This was reversed under Thatcher. In the US, manufacturing was much more profitable than the rest

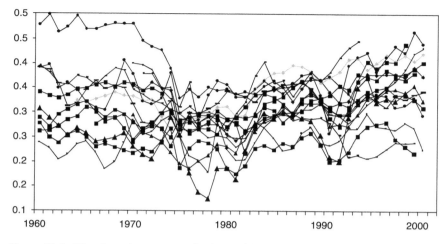

Figure 11.6 Manufacturing gross profit shares: 16 OECD countries 1960–2001.

of the economy until the 1970s and first half of the 1980s. But the subsequent recovery in US manufacturing brought a return to the high profit rates relative to the US economy, and for the first time distinctly higher profitability than in Germany and Japan its main manufacturing rivals (see Brenner 1998, 2002 for an account that places great emphasis on the waxing and waning of external competitive pressure on US manufacturing).

3 Manufacturing profits and real exchange rates

Figure 11.6 explores the behavior of manufacturing profitability by reporting the gross profit share for 16 OECD countries. This measure is the most broadly available indicator and is not dependent on assumptions about asset lives.[7] The chart suggests a general decline in profitability until the early 1980s and the widespread (but not universal) recovery subsequently. Across the 15 countries which have data for the whole period the (unweighted) mean profit share fell from 0.317 to 0.260 between 1970 and 1981 and then recovered to 0.346 in 1999. Thus, many European countries (and indeed Australia and New Zealand) behaved more like the UK, with a strong manufacturing profits recovery, than like Germany or Japan.

This panel data for profitability allows two further issues to be explored. First, has the dispersion of profitability across countries tended to decrease, as might result from greater international competition? Of course the gross profit share is not an ideal indicator – it could differ across countries reflecting different output capital ratios rather than different profit rates. Nevertheless a strong convergence in profit rates would be expected to show up in the pattern of gross shares. Second, it might be anticipated that profitability would become more volatile within countries as international competition became a more important source of "shocks." In

Table 11.1 Variability of manufacturing profitability

Standard deviations of gross profit shares, 10 year averages, 15 countries	1960s	1970s	1980s	1990s
Across countries	–	0.054	0.045	0.054
Across countries (excluding Japan)	–	0.047	0.044	0.055
Within countries (10 year average)	0.020	0.032	0.028	0.031

Note
Data for the 1960s is available only for eight countries, which precludes meaningful comparisons across countries; within country variability is estimated from the eight countries and linked to the broader series for the 1970s.

both cases the restriction of coverage to manufacturing is an advantage, as international competition would be expected to show up most strongly there.

Table 11.1 shows the ten-year averages, for the 15 countries with data covering the whole period, of (1) the yearly standard deviation of profit shares (to measure profit variability across countries); (2) the standard deviation of profit shares within each country (to measure variability within the country over the ten years).

Variability across countries decreased in the 1980s but then rose again in the 1990s. The earlier decrease reflects the influence of the extremely high profit shares in Japan in the earlier 1970s discussed earlier. If Japan is left out then variability across countries seems to have declined a little in the 1980s but risen in the 1990s. Variability within countries changed less, but after a small increase in the 1990s it was still as great as in the turbulent 1970s and half as large again as in the 1960s.

Globalization could help explain such patterns. Perhaps the least disputed aspect of the current phase has been the growth in capital flows which have contributed to long swings in the real exchange rate (the vagaries of the dollar being a prime example). The best measure of the real exchange rate is an index of relative unit labor costs in manufacturing (RULC), year-to-year fluctuations in which are dominated by movements in the nominal exchange rate. Table 11.2 shows the results of regressing manufacturing gross profit shares, as shown in Figure 11.6, on RULC using country fixed effects.[8]

RULC has a significant effect on the gross profit share for the period as a whole and in subperiods. A coefficient of –0.05 implies that a 1 percent rise in cost competitiveness increases the profit share by half percent or about 0.15 percent points. It is interesting that RULC has a slightly greater effect on profit shares in the 1990s than before. This is consistent with international competition having become increasingly intense making faster costs increases (whether emanating from wages or the exchange rate) increasingly difficult to pass on in higher prices. It is also consistent with the result of Carlin *et al.* (2002) that RULC had a slightly stronger effect on export market shares of OECD countries in the 1990s than in the 1980s.

Table 11.2 Regressions of gross manufacturing profit share on RULC

Dependent variable log (gross profit share)	Coefficient of logRULC	Memo item: mean of the absolute value of the annual change in logRULC	No of observation (14 countries)
Pooled regressions		(1964–70=0.031)	
1970–2001	−0.452 [0.000]	0.050	455
1970–79	−0.551 [0.000]	0.062	125
1980–89	−0.562 [0.000]	0.047	150
1990–2001	−0.679 [0.000]	0.045	180
Country regressions			
USA	−0.290 [0.003]		32
Japan	−0.133 [0.118]		32
Germany	−0.315 [0.060]		31
UK	−0.108 [0.339]		31
Sweden	−2.231 [0.000]		30

Note:
p values shown in [ ].

Table 11.2 also reports the degree of year to year variation of RULC: It was noticeably higher in the 1970s than in the two subsequent decades reflecting the turmoil in exchange rates and labor costs of that decade. Given the convergence of inflation rates in the OECD through the 1980s it might be expected that the variability of RULC would have declined further in the 1990s. The continued instability of nominal and thus real exchange rates must account for the continued high level of variability – on average cost competitiveness of a country continued to vary by over 4 percent per year. Because variations of RULC had a slightly stronger effect on profitability, it is plausible that international financial volatility was contributing more to the variability of profits in the 1990s.

The table also records the impact of RULC on manufacturing profitability of the four countries discussed earlier. The very weak effect in the UK is surprising. Sweden is also reported in the table because of the extreme sensitivity of profit shares to RULC. Of course this is a very simple regression and the correlation of RULC with other relevant factors (such as the business cycle) can bias the result in either direction. Even so the fact that there is a significant impact of RULC on profits in the relatively closed USA is interesting. Together with the very interesting findings of Michael Klein *et al.* (2000) on the strong impact of the exchange rate on gross job destruction this supports due emphasis being placed on the exchange rate.

It was noted at the outset that the focus of this short paper is the ACCs. The OECD's STAN data set does contain some recent profit information for a handful of NICs and transition economies (all OECD members), which gives a flavor of how interesting a fuller analysis could be. Figure 11.7 suggests that Korea has

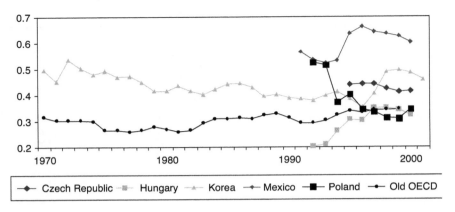

Figure 11.7   Manufacturing profit shares: NICs etc.

maintained a high profit share (very comparable to that of Japan up to the early 1970s), but with some decline in the 1970s and sharp upswing after 1996. Mexico's profitability appears to be higher still.[9] Of the East European economies, Poland and Hungary reached, from quite different starting points, profit shares rather comparable to the average of the "old OECD" analyzed earlier, whereas the Czech rate has stayed a good deal higher. A serious comparative study of the profitability of the manufacturing sectors in high and low wage countries is long overdue.

4   Conclusions

Section 2 suggested that economy-wide profitability in the three most important ACCs declined since the 1950s or 1960s peaks but, less well known, has been within a surprisingly narrow band over the last decade. The fall was heavily concentrated in manufacturing and tended to erode the differential in favor of that sector. This is consistent with growing competitive pressure in manufacturing, much of which must have come from international competition. However, the fall in manufacturing profitability was not offset by a rise elsewhere in the economy and this shows that this was not simply an equalization among sectors but had other causes.

Section 3 showed the rather widespread nature of the recovery in manufacturing profitability since 1980s despite this period being heralded as a new epoch of globalization. Of course globalization also affects workers' bargaining power through the greater mobility of production especially when combined with widespread mass unemployment.[10] Despite the closeness of overall profit rates in the USA, Germany, and Japan in the 1990s, manufacturing profitability in the larger group of OECD countries was actually more dispersed in the 1990s than in the 1980s. Profitability has also remained much more variable within countries on a year-to-year basis than in the 1960s despite the generally less turbulent macroeconomic conditions in the 1990s. The continuing variability in the real exchange rate, combined with the fact that the link between cost competitiveness and profitability seems to have become stronger, helps to account for this.

The above suggests there have been two postwar phases of globalization for the ACCs. The first, lasting through the 1970s, saw increasing competition, primarily through manufacturing trade, erode monopoly positions. Profits took the hit as high employment and stronger unions allowed manufacturing workers to maintain and enhance their position. In the second phase, after 1980 capital mobility has been much more prominent with two important implications. First, greater mobility of international production – the "threat effect" – combined with mass unemployment and political attacks to weaken workers bargaining position. In many countries these labor market developments dominated greater product market competition and allowed some recovery of profits – a process so far delayed in Germany and in Japan. Second, flows of financial capital kept exchange rates very volatile despite the generally more stable macroeconomic conditions. This has meant that manufacturing profits have not regained the degree of stability seen in the 1960s which must have had an inhibiting effect on capital accumulation.

Notes

1 Leaving out the old East Germany and the UK's North Sea oil fields (where profit rates were 30 percent) would boost the German profit rate by about 1 percent and reduce the UK rate by a similar amount, and the UK's rate would be reduced by a further 1 percent if public corporations were included in the series (as they are in other countries). The UK profit rate still looks surprisingly high.
2 In the USA between 1965 and 1982 (the peak and trough for the profit rate) the profit share fell by 34 percent and the output capital ratio by 27 percent; in Germany between 1955 and 1982 the profit share fell by 55 percent and the output capital ratio by 38 percent.
3 The series for manufacturing profit rate for Japan is not strictly comparable (referring to the gross rate of return rather than the net, though these generally are close together) and has to be quite roughly estimated for both the 1950s and 1990s. Even so the series probably represents the broad picture.
4 Glyn and Sutcliffe (1972) saw labor market pressures (labor shortage, worker militancy) as the hammer and international competition as the anvil in the profit squeeze. Brenner's almost exclusive emphasis on the product market (1998, 2002) seems one-sided, as Arrighi (2003) has recently argued.
5 This is important for this analysis, as inventories are both more important in manufacturing and decline more than outside.
6 Little significance should be attached to the edging ahead of manufacturing profitability in the 1990s as it partly reflects the revised German national accounts system.
7 In the few countries for which capital consumption data is published its share tended to rise, for example in both the USA and Germany from some 9 percent of value added to 14 percent over the 30-year period. This reflected falls in the output capital ratio, especially in the earlier part of the period, and a shift of asset composition toward shorter-lived assets. The chart is deliberately drawn on a scale starting at 0.1 because 10 percent is a typical figure for the share of capital consumption in value added and thus the chart gives an idea of the *proportionate* changes in the profit share net of capital consumption.

8 RULC is just an index with no attempt to use PPP to measure productivity so that there is no levels information in RULC. There is thus no meaningful interpretation of the country dummies which are not reported. Fixed effects examine how deviations of the profit share from its mean value for the country have been correlated with the deviations of RULC from its average level for the country.

9 There is some doubt in the STAN data about whether the value added data for Mexico really is at (or close to) factor costs. If it includes a substantial indirect tax element the measured profit share will be inflated.

10 Glyn (1997) found manufacturing profitability to be significant increased by unemployment as well as by greater cost competitiveness.

References

Armstrong, P., Glyn, A., and Harrison, J. (1991; 2nd ed.) *Capitalism Since 1945*, Cambridge, Massachusetts: Basil Blackwell.

Arrighi, G. (2003) 'Tracking Global Turbulence', *New Left Review*, March/April, pp. 5–72.

Brenner, R. (1998) 'The Economics of Global Turbulence', *New Left Review*, May/June, pp. 1–229.

—— (2002) *The Boom and the Bubble: The U.S. in the World Economy*, New York: Verso.

Carlin, W., Glyn, A., and Manning, M. (2002) 'Cost Competitiveness and Export Performance in OECD Economies: How Does the UK Compare?', *Mimeo*, University College London.

Glyn, A. (1997) 'Does Aggregate Profitability *Really* Matter', *Cambridge Journal of Economics*, 21(5): 593–619.

Glyn, A. and Sutcliffe, R. (1972) *British Capitalism, Workers and the Profit Squeeze*, Middlesex, UK: Penguin.

Klein, M., Schuh, S., and Triest, R. (2000) 'Job Creation, Job Destruction and the Real Exchange Rate', NBER Working Paper 7466, Cambridge, Massachusetts: National Bureau of Economic Research.

Wood, A. (1994) *North South Trade, Employment and Inequality*, Oxford: Clarendon Press.

Data appendix

Net profit rates for nonfinancial companies

USA – Bureau of Economic Analysis. National Income and Product Accounts. Table 1.16 Capital Stocks Tables 4.1, Inventories 5.12A.

Germany – Net Rate of Profit on Non-Agricultural Business Capital Stock. German National Accounts tables. From 1994 refers to all Germany and omits a small element of services. For years before 1960 and after 1994 ratio of inventories to net fixed capital assumed constant.

Japan – National Accounts of Japan tables for Income Accounts and Balance Sheets of Non-Financial Corporations. For pre-1970 linked to nonagricultural business series from Armstrong *et al.* (1991).

UK – ONS Website Profitability of Private Non-Financial Corporations. Series linked back from 1965 to corporate profit rate series in Armstrong *et al.* 1991.

Net profit rates for manufacturing

In each case operating surplus is adjusted to take out an attributed average wage for the self-employed.

USA – Bureau of Economic Analysis. Gross Product Originating Accounts for operating surplus net of business taxes (these data are allocated by industry of each establishment rather than by industry of the corporation whereas in the National Income and Product Accounts corporate profits are by industry of corporation although employee compensation is by establishment as are Capital Stocks in the Fixed Asset tables).

Germany – National Account tables From 1994 refers to all Germany. For years before 1960 and after 1994 ratio of inventories to net fixed capital assumed constant.

Japan – Gross Profit Rate from OECD National Accounts data 1965–92. Updated using gross profit share from Japan National Accounts Income Generated by Industry and estimating output capital ratio from partial value added and capital stock data. Inventories in Japanese manufacturing are assumed to represent the same ratio to gross fixed capital stock at current prices as in the USA and Germany.

UK – ONS Website Series linked back from 1965 to series in Armstrong *et al.* 1991.

Gross profit shares in manufacturing

These are estimated from the March 2003 issue of OECD's STAN database, with a correction for self-employment. For the USA, Germany and Japan, and UK series were re-calculated directly from national account sources as given above. The data for before 1970 was spliced on from OECD sources as reported in Glyn (1997).

Index

For Product Safety Concerns and Information please contact our EU
representative GPSR@taylorandfrancis.com
Taylor & Francis Verlag GmbH, Kaufingerstraße 24, 80331 München, Germany

www.ingramcontent.com/pod-product-compliance
Ingram Content Group UK Ltd.
Pitfield, Milton Keynes, MK11 3LW, UK
UKHW021621240425
457818UK00018B/680